Elections and Distributive Politics in Mubarak's Egypt

Despite its authoritarian political structure, Egypt's government has held competitive, multiparty parliamentary elections for more than thirty years. This book argues that, rather than undermining the durability of the Mubarak regime, competitive parliamentary elections ease important forms of distributional conflict, particularly conflict over access to spoils. In a comprehensive examination of the distributive consequences of authoritarian elections in Egypt, Lisa Blaydes examines the triadic relationship between Egypt's ruling regime, the rent-seeking elite that supports the regime, and the ordinary citizens who participate in these elections. She describes why parliamentary candidates finance campaigns to win seats in a legislature that lacks policy-making power, as well as why citizens engage in the costly act of voting in such a context.

Lisa Blaydes is Assistant Professor of Political Science at Stanford University. Her work has appeared in *International Organization, Middle East Journal, World Politics*, and other journals. The dissertation on which this book is based received the 2009 Gabriel Almond Award for best dissertation in the field of comparative politics from the American Political Science Association. Blaydes received her PhD in political science from the University of California, Los Angeles, in 2008. From 2008 to 2010, she was an Academy Scholar at the Harvard Academy for International and Area Studies.

To my parents

Elections and Distributive Politics in Mubarak's Egypt

LISA BLAYDES
Stanford University

CAMBRIDGE UNIVERSITY PRESS
Cambridge, New York, Melbourne, Madrid, Cape Town,
Singapore, São Paulo, Delhi, Mexico City

Cambridge University Press
32 Avenue of the Americas, New York, NY 10013-2473, USA

www.cambridge.org
Information on this title: www.cambridge.org/9781107000551

First published 2011
Reprinted 2011, 2013

A catalog record for this publication is available from the British Library.

Library of Congress Cataloging in Publication Data

Blaydes, Lisa, 1975–
Elections and distributive politics in Mubarak's Egypt / Lisa Blaydes.
    p. cm.
Includes bibliographical references and index.
ISBN 978-1-107-00055-1 (hardback)
1. Elections – Egypt.   2. Political Participation – Egypt.   3. Egypt – Politics and
government – 1981–   I. Title.
JQ3892.B53   2010
324.962'055 – dc22   2010024846

ISBN 978-1-107-00055-1 Hardback

Contents

Figures

Tables

Acknowledgments

I have been the fortunate recipient of much sage advice and numerous types of support over the years it has taken to write this book. I owe a huge debt of gratitude to the original supporters of this project, which began as a doctoral dissertation in the Political Science Department at the University of California, Los Angeles (UCLA). The co-chairs of my dissertation committee, Leonard Binder and George Tsebelis, have been tireless supporters of both my work and my professional development. I am incredibly thankful for the unique contributions each has made to this project. Barbara Geddes has been a supportive critic and mentor over the years; her thoughtful comments have improved this project greatly. I also benefited tremendously from my interactions with James Honaker and Jeff Lewis at UCLA.

Josh Cohen, Jim Fearon, David Laitin, Beatriz Magaloni, and Peter Stone at Stanford all provided useful ideas and suggestions. Many thanks as well to Carles Boix for helpful comments on Chapter 3 at a Princeton conference on "Dictatorships: Their Governance and Social Consequences." Sean Yom contributed important insights on qualitative methodology. Monika Nalepa and Nahomi Ichino thoughtfully commented on the Introduction. Steve Haber, Kevin Koehler, and Robert Springborg all deserve special thanks for offering their thoughts on the entire book.

I am particularly grateful to Jorge Dominguez, Kathleen Hoover, and Larry Winnie at the Harvard Academy for International and Area Studies for hosting me during the 2008–2009 and 2009–2010 academic years. In addition to providing an outstanding environment for completing this book, the Academy sponsored a book conference that allowed me to share the project with Nathan Brown, Steve Levitsky, Roger Owen, Mustapha Kamal al-Sayyid, Lisa Wedeen, and Daniel Ziblatt. I thank each of them for taking the time to read and comment on my work. It was ultimately their support that gave me the confidence to send the book out.

I gratefully acknowledge the financial support of the Fulbright–Hays Doctoral Dissertation Research Abroad Fellowship, which sponsored my field research in Egypt in 2005. While in Egypt, the Binational Fulbright Commission provided administrative and other support in an incredibly professional manner. The Centre d'Etudes et de Documentation, Economiques, Juridiques, et Sociales in Cairo gave me the opportunity to participate in a conference that analyzed the 2005 elections, allowing me to make another trip to Cairo in April–May 2006. A National Science Foundation Dissertation Improvement Grant supported me during an additional stint of fieldwork in April–May 2007. The Roy and Dorothy John Doctoral Fellowship, Alice Belkin Fellowship, and Foreign Language and Area Studies Fellowships, all administered by the UCLA International Institute, provided funding during my years of coursework and eventual dissertation writing. I would also like to acknowledge the financial support of the Institute on Global Conflict and Cooperation and the UCLA Graduate Division.

While in Egypt, I relied on the knowledge of many incredible individuals, each patient enough to sit with me and share their understanding of Egyptian politics. Thanks to Hassan Abu Taleb, Sonia 'Ali, Gehad Auda, 'Ali Fatah al-Bab, Mohammed al-Batran, Ossama al-Ghazali Harb, 'Ali al-Din Hilal, Mohammed Kamal, Gouda 'Abdel Khalek, Karima Koriyem, Mahmoud Nur, Mohammed Omran, Gasser 'Abdel Raziq, Mohammed al-Sawi, Mustapha Kamel al-Sayyid, Gamal Siam, Samer Soliman, Sherif Wali, and Moheb Zaki for being particularly helpful. Some of my best friends during this time were my fellow graduate students at universities in Egypt. Thanks go to Iman al-Ayouty and Atef al-Saadawi of the Faculty of Economics and Political Science of Cairo University, Mohammed Habib of Al-Azhar University, and Mohammed Bashandy of Helwan University. Noha Saleh Salem, Shimaa Ahehta, and Rasha al-Sherif were wonderful friends during my time in Cairo. Although our conversations did not generally venture into the realm of politics, we had much to talk about. Ossama al-Batran and Safinaz al-Tarouty deserve special thanks. I also want to express appreciation to the al-Batran and al-Tarouty families of Giza, who warmly and repeatedly opened their homes to me and my family.

Eric Chang, Jennifer De Maio, Katja Favretto, Hazem Kandil, David Karol, Mark Kayser, Marisa Kellam, Shuhei Kurizaki, Drew Linzer, Larry Rubin, Rob Salmond, Liz Stein, and Jana von Stein were all wonderfully smart and supportive colleagues at UCLA. Florian Kohstall, David Patel, and Stacey Philbrick Yadav also are valued friends and colleagues.

My family is owed particular thanks. I am grateful to my brother, Bernard, for editing the entire book and assisting in the preparation of the index. My mother and mother-in-law generously provided many hours of childcare over the years. In my husband, Josh, I have found the most supportive academic spouse that anyone could ever ask for. His willingness to pack up and move our small family to Egypt and his acceptance of continued travel back and forth to Egypt over the years are truly appreciated. He never questioned the wisdom of my academic pursuits but instead quietly supported my efforts. My son, Jonah, has been living with this project his whole life and I am grateful for his love and patience. Ethan joined us at the very end of the process and I am grateful to him as well.

1

Introduction

The existence of electoral competition, at times fierce and expensive, seems paradoxical in an authoritarian context, where the selection of regime leadership has already been made. Yet nearly all autocrats hold some form of elections, and hegemonic party regimes – such as the one in Egypt – represent one of the most common forms of dictatorship in the world (Magaloni 2006). This book seeks to unravel a series of interrelated puzzles about elections in Egypt: In what ways does the authoritarian regime benefit from holding elections? Why do candidates spend scarce resources to run for a seat in a parliament that does not make policy? Why do citizens engage in the costly act of voting in such a context? And do we observe patterns of economic change surrounding autocratic elections that resemble the trends observed in democracies? The answers to these questions are critical to understanding the mechanics of authoritarian survival, both in Egypt and elsewhere. I argue that the authoritarian regime in Egypt has endured *not despite* competitive elections, but, to some degree, *because* of these elections.

A number of themes run throughout this project. The first is that the authoritarian regime in Egypt has made increasing use of competitive, market-style mechanisms to mediate political relationships over time. Second, economic change and a generalized withdrawal of the Egyptian state from its hegemonic economic role in society have both had an impact on the nature of relations among the regime, elite, and citizenry. Finally, although electoral authoritarianism in Egypt is currently stable, the by-products associated with this equilibrium – such as institutionalized corruption and budget-cycle–induced inefficiencies – have the potential to undermine its stability over time.[1]

---

[1] Greif and Laitin (2004) argue that an institution can endogenously affect aspects of a political, economic, or social situation apart from the behavior in the transaction under consideration. For Greif and Laitin, such factors should be considered as variables in accounting for the self-reinforcement (i.e., long-term stability) of that equilibrium. They are thus quasi parameters.

1.1 THE ARGUMENT

The central argument here is that competitive parliamentary elections in Egypt represent a rational, and perhaps even best, response for an authoritarian regime that faces a number of political challenges.[2] A primary reason for this is that elections ease important forms of distributional conflict, particularly conflict over access to spoils within Egypt's broad class of elite, that represent an important source of support for the regime.[3] The easing of distributional conflict is not, however, the only benefit of a competitive electoral market; elections institutionalize dominance through formal channels, provide important information for the regime regarding the performance of party leaders and rank-and-file cadre, offer a focal point for the redistribution of wealth to state employees and the citizenry,[4] provide a façade for high-level corruption, and enhance the international reputation of the autocrat while strengthening his political hold. This is not to say that holding elections is without risk for the authoritarian leadership. There exists a trade-off between intra-elite peace and other benefits I describe, on the one hand, and costs related to the ways that elections exacerbate state–society relations, particularly relations between the state and supporters of the Muslim Brotherhood, on the other hand. Yet even given the escalation of such state–society tension, I argue that the benefits of elections to the authoritarian leadership exceed the costs.[5] All significant political actors in Egypt prefer the existence of competitive parliamentary elections to the elimination of these elections in both the short and medium term. In fact, the elimination of elections would represent a utility loss for nearly all major actors and societal groups that have come to rely on competitive electoral institutions. Elections, then, have a distinctly functional utility that

[2] Parliamentary elections exist within the context of a broader electoral structure in contemporary Egypt. In addition to lower-house elections, upper-house, municipal council, and, beginning in 2005, multicandidate presidential elections all take place. This is in addition to elections for the leadership of professional syndicates, sports clubs, and for leadership of other nonpublic institutions. Although most of the arguments of this book refer primarily to lower-house parliamentary elections, many of the processes are present in other types of elections as well.

[3] Although conflict over the distribution of resources is not the only dimension of political relevance in contemporary Egypt, it is, perhaps, the most important and remains the focus of a number of prominent studies of how and why autocracy persists (Boix 2003; Acemoglu and Robinson 2006).

[4] Schelling (1960) describes a focal point as a solution that individuals will converge upon in the absence of communication because that particular solution seems to be natural or relevant. Whereas a focal point typically refers to an individual's expectation regarding the actions of other individuals, here, individual and regime convergence on a common action based on their mutual expectations is intended. In timing government giveaways, election season has come to be seen as a natural and relevant time for such giveaways to take place.

[5] For some authoritarian regimes, the benefits associated with competitive elections do not exceed the costs. This is particularly the case in weakly institutionalized autocracies that hold elections primarily as a result of external influence. In such contexts, the destabilizing effects of competitive elections often outweigh the functional benefits. See Levitsky and Way (2010) for more details on the impact of elections for such regimes.

complements the preferences of a variety of different actors.[6] The counterfactual claim implicit in this work is that, absent elections, the regime would not be so durable. A main reason for this is that the rent-seeking elite – which emerged as the regime's key constituency under former President Anwar al-Sadat and has remained so under Hosni Mubarak – has required a system of resource allocation that minimizes the potential for destabilizing distributional conflict.[7] Elections are a public, and credible, way to commit to such allocation. Managing concerns over access to material enrichment, in fact, lies at the very core of the regime's stability.

These ideas build on a number of existing scholarly works, yet stand in contrast to both the dominant explanations for authoritarian persistence in Egypt and alternative theories regarding the functional role of elections in autocratic regimes. For example, this book expands on the important work of Geddes (2005), who has argued that dictators expend scarce resources on parties and elections – despite the risks – because these institutions help regimes solve problems. As a result, parties and elections are a central part of an "autocratic survival strategy" (Geddes 2005).[8] Geddes primarily emphasizes the use of parties and elections as a counterbalance to the military or factions within the military. Although I concur with her general conclusion about the use of elections for solving intraregime conflict, my research focuses on the importance of elections as a mechanism for distributing rents and promotions, as a focal point for economic redistribution to the citizenry, and as a source of information for the autocratic regime, rather than the use of parties and elections as a balance to the military. In addition, my argument is distinct from that of Brownlee (2007), who finds that it is effective *parties*, not elections, that matter for solving intra-elite conflict. Although parties may be important venues for negotiating the role of elites, this book finds that the electoral process *itself* serves as a key mechanism for containing intra-elite competition as elections aid in the distribution of both rents and coveted positions within the regime, among other functions. This argument also complements, but is distinct from, the findings of Lust-Okar (2006), who focuses primarily on the distributive benefits of elections from the nonelite perspective, particularly how local constituents have come to expect parliamentarians to deliver pork and

---

[6] Elster (1982) criticizes the use of functional explanations in social science, arguing that all social phenomena can be explained in terms of the goals, properties, and behaviors of individuals. Giddens (1982) suggests that the "weak" functionalist paradigm is probably not worth regarding as a form of functionalism. The weak paradigm, consistent with the discussion of authoritarian institutions described in this book, states that a pattern of behavior may have consequences that – although unintended or unforeseen by those initiating the pattern of behavior – confer some benefit. According to Giddens, Elster's real objection was to the "strong" functionalist paradigm, in which patterns of behavior have a function and this function explains why behaviors exist in the first place, a tendency particularly apparent in Marxist and radical social science.

[7] See Hinnebusch (1988a) and Springborg (1989) for more on the importance of the rent-seeking elite to the regime.

[8] Also see Lust-Okar (2006), Magaloni (2006), and Greene (2007). See Gandhi and Lust-Okar (2009) for a review of the literature on authoritarian elections.

other benefits.[9] My argument joins an increasingly well-established view that dictators create powersharing arrangements with their "loyal friends" and that parties and elections help serve this role (Magaloni 2006; Boix and Svolik 2007; Magaloni 2008).

Magaloni (2008) considers the role of authoritarian institutions and argues that both parties and elections mitigate "the commitment problem" that exists between a dictator and his ruling coalition. She argues that autocracies with parties and elections are more stable because of their ability to establish "power-sharing deals," in which these institutions serve as the contract between the dictator and his coalition.[10] Parties and elections, then, can serve as a contract between an autocrat and his coalition of elite supporters via institutions that are negotiated over rights to intangible, often economic, forms of property.[11] Competitive parliamentary elections, and the informal norms that have developed surrounding these elections, commit the regime to a decentralized mechanism for patronage sharing with the politically relevant elite.[12] Elections are a credible mechanism of selection because canceling elections would entail significant costs for the regime, both domestically and internationally.

In addition to the importance of elections as an institution, this book also builds on an emerging literature that argues that elections are important sources of information for the regime. Magaloni (2006) makes two important contributions to this literature. Referring to the overwhelming electoral victories of the Partido Revolucionario Institucional (PRI) in Mexico, Magaloni argues that elections communicate information about the regime's strength, discouraging defections from the hegemonic party. To achieve huge margins of victory,

[9] Lust-Okar (2006; 2008; 2009a) argues that elections are best understood as an arena of competition over access to a pool of state resources, or what she calls "competitive clientelism." She argues that citizens vote for candidates who can provide them with *wasta*, or mediation, and tend to be individuals from their families, clans, or tribes. The hope is that, by electing a candidate with whom they enjoy a personal tie, the voter will gain access to a government job and discretionary funds (Lust-Okar 2006, 459). One factor left unexplained by the Lust-Okar explanation involves why citizens vote when only some relatively small fraction of voters will enjoy a benefit from their participation.

[10] Boix and Svolik (2007) make a related but slightly different point; they argue that legislatures provide the forum within which notables exchange information, and elections serve as a signal of the influence of individual notables. There is some question regarding a) the extent to which notables need a separate forum within which to share information, as they may already have overlapping social networks, and b) why a public forum, like a legislature, would be preferable to private fora for communication between notables.

[11] According to North (1993), institutions are constraints that structure human interaction, reducing the uncertainty arising from that interaction.

[12] Although formal institutional rules are openly codified, Helmke and Levitsky (2003) define informal institutional rules as those "socially shared rules, usually unwritten, that are created, communicated, and enforced outside of officially sanctioned channels." Pioppi argues that limiting analysis to just the formal sector would suggest corruption and clientelism are signs of state weakness, whereas instead they should be viewed as "indicative of the efficiency of a system of power" (2007, 140). This is consistent with others who have argued that, in Egypt, informal norms and political institutions are as significant as formal institutions and key to the authoritarian regime's survival (Blaydes 2005; Koehler 2008).

the PRI had to produce high turnout as well as high levels of support, even though this process was quite costly.[13] Second, elections provide information about supporters and opponents of the regime.[14] Using information about the geographic distribution of dissent, the PRI in Mexico was able to reward supporters with access to government funds, as well as to punish defectors. Magaloni writes that "elections are employed as means to distribute power among lower-level politicians. Autocratic regimes reward with office those politicians who prove most capable in mobilizing citizens to the party's rallies, getting voters to the polls, and preventing social turmoil in their districts" (2006, 8). In this book, I argue that elections serve a very similar purpose in Egypt, where they reveal information about the competence and loyalty of both bureaucratic officials and party cadre, providing the authoritarian leadership with what is perceived as an even-handed way for the autocrat to decide who should receive party appointments. In addition, I find evidence to suggest that there also exists a "punishment regime" in Egypt, namely areas that supported the regime's political opposition group were subsequently neglected when decisions regarding critical infrastructure distribution, like water and sewerage lines, were made.

Hermet, Rose, and Roouquie have argued that elections in authoritarian countries provide a rare opportunity to analyze the public manifestation of a regime's attempt to perpetuate its control (1978, 9). The authors ask: "Are elections, considered as one of the most significant fields of analysis in Western multi-party states, so deprived of meaning in other regimes that they are not worth studying" (1978, 8)? This book finds that elections in an authoritarian context convey a great deal about the functioning of that regime and should be analyzed more for what they can tell us about the perpetuation of autocratic governments than as an indication of democratic transition. In fact, the elections solve political problems that have nothing to do with democracy. In Egypt, politics revolves around the complex interaction between a number of important societal actors, where elections have important implications for all.

---

[13] This theory makes particular sense in the Mexican setting, where the electoral contest of interest was the presidential race. Because no president could serve more than one six-year term, the PRI was forced to choose a new candidate every election cycle. Political entrepreneurs interested in someday competing for high office would recognize the invincibility of the PRI and choose not to defect. Although the idea is broadly applicable to a wide variety of cases, its focus on the dynamics of presidential elections makes this aspect of the theory less relevant for authoritarian countries with competitive parliamentary, but not presidential, elections. For example, multicandidate presidential elections were not introduced in Egypt until 2005, although competitive parliamentary elections have been in place for a much longer period. Do supermajority victories on the part of the hegemonic party deter challengers and defections at the parliamentary level? Not in Egypt, where both hegemonic party defectors and independent candidates associated with the Muslim Brotherhood often fare well in parliamentary contests.

[14] Keshavarian (2009) makes an interesting and related argument that, in Iran, the regime uses elections to gather information about the popularity and viability of allies.

1.1.1 Actors and Preferences

This book analyzes the triadic relationship between the leadership of the authoritarian regime, the rent-seeking elite that represents a critical pillar of support for this regime, and the broader Egyptian citizenry. In particular, it considers how both formal institutions – such as elections and the rules governing the prerogatives of parliamentarians – and informal norms mediate these relationships. Other relevant actors include the opposition Muslim Brotherhood and foreign actors such as the United States.

The Ruling Regime. Defining what constitutes the ruling regime in an authoritarian setting is a potentially treacherous undertaking, particularly because it is impossible to precisely identify the core of individuals who make up this body. The ruling regime in Egypt refers to those individuals who "exercise power"; this includes some actors who are not part of the formal state apparatus, and, conversely, there are many agents of the state who are not part of this elite grouping (Kienle 2001, 6). The regime in Egypt consists primarily of the president, his close family, and the small cadre of "super" elite that surround him, including selected senior military, party, and intelligence officers. This book will show that promotion decisions within the party and state structure are made on the basis of performance and revealed competence, and core membership in the regime elite is based on family ties, established loyalty, and personal connections. It is also noteworthy that the president serves as "patron-in-chief"; Kassem argues that the president's powers combined with the patronage he can bestow on others has created a clientelist structure that renders him the "ultimate patron" (2004, 168). The National Democratic Party (NDP), created and re-created by the regime, helps maintain this network of clients (Kienle 2001, 8).

The relationship between the regime and the state is a complicated one, particularly given the fact that the Egyptian state is large, porous, and has a tendency to promulgate policies that appear to contradict each other.[15] This suggests that the regime in Egypt sometimes finds itself in conflict with the very institutions that it has created (Bianchi 1989). At the start of my fieldwork for this book, I was troubled by this contradiction and concerned with the question of the intentionality of institutional selection. In other words, why would an authoritarian regime create or delegate power to institutions that either did not share its preferences or could not guarantee its preferred outcome? Over time, I came to realize that the policies put forth by the Egyptian regime, although they sometimes appeared ad hoc, represented a rational response to

---

[15] Poggi defines the modern state as "a set of complex institutional arrangements for rule operating through the continuous and regulated activities of individuals acting as occupants of office. The state, as the sum total of such offices, reserves to itself the business of rule over a territorially bounded society" (1978, 1). An important goal of the state as an institution is to make allocation processes "relatively predictable and stable," thus reflecting "consensus among all participants" (Poggi 1978, 2).

the day-to-day political events it was facing.[16] As political actors work to solve problems, a series of short-term decisions accumulate into a set of policies and institutions.[17] It also appears that the regime has engaged in a mixing of strategies, or what Magaloni, Diaz-Cayeros, and Estevez (2007) describe as a "portfolio diversification" of authoritarian tactics. The result is what Wedeen might characterize as "strategies without a strategist" (1999, 153), and, in many ways, the regime has used a process of trial and error in the creation of the formal and informal political institutions that have come to characterize its rule.

Although the challenges facing the authoritarian regime in Egypt have changed and continue to change over time, since the mid-1970s, certain political exigencies emerged that resonate to this day. First, there exists a relatively large class of rent-seeking support elite, in which many individuals have a quasi-legitimate claim to state spoils.[18] This class emerged in the period following Sadat's open-door economic policies and grew in size with increasing economic liberalization. Second, the regime faces the challenge of millions of underemployed, poor citizens whose economic insecurity encourages a preference for small, targeted economic rewards immediately over the discounted value of programmatic benefits in the future.[19] This comes in the context of a generalized withdrawal of the Egyptian state from its dominant role under President Gamal 'Abd al-Nasser and growing income inequality. Third, the regime faces the challenge of a popular Islamist opposition movement with a desire to express its support for political change. Channeling and neutralizing this movement, while simultaneously using elections as an occasion to gather critical information about popular support and cadre competence, provide both a challenge and an opportunity for the regime. Finally, Egypt increasingly exists in an external environment that encourages competitive elections.[20]

Why do elections represent a rational response for the regime given the challenges it faces? Competitive parliamentary elections are a cornerstone of the regime's political process and provide a myriad of benefits. It is not my contention that competitive elections were introduced for the purposes described

---

[16] This is not unlike the way Barkey describes Ottoman leaders responding to the challenges they encountered (1997, 57).

[17] As Pierson points out, "we should anticipate that there will be sizable gaps between the ex ante goals of powerful actors and the actual functioning of prominent institutions" (2004, 15).

[18] Of course, the implicit comparison in this statement is to other regimes of this type rather than to the size of the elite in Western democracies. Thanks go to Jorge Dominguez for making this point.

[19] See Desposato (2006) for a full description of this argument in the Latin American context. Levitsky (2007) further argues that, in contemporary Latin America, clientelist linkages are highly compatible with market-oriented economic reforms; one reason for this is that, in environments of large informal economies and widespread unemployment, clientelist links are particularly effective for winning votes.

[20] See Levitsky and Way (2005) for a description of the increasing cost of authoritarianism given a changing international environment.

in this book.[21] Rather, the benefits of competitive electoral institutions became apparent and evolved over time. Many of the benefits of elections are related to the distributive choices faced by the regime in the context of a financially stretched, postsocialist Egyptian state. In particular, elections contribute to regime health by removing some aspects of social control from the hands of the regime and delegating them to the electoral market. The institutionalization of these difficult allocation decisions creates what Huntington would call an adaptable and coherent political system that can be "effective, authoritative [and] legitimate" (1968, 2).

Although authoritarian regimes like the one in Egypt are typically described as "rigid and inflexible," it is increasingly clear that such regimes have the capacity to adapt in politically meaningful ways (Heydemann 2007b, 21). The existing institutions in Egypt enjoy a type of equilibrium yet are not static. Rather, change over time is in important part of the narrative as particular types of institutions, particularly ones that encourage a competitive political market, prevail.[22] At the same time, there exist endogenous by-products of this equilibrium that have the potential to undermine its stability over the long term.

The Rent-Seeking Elite. Writing about authoritarian regimes in general, Egyptian commentator Ayman al-Amir describes the logic of authoritarian survival for the regime in the following way:

> Autocracies perpetuate themselves in power through a supporting, beneficiary elite. This is not the standard electorate that votes governments and presidents in and out of office in decent democracies. Rather, they consist of exclusive special interest groups and include security officials, business tycoons, regime propagandists and self-serving political aspirants. To guarantee loyalty, the elite have to be awarded special privileges and lucrative incentives. They often stand to lose everything, and risk legal prosecution, should the alliance of interests collapse. So they are bonded to the regime and become its main apologists.[23]

In Egypt, the rent-seeking elite includes influential family heads, tribal leaders, successful businessmen, and senior bureaucratic appointees, referred to by

---

[21] Mahoney, for instance, has argued for the importance of distinguishing between the circumstances that led to the creation of an institution and the process by which that institution persists (2000, 512). Gandhi and Lust-Okar (2009) suggest that the factors associated with the emergence of a particular set of institutions do not necessarily explain their functioning over the long term and that, in fact, the institutionalization of elections and parliaments frequently preceded the development of ruling regimes.

[22] A primary critique promoted by Elster of functionalist explanations is that they do not deal adequately with the dynamics of change. Berger and Offe, however, argue that the extent that "social arrangements can be compared to biological selection mechanisms, as is certainly possible in the case of market competition, functionalist explanations in the strict sense (that is, without any actor-related qualifications) appear to be perfectly admissible" (1982, 523), and, in fact, are beyond the scope of Elster's critique.

[23] *Al-Ahram Weekly*, April 10–16, 2008.

Baaklini, Deroeux, and Springburg as the loyal "foot soldiers" of the regime (1999, 237–8).[24] One editorialist deems them the "intermediates" (*taḥtāniyîn*), or the level of people between the ruling regime in Cairo and the citizenry.[25] This class of elite is a critically important base of support for the ruling regime because the elites mediate the potentially contentious relationship between the regime and society.

The various iterations of hegemonic party structure that have emerged since the 1952 Free Officers' Coup have provided important venues for the interests of this elite.[26] Egypt's hegemonic party has drawn supporters as a result of its "inextricable ties to the state and the latter's control of vast resources," where "material interest and opportunism" are the main draws (Beattie 1991, 42–3). Beattie (1991) asks a powerful question: What happens to this support network when state resources dry up? Writing in the early 1990s, he predicts that support for the party would also evaporate (Beattie 1991, 42–3). This seems entirely reasonable given the experience of countries like Mexico, where single-party dominance as an equilibrium was unsettled by changing economic conditions (Magaloni 2006; Greene 2007). Yet even in the context of a postsocialist Egyptian state, the ruling regime in Egypt has been able to adapt and secure the continued loyalty of the rent-seeking elite. Competitive parliamentary elections, particularly elections that provide opportunities for competition within the NDP, emerged as the primary mechanism by which the authoritarian regime in Egypt makes difficult decisions about the allocation of spoils in the context of a broad, rent-seeking elite support base.

Competitive parliamentary elections – in contrast to lotteries, queues, or other allocation mechanisms – serve this purpose quite well. Highly contested elections in Egypt closely resemble an all-pay auction, with bidders (parliamentary candidates) paying for a shot at the prize (the parliamentary seat). The bid that candidates pay is the cost of the electoral campaign, which is not financed by the hegemonic party. Rather than payment going to the regime directly, however, the largest expense associated with a campaign involves side payments to supporters as part of election mobilization. In this way, the cost of popular mobilization at election time is passed on to elite office seekers, who are required to construct their own local support networks to win office. From the perspective of the authoritarian regime, this is a positive externality created by electoral competition that lotteries, queues, and other allocation mechanisms would not generate. From the perspective of the rent-seeking elite, allocation

---

[24] This is not to say – quite cynically – that all family heads, tribal leaders, bureaucrats, and successful businessmen in Egypt are concerned only, or even primarily, with rent seeking. Many are motivated by status, prestige, and the desire to effect political change and improve living conditions of the poor. The importance of rent seeking as a political activity among individuals of this class is important enough, however, that it is a focus here.

[25] *Al-Masry Al-Youm*, March 19, 2008.

[26] My use of the term "hegemonic" party is not intended to make a statement about a regime's use of power, rather than force, to achieve its political goals. Rather, I adopt the expression in continuity with previous scholarly work.

decisions are made according to established norms and expectations; individuals who engage in the largest amount of redistribution within their districts are given the opportunity to reap the benefits of membership in parliament. Elections, then, are a decentralized distribution mechanism that aids authoritarian survival by regularizing intra-elite competition, while at the same time outsourcing the cost of political mobilization and redistribution.

What kinds of benefits can one expect as a result of holding office? Holding a parliamentary seat in Egypt does not afford one the opportunity to influence policy in a meaningful way. Rather, the benefits of holding a parliamentary seat come from the informal access and preferential treatment given to legislators, particularly Egypt's high guarantee of parliamentary immunity, which protects parliamentarians from arrest, detention, or charge of criminal activity. In other words, holding a seat in parliament offers important opportunities for rent seeking simultaneously with protection from charges of corruption.[27] This arrangement is more credible than simply investing the elite in graft. In order for parliamentary immunity to be lifted, two-thirds of the assembly must vote to do so, and most parliamentarians, given the state of their own financial dealings, are reluctant to lift their colleagues' immunity in all but the most egregious cases. As a result, members of the rent-seeking elite spend a significant amount on their parliamentary campaigns. In 2005, the average campaign was reported to cost more than LE 12 million.[28] As one opposition journalist put it, parliamentary hopefuls spend millions to reap billions.[29]

Much of the competition for these seats takes place within Egypt's hegemonic party as NDP official candidates compete with NDP independents, who rejoin the party upon winning their seat. Independent candidacy has become exceedingly common, particularly for NDP-affiliated individuals who are not able to secure a place on the official party list. In 2005, 85 percent of all candidates running were independents, many of them affiliated with the NDP (Teti, Gervasio, and Rucci 2006).

By investing members of the rent-seeking elite in corrupt or, at the very least, below-board economic activity, members of this class become vulnerable to charges of economic crimes either under the current regime or under some future democratic or authoritarian government. As a result, current and former parliamentarians who engage in semi-licit or illicit activity find it harder to defect against the ruling regime, which maintains an extensive apparatus for collecting information on the dealings of these individuals. Thus, in the context of the declining role of the Egyptian state in the economy, the ruling regime has – to a large, but not total extent – substituted distribution of state largesse for

---

[27] A parliamentarian earns benefits that are a function of his effort and skill at taking advantage of the opportunities afforded by holding office. This is not unlike Akerlof's description of the "rat race" (1976), where there are wage differentials for workers who are able to work more quickly or under more difficult conditions.

[28] *Egyptian Gazette*, February 5, 2007; the exchange rate at the time was about LE 6:US$ 1.

[29] *Al-Wafd*, September 20, 2005.

access to market-based corruption via parliamentary office.[30] Noted Egyptian economist Galal Amin describes corruption in Egypt over the past four decades in the following way:

> While corruption in Nasser's era, especially in the aftermath of the 1967 defeat, was still in its infancy and was met with strong condemnation, it turned into a big festival in Sadat's era as people enjoyed every possible opportunity [to commit corrupt actions] fearlessly. In Mubarak's era, however, condemnation of corruption has disappeared ... corruption has become part and parcel of the regime itself ... in other words, since the 1980s corruption has been gradually legalized.[31]

Amin's observations and the prevailing political wisdom in Egypt both suggest that elite corruption has emerged as a growing trend. Editorialist Soliman Gouda has gone so far as to describe parliament as a greenhouse for below-board business interests, where corruption is allowed to flourish.[32] Competitive elections serve as a façade for elite corruption, creating an alliance that binds the highest levels of the Mubarak regime and Egypt's rent-seeking elite.

The Citizenry. Citizens face a complex set of factors when making decisions about how they should participate in electoral contests within an authoritarian context. On one hand, elections provide an opportunity for public expression, even if limited. Supporters of Egypt's opposition Muslim Brotherhood have the chance to vote their candidates into office, raising the profile of the group. Voters also have the opportunity to send a signal to the regime (or to corrupt vote buyers) by spoiling their ballots. In addition, citizens have the opportunity to gain material rewards through their participation in the competitive elections. This is not a new phenomenon in the Egyptian context. Noted playwright Tawfiq al-Hakim commented that the biggest beneficiary of the 1938 elections was the "poor peasant ... this neglected, forgotten, and despised being is only valued on voting day. At any other time, his voice is lost in the wind, but on this particular day price is a function of demand."[33] Vote buying remains a common phenomenon in Egyptian elections, and the electoral season becomes a key opportunity for the masses to interact with elites.[34] Elections serve as a focal point for other types of giveaways as well, particularly increases in bonuses and incentive pay for state sector employees in the run-up to parliamentary contests. These small increases in salaries and other benefits offer

---

[30] This type of substitution has not occurred in all authoritarian regimes undergoing economic liberalization, however. For example, Greene argues that, in the Mexican case of economic liberalization, privatization of state-owned enterprises caused "well-greased patronage networks to run dry" (2007, 33-4).

[31] *Al-Ahram Weekly*, April 3–9, 2008.

[32] *Al-Masry Al-Youm*, September 23, 2008.

[33] Quoted in *Al-Ahram*, November 8, 2000.

[34] *Al-Masry Al-Youm*, June 28, 2007.

the possibility of a gradual improvement for public sector workers and other beneficiaries.

On the other hand, participation in elections is a potentially costly act. Elections are often accompanied by violence, as the hired thugs of various candidates jockey outside polling stations, and the government – in some cases – works to stem the success of candidates associated with the Muslim Brotherhood. Even under the best circumstances, voting often requires a lengthy wait in line. As a result, participation in parliamentary elections has been confined largely to a) poor individuals who believe that the material rewards associated with their participation outweigh the costs and b) ideological supporters of the opposition Muslim Brotherhood. Large blocs of the middle and upper-middle classes have been left out of the electoral equation (Soliman 2006). Survey results suggest, however, that 98 percent of a representative sample of Egyptians believe that democracy is a very good or fairly good way to govern their country, where elections are closely associated with democracy (Tessler and Gao 2005). The direct benefit from elections for poor Egyptians who sell their votes to local political entrepreneurs is the cash or favor they receive and use to meet their immediate financial needs. The long-term cost of these elections, in terms of how they perpetuate the authoritarian regime, is less obvious and more dispersed.

Other Actors. Although the focus of this book is on the triadic relationship between the ruling regime, the rent-seeking elite, and the broader citizenry, other relevant political actors are considered in the analysis. These actors include the Muslim Brotherhood, liberal intellectuals, and external actors such as the United States. The Muslim Brotherhood participates because elections are seen as an opportunity for the organization to establish itself as the most viable opposition group in the country, without posing a direct challenge to the existing regime. Liberal intellectuals have not challenged the authoritarian status quo more forcefully because they find democratic transition less appealing than their counterparts in other parts of the world. This is because the results of a free election might bring Islamist parties to power, and they have a history of censoring important forms of intellectual output, such as philosophy, art, and literature. This suggests that democracy – as a reflection of the preferences of the median voter – has the potential to impact the distribution of rights and civil liberties in important ways that hinder democratic transition. Finally, I find that electoral authoritarianism is incentive compatible for the United States, a key ally of and major foreign aid donor to Egypt.

1.1.2 Existing Explanations for Autocratic Resilience in Egypt

Theories to explain the resilience of authoritarianism in Egypt generally fall into one of two categories. The first contains essentialist explanations that consider authoritarianism in Egypt either a historic by-product of Egypt's natural environment or an outgrowth of Egypt's religious or cultural tradition. Some of these theories trace the authoritarian nature of Egyptian government back to antiquity, when pharaohs enjoyed an exalted position and power was highly concentrated in a single individual. Karl Wittfogel, in his classic text entitled *Oriental Despotism*, called Egypt a hydraulic society in which a powerful and centralized state is responsible for the large-scale government works needed for irrigation and flood control of the Nile (1957). This theme is also reflected in Gamal Hamdan's *Shakhsiat Miṣr (The Personality of Egypt)* (1967). Others in this category have argued that Islam is associated with authoritarianism, both in an older generation of scholarship and more recently. The adage "one-thousand nights of despotism is preferable to one night of anarchy" is attributed to Islamic thought; others point to Koranic sources regarding the need for Muslims to obey their rulers as an explanation for authoritarian stability. In the contemporary literature, Fish (2002) argues that Muslim countries are demo-cratic "underachievers" and suggests that Islam's "subordination of women" may be the causal explanation for the Muslim world's authoritarian status. Even among contemporary Egyptian social scientists, there is a sense that "authoritarian beliefs are deeply embedded in the Egyptian culture" (Zaki 1998, 116). Zaki identifies both submissiveness to authoritarianism and toler-ance as two broad characteristics of Egyptian political culture that are ingrained in Egyptian consciousness as a result of Egypt's Islamic legacy (1995, 137). There is also the sense that *fitna*, or discord, cannot be tolerated in Islam. According to Zaki, "the fear of *fitna* has inculcated Egyptian society with a deep aversion to opposition and division and an appreciation of strong author-ity" (1995, 139).

The second category of explanations focuses on the impact of repression and fraud to perpetuate the existing regime. Journalistic accounts of authoritarian-ism in Egypt tend to emphasize the repressive prowess of the state and the use of force and electoral manipulation. There is no question that the country's domestic security services are key to safeguarding the regime. The tragedy of modern dictatorship in countries like Egypt, however, is that repressive mea-sures (or the threat of repressive measures) are not even necessary for the vast majority of the population, because many citizens either abstain from polit-ical participation or turn out to support the ruling regime and its political allies.[35] This has led Zartman to call on scholars to look "beyond coercion" to explain the durability of the Arab state (1988a). I find that, unlike popular and journalistic portrayals of authoritarian rulers as despised and dependent on repression and electoral fraud to perpetuate their power, authoritarianism in Egypt is sustained through more subtle, though equally effective, systematic and institutionalized channels. As a result, electoral institutions have been a key element of the Mubarak regime's longevity.

This book builds on a variety of works that focus on the institutional sources of authoritarian stability in Egypt. Whereas some have focused on the role of

---

[35] This is what Diaz-Cayeros, Magaloni, and Weingast (2003) call the "tragic brilliance" of hegemonic party regimes.

informal institutions (Singerman 1995), others have considered how political pluralism (Kassem 1999; Albrecht 2005; Koehler 2008) and the authoritarian party structure (Brownlee 2007) reinforce autocracy in Egypt. Writing about Egypt in the context of the broader Arab world, Lust-Okar (2005) seeks to explain opposition pressure for political reform, given a state of prolonged economic crisis. An implication of her argument is that opposition pressure is a precursor, or perhaps even a necessary condition, for regime change. Lust-Okar finds that countries that allow managed political liberalization are able to effectively control their opposition. This occurs because moderates come to enjoy the benefits of participation in government institutions and are thus reluctant to join radicals in their fight against the regime. Although Lust-Okar does not argue that this is why countries have competitive elections, political liberalization is typically associated with competitive electoral contestation.[36] Although the mechanisms that I describe for the persistence of autocracy in Egypt differ from those mentioned by Lust-Okar (2005), they share a common focus on the use of seemingly democratic political institutions to perpetuate authoritarian rule.

1.1.3 Alternative Theories for the Role of Elections in Autocracies

Although some scholars have considered electoral authoritarianism an unstable "halfway house" between democracy and autocracy, the idea that countries move along a democratic trajectory has been challenged (Levitsky and Way 2003).[37] It is becoming increasingly clear that many authoritarian regimes that hold elections are not democratizing at all; rather, they are simply "well-institutionalized authoritarian regimes" (Geddes 2005). In fact, increasingly, scholars of authoritarian regimes find that autocratic elections stabilize these regimes (Lust-Okar 2006; Magaloni 2006; Greene 2007).

The longevity of many electoral authoritarian regimes has led to a burgeoning literature on the reasons authoritarians hold elections and the political and other effects that these elections engender. Whereas some works have attempted to characterize these regimes definitionally and theoretically, others have sought either to explain the inner workings of these regimes or to generalize about some larger set of cases. Cox (2008), for example, focuses on

---

[36] In the 1990s, the regime faced an almost decade-long battle against an extremist Islamist movement. The moderates, although often conflated with radicals in government propaganda and repression campaigns, did not join in this fight, however. The cost of joining the radicals was simply too high. In fact, over time, we see the endogenous formation of preference for these groups; Egyptian radicals eventually came to moderate their political views, and some even stood for parliamentary seats in the 2005 elections. See Blaydes and Rubin (2008) for a more thorough discussion of the deradicalization process.

[37] The idea of liberalized authoritarianism as an unstable "halfway house" was promoted by Huntington (1991, 137). Diamond (1989) has argued that low levels of institutionalization make pseudo-democratic regimes unstable.

an autocrat's desire to maintain his personal safety, arguing that authoritarian rulers agree to electoral risk to reduce the likelihood of violent removal from office via coup or revolution. Lust-Okar (2005) argues that dictators use the rules surrounding authoritarian elections to create "divided structures of contestation," where parties that participate in these contests become more invested in the regime.

As Geddes (2005) points out, authoritarian regimes that hold elections tend also to have political parties and some form of legislature. As a result, there is significant overlap in the relevant literature. Here, I review three major themes in the existing literature that theorize how authoritarian regimes use electoral and related institutions in an effort to explain why the existing literature does an inadequate job of handling the Egyptian case – a case that I believe is emblematic of many Middle Eastern and other autocracies.

Cooptation through Legislative Policy Sharing. Gandhi and Przeworski (2001; 2006) and Gandhi (2008) are associated with the idea that political opposition is coopted through its participation in policy-influential legislatures by way of electoral competition. They argue that when the opposition is strong, dictators make more extensive policy compromises to keep the opposition from rebelling. "Policy concessions require a forum in which demands can be revealed and agreements can be hammered out. Hence, we assume that the presence of institutions, especially of parties in legislatures, is an indicator of policy concessions" (Gandhi and Przeworski 2006).[38] Although this may be the case in some authoritarian countries, the assumption that legislatures legislate is an inaccurate characterization for many autocracies, particularly those in the Middle East.[39]

Although the Egyptian legislature enjoys broad policy-making authority in principle, in practice, the president controls a docile majority in parliament, which generally renders his legislature prerogatives into formal laws. The president is considered to be above parliamentary authority, and he has many options for pushing his policy agenda. For example, the president can legislate by decree when parliament is not in session and can also bypass parliament through a government-sponsored referendum. Although Article 151 of the constitution stipulates that parliamentary approval is necessary for international

---

[38] Wright (2008) convincingly argues that, although much of the previous literature on authoritarian institutions assumes that authoritarian legislatures serve the same purpose in all kinds of regimes, in fact, there are important distinctions to be made between different types of authoritarian legislative institutions. He finds that legislatures improve economic performance in dominant-party and military regimes but not in personalist dictatorships and monarchies, arguing that different types of authoritarian legislatures serve different functions.

[39] For example, although the authors use the existence of Islamist parliamentarians in the Jordanian parliament as evidence that policy compromises were taking place, Jordan specialists cast doubt on this evidence by reporting that Jordanian parliamentarians (and the public more generally) view the job of legislators as providing jobs and delivering services to their local constituents and families, not making policy (Lust-Okar 2006).

agreements, this is not enforced. In 1997, for example, the parliament rubber stamped eighty-seven international agreements in one parliamentary meeting, and eighteen were never even discussed at that meeting (Fahmy 2002, 52). Likewise, defense and foreign policy matters are reserved for the executive. The situation is similar regarding domestic and budgetary issues, leaving little room for opposition policy influence. This suggests that parliaments and the elections that bring them to power, in cases like Egypt, exist to serve some other purpose than cooptation via a shared policy space.

Demonstration Effects. A number of works describe the demonstration effects of authoritarian elections and how these effects shore up support for an autocratic regime (Geddes 2008; Magaloni 2006; Wedeen 2008). One important theory regarding the way authoritarians use elections involves electoral institutions as a means to perpetuate certain types of "national fictions," particularly with regard to the popularity and strength of an authoritarian regime or leader. Wedeen writes that scholars who study the political importance of symbolic acts argue that these acts operate to produce forms of legitimacy and hegemony, enabling authoritarian leaders to strengthen their rule (1998, 505–6). Wedeen takes this argument one step further and finds that, in Syria, the Asad regime engages in similar behavior, but no one actually believes the fictitious public pronouncements and election results that come about from these institutions. Rather, citizens behave *as if* they do, and this ability to force citizens into particular symbolic acts serves as a mechanism of coercion (Wedeen 1998, 519). For Wedeen, elections are part of a subtle coercive apparatus. For example, former President Asad was congratulated for winning 99 percent of the vote. These "requirements of public dissimulation" are imposed on regular citizens, who are forced to participate in the authoritarian's rule (Wedeen 1998, 504). Wedeen writes:

> Political practices that encourage dissimulation register the participants' fluency in the rhetorical operations that the regime puts forth. The regime's power resides in its ability to sustain national fictions, to enforce obedience, to make people say and do what they otherwise would not. This obedience makes people complicit. It entangles them in self-enforcing relations of domination, thereby making it hard for participants to see themselves simply as victims of the state's caprices (1998, 519).

For Wedeen, the use of symbolic power represents a weapon in the authoritarian arsenal alongside the use of various inducements and punishments. In other words, in the absence of the cult, other – perhaps more costly – disciplinary forms are required to sustain obedience (Wedeen 1999, 153). She writes: "Asad's cult is an effective mechanism of power because while economizing on the actual use of force, it also works to generate obedience.... In other words, political systems are upheld not only by shared visions, material gains, and punishments, but also by unstable, shifting enactments of power and powerlessness, which are no less real for being symbolic" (Wedeen 1999,

146–7).[40] In the less overtly authoritarian context of Yemen, Wedeen finds
that controlled electoralization of the political scene has been used to empty
democratic procedures of what one would expect to be their true content – free
and fair representation of voters (2008, 74). For Wedeen, the Yemeni regime's
ability to carry out a credible presidential election creates power "by demonstrating to regime officials and citizens alike that the regime could get away
with the charade" (2008, 77). Whether regimes are sustained via habituation
through symbolic acts (Wedeen 1998) or systematic depoliticization through
competitive yet hollow elections (Wedeen 2008), neither explanation tackles
the important material and distributive implications of contested elections,
which are key in the Egyptian case.

Magaloni (2006) argues that elections disseminate public information about
the strength of the regime's hegemonic party and that this helped the PRI,
Mexico's hegemonic party, to create an image of invincibility that deterred
potential entrants to the political market. To demonstrate this, high turnout
and a supermajority victory were required for each election; at times, the PRI
actually stuffed ballot boxes to create the impression of higher turnout without
changing the relative distribution of votes. Geddes (2005) concurs, arguing
that "high turnout and supermajoritarian election outcomes signal that citizens
remain acquiescent," thus deterring both civilian and military rivals. Yet, what
happens when turnout is low and the hegemonic party cannot win a majority
without reincorporating party defectors? Would elections of this type, as are
common in Egypt, actually send the opposite signal to potential opponents?
Geddes (2008) focuses on the positive demonstration effects that parties and
elections can afford an incumbent authoritarian. She finds that the creation
of a party increases the risk that a coup attempt will fail for two reasons:
a) such parties increase the number of citizens who have something to lose
from the ouster of the dictator, and b) such parties can mobilize citizens in
street protests if needed at the time of a coup. Yet, coups happen very quickly,
often more quickly than parties can organize proregime street demonstrations.
Geddes (2008) also argues that elections serve the same basic function as street
demonstrations in that they influence potential opponents' perceptions of how
hard it would be to take down the regime. Yet, in both Geddes (2008) and
Magaloni (2006), for elections to matter in the way that they describe, both

---

[40] Rather than obedience becoming habitual via symbolic acts, as suggested by Wedeen (1998),
Kuran argues that a lack of information about others' preferences sustains authoritarian rule.
Kuran argues that citizens living under authoritarian rule very often engage in the act of
preference falsification, or the act of misrepresenting one's genuine wants under perceived
social pressures (1995, 3). Kuran contends that, when privately held preferences are revealed,
the overthrow of an unpopular regime is a likely outcome (1995, 89). Application of Kuran's
ideas may be limited to the few, but nontrivial, examples of authoritarian regimes that also
place considerable limits on political and press freedom. An increasing number of authoritarian
countries, however, are sustained despite considerable freedom of expression, where citizens
are able to reveal their private preferences to one another. For example, Egyptian political life is
meaningfully open. Anti-Mubarak articles, jokes, placards, blogs, and e-mails routinely make
the rounds in ways that do not suggest citizens are particularly fearful of retribution.

turnout and election results should favor the dominance of the hegemonic party. When elections typically mobilize less than a quarter of eligible voters – as is common in Egypt – it is hard to imagine that these displays have the meaningful deterrent demonstration effects, suggesting a different mechanism or series of mechanisms at work.

Parties and Elections to Balance Military Strength. In a pair of papers, Geddes (2005; 2008) argues that parties and elections are used by autocrats to counterbalance the threat of the regime's most formidable potential foe – the military or factions within the military. Geddes (2005) writes that "because of its control of weapons and men, the military is always a potential threat, even to dictators who are officers themselves." The logic of her argument is that coup attempts are less likely to succeed in countries with party institutions because citizens are vested in the existing organizational structure of the regime (2005) and because of the positive demonstration effects that the party can create (2008). The implication is that "even when authoritarian parties are filled with opportunistic cadres who joined the party to get ahead...they still make a contribution to dictatorial longevity" (2005). The assumption that authoritarian institutions – like parties, parliaments, and elections – exist to balance potential threats from within the military is worth discussion independent of the mechanism elaborated previously. This is particularly so for the Egyptian case, where the military appears to be the final guarantor of the existing authoritarian regime. In fact, a similar argument was made about the Egyptian context by John Waterbury, who wrote that "Nasser had to build up the ASU (Arab Socialist Union) as a civilian counter to the military" when he was faced with the growing influence of Field Marshall 'Abd al-Hakim 'Amr (1983, 316).[41] My primary argument here is that, although it is possible – and perhaps even likely – that the hegemonic party served as a counterbalance to Egypt's military in the Nasser era, in more recent years, the development of the party and the regime's decision to continue holding multiparty elections are, in fact, consistent with the military's objectives. As a result, my arguments and Geddes's theory of parties for "coup-proofing" are not mutually exclusive, as Geddes refers primarily to the early periods of authoritarian consolidation.

[41] Although Waterbury describes the ASU as a counterweight to the military, he acknowledges that the military and the party were allies in at least some domains, particularly when it came to accepting policy packages that conformed with Soviet expectations in exchange for arms acquisitions (1983, 337). Cook disagrees with the argument that the ASU was established as a counterweight to the military (2003, 154). Leonard Binder makes the parallel but opposite argument to that put forward by Waterbury. Binder argues that 'Amr was called upon by Nasser to limit the activities of the leftists (1978, 343). The two organizations, therefore, appeared to serve as a left–right balance within the regime, although there is also evidence that Nasser may have been balancing left–right elements within the ASU simultaneously. Binder argues that the decision to use elections to restructure the ASU was in response to a growing leftist element that supported appointments based on Marxist credentials rather than popular support (1978). This suggests that elections may not have been implemented to balance the military but rather to balance leftist elite elements within the hegemonic party structure.

The most compelling argument for a confluence of regime–military interests in the Mubarak era is presented by Cook (2003; 2007). He argues that the Egyptian military has a clear "hierarchy of interests" with regime survival as the top objective. He finds that, in Egypt, the military did not object and may even have anticipated the benefits from this type of change (Cook 2007). In particular, the military will only respond to elections in a reactionary fashion when it perceives an encroachment on its core issue areas – most importantly, a threat to the political order (Cook 2007). For example, the hegemony of the NDP in the People's Assembly did not serve as a threat to the military, particularly because the parliament had increasingly become an "extension of the executive branch," according to Cook (2007, 70). The establishment of a dominant single-party structure via elections, therefore, served the overall interests of the regime and, as a result, the interests of the military as well.[42]

Cook also argues that there may actually be benefits to the military from the development of parties and elections. Greater political openness was accompanied by a more liberal economic environment, and this economic openness has provided the Egyptian military with some significant opportunities. Sadat's open-door economic policy allowed the military establishment to benefit from the "commissions game," permitting officers to get rich with lucrative military contracts (Cook 2007, 19). The military also got into the business of arms production and the manufacturing of civilian goods. By the late 1980s, defense industries sold civilian goods, including refrigerators, heavy turbines, and food products, worth hundreds of millions of Egyptian pounds annually (Waterbury 1993, 105). In these ways, Egypt's military regime "groped its way toward some form of state capitalism" (Waterbury 1993, 60). According to Brommelhorster and Paes, this is not unusual in the developing world, where "the special status enjoyed by members of the armed forces in many countries...gives them a degree of political leverage and economic privilege over and above their private sector competitors or other state enterprises" (2003, 1).[43]

Finally, the existence of semicompetitive parliamentary elections also helped to ease the relationship between the Egyptian regime and its most important

---

[42] In addition, Cook argues that there is a type of flexibility associated with maintaining a democratic façade. In particular, Mubarak and his allies believe that allowing the Muslim Brotherhood to participate in politics would reduce the willingness of Islamist activists to express themselves through strikes and more violent actions (Cook 2003, 167).

[43] For example, by 1994, the military-controlled Administration of National Service Projects in Egypt ran more than a dozen factories that employed tens of thousands of workers and produced everything from agricultural machines to medications to ovens (Frisch 2001). Increased foreign direct investment and rent streams from the United States were particularly important to the military in the development of these industries (Cook 2003, 177). Siddiqa (2007) describes the extensive business interests of the military in Pakistan. In Pakistan – like in Egypt – the military runs a commercial empire. The military in Pakistan derives a number of benefits as a result of the economic interests of the organization. These benefits include state land transferred to military personnel as well as military resources spent on perks and privileges for personnel. In Pakistan, these items are not on the official defense budget.

aid donor – the United States. In fact, Frisch (2001) and others have argued that the Egyptian military has been modernized almost completely at the expense of the United States and that this is particularly the case for "big ticket" and prestige items. Zaki argues that, to ensure the continued support of the military for his regime, Mubarak strove to preserve uninterrupted access to advanced weapons, training, and other benefits from the United States; this guaranteed that the army would have a direct stake in both his rule and the relationship to the United States (1995, 131). This suggests that the military may have come to appreciate the "range of pseudo-democratic institutions and representative structures," which served to insulate them from politics (Cook 2003, 168). Public dissatisfaction could be directed at other institutions, perhaps allowing the military to focus on its core interests, such as force development and rent seeking.[44]

The viewpoint presented here challenges existing conceptions that the hegemonic party and the military are competitors. Perhaps more important than the balancing of the military with political parties is the balancing that takes place between competing and overlapping institutions in related spheres of influence. For example, the oversight role of the parliament has been strengthened at various points in time to provide a counterweight to the hegemonic party. Nasser bolstered the powers of the parliament vis-à-vis the ASU by dropping ASU membership as a requirement for serving in parliament (Beattie 2000, 84). In addition, the Ministry of Interior's Central Security Forces (CSF) provide an important counterbalance to the conventional armed forces.[45] Springborg argues that Sadat's policy of demilitarization worked in favor of the Ministry of Interior (Springborg 1989, 140), and Mubarak continued to build up the CSF in order to balance military power (Frisch 2001).

[44] In addition, the Egyptian military has also witnessed a change in its role over time. Although the Egyptian military was a crucial pillar of the regime at its establishment, since its 1967 defeat by the Israelis, the military has maintained a relatively low profile (Cook 2003, 136–7). Beginning with Nasser and intensifying under Sadat, the Egyptian military has been intentionally and systematically depoliticized and professionalized, with little resistance (Zaki 1995, 128–9). Although the military played a more active role in the day-to-day activities of the regime in the pre-1967 period, post-1967 the military was largely absent from politics, perhaps in a bid to appear above the political fray. Waterbury has argued that the "tentacular spread of the military into the civilian sphere sapped it of its fighting capacity" (1983, 337). By the 1980s, the military was "merely one of a number of institutional interest groups and, if its claim on the budget, which slightly declined as a proportion of total spending and GNP, was any indicator, one carrying little privileged weight" (Hinnebusch 1988a, 131). Although still a key pillar of the regime, what Bianchi calls the "entrepreneurial army" (1989, 5) is also increasingly a bourgeois enclave with ready access to consumer goods and special housing (Beattie 1991). For example, the Egyptian army has constructed at least seventeen military cities to physically isolate the military enclave from the civilian population (Frisch 2001).

[45] The CSF is a paramilitary force responsible for the protection of public buildings, foreign embassies, and tourist attractions.

1.2 WHY EGYPT?

Why does Egypt make a good subject for the study of electoral authoritarianism? With more than 80 million citizens, Egypt is the largest country in the Arab world and one of the largest and most politically significant in the Middle East. Egypt has long served as a political leader to countries in the region. In particular, political institutions that have developed in Egypt often find their way to other Arab states. As a result of its role as a bellwether for political developments across the Middle East, Egypt, as a subject of academic research, has been the subject of intense scrutiny. And with many of the world's remaining authoritarian regimes found in this region, examining autocracy in such a context is useful for both theory building and empirical testing.

From a theoretical perspective, studying Egypt offers a number of important opportunities. First, Egypt's institutional arrangements closely resemble the modal authoritarian regime that exists in the world today. As a result, Egypt has been described as the "perfect model" of semi-authoritarianism (Ottaway 2003, 31). Whereas the Egyptian case may be definitionally distinct from examples of "competitive authoritarian" regimes, as described by Levitsky and Way (2002), electoralization in Egypt bears important similarities to electoral processes in competitive authoritarian regimes, such as Malaysia, Mexico under the PRI, and Russia. In addition, Egypt also represents an excellent case for the study of comparative clientelism. Kitschelt and Wilkinson (2007) find that there has been a lack of scholarly attention paid to patterns of linkage among politicians, parties, and citizens, particularly in authoritarian regimes, and this book seeks, in part, to address that omission.

In the introduction to *Autocracy*, Gordon Tullock correctly points out that collecting information in a nondemocratic setting is highly challenging and that these difficulties explain why the existing literature on nondemocracies tends to be sparse and poor (1987, 31). There is no question that researching authoritarianism in Egypt poses similar challenges, yet the setting also offers a number of important opportunities. First, the institutions that constitute the government and regime in Egypt are, as I have mentioned, both large and porous, offering multiple openings for a researcher to collect data and interview participants. In addition, Egypt's storied bureaucratic tradition means that certain types of data are available to a greater extent than in other authoritarian settings. During the period under study, Egypt also enjoyed a relatively free press and an extensive state-associated media bureaucracy responsible for publishing multiple daily and weekly newspapers as well as news magazines. As a result, this project makes considerable use of state, opposition, and independent media, both as sources of empirical information as well as to gauge elite and popular opinion on a variety of issues.

Although the questions that this book addresses are general, my methodological strategy has been to test these broad theories in very narrow, focused, and specific circumstances that allow for a degree of experimental control. The datasets I have collected exploit variation in Egypt across time (yearly and, in some cases, monthly data) and across space (governorates, neighborhoods, and electoral districts as units of analysis). I complement the quantitative analysis with more than eighty interviews conducted with Egyptian politicians, government employees, local council leaders, journalists, human rights activists, and academics during a year of field research in Egypt[46] and a close reading of the highly informative Egyptian press. Although a number of excellent projects have sought to develop sophisticated formal models of authoritarianism, or have employed large-N statistical analysis with country or regime as the unit of observation, few scholarly works have sought to develop theory and test the empirical implications of that theory within an authoritarian setting.

1.3   THE PLAN OF THIS BOOK

This book is organized as follows. Chapter 2 provides a brief history of economic and political change in Egypt since 1952 with an eye toward two overarching themes: the long-term trend toward more competitive electoral institutions and the gradual withdrawal of the state from its dominating role under Nasser. It is not a primary goal of this book to explain *why* competitive elections first emerged in Egypt. Describing the changing nature of political and economic institutions, however, elucidates the goals and priorities of the regime, particularly the need to establish and maintain an elite base of support. In particular, Chapter 2 seeks to explain how Egypt has converged on a particular set of electoral authoritarian institutions.

Chapter 3 describes some of the benefits that the authoritarian regime in Egypt derives from holding competitive elections. A primary argument of Chapter 3 is that parliamentary elections serve as an important means for distributing access to rents and opportunities for graft and, as a result, ease certain types of distributional conflicts, particularly within Egypt's hegemonic party – the NDP. Since 1990, official NDP candidates have competed vigorously with both NDP-affiliated and opposition candidates in expensive electoral races. Elections act as a kind of auction where the candidates who are willing to engage in the largest amount of economic redistribution to their districts are able to win parliamentary seats.[47] The benefits of holding office include access to rents and influence as well as parliamentary immunity from criminal prosecution, which is often used by office holders to avoid prosecution for corruption. In Chapter 3, I will also show how election results provide important information to the authoritarian regime regarding the competence of bureaucratic and party apparatchik.

Chapter 4 describes how election results provide the regime with a map of areas of political support for the opposition. Using election results and

---

[46] The primary fieldwork for this project took place March–December 2005 with follow-up trips in April–May 2006, April–May 2007, and August–September 2009.

[47] NDP and NDP-affiliated candidates finance campaigns out of their own pockets.

data from the Egyptian census, I find that, between 1986 and 1996, areas that supported the opposition subsequently saw smaller improvements by the government to their water and sewerage infrastructures than areas that supported regime candidates. The results of this analysis are consistent with core-voter models, where the incumbent elite reward loyal constituencies and punish opposition constituencies.

Chapter 5 considers the following question: Does the authoritarian regime in Egypt manipulate economic policy in the run-up to parliamentary elections? Although empirical evidence for the existence of electoral budget cycles is inconclusive in democratic countries, increasingly, the strongest statistical evidence for the phenomenon has been in authoritarian regimes. In Chapter 5, I argue that Egypt – with a highly centralized process for economic policy making – exhibits such patterns. Through analysis of both qualitative and quantitative data, I describe the particular strategies used by the regime for orchestrating economic incentives to induce support prior to elections.

Chapter 6 considers why citizens vote in Egyptian elections and under what circumstances ballots are spoiled. In Egypt, vote buying is common and, in line with the argument that a poor person benefits from a consumption good more than a wealthy person, I expect the poor to be more responsive to targeted rewards. In addition, I find that formal institutional factors, like the threat of economic sanction for failing to turn out, and informal norms, like the use of state media to support regime candidates, make the poor more likely to vote. In order to test my arguments, I have collected data on voter turnout for the 2000 parliamentary, 2002 municipal, and 2005 parliamentary and presidential elections at the local level. Using the appropriate ecological inference techniques, I find that illiterate people vote at nearly twice the rate of literate people in Egyptian elections. I also investigate the likelihood of ballot spoiling, or the intentional defiling or marking of a ballot to make it invalid. I argue that some vote sellers intentionally spoil their ballots as a political signal. Using data on spoiled ballots from more than 200 electoral districts for the 2005 parliamentary elections and 26 governorates for the 2005 presidential elections, I find empirical support for this theory.

Chapter 7 describes more fully why political entrepreneurs run for parliament when legislative institutions have little influence on policy. I argue that formal institutions and informal norms regarding the perks of holding office have made personal economic enrichment a primary motivation for seeking a seat in parliament. For a significant swath of the rent-seeking elite, elections provide a façade for political corruption; political entrepreneurs compete for parliamentary immunity, which allows them to engage in illegal profiteering with little fear of prosecution. In this way, the rent-seeking elite have come to enjoy a tacit alliance with the authoritarian regime that protects them from prosecution for graft.

Chapter 8 seeks to explain why the Muslim Brotherhood participates in parliamentary elections that, I have argued, work to stabilize the authoritarian regime as well as what factors explain the propensity of individuals to turn

out to vote for a programmatic, Islamist agenda. The vast majority of ideological voters support candidates from the opposition Muslim Brotherhood. I find
that participation in competitive parliamentary elections presents an opportunity for the Brotherhood to advance its agenda and signal its willingness to
cooperate with the regime leadership. A second part of Chapter 8 examines
both the structural factors that lead individuals to support the Brotherhood in
elections as well as the specific strategies the Brotherhood employs to encourage individuals to turn out in support of its candidates. Using a selection model
that considers the decision to run in a district as well as the determinants of
electoral success once the commitment to run has been made, I find that the
Brotherhood targets districts that are populated by their core constituency –
individuals that are literate but relatively underprivileged. Their ability to win
in a particular district, however, is a function of the level of regime repression.

Chapter 9 considers the implications of democratic transition for the distribution of civil rights and liberties to Egyptian artists and liberal intellectuals.
I argue that, although artists and liberal intellectuals have played an influential, if not pivotal, role in transitions to democracy in many countries around
the world, Egyptian artists and intellectuals have been reluctant to push for
democratic change because free elections are likely to bring to power Islamist
organizations that have a history of censoring important intellectual outputs,
such as philosophy, art, and literature. Which groups, then, have the incentive
to challenge the authoritarian regime more forcefully for democracy? I argue
that labor organizations, peasants, and university students are most likely to
lead an effective grassroots, anti-authoritarian movement in Egypt, potentially
in alliance with Islamist groupings.

Chapter 10 argues that the distributive significance of electoral competition extends beyond the domestic sphere to Egypt's relationship with external
actors, including foreign aid donors like the United States, that play a critical
role in providing financial assistance for the regime. Particularly, this chapter
seeks to explain why foreign government efforts to promote democratization
in Egypt have been so unsuccessful. To answer this question, I develop an
agenda-setting model of democratization in authoritarian regimes, where foreign actors, such as the United States or international financial institutions,
serve as veto players along with the regime leadership. I argue that foreign
actors tend to promote the electoralization of authoritarian regimes rather
than policies that diminish regime dominance. This is because authoritarians
are the agenda setters, and they have the ability to select their preferred point
(i.e., the set of institutions) after considering the winset of the foreign actor as
a constraint.

Chapter 11 considers the Egyptian experience in a broader comparative
perspective. I find that there are four primary types of electoral–institutional
arrangements across the authoritarian states of the Arab world: a) hegemonic
party regimes with high levels of political contestation, such as Egypt; b) constitutional monarchies with high levels of contestation; c) single-party regimes
with limited electoral competition; and d) nonconstitutional monarchies

with low levels of electoral contestation. I describe how Egypt's experience with electoral competition compares with that of other states in the region. Chapter 11 also offers some tentative conclusions regarding where and when we would expect to see competitive authoritarian elections emerging across the Arab Middle East. I argue that two factors stand out as being of particular importance when describing observed variation in electoral competition across Arab states. The first is the relative wealth of citizens in the polity, which tends to be largely a function of access to external rents, such as oil revenue. In countries with higher levels of natural resource wealth, authoritarian regimes are less in need of mechanisms to distribute patronage as individuals are more likely to have their financial needs met. The second dimension of interest involves the size and nature of the ruling coalition. Regimes that are ruled by a minority group – whether ethnic, religious, geographic, tribal, or otherwise – may already have mechanisms for patronage distribution in place, minimizing the need for elections to serve this role. In such regimes, the size of the elite may be fairly small, easing certain types of patronage distribution pressures.

Chapter 12 discusses the possibility for future political change in Egypt through an exploration of how the electoral authoritarian equilibrium that I have described contains within itself undermining factors that have the potential to destabilize this equilibrium over time.

2

Political and Economic Change since 1952

Although parliamentary elections took place in Egypt during the late 1800s, historians have identified two significant periods of multiparty politics in the country (Beattie 2000). The first occurred following the promulgation of the 1923 constitution, after the British declared an end to the protectorate and Egypt became an independent state.[1] The second began in 1976 under President Anwar al-Sadat and continues through the rule of Hosni Mubarak. Although the focus of this book is on an electoral authoritarian equilibrium that has emerged under Mubarak, this chapter seeks to explain some of the dynamics that have led the authoritarian regime in Egypt to converge on this particular set of institutions.[2]

The history of institutional change in Egypt suggests two seemingly contradictory facets. On one hand, the Egyptian experience supports Heydemann's contention that authoritarianism has proven to be an adaptive, highly flexible style of rule (2007b, 22). Egyptian political institutions have evolved over

---

[1] Egyptian political reformers, such as NDP defector Ossama al-Ghazali Harb, have described this period as a potential model for competitive party politics in Egypt in the future (interview with Ossama al-Ghazali Harb, editor and Shura Council member, May 2, 2006). Although not a focus of this book, there exist some interesting parallels between elections during the pre–1952 era and later elections. For example, the parliamentary elections of 1931 – among the most controversial and best documented of the period – have been described as a bitterly fought competition between local notables (Brown 1990, 154). How did the local elite convince rural Egyptians to turn out to vote? Brown writes that the elite mobilized the peasant vote through a combination of carrots and sticks. "Peasants voted not because they felt any inclination to do so, but because officials and notables enticed and on occasion even coerced them to vote" (Brown 1990, 150). In other words, many Egyptians either voted in exchange for favors or to escape punishment, a situation that mirrors contemporary Egypt and is described more fully in Chapter 6.

[2] Although in many ways 1976 would appear to be a natural starting point for a research project focusing on the distributive consequences of elections in Egypt, this book focuses on electoral competition during the rule of Mubarak. By focusing on the Mubarak era, I am able to hold constant factors that may be idiosyncratic to Mubarak as a political leader.

time to accommodate changing circumstances and exigencies. At the same time, Egyptian institutions have also exhibited a degree of path dependence.[3] Pierson (2004) argues that there tends to be some institutional stickiness associated with inherited social arrangements; in other words, there is a status quo bias in political institutions. In the case of Egyptian electoral institutions, options available to the ruling regime have been constrained, to some degree, by the country's past political experiences and institutions. Whereas this might imply that elections represent a suboptimal outcome from the perspective of the ruling regime, this need not be the case. Indeed, the desire to avoid the costs associated with undoing an existing institution (e.g., elections) may have actually encouraged the ruling regime to innovate in ways that have made existing institutions work for stability. And given the variegated institutional options associated with electoralization, the ruling regime seems to have suffered little because of this institutional stickiness. As a result, the flexible and evolving nature of these institutions suggests that political change can take place within the historical constraints of Egypt's institutional legacy.

Mubarak inherited a regime that had witnessed the rise of internal, electoral competition beginning in the late Nasser period and intensifying under Sadat. This overall trend of increased electoral competition is apparent despite periods of deliberalization. The increase in electoral competition over time has been concomitant with a second general trend of economic liberalization and increasing economic competition in Egypt. A primary argument of this chapter is that a growing reliance on market mechanisms in the economy has reinforced increasing competition in the electoral market in a number of important ways. Most significantly, economic and political liberalization has worked to empower Egypt's rent-seeking elite as a key base of support for the authoritarian regime. At the same time, the diminished role of the Egyptian state in the economy has left the regime with fewer resources to buy the support of this critical constituency; elections have emerged as an important way to distribute resources in the face of the state's withdrawal. As a result, economic and political liberalization go hand in hand, but not in a way that destabilizes authoritarianism. Rather, economic liberalization encourages the development of clientelistic relationships throughout the political system in an environment of increasing resource scarcity.

My arguments about Egypt suggest that economic liberalization need not serve as a driver of regime change or democratization. Proponents of such a position typically argue that policies that liberalize the domestic economy – like privatization of state-owned enterprises – create economic crises that

---

[3] Whereas the institution of elections might be thought of as "path dependent" in the loose sense of the term, it is not clear that electoral institutions in Egypt would meet Mahoney's definition of path dependence as "those historical sequences in which contingent events set into motion institutional patterns or event chains that have deterministic properties" (2000, 507). In particular, authoritarian elections in Egypt appear to contain within them both self-reinforcing properties as well as self-undermining ones.

can be politically destabilizing (Haggard and Kaufman 1995). According to Haggard and Kaufman (1995, 8), this is because such crises damage the "coalition of interests" that sustain the status quo. Given the unpopularity of economic liberalization, policies of this type are thought to undermine an existing authoritarian regime (Fish and Choudhry 2007). Indeed, in Egypt in both 1977 and 1986, economically driven riots posed an important challenge to the regime. In both cases, however, the regime was able to recover from the popular challenge through its continued reliance on a coalition of elites. Discussing the case of Mexico, Greene (2007) considers what happens when a state is unable to maintain control over the domestic economy as a result of economic liberalization. According to Greene, "a leaner federal public bureaucracy yielded fewer patronage jobs," causing the PRI's system of patronage to run out of the funds needed to sustain itself (2007, 8). In this way, economic liberalization created an opening for left-wing opposition parties to emerge (Greene 2007, 91) and was a proximate cause of the PRI's decline. My analysis of Egypt suggests one route whereby economic liberalization both a) allows an authoritarian regime to reconstitute its ruling coalition and b) reinforces a system of electoral competition with clientelistic relationships at its core.

This argument complements a series of scholarly works linking economic liberalization to clientelism, neopatrimonial political institutions, and continued authoritarianism. For example, Ehteshami and Murphy (1996) argue that economic liberalization makes autocratic states simultaneously more internally competitive and more authoritarian. In the context of Latin American politics, Levitsky (2007, 209) finds that clientelist linkages are "highly compatible" with market-based economic liberalization in contrast to the conventional wisdom, which suggests that, as societies modernize, clientelism should recede. Schlumberger (2008) argues that structural adjustment in Middle Eastern countries, like Egypt, has created a personalized system of political rule whereby private-sector elite are linked to the ruling regime through informal clientelist networks that are central to the authoritarian system. In a discussion of Egypt, Hinnebusch (2001a, 118) has argued that, as neoliberalism has widened "state dependence on the market economy, the more state interests – in stability – may be seen to coincide with bourgeois class interests."[4]

In the sections that follow, I discuss the use of elections under Nasser, then the conditions under which multiparty politics were first introduced under Sadat. Next, I consider the factors contributing to Mubarak's decision to continue holding multiparty parliamentary elections after Sadat's assassination and changes to political institutions during the Mubarak era. I also trace trends in economic liberalization throughout each of these periods and connections between liberalization with management of elite interests.

---

[4] Clark and Kleinberg (2000) also challenge the conventional wisdom that economic liberalization promotes democratization. They argue that, for a wide swath of cases, including a number in the Middle East, the withdrawal of the state from a prominent economic role does not encourage the type of civil society development that promotes democracy.

2.1   SINGLE-PARTY POLITICS AND ELECTIONS UNDER NASSER

The current Egyptian regime came to power in 1952 with a coup undertaken by the Free Officers, a cabal of military officers advocating nationalist and socialist policies. Although the land reform undertaken by the regime created a significant link between the regime and the masses, the 1952 coup is not considered a popular revolution by most historians (Vatikiotis 1961, 74–5). The Free Officers abrogated the constitution that had been in place under the monarchy and replaced it with one that granted strong executive authority to the president. During a transition period from 1953 to 1956, the Revolution Command Council – which represented little more than a reconstitution of the Free Officers' executives – together with the cabinet, took on the task of setting national policy (Vatikiotis 1991, 382).

The new regime undertook a series of economic policies – particularly nationalizations – which resulted in a largely state-controlled economy (Waterbury 1993, 60). Prior to this, production and investment had been largely in the hands of the urban bourgeoisie. Following nationalizations, however, state actors took the lead in economic decision making (Migdal 1988, 229–30). Land reform, a cornerstone of the new regime's policy profile, was implemented with the goal of undermining the large landowners who had historically dominated Egypt's political and economic life. According to Waterbury, the reform had twin goals of consolidating power at the expense of the old aristocracy while at the same time supporting the stratum of small-scale farmers who could provide political support in the countryside (1993, 60–1).

Scholars of this era have encouraged a nuanced view of the economic policy changes promoted by Nasser. Ayubi writes that it would be incorrect to think of leaders like Nasser as devoted socialists; rather, left-leaning policies were promulgated with the goal of eliminating the large landlord as a politically influential force more than out of ideological commitment (1995, 202). As a result, certain market practices were retained despite the significant expansion of the state economy. Nowhere was the expansion of the state more obvious than in terms of the commitments and entitlements that came to dominate social policy. For example, all levels of public education were offered free-of-charge, and any student who successfully passed the secondary school exam earned the right to attend a university. Beginning in 1964, a public sector job was guaranteed to anyone graduating from a university or a technical institute. The public sector came to account for more than 35 percent of the gross domestic product (GDP), dominating the country's economic activity.[5]

During this period of economic policy change, political parties were banned. Waterbury writes that, for the regime, there was a need to formally structure political life with the goal of both controlling and preempting potential competitors (1983, 308). As a result, the ruling junta created a series of

---

[5] See Ayubi (1995) for more details.

one-party organizations.[6] Cooper writes that these mass political organizations were developed and reconstituted continuously with every incident of elite discord (1982, 30). The single party in Egypt, therefore, helped the regime to manage challenges involving the political elite in potentially significant ways.

2.1.1   The Liberation Rally and the National Union

The first of these mass political organizations, the Liberation Rally (LR), was developed and promoted by the regime beginning in 1953. Neither the LR nor its successors were created to grant political voice to party members or citizens. Rather, the LR was created with the intention of serving a number of functions related to the survival of the regime, only some of which were apparent when the organization was first established:

> The mass parties were means of mobilizing sentiment for the regime and means of rendering the masses unavailable to alternative leaders. Later, when the security of the regime was better established, additional uses of the mass party were recognized. Only in the fields of interest-groups coordination and the redress of individual grievance did the mass party appear to serve anyone but the government itself (Binder 1978, 41).

The LR successfully organized student groups into mass demonstrations (Vatikiotis 1961, 83) and incorporated labor unions into the state's corporatist apparatus (Waterbury 1983, 312). Tangible benefits beyond that are difficult to identify, although there is some evidence that the LR provided an arena for elite competition (Harik 1974, 68–9).

The LR was dismantled by 1956 and replaced by the National Union (NU), which was considered a more serious organization than its predecessor (Waterbury 1983, 313). All Egyptian adults were members of the hierarchically organized NU, which had a presence in both villages and provincial capitals. In the countryside, the NU was dominated by well-established local elites (Waterbury 1983, 313), who Binder calls the second stratum (1978). Binder defines the second stratum as the rural nobility who came to dominate positions of power in the NU; the second stratum was not the ruling class but rather the pool from which political officials were chosen (1978, 11, 28).

The NU did not make policy or exert influence over important policy decisions (Waterbury 1983, 313–4). If the mass organization did not have any influence on policy, why did individuals seek membership and positions within the party? Binder writes that members approached the party pragmatically, without ideological aspirations. In particular, individuals joined the party to seek restitution for grievances and protect existing rights and privileges (Binder 1978, 42).

---

[6] None of the mass political organizations developed and promoted under Nasser were actually called "parties," as the term political party (*ḥizb*) harkened back to the previous liberal era. Binder writes that, although they were not called parties, they operated as such (1978, 36), and I refer to these organizations as parties in this chapter.

Because all citizens were considered members of the NU, membership was not a very effective tool for determining commitment to the regime or the organization. For local political entrepreneurs, NU membership and, more important, approval became critical for personal advancement. For example, the NU served as a gatekeeping organization for candidacy in elections to Egypt's National Assembly.[7] Parliamentary elections took place within the context of the party because candidates were prescreened and representatives served in single-party assemblies. Candidates for parliament had to seek the approval of the NU Executive Committee. In fact, NU approval was a requirement for participation in important governing or steering committees of the government (Vatikiotis 1961, 113), including town and village mayors (Fahmy 2002, 57). Individuals suspected of opposition to the regime were disqualified from participation in such posts.

The Nasser regime did not depend on mass organizations like the NU for its power or position; rather, this support was "supplemental and stabilizing" (Vatikiosis 1961, 102). Eventually Nasser decided to "discard the experiment" (Waterbury 1983, 314), eventually replacing the NU with the ASU.

2.1.2 The Arab Socialist Union

The ASU represented a more ambitious party-building effort than its predecessors. Waterbury writes that Nasser established the ASU with a broader mandate; with the ASU, Nasser sought to constrain the development of opposition political forces through controlled mobilization of the masses (Waterbury 1983, 322). Nasser had learned from the failings of the previous two organizations, and this understanding informed decisions about the creation of the new party. Waterbury writes:

> The Liberation Rally and the National Union failed in part because universal, compulsory membership meant that no citizen could take any particular pride or derive kudos from identification with the organizations. The ASU, while maintaining the principle of universality, instituted different grades of membership, eventually moving toward the formation of a "vanguard." Moreover, membership was made voluntary. Prospective members had to apply to the ASU and pay annual dues. At the time of parliamentary elections in 1964, for example, there were over 4 million active members in the ASU but over 6 million eligible voters (1983, 314).

Because ASU membership was not compulsory, one's membership status and level of participation within the structure conveyed political information to the regime. Although all Egyptians were technically eligible for membership, less than a quarter ever joined the ASU or passed the rigorous screening required of

---

[7] Prior to 1971, the Egyptian parliament was formally known as the National Assembly.

members (Dekmajian 1971, 146). In addition, the ASU classified members into a variety of membership levels. Twenty thousand members were part of the political vanguard (Dekmajian 1971, 146). From a 1,500-member National Congress, 250–300 were selected for the General Central Committee, with 25 selected for the Supreme Executive Council (Dekmajian 1971, 145–6).

Harik describes the single-party system in Egypt as one where regional leaders recruited local leaders into the party, offering a mechanism for both identifying and organizing allies of the regime (1973, 81–2). And, like its predecessors, the ASU served as a gatekeeping organization. Membership was a precondition for political activism, and dismissal from the party represented a form of political punishment (Cooper 1982, 32). The party continued to screen those who would be eligible to run for parliamentary and other office. Beyond that, individuals sought high positions in the official party "for purposes of self-protection, influence, status, and privilege – especially when dealing with the government bureaucracy" (Harik 1973, 90).[8] The ASU also organized relations between the government and rural areas. Harik writes that the party organization served as a "contract" between regionally and locally influential elite (1973, 81–2).[9] Harik argues that the collaboration of local leaders as an "auxiliary base for political support and for the implementation of policy" (1974, 65) was important for the regime. Loyalty of local leaders was rewarded with material benefits (Sonbol 2000, 138).

One of the most consequential decisions made during the Nasser era involved the use of elections to promote party cadre within the ASU. Until 1968, ASU leadership was appointed, not elected. In 1968, the March 30 Program provided the basis for a reorganization of the party, including the implementation of within-party elections. Nasser's decision to make this important institutional change can be linked, in part, to Egypt's defeat by Israel in 1967. Internal elections served a number of important functions. Delegitimized after the military defeat, the elections provided an opportunity to institutionalize forms of accountability, at least within the party structure (Dekmajian 1971, 269). In addition, internal elections eased aspects of elite management, an issue that had concerned Nasser since at least 1965 (Binder 1978, 336). In particular, the elections created a "routinized and dependable" way to manage the party cadre (Cooper 1982, 55). The choice to use elections rather than appointment in leadership selection was also part of Nasser's need to balance left- and

---

[8] Ayubi argues that ASU appointments were a function of a combination of factors, including personal connections, acceptance by the security organs (1980, 449), and efficiency in administrative work (1980, 441). The ASU also offered an alternative to traditional centers of power, especially in rural areas (Hopwood 1985, 92). El-Karanshawy writes that the ASU was a vehicle of upward mobility for some individuals who were able to influence local politics and win office via their party connections (1997, 8–9).

[9] Harik writes that the ASU served as a location where complaints and problems were reported (1973, 90). This idea of political institutions, like the party, functioning like a "fire alarm" to balance the power and abuses of the bureaucracy is a theme that I will return to in other sections of this book.

right-wing elements within the elite (Binder 1978, 338). Whereas leftists sought the advancement of a structured, class-conscious party cadre, a more liberal, right-wing element of the elite pressed for competitive elections and civil liberties (Binder 1978, 348). The March 30 Program represented a first step in the reorientation of the regime away from the left in a bid to gain support among the urban elite (Ansari 1986, 151) and the right.[10] Cooper characterizes this shift as one that represents a decrease of popular appeal but an increase in reliable support (1982, 55).[11] Therefore, although the strength of the regime lay in the personalist and bureaucratic nature of Nasser's rule, the regime was not able to entirely forego institutional infrastructure (Hinnebusch 1988a, 18).

2.2 SADAT AND THE INTRODUCTION OF MULTIPARTYISM

As weak as the ASU may have been, the existence of the mass party may have helped to maintain stability in the wake of regime crises, such as the death of Nasser in 1970 (Cooper 1982, 32). Following Nasser's death, elite struggles posed perhaps an even greater threat to the stability of the regime. Sadat faced a power struggle between the two major camps at the time: a) the leftists, identified most prominently with the ASU's 'Ali Sabri; and b) a numerically large but diffuse conservative grouping led by Sadat (Hinnebusch 1988a, 40–1). The Sabri camp, which included the minister of interior and many military officers (Waterbury 1993, 166), preferred continued alliance with the USSR, whereas the conservatives turned increasingly to the United States (Hinnebusch 1988a, 42). Sadat dismissed nearly all existing bureaucratic leadership in what was known as the "corrective" revolution. After consolidating his power, Sadat undertook a series of high-profile new policy initiatives. One of Sadat's first acts was to return some of the property seized from wealthy families under sequestration. Economic liberalization created rent-seeking opportunities for a new distributive coalition (Heydemann 2004, 6, 12). In July 1972, Sadat expelled Soviet advisors in a reorientation of Egyptian foreign policy toward the West. Egypt crossed the Suez Canal in the 1973 war, paving the way for the eventual peace process with Israel.

Domestically, it was becoming increasingly clear that the old ASU would not be an effective vehicle for Sadat's needs. Sadat purged the ASU of Sabri and his allies (Fahmy 2002, 61). During the 1971 parliamentary elections, many leftists were not permitted to seek office (el-Mikaway 1999, 28). Student riots in 1972 were followed by meetings to determine the future course of the

---

[10] At this point in time, the left–right political dimension was the main political dividing line in Egyptian political life (Cooper 1982, 91). This is in contrast to more recent times when a secular–religious divide and democratic–autocratic divide are more salient.

[11] For example, Waterbury writes that peasants saw a multiparty system as a "lightly veiled pretense for counterrevolutionary forces to eat away at the benefits of the revolution" (1983, 358). Traditional left-leaning constituencies, like organized labor and university professors and students, also feared the political implications of internal elections (Waterbury 1983, 358).

ASU (Waterbury 1978, 355). Sadat began the process of reinventing Egypt's party structure by initiating a period of open dialogue following the circulation of a regime-disseminated white paper on the future of the ASU (Waterbury 1978, 356). Sadat thereby opened up debate over political reform to collect information about elite preferences and to inform regime policy and institution formation. Sadat also engaged in economic liberalization, which helped to solidify support from his base – the right-leaning political classes.

2.2.1 Open-Door Economics

Upon assuming office, Sadat began promoting the interests of the private sector, and the relative success of the 1973 war gave Sadat the legitimacy to continue that effort (Dessouki 1981). *Infitāḥ* – or the open-door economic policy – was launched in 1974. Goals of the policy included attracting investment from the Gulf and encouraging joint ventures between Egyptian firms and foreign companies (Waterbury 1985). Law 43 of 1974 was the main legislation governing *infitāḥ*. It opened Egypt to some foreign investment, offering foreign firms protection against nationalization as well as greater opportunities for foreign-exchange transactions (Abdel Khalek 1979).

However, heavy state involvement in the economy persisted, and many of the policies of Nasserism were reasserted (Ansari 1986, 178).[12] Sonbol writes that *infitāḥ* was not intended to undermine Nasser's brand of socialism, per se. Rather, it was believed that state socialism for the masses could survive contemporaneously with free market opportunities for the business elite (Sonbol 2000, 160–1). *Infitāḥ*, therefore, represented a step in undoing aspects of the socialist state, but in a way that eliminated few of the welfare benefits established under Nasser. The economic reform program offered the elite access to the benefits of the new economic policies (Heydemann 2004). In particular, liberalization favored the development of the business elite, allowing some to make money in real estate and imports (Hamed 1981). But by the end of 1976, only $77 million had been invested (Hamed 1981), and critics complained that the policies had done little more than exacerbate class cleavages (Waterbury 1985).

The impact of *infitāḥ* on the economic well-being of everyday Egyptians has been the subject of considerable debate, but there is substantial evidence to suggest that the most important political impact of *infitāḥ* was the creation of a new class of speculators and private-sector profiteers (Waterbury 1985). As a result, the 1970s were a period of growth of Egypt's business community (Sadowski 1991, 93). These individuals thrived as middle men for imported goods and commissions agents (Heikal 1983), and eventually this class became

---

[12] Just as Nasser's nationalizations did not completely eliminate free-market capitalism in Egypt (Binder 1988), Sadat's program of economic liberalization did not fully undo Nasser's socialist legacy.

an important source of political support for Sadat as he worked to silence critics on the left.[13]

2.2.2 Open Dialogue: A Prelude to Political Liberalization

In the run-up to multiparty competition, Sadat initiated a phase of relatively open debate regarding elite preferences. Cooper writes that nearly two years of heated, contentious discussion took place focusing on the future of national political institutions (1982, 179). During this period, Sadat invited the political elite to engage in the debate without revealing his own preferences. Nearly all major elite actors made their views known (Waterbury 1978, 251). Waterbury writes that Sadat's strategy was to "set the rules of debate without predetermining the conclusions that are to be drawn, for the course of the debate itself will inform him what concrete steps are warranted" (1978, 249). In this way, Sadat learned how a broad range of politically relevant groups felt about the future, "all the while reserving to himself the right to decide how fast and in what direction to reorient the polity" (Waterbury 1978, 251).

This period was marked by political activism, particularly among the elite (Hinnebusch 1988a, 53). For example, a parliamentary committee tasked with discussing these issues offered an opportunity for professionals and intellectuals to call for expanded political liberties and more intense competition (Baker 1978, 164). On the other hand, farmers' and workers' organizations, which feared a multiparty system might undermine their position, continued their opposition to party competition (Baker 1978, 164). Hinnebusch writes that, "the debates revealed several distinct tendencies in elite opinion" (1988a, 159). Baker finds that, during this period, Sadat remained "aloof from the turmoil," but that the debate continued with his "implied blessing" (1978, 155). Highly tactical, Sadat preferred to let others reveal their hand before revealing his own preferences and strategy (Beattie 2000, 38). It was only after this period of open debate that Sadat made the move to multipartyism.

2.2.3 Sadat and Elections

Early in 1976, Sadat convened a committee to discuss political reform. By March 1976, three platforms, which eventually became parties, were allowed to emerge and became the basis for competitive multipartyism in Egypt. Importantly, independent individual candidacy was also allowed.

There exists only limited consensus in the previous literature regarding why Sadat chose to implement competitive multiparty parliamentary elections in 1976. Most, but not all, scholars acknowledge the influence of multiple factors

---

[13] This is not to say that business opportunities did not exist under Nasser. Sadowski writes that businessmen welcomed some of the interventions of the Nasser era, taking advantage of some aspects of the state-directed economy (1991, 102).

in the decision. A first line of reasoning emphasizes domestic political considerations and Sadat's desire to accommodate conservative elite preferences for greater political expression. As Sadat sought to move beyond the leftist bases of support enjoyed by Nasser, he turned increasingly to conservatives, who supported a more open political environment, as the base of his support. A second line of reasoning focuses on external factors. Proponents of this theory argue that, in order to effectively make the transition from the Soviet orbit of influence to ally of the United States, Sadat introduced a more open political system.

Egyptian politicians and analysts tend to emphasize the importance of external influences on the decision to hold multiparty elections, although they point out that external factors do not influence the political behavior of the president unless there is also a domestic regime utility view.[14] In other words, when external pressure is coupled with an opportunity to improve a domestic political situation, then change occurs. The way that change occurs is also subject to the strict agenda control of the authoritarian regime, even when a foreign influence serves as the impetus for the change.[15] Western academics have also focused on foreign influences and Sadat's reorientation toward the West. McDermott writes that "Sadat had in mind a European and Western audience in this particular exercise.... he was conscious of wanting to show the world that Israel did not have the monopoly of multiparty systems" (1988, 109). Beattie has also argued that being in the American camp was a critical component of Sadat's larger political plan (2000, 88) and that "much of Sadat's motivation came from wishing to please the West" (2000, 223).

The majority of historical studies of this decision by both Western and Egyptian scholars, however, tend to focus on important domestic considerations, particularly a desire to manage the ideological preferences of various elite actors and groups. In particular, Sadat was seen as courting right-leaning elements of society in an effort to balance leftist rivals for power. In 1974, Sadat undertook his open-door economic policy (*infitāḥ*), which empowered Egypt's bourgeoisie. Sadat viewed this group as a "friendly force," accommodating their interests and offering privileged access to power (Hinnebusch 1988a, 228–9). This group furnished Sadat with an important source of support as he continued to consolidate power (Abdelrahman 2004, 197–8). The shift toward economic liberalization privileged the entrepreneurial class (el-Mikaway 1999, 30), introducing a period of growth for the Egyptian business community (Sadowski 1991, 93). Springborg argues that Sadat undertook liberalization because "it was in the interest of the class upon which his power was based" (1988, 138).

[14] Interviews with Moheb Zaki, Ibn Khaldun Center for Development Studies, April 30, 2006; Gehad Auda, NDP Media Secretariat and Professor of Political Science, Helwan University, May 1, 2006; and Mohammed al-Batran, former member of the People's Assembly and Shura Council, May 1, 2006.
[15] This argument is developed more fully in Chapter 10.

Cooper sees external and exogenous crises as precipitating Sadat's move toward liberalization but the impetus for liberalization as largely domestic. He writes: "In brief, the pressure on the regime and the particular way that interests were juxtaposed, especially in the tension-filled months after the June 1967 defeat and the death of Nasser in September 1970, pushed toward liberalization" (1982, 134). The goal, therefore, was to build consensus around specific policy objectives (Cooper 1982, 132). Tucker argues that political liberalization served as a substitute for the failures of *infitāḥ*; because Sadat was not able to improve the material condition of most Egyptians, he refocused attention on undoing Nasser's totalitarianism (Tucker 1978). Waterbury emphasizes the informational aspects of holding elections. He writes that Sadat was willing to sacrifice some of the control that obsessed Nasser in order to "see more clearly the forces that warranted control" (1978, 354).

Hinnebusch argues that the party elite had moved to the right, although conservative tendencies were based primarily on pragmatic rather than purely programmatic concerns (1988a, 120–1, 161). Many of these individuals represented the business elite. He writes that this group sought

> enough political liberalization to protect itself from the arbitrary power of the ruler and allow it greater freedom of political expression, and that Sadat sought to accommodate it; but both feared that excessive liberalization might result in the erosion of authority or the mobilization by counter-elites of a mass challenge to the policies they favored. Hence they wanted a strictly limited liberalization confined to elite levels which would not result in the pluralization of the mass political arena (1988a, 119).

In addition to a desire to accommodate the business elite at the expense of the masses, Hinnebusch also acknowledges the importance of the external environment. He writes that Egypt needed to cultivate Western goodwill, in order to garner Western support for his foreign policy agenda (Hinnebusch 1988a, 135). The plan to open up the system of multiparty competition at the parliamentary level, therefore, satisfied multiple objectives, including the desire to "differentiate his regime from Nasser's, satisfy participatory pressures, win support from liberal elements of the bourgeoisie, please the Americans on whom his diplomatic initiative depended and encourage the economic liberalization he was launching" (Hinnebusch 1988a, 158–9). Others, like Fahmy, have also emphasized the importance of seeking funds from the United States (2002, 63–4).

The elections, therefore, were introduced during a time when there still existed fairly clear ideological distinctions between two important factions of Egypt's political elite, although these ideological differences may have been strongly motivated by pragmatic concerns. The move toward elections was seen as a shift in favor of right-leaning and business-oriented elements of this political class. It is this class, in fact, that continues to dominate the Egyptian elite. Although the importance of external factors – particularly the desire to court the West – cannot be ignored, the decision to hold elections was rooted, at least to some extent, in a desire to manage the country's political elite. Then, once the right-leaning business elite came to enjoy a dominant position, the nature of intra-elite conflict became increasingly focused on the distribution of resources (and access to resources) within the rent-seeking elite, and this tendency was exacerbated by the increased opportunities for private wealth accumulation that accompanied structural adjustment.

2.3   ELECTIONS AND ECONOMIC CHANGE UNDER MUBARAK

Following the assassination of Sadat in 1981, Egypt's most important political and economic policies changed little (Dawisha and Zartman 1988). Hinnebusch describes the Mubarak era as one of continuity during which the initiatives introduced by Sadat "crystallized"; the most important of these legacies included the open-door economic policy, the growth of a new bourgeoisie, and growing political and financial dependence on the United States (1988a, 298). Part of this legacy included the multiparty parliamentary elections that Sadat had introduced. Early on, Mubarak signaled some continued commitment to pluralism; opposition candidates competing in two by-elections held in the early 1980s considered the elections to have been fairly run (McDermott 1988, 77). The right-leaning political elite also intensified their demands for pluralism during this period (el-Mikaway 1999, 42). The Wafd opposition party won a lawsuit in 1983 that allowed the party to contest the 1984 election. In coalition with the Muslim Brotherhood, a Wafd–Brotherhood alliance won 58 seats and 15 percent of the total vote.[16] In fact, Ayubi suggests that the Mubarak era truly did not begin until 1984, following the fiercely contested parliamentary election (1989, 13) considered by many to have been open and fair (McDermott 1988, 77).[17]

Why did Mubarak continue the multiparty politics experiment and allow even more intense forms of contestation than had been permitted under Sadat? Springborg posits a number of possible hypotheses (1989, 135–7). First, he suggests that the president lacked the power to reverse Sadat's efforts to deconstruct Nasser's political legacy. A second explanation is that Mubarak implemented greater political pluralism as a counterweight to tightening economic conditions, where pluralism would serve as a political safety valve for economic discontent. Although Springborg does not offer an unequivocal answer, he most strongly suggests that Mubarak inherited an NDP that served as a vehicle for the interests of business-oriented Sadatists (1989, 157) and that this

[16] The Wafd was formally reintroduced in 1978, but disbanded shortly thereafter when Sadat issued a security law barring anyone who had held a ministerial position before 1952 from participating in politics. This law was overturned in 1983 by the Egyptian courts (Goldschmidt and Johnston 2004, 415).
[17] The regime's ability to manage the 1984 elections made it clear that Mubarak and the ruling party could control a system characterized by considerable contestation (Ayubi 1989, 13).

group could be mobilized in support of the regime. The 1984 elections represented an elimination of the left while simultaneously introducing opposition on the right (Zartman 1988a, 76). Over time, it would be this challenge from first an alliance of the Wafd and Muslim Brotherhood, and increasingly from just the Muslim Brotherhood, that would become the relevant, ideological split in the elite. The rent-seeking elite came to be the base of the Mubarak regime, and keeping this class of individuals in tacit alliance with the authoritarian leadership became the key to continued stability.

Following Sadat's decision to support right-leaning elements of the party in the 1970s, this rent-seeking class came to dominate the political elite in Egypt and, to a large extent, still dominate Egypt in the present period. During the Mubarak era, therefore, the regime's focus was not on whether elections would occur, but rather on the various tools and tactics the regime could employ to manage and manipulate those elections.

2.3.1 Changing the Rules of the Game

Attempts to control the outcome of elections were made largely through changes to the formal political institutions governing electoral contests.

A Preference for Formal Institutionalized Changes. Even though many autocrats have the institutional capacity to impose policies without the formal consent of other societal groups, it is often preferable to implement policies under the cover of formal institutions. In Egypt, as in other autocracies, there is surprising attention paid to issues like procedural integrity, even when passing the most draconian and undemocratic of laws.[18] The policy and other preferences of Mubarak and his cadre of advisors are expressed and often made into law via the legislature. Some may ask, why bother? The Egyptian president has the ability to legislate by decree in "emergencies" (very loosely defined) and when parliament is not in session. Yet, deviations from policy change via parliamentary channels are potentially costly. Such actions lack the political cover provided by parliamentary action and open the regime up to criticism from opposition newspapers and opposition elite. The preferred method, then, for securing policy objectives is through an elected supermajority in parliament. Parliamentary elections legally create the legislative supermajority needed to pass constitutional amendments and to rubberstamp initiatives put forth by the president.[19]

---

[18] Authoritarians show a penchant for collecting the most dazzling array of laws and stipulations from democratic constitutions around the world that, when used together, have an entirely undemocratic effect.

[19] For example, the regime's introduction of multicandidate presidential elections in 2005 was a first step in institutionalizing the dominance of the NDP with the goal of moving away from the personalist aspects of the regime identified with Hosni Mubarak to pave the way for the possible succession to power of his son, Gamal. The ninth congress of the NDP saw the continued rise of Gamal with his appointment to the party council from which candidates for the

Although Mubarak has allowed the opposition to win seats, his regime would never permit the opposition enough seats to block legislation. For example, constitutional amendments need to be approved by two-thirds of the People's Assembly; therefore, the regime has sought to maintain a dominant majority of seats in the legislature. Upward of 85 percent of parliamentarians elected in 2000 were associated with the NDP.[20] In 2005, the NDP majority dropped to about 70 percent, although this was still sufficient for meeting the crucial two-thirds needed to pass constitutional changes.

Controlling the Terms of Contestation. The terms of contestation under Mubarak have provided opportunities for serious competition between individual candidates; at the same time, the nature of this competition has been closely controlled to ensure the ruling elite's overall objective of maintaining a supermajority in parliament. This occurs on a number of different levels and through a series of institutionalized channels. First, the government strictly controls which groups are allowed to form licensed political parties. Second, the regime has shown a willingness to manipulate and alter electoral institutions in ways that are expected to favor the hegemonic party. Finally, selective implementation of various legal and constitutional injunctions are used to control the extent of competition.

One of the most important ways that the regime under Mubarak controls the nature of political competition relates to the ability of groups to form political parties.[21] Egypt's political parties' law puts serious limitations on the ability to create new parties and on existing party activity.[22] Legislation states that new parties have to be distinct from existing parties, cannot be based on class or religion, and should promote national unity and social peace and accept the results of referenda (Ayubi 1989, 15). Furthermore, parties also have to accept the principles of Islamic law as Egypt's main source of legislation (2001). Rif'at al-Sa'id – leader of the Tagammu' party – has said that freedom to establish political parties is extremely constrained and the criteria used for licensing parties are not clear (Hussein, Al-Said, and Al-Sayyid 1998, 77). Although candidates can run as independents, Al-Sa'id says that legal status matters as approved parties are also allowed to publish a newspaper (Hussein et al. 1998, 77), which can be a source of funds for the organization.

To date, the regime has shown a preference for liberal elite parties over leftist and religious parties. For example, the committee approved Ayman Nour's liberal Ghad Party in October 2004, and, in May 2007, it approved Ossama al-Ghazali Harb's liberal secular Democratic Front Party. Recent parties rejected by the committee include the Islamist-leaning Wasat party (on the grounds

---

2011 presidential election will be chosen. See *Al-Ahram Weekly*, December 27, 2007–January 2, 2008.

[20] This includes individuals who ran as independents but rejoined the NDP after winning office.

[21] See Stacher 2004 for a detailed discussion of restrictions on political parties in Egypt.

[22] Human Rights Watch, *Monopolizing Power: Egypt's Political Parties Law*, January 2007, Number 1.

that it had a platform too similar to existing parties) and the Nasserist Karama party (on the grounds that it advocated a radical ideology).[23]

In addition, the Mubarak regime uses a variety of electoral rules to ensure the NDP's continuing parliamentary majority.[24] Egyptian elections under Sadat had been characterized by a relatively large number of independent candidates. In an effort to stem this trend and to exert the influence of the hegemonic party structure, the electoral system was altered. In 1983, Egypt's "first past the post" run-off system was replaced.[25] The new law mandated a party-list proportional representation (PR) system and reduced the number of constituencies from 176 to 48. In addition, parties were required to achieve an 8 percent minimum threshold of the nationwide vote. If they did not, their members were barred from the People's Assembly, and votes for such a party would automatically transfer to the largest party (i.e., the regime's party). Posusney (1998) writes that "Mubarak's 1984 election law closed the door on independent candidacies, while limiting the chances for opposition parties." The NDP won 87 percent of the contested seats in the 1984 election, despite having only received 73 percent of the popular vote. The gap reflects the NDP's receipt of votes cast for parties that failed to reach the 8 percent threshold. Only one opposition group (the Wafd–Muslim Brotherhood alliance) received more than 8 percent of the vote, earning 13 percent of the seats.

Opposition party lawyers offered a legal challenge to the PR system, and, in 1987, the regime changed the electoral law preemptively (Makram-Ebeid 1989, 22). The new law mandated that one seat in each constituency would be reserved for independent candidates, although parties would be permitted to contest these seats (Posusney 1998). Winners were to be chosen on a plurality basis, with a run-off if the top candidate did not earn more than 20 percent (Posusney 1998). Although the creation of individually contested seats did provide an opportunity for the smaller opposition parties to obtain seats by running locally popular candidates as independents, Kassem argues that the amended law did not differ significantly from its predecessor because only a fraction of independent seats were acquired by genuine independents (2004, 60). The NDP continued to enjoy a supermajority that allowed easy passage of regime-sponsored legislation (Posusney 1998). Egypt's Supreme Constitutional Court eventually ruled that the 1987 election law was discriminatory toward independent candidates, calling into question the legitimacy of the sitting parliament. Mubarak suspended parliament and appointed a committee of legal experts to draft a new election law. Following this review, the regime reinstated an individual candidacy system and increased the number of districts from 48 to 222.[26] Kienle argues that, during this period, the Mubarak regime became

---

[23] Ibid.

[24] See Owen 2004 for a complete discussion of changes to Egypt's electoral rules under Mubarak.

[25] See Kassem 2004 for more details.

[26] Each constituency has two parliamentarians, one representing the category of worker or peasant and the other a professional. Voters were allowed to cast their ballots for two candidates. This electoral system continued to be used through the 2005 parliamentary elections.

more active in its management of elections, allowing the regime to enlarge its constituency (2001, 5).

In reaction to only limited independent supervision slated for the 1990 elections, the overwhelming majority of opposition parties boycotted the contest. The 1990 election used a two-round electoral rule. Those candidates who received an absolute majority of votes in the first round were elected. If no candidate received an absolute majority, a second round of voting occurred and the winner of this round was elected. The number of independent candidates running in 1990 exploded following the move away from party lists; in fact, when the campaign period opened, there were 2,486 independent candidates compared with only 589 official party candidates (Auda 1991, 75). Although the electoral system governing the election of the lower house of parliament in Egypt has been largely retained since 1990, regime insiders more recently have considered a reengineering of the rules.[27]

In addition to the law on political parties and willingness to manipulate electoral institutions, a series of other laws, amendments, and court rulings aid the electoral objectives of the ruling party. First, Egypt has been under emergency law continuously since 1981. This gives the government the power to arrest at will and hold suspects without trial for long periods of time. Emergency rule was especially important during the 1990s, when the regime was engaged in a public battle with Islamist elements of society.

In 2007, the regime initiated an amendment to the Egyptian constitution. One important affected area involved judicial monitoring of elections. The constitution previously specified the supervisor of each main polling station be a member of a judicial body.[28] The new constitutional amendment was not explicit regarding the definition of judicial supervision, however. Although a number of prominent legal scholars and civic activists insisted that only bench judges could serve as monitors, the government used nonjudge legal officers to supervise the vote in many places (el-Ghobashy 2006). Despite the government's attempts to use legal officers, rather than bench judges, as polling station supervisors, the overall influence of judicial supervision resulted in more free elections in 2000 and 2005 (Soliman 2006). Under a more recent amendment, bench judges supervise primary polling stations, leaving the vast majority of polling locations supervised by lower-level bureaucrats and others.[29]

In sum, the ruling regime alters political institutions, including electoral rules, to favor the hegemonic party. There is a preference for changes to formal institutional arrangements over post hoc solutions. The regime has a very strong incentive to maintain a supermajority in parliament so that it can continue to alter the formal institutional arrangements at its discretion. Although the

---

[27] Interview with Mohammed Kamal, NDP Policies Secretariat and Professor of Political Science, Cairo University, May 3, 2006.

[28] In July 2000, a court ruled that judicial supervision would only be effective if it extended to auxiliary as well as main stations (el-Ghobashy 2006).

[29] *Al-Ahram Weekly*, March 22–28, 2007.

regime is willing to allow the opposition to win some seats, incumbent leaders have no interest in seating an opposition strong enough to block action.

2.3.2 Withdrawal of the State

The undoing of the socialist policies introduced by Nasser continued under Sadat through the rule of Mubarak. *Infitāḥ* and desequestration measures undertaken by Sadat reversed some aspects of Nasser's socialist legacy (Ansari 1986, 172). Sonbol provides a particularly compelling picture of the general withdrawal of the state during this period and describes the changes in terms of what she sees as the key actors in Egyptian society – the *'amma*, or general public, and the *khāssa*, or the privileged classes. She argues that, although the Nasser-era social contract provided the *'amma* with free education, health services, social security benefits, agricultural subsidies, and public sector jobs, "with population growth, poor industrial production, and a static foreign aid package, the government faced severe problems in its efforts to continue satisfying these obligations" (Sonbol 2000, 167). My contention is that the regime chose to narrow its base under Sadat, both in an attempt to counterbalance Nasserite dissension and also out of a realization that courting the *amma* was not financially tenable.

This trend became particularly apparent with the implementation of Egypt's structural adjustment program. Egypt signed agreements with the International Monetary Fund (IMF) in 1976, 1978, and 1987 in an attempt to reduce a debt that had begun to overwhelm the state beginning in the late 1970s (Seddon 1990). By the late 1980s, investment and GDP growth had declined under the burden of unmanageable foreign debt (Korayem 1997). Egypt's Economic Reform and Structural Adjustment Program (ERSAP) was signed with the IMF and World Bank in 1991. The ERSAP imposed strong conditionality and called for change in a number of areas, including macroeconomic policy adjustment, removal of consumer subsidies, elimination of price controls, and foreign trade liberalization. Privatization of state-owned enterprises was a cornerstone of the reform program (Khattab 1999). Between 1991 and 1999, 33 percent of state-owned companies were privatized (Khattab 1999). By 2001, Egypt had either partially or fully privatized 158 companies (Goldschmidt and Johnston 2004), and the changing economic scene provided opportunities for some to make a great deal of money in a short period of time (Beattie 2000, 150–1). Changes in the Egyptian economy were reinforced when Egypt joined the World Trade Organization (WTO) in 1995 (Rutherford 2008, 199).[30]

According to Korayem, the structural adjustment program has had a profound negative impact on Egypt's poor, particularly by increasing income

---

[30] How were all of these changes accomplished? Moustafa (2007, 36) argues that a series of Egyptian Supreme Constitutional Court rulings enabled the regime to overturn socialist-oriented policies without having to face direct opposition from social groups that were threatened by economic liberalization.

inequality (1995). For example, "many families stopped sending their children
to school ... particularly girls" as a result of changes induced by structural
adjustment.[31] Increasingly, young girls can be found working as housekeepers
earning between LE 300 and LE 500 per month.[32] Neoliberalism also led to a
relocation of welfare provision and development work away from the government to the private sector and nongovernmental organizations (NGOs) (Ismail
2006, 71). In many cases, Islamically oriented organizations have become
important in the provision of social services.[33] The proliferation of squatter
settlements around Cairo also speaks to the withdrawal of the Egyptian state
during this period. In sum, state safety nets that were put in place during the
Nasser era were gradually withdrawn (Bayat 1996).

Eminent Egyptian jurist Tariq al-Bishri has argued that the state has aban-
doned its duty to provide basic services, such as education and health, to the
citizenry.[34] One NDP insider has said that a "new style of government" has
emerged in Egypt that no longer provides social services.[35] Whereas socialist-
style benefits were not explicitly withdrawn in all cases, they were often watered
down to the point of worthlessness. For example, subsidized foodstuffs are
provided in short supply, leading to long lines and widespread shortages.[36]
According to one press report, Egyptians are waiting in longer lines than ever
for regime-subsidized goods or services at locations like bakeries, petrol stations, public offices, and hospitals.[37] As the world-market price of oil increased
in 2008, for example, shortages of fuel – which is heavily subsidized by the
state – became common.[38] Rather than eliminating the subsidy, the government
left taxi and microbus drivers visiting multiple petrol stations in search of the
highly subsidized 80-octane fuel; the more expensive 90-octane fuel, however,
was readily available.[39]

The undermining of free public services has increased families' private
expenses for both health care and education (Bach 2002). The quality of health
services has declined (and continues to decline) at state-run hospitals, leading
to an increasing privatization of medical services. Students who received high
marks in the 2007 *thānawiya 'amma* examinations, which determine university admission, conceded that private lessons were a key to their success; the
independent newspaper *Al-Masry Al-Youm* ran the headline that translates to

---

[31] *Egyptian Gazette*, August 3, 2008.
[32] Ibid.
[33] See Fahmy 2004 for more details on this point.
[34] *Al-Ahram Weekly*, December 28, 2006–January 3, 2007.
[35] Interview with NDP official, May 1, 2007.
[36] This is not to say that the government no longer provides welfare benefits to Egyptians. An
Egyptian official in 2007 said that the government still spends 13 billion LE a year to subsidize
bread and cooking gas (*Al-Masry Al-Youm*, September 27, 2007). Nonetheless, the overall
trend in government welfare provision appears to be on a decline.
[37] *Egyptian Gazette*, August 10, 2008.
[38] *Egyptian Gazette*, July 12, 2008.
[39] Ibid.

"The Death of the Public School and the Victory of Private Lessons."[40] According to a 2007 government study, 60 percent of families with children in preuniversity education have to spend at least LE 100 a month on private lessons.[41]

Ismail describes the retreat of the state as including "the freezing of health spending, the masked privatization of schooling, a cap on public sector hiring, and an accompanying informalization of labor leading to the disappearance of social security for greater numbers of the working poor" (2006, 71). One statistic that illustrates this trend over time is general government expenditure as a percentage of GDP.[42] Although more than 30 percent at the peak of public sector power, the government's footprint on the overall economy has declined significantly since the Sadat era, leveling off in the mid-1990s to about 12 percent.

Although there has been an expectation that changes in economic policy would lead to a trickle-down benefit for the lower and middle classes (Bayat 1996), upper classes have been most helped by economic developments related to the withdrawal of the state, particularly private sector interests that grew in strength and importance under Sadat and Mubarak.[43] Mitchell argues that Egypt's economic reform offered new opportunities for some through a complicated readjusting of economic networks (2002, 281). Sonbol describes the beneficiaries of this readjustment as a class of private entrepreneurs she calls the *khāṣṣa* (2000, 158). This includes professionals with private business interests, such as the *tujjār* (trading class), who became partners with government organizations and grew influential (Sonbol 2000, 158), as well as high-ranking elements of the *multazim* (bureaucracy), who have benefited from their role brokering financial deals (Sonbol 2000, 167). The net result is that modest affluence extends to just 5 percent of the population, and 3 percent of the population accounts for half of all consumer spending (Mitchell 2002, 286–7).

The inconsistency between what neoliberal economists claim as Egypt's officially reported high GDP growth and the declining living standards of most Egyptians has also caused growing political instability. On one hand, BMW reported a 20-percent annual growth in sales to Egypt in 2007.[44] According to auto industry executives, luxury cars used to make up just 5 percent of total auto sales in Egypt. In the first half of 2008, however, luxury cars accounted for 50 percent of cars sold.[45] In 2007, there were 500 billionaires and 1 million

---

[40] *Al-Masry Al-Youm*, July 17, 2007.

[41] *Egyptian Gazette*, September 21, 2007.

[42] General government final consumption expenditure includes all current spending for purchases of goods and services (including wages and salaries). It also includes most expenditures on national defense and security, but excludes government military expenditures that are part of government capital formation.

[43] Interview with Egyptian Foreign Ministry official, May 22, 2007.

[44] *Washington Post*, April 5, 2008.

[45] *Egyptian Gazette*, August 24, 2008.

millionaires living in Egypt.[46] On the other hand, in 2007, 40 million Egyptians lived on less than $2 a day,[47] and declining living standards have led to numerous public displays of economic stress, including strikes and economic protests.[48]

The political implications of the withdrawal of the state from its traditional role became particularly acute in late 2007 and early 2008. By the end of 2007, it was clear that higher world food prices were a major problem for the Arab world, and Egypt in particular.[49] By January 2008, the government had already spent 88 percent of the funds allocated to subsidies for the 2007–2008 budget with six months left in the fiscal year.[50] The government stopped subsidizing the *fino*, or refined, bread loaf popular for use in sandwiches.[51] Government statements by both Prime Minister Ahmed Nazif on Radio Cairo[52] and sources in the Ministry of Social Solidarity in early December had said that the government was considering turning commodity subsidies into cash transfers directed at the poor.[53] The government came under attack for suggesting that cash subsidies might take the place of subsidized foodstuffs.[54] Nazif made a public statement that subsidies would not be canceled and called for a national dialogue with the goal of redirecting subsidies to eligible target groups.[55] A ministerial committee was formed to investigate the matter, and the Minister of Social Solidarity stated that the government did not have a clear vision of subsidy reform but was considering a number of alternatives.[56]

As the price of wheat doubled between 2007 and 2008, Egypt – the world's second-largest importer of wheat – entered a state of crisis in the spring of

---

[46] *Egyptian Gazette*, March 7, 2008; based on $US.

[47] Ibid.

[48] Adam Morrow and Khaled Moussa al-Omrani, "Can't wait a generation to eat," *Inter Press Service*, March 26, 2008.

[49] *Al-Hayat*, December 31, 2007.

[50] Rehab el-Bakry, "Public outcry over talk of subsidy reform," *Business Monthly*, American Chamber of Commerce in Egypt, January 2008.

[51] *Al-Masry Al-Youm*, December 12, 2007.

[52] Ibid.

[53] *Al-Masry Al-Youm*, December 3, 2007.

[54] *Al-Ahram Weekly*, December 13–19, 2007.

[55] *Al-Masry Al-Youm*, December 11, 2007.

[56] No doubt fearful of the public response if the subsidy issue was poorly handled, the government worked to preview reaction to a change in policy through focus groups. The National Council for Women's Governorate Committee conducted 155 meetings with 13,374 participants across Egypt to discuss the issue of subsidies. The dialogue that took place in the meetings emphasized that food subsidies were vital to both promoting political stability as well as providing legitimacy to the political system. More than 85 percent of those surveyed felt that cash subsidies would not work, and many feared that inflation associated with the cash transfer program would leave them worse off than under the current system. A 60-year-old housewife told one reporter that, "prices are in continuous rise so the cash provided by the government will never be enough to buy the same goods at the market price." See *Al-Ahram Weekly*, December 6–12, 2007, December 27, 2007–January 2, 2008, and January 24–30, 2008, for more details on the subsidy issue.

2008.[57] Following the deaths of at least six people in bread lines, Mubarak delegated the baking and distribution of bread to the military and security apparatus.[58] The security services were charged with receiving flour quotas in each governorate, producing the bread in bakeries run by the Interior Ministry, and then packaging and distributing the bread at designated outlets.[59] According to an official at the United Nations (UN) World Food Program, 55 percent of Egyptians suffer from an iron deficiency due to poverty and malnutrition,[60] suggesting that issues related to obtaining basic foodstuffs remain of vital importance to many Egyptians.

The withdrawal of the state from its traditional role has had profound implications for the nature of electoral competition and the rise of new political powers. By the mid-1980s, it was increasingly clear that the distribution of public goods in Cairo was plagued by a crisis of scarcity (Singerman 1995, 244). Economic reform continued a general trend of the withdrawal of the Egyptian welfare state, particulary through a strategy of diluting "gains offered by the system, rather than any decisive retreat from it" (Wickham 2002, 51).

2.4 CONCLUSIONS

The move to relatively freely contested parliamentary elections represents the culmination of a gradual electoralization of Egyptian politics that began under Nasser and has continued – though sometimes irregularly – through to the rule of Mubarak. A variety of political and economic factors have contributed to the regime's effort to narrow its political base over time. Liberalization of the economy has reinforced electoralization by simultaneously empowering the rent-seeking elite, while leaving the regime with fewer resources with which to buy support. In this way, elections have emerged as an important way to distribute resources. This perspective stands in contrast to the view that economic liberalization works to advance the interests of democratic representation. The next chapter takes this narrowed political base as a starting point and discusses how the regime manages its ruling coalition in this environment of resource scarcity.

[57] *Washington Post*, April 5, 2008.
[58] Ibid.
[59] *Al-Masry Al-Youm*, March 27, 2008.
[60] *Al-Masry Al-Youm*, April 11, 2008.

3

Elections and Elite Management

The long-standing conventional wisdom regarding why authoritarian regimes establish parties, hold elections, and convene legislatures is that these institutions convey an aura of legitimacy, both domestically and to the outside world. Domestically, most autocrats enjoy the power and institutional capacity to impose their policy preferences autonomously. Nevertheless, it is often preferable to rule under the cover of formal legislative institutions with ruling parties comprising a parliamentary majority. In fact, in many authoritarian regimes, there is surprising attention paid to issues of procedural integrity, even when passing the most undemocratic of laws. The existence of elections and parliaments also conveys an appearance of legitimacy to the outside world.[1] Authoritarians reap the benefits associated with perceived liberalization through establishing institutions that appear democratic. The United States and Europe then offer aid or preferential trading arrangements in exchange for such liberalization, and international financial institutions offer cut-rate loans. A number of scholars assume or even actively promote the idea that elections confer legitimacy on authoritarian and "transitioning" regimes in Africa (Mozaffar 2002; Moehler 2005), Central Asia (Schatz 2006), China (Heberer 2006), the Arab world (Hudson 1991), and more generally (Schedler 2002).

My contention, however, is that the quest for legitimacy is only half the story.[2] There is, in fact, a more compelling explanation, namely, that elections

---

[1] Levitsky and Way (2003) argue that, following the collapse of the Soviet Union, a period of Western liberal hegemony began during which the costs associated with the "maintenance of full-scale authoritarian institutions" rose considerably.

[2] Political legitimacy can have a number of related but distinct meanings, including the following: a) the popularity of an incumbent ruler or regime, b) the moral right to govern, and c) a belief in the appropriateness of a particular system. As a result, legitimacy, as a political attribute, suffers from both conceptual fuzziness and measurement difficulty. See Magaloni (2006, 12–3) for more on why arguments about legitimacy are particularly hard to test empirically. An important area of future research will be refining the concept of legitimacy to allow for greater theoretical and empirical precision.

are a tool to manage domestic political elite, upon whom the authoritarian relies for regime stability. I argue that competitive parliamentary elections in Egypt serve as an important device for the distribution of rents and promotions to important groups within Egypt's politically influential classes, including family heads, businessmen, and party apparatchik. For party cohort, the ability to limit opposition voteshare serves as a signal of competence and loyalty to regime leadership, and party officials are promoted and demoted on this basis. For members of Egypt's politically influential upper class, parliamentary elections work as a kind of market mechanism for the selection of individuals who will be allowed to extract state rents in the future. In addition to the quasi-legitimate benefits of holding office, elections resemble an auction in which members of the elite compete for the right to parliamentary immunity. Under the cover of parliamentary immunity, individuals who have won office have the ability to engage in corruption with little fear of prosecution. I believe that economic liberalization has increased the perceived or real value of holding a parliamentary seat over time, and I find that parliamentary incumbency rates reflect this trend.

3.1 THEORETICAL CONSIDERATIONS

This chapter deals with the general question of how to allocate resources across a set of individuals who, collectively, may be considered the "selectorate" for the existing regime in Egypt.[3] This class of individuals – which I deem the rent-seeking elite – includes influential family heads, business elite, and senior bureaucratic appointees.[4]

The question of how to distribute scarce goods across a relatively large set of individuals, who each has a claim on the regime, requires careful consideration. It may seem odd to discuss distributive or allocative justice in the context of dividing the spoils of an authoritarian regime; yet, from the perspective of political entrepreneurs operating in this environment, maintaining norms of fairness and transparency is of surprising importance.[5] As members of the elite pursue their political careers, conflict over access to state resources has the potential to destroy the incumbent's coalition of support. Thus, equity, particularly the consistent application of norms for distribution of some set of resources or rights, is a condition for social stability (Young 1994, 153), even in an authoritarian setting. In an ideal world, the scarce good or resource would be allocated "in proportion to each claimant's contribution"

---

[3] The term "selectorate" refers to the subset of individuals within the population who, in principle, have control over the choice of leadership (Bueno de Mesquita et al. 2003). It is possible to argue that, in Egypt, the winning coalition represents a fairly large proportion of the selectorate.

[4] An additional group with considerable influence is the leadership of the Egyptian military.

[5] This also suggests that it is possible for a group to observe norms internal to that group but not outside of it. In other words, norms of egalitarianism or in-group fairness may be relevant for intra-elite matters, but not applicable to elite–mass relations.

(Young 1994, 9). Yet, determining the relative contribution each member of the elite makes to broader regime stability is an impossible undertaking.

There are a number of strategies by which an authoritarian regime might distribute resources to its broad coalition of elite supporters. For example, Stone (2007) argues that lotteries are a "uniquely just" way to allocate certain benefits. The use of lotteries for the distribution of political power and access is not unprecedented; political representatives were chosen by lot in some Greek and Italian city states (Elster 1989, 63–4). Why lottery over other mechanisms of selection? According to Elster, "political lotteries were used to prevent or dampen the murderous conflicts among factions of the oligarchy" (1989, 104). On the other hand, lotteries can introduce certain types of perversities. In particular, uncertainty over the future can produce inefficiencies (Elster 1989, 111), and political actors may feel as though they lack agency. As I will argue, lotteries also fail to generate certain positive outcomes that are only possible under market competition.

Queuing – or a system that favors seniority – provides an alternative to lottery. Queuing is allocation by effort and, as such, is seen as more fair by some, despite the fact that the effort associated with queuing is relatively unproductive (Elster 1989, 71). Shepsle and Nalebuff (1990) emphasize seniority – a form of queuing – in assignment to U.S. congressional committees. In an authoritarian context, a system of rewards based on queuing or seniority has both benefits and drawbacks. On one hand, long-term loyalty, a trait highly valued in such a context, is rewarded. On the other hand, if the selectorate is large enough, there may be too many people in the queue to make distribution by this strategy meaningful. In addition, the deterministic certainty of a queue would be disadvantageous to young, up-and-coming supporters of the regime who may also be the constituency most likely to overthrow the ruler.

Rather than using lotteries or queues, competitive markets, such as auctions, are a third avenue for making allocation decisions (Milgrom 1989, 19; Klemperer 1999). Indeed, competitive allocation, which operates through market mechanisms, is often supported on grounds of equity and constitutes the "only efficient and consistent" method of allocation that "leaves everyone at least as well off as he was initially" (Young 1994, 19). Highly contested elections have emerged as a primary mechanism for managing intra-elite competition over allocation decisions in Egypt, where elections closely resemble an all-pay auction as bidders (i.e., parliamentary candidates) pay regardless of whether or not they win and receive the prize (i.e., the parliamentary seat). The bid that candidates pay is the cost of the electoral campaign.[6] Rather than payment going to the regime directly, however, the largest expense associated with a campaign involves side payments to supporters as part of election mobilization. In this way, the cost of popular mobilization at election time is shouldered by elite office seekers who construct their own local support networks

---

[6] I use the term "bid" here consciously as elections are generally won by the individuals who are able to buy the largest number of votes.

to win office. From the perspective of the authoritarian regime, this is a positive externality created by electoral competition that lotteries and queues do not generate. The electoral auction creates a market system for difficult allocation decisions in which channeled competition between members of Egypt's hegemonic party and party-affiliated independents takes place according to well-established norms and expectations. Individuals who engage in the largest amount of redistribution within their districts are given the opportunity to reap the benefits of parliament. Elections, then, are a decentralized distribution mechanism that aids authoritarian survival by regularizing intra-elite competition, while at the same time outsourcing the cost of political mobilization and redistribution to the rent-seeking elite. Because of their public nature, elections also represent a more credible way to commit to promised redistribution than alternatives.

This argument is consistent with Weingast's contention that "appropriately specified political institutions are the principal way in which states create credible limits on their own authority" (1993, 288) as well as Haber's argument that the creation of a property rights system is key for stability in an autocratic regime (2006). Can a system of property rights be so broadly construed as to include the right to patronage distributed via competitive election to parliament? Haber (2006) writes that authoritarians often protect the right to "jobs, loans from government-run banks, the opportunity to receive bribes and kickbacks, selective allocation of trade protection, and tax preferences," all under the broad rubric of property rights. This wide range of "emerging new property forms" blurs traditional conceptions of private property rights (Lawson 2007, 113). Crony capitalism, a system in which those close to the political authorities receive favors that have large economic value, solves a political problem by allowing the government to "guarantee a subset of asset holders that their property rights will be protected" (Haber 2002, xii–xiv). Haber describes this as an "implicit contract between government and the privileged asset holders" (Haber 2002, xv).[7] Access to the ruling elite is open to businessmen through parliament, facilitating clientelist connections that fuel crony capitalism (Hinnebusch 2007, 24).

In Egypt, there exist a series of reinforcing political and economic ties between the regime and the elite. Channels of patronage "filter down" from the president and reinforce a system of rewards and punishments built into the hegemonic party structure (Tripp 2001, 211). Political entrepreneurs can seek one of two paths to personal enrichment. By running for parliament, members of the regime's broad coalition have a chance to bid for access to rents and opportunities for graft via elected office. Members of the elite coalition may also choose to operate in bureaucratic or party channels, seeking political

---

[7] Haber, Razo, and Maurer (2003) describe how a dictator and political entrepreneurs can maintain a stable authoritarian regime by creating a property rights system that is based on the generation and distribution of economic rents; third-party enforcement is critical to maintaining this equilibrium. In the Egyptian case, both the domestic coalitional and international reputation costs associated with shutting down or heavily rigging elections are high and becoming higher as the benefits from parliamentary membership increase.

appointment to high-level positions that afford them influence and opportunities for rents. Using elections as the primary mechanism, distributing these opportunities provides two important benefits to the regime. First, competitive markets, including electoral markets, provide information. McMillan (ND) writes that "well-functioning markets remove the need, in other words, for the government to pick winners." This is particularly important in an authoritarian setting, where making poor choices about these issues has particularly high stakes. Second, performance in elections provides a clear and public pattern of merit that is rewarded. Under a system of competitive electoral competition, all potential political entrepreneurs have a chance to bid for public office. Bureaucrats and party cadre who can prove both their competence and loyalty are able to compete for positions. Using election results and performance as criteria for rent access is perceived as largely impartial.

To summarize, the authoritarian regime in Egypt uses a highly competitive electoral market as an indirect mechanism for the allocation of rents, access to rents, and party positions – all relatively scarce resources – to members of Egypt's broad elite coalition.

3.2 MANAGING DISTRIBUTIVE EXPECTATIONS VIA ELECTIONS

Why do political entrepreneurs in Egypt spend huge sums of money to run for parliamentary seats in a legislature that does not make policy? In Egypt, elections are highly contested by multiple candidates from both within and outside of the hegemonic party. Intense within-party electoral competition emerged in 1990, when the proportional representation system that had been used in the 1984 and 1987 elections was deemed unconstitutional.[8] Under the new system, NDP party members who did not receive nomination as the party's "official" candidate in a district now had the opportunity to run as independents. In the 1990 election, independent candidates far outnumbered official party candidates, even among NDP members (Auda 1991, 75). Although the official NDP slate won only 57 percent of seats, electorally successful NDP independents rejoined the party once in parliament, providing the NDP with a supermajority (Auda 1991, 75–6). According to Auda, electoral competition came to be "viewed less as a means of reforming the government or the economy than as a way to enhance social prestige and personal wealth and influence" (1991, 76). The 1995 election saw a further increase in the number of independent candidates; an extra 100 seats were added to the NDP majority when these NDP independents rejoined the party following the election (al-Awadi 2004, 171). By 2000, 79 percent of all candidates ran as independents (Langohr 2000). And, although only 39 percent of official NDP candidates won their seats,

---

[8] In 1984, individual candidacy was not permitted, and, in 1987, strict limits were placed on opportunities for individual candidates. The 1987 election used a parallel system that included the opportunity for a limited number of independents (48 seats) as a result of a previous court ruling. The rest of the seats were distributed via a proportional representation system.

after NDP independents rejoined the party, the NDP enjoyed an 88 percent majority.[9] In 2005, 4,300 independents contested the election; Koehler calls competition between official and independent NDP candidates the "real" story of these parliamentary elections (2008, 984).[10]

Electoral manipulation takes place in a limited number of cases (usually aimed at the opposition Muslim Brotherhood), and, as such, the majority of the 444 electoral contests are genuinely competitive. This is particularly the case for districts where NDP official candidates face off against NDP independents. Elections allow the regime to manage distributive expectations for Egypt's rent-seeking elite, particularly with regard to the distribution of power, promotions, rents, access to state resources, and immunity from criminal prosecution for corrupt practices. In this way, elections provide a well-structured environment for elite competition and preempt more serious conflict between individuals and groups. At the same time, elections allow the authoritarian leadership to push off some of the costs of political mobilization onto this elite class. Elections, therefore, contribute to the health of an authoritarian regime in a variety of ways.

3.2.1   Distributing Access to State Rents

The political elite in Egypt can be divided into a number of categories. The most significant grouping is the set of influential family heads and businessmen that I call the rent-seeking elite. The categories of family head and businessman are not mutually exclusive (in fact, almost all elite Egyptians have extensive business dealings), and these individuals are the present day successors to the entrepreneurial Sadatists of the 1970s. They compete vigorously for the chance to serve in parliament and spend millions of Egyptian pounds on expensive election campaigns, leading one commentator to suggest that there is a "flourishing electoral economy" in Egypt, where citizens witness a "war of the wallets" at ballot time (Boutaleb 2002). In 2000, average candidates spent LE 3–5 million buying votes (Boutaleb 2002), with the cost of candidacy rising even higher in 2005. It is rumored that, in 2005, a wealthy hotelier in Cairo spent more than LE 20 million on the day of the parliamentary election in her district alone.[11] Local press reports suggest that candidates in other districts spent upwards of LE 10 million on their campaigns.[12]

So why do candidates go to such lengths to secure seats in a parliament that is known to be little more than a rubber stamp for the prerogatives of the authoritarian regime? With highly circumscribed policy influence, on the surface, it would appear irrational that candidates would expend such effort

[9] Arab Strategic Report 2001, Al-Ahram Center for Political and Strategic Studies.
[10] See Collombier (2007) for a description of how the 2005 elections represented an opportunity to evaluate internal struggles within the NDP.
[11] In 2005, the $US–LE exchange rate was approximately 6:1.
[12] *Al-Ghad*, November 23, 2005.

and resources. In fact, expensive campaigns are not irrational at all given that elections in Egypt are a sorting mechanism for the distribution of resources and access to state largesse. The authoritarian leadership needs a mechanism to provide members of the political elite with continued "payment" in exchange for their support. One strategy to accomplish this might have been to appoint individuals to parliament or some other body and distribute benefits on this basis. However, those that would have been excluded from the distribution of spoils could have become embittered and sought strategies for the overthrow of the leadership. In addition, the regime would continually face the challenge of picking the right people. Through elections, on the other hand, the regime distributes access to state resources in what is perceived to be a fairly free and competitive basis. Here, disgruntled individuals have little recourse or basis for complaint. In a 2007 interview, NDP heavyweight Fathi Sorour characterized parliamentary elections in Egypt as survival of the fittest.[13] Those who spend the most on campaigning are most likely to prevail. The party does not finance these election campaigns, and often candidates compete against "independents" who are in truth aligned with the NDP, making ideological considerations irrelevant.[14]

What kinds of benefits can one expect as a result of holding office? Individuals seeking material advancement in Egypt are often dependent on state channels for access to privilege. A position in parliament provides numerous opportunities for money making and influence. Parliamentarians capture state resources through both authorized and informal channels. Holding a seat in parliament provides potential opportunities to barter or sell appointments and jobs. Parliamentarians are often able to expedite the issuing of permits, allowing them to expand their businesses. Parliamentarians are sometimes bribed for their influence or access to ministers who can provide services to districts. Wurzel writes that political entrepreneurs enter parliament to do their own deals, with no systematic interest in political reform (2004, 125). Loans without interest or collateral are also reported to have been negotiated between bank officials and parliamentarians (Kienle 2004, 288).[15]

In addition to these – what I would describe as "typical" – avenues of influence and benefit, parliamentarians also use legal immunity granted to office holders for more nefarious purposes. As a result, it is widely believed that more important than the legal or quasi-legal benefits of holding a parliamentary seat are the myriad of illegitimate opportunities available to parliamentarians as a

---

[13] *Al-Masry Al-Youm*, March 24, 2007.

[14] See Blaydes and el-Tarouty (2008) for more details on the impact of intraparty competition on election campaigns in Egypt.

[15] A similar pattern has been observed in Pakistan. Using loan-level data of 90,000 firms in Pakistan (representing the entire universe of corporate lending between 1996 and 2002), Khwaja and Mian (2005) find that politically connected firms receive preferential treatment in access to government loans. The more powerful and successful a politician, the more influence he or she has on the banks; a parliamentarian, for example, enjoys greater influence on the banks than someone who is simply a member of the ruling party.

result of their protection from prosecution for corruption. Norms establishing unusually high guarantees of parliamentary immunity (*ḥaṣāna*) in Egypt, therefore, are a major motivation for legislative office seeking.[16] Whereas the formal institution of parliamentary immunity – or the granting of protection from prosecution for their actions as parliamentarians – has historically been used to protect legislators from civil actions for libel or defamation, the authoritarian leadership has encouraged informal norms to emerge that allow parliamentarians to engage in corrupt and illegal activities with impunity.[17]

Under the protection of immunity as it exists in Egypt, parliamentarians engage in relatively minor infractions and large-scale fraud and embezzlement. Parliamentarians have been accused of illegally importing large quantities of the drug Viagra.[18] Others have been found selling illegal permits for the pilgrimage to Mecca, bouncing thousands of dollars in checks, and many other infractions.[19] Parliamentarians have been suspected of evading payment on the purchase of property, embezzlement, and other crimes.[20] In el-Karanshawy's ethnographic account of village politics, he writes that the candidate who won the 1987 election in a village under study was one of the most powerful drug dealers the area had ever known (1997). In a particularly tragic case involving high-level corruption, more than 1,000 Egyptians perished in 2006 when a ferry boat owned by parliamentarian Mamduh Isma'il sank in the Red Sea while traveling between Saudi Arabia and the Egyptian coast. Subsequent reports on the causes of the disaster have suggested that negligence sank the vessel. Isma'il was able to flee to Europe as a result of his parliamentary immunity.[21] Many such examples exist.

Egyptian economic policy has made the offer of parliamentary immunity even more enticing over time. Egypt's implementation of an IMF-mandated privatization and economic liberalization program beginning in the late 1980s had a significant effect on the increasing influence of money and corruption in politics. Egypt's inability to finance its debt led to the introduction of an IMF structural adjustment program (SAP) that included, among other things, "a reduction in government spending, the gradual cutting of subsidies, privatization of the economy, a contraction of government intervention in the economy

---

[16] In countries influenced by the British legal tradition, parliamentarians are only protected for acts related to legislative activity. For example, a legislator would be protected from accusations of slander and libel for speeches made on the floor while discussing legislation. Countries like Egypt that have taken the French system as a basis for their constitution offer parliamentarians even greater protection, including severe restrictions barring the police from arresting, detaining, or otherwise charging parliamentarians of crimes. In order for prosecution against a parliamentarian to proceed, a court or often the parliament itself must lift immunity first (Wigley 2003).

[17] Migdal, writing of Egypt, argues that "corruption tolerated by state leaders on the part of those they have co-opted can be a further source of political control" (1988, 220).

[18] *Al-Ahram Weekly*, March 16–22, 2006.

[19] Vickie Langohr, *Middle East Report*, November 7, 2000.

[20] *Al-Ahram Weekly*, August 19–25, 1999.

[21] Isma'il was later sentenced in abstentia to seven years in prison.

and a much greater reliance on market mechanisms" (Zaki 1995, 164). Rather than creating growth for large segments of the population, economic liberalization gave rise to a new, wealthy, and corrupt capitalist class (Zaki 1995, 166). Zaki writes:

> Running parallel with the government's successful achievements in its SAP [structural adjustment program] is a stream-flow of corrupt practices, (with) most stories implying the existence of interlocking interests between certain elements of big business, and certain members within the ruling circles (1998, 147).

Analyst 'Amr al-Shoubaki argues that, in the years following Sadat's decision to hold multiparty elections, parliamentarians came to play an important role in negotiating services and infrastructure improvements, including roads, hospitals, and schools, and helping people find jobs, in order to win support from constituents.[22] These parliamentarians are often referred to as "service deputies" (*nā'ib al-khadamāt* – singular). Al-Shoubaki writes that, over time, this strategy began to fail because parliamentarians found themselves less able to provide these services as the ministers of various agencies, who served as gatekeepers to public funds, became unwilling to make the same types of concessions as before.[23] Whereas al-Shoubaki does not attribute this belt tightening to any particular factor, Zaki argues that it was the economic crisis and subsequent SAP that decreased the level of funds available for patronage activities (Zaki 1995, 229). Al-Shoubaki writes:

> This situation was behind the emergence of a new pattern of parliament members who gained seats through direct vote buying rather than promises to provide services to the people. Thus, an unprecedented process of vote buying appeared on the surface to reflect the absence of people's confidence in deputies with political discourse as well as those of services. Because voters were sure that they would not see candidates again, they preferred to directly sell their votes to those who can afford them. The third significant phenomenon was the dominant role of cash money, which came to substitute for the services that were usually offered to residents of many electoral constituencies.[24]

Ever since, electoral campaigns have grown more and more costly (Ouda, El-Borai, and Seada 2002, 65). Economic estimates suggest that total candidate expenditure in the 2000 election was LE 10 billion, compared with LE 4 billion in the 1995 election, and that the number of businessmen doubled in parliament between 1995 and 2000 (Ouda et al. 2002, 66). The price of a parliamentary seat is commensurate with the value that political elite expect to receive as a result of holding that seat. An increasingly liberalized economy combined with immunity from prosecution has driven up the cost of a parliamentary seat over time. The ability to engage in corruption under more open economic conditions

---

[22] 'Amr al-Shoubaki, "Legislative Elections in Egypt: Indicators and Consequences," Al-Ahram Center for Political and Strategic Studies, Issue 46, December 2005.

[23] Ibid.

[24] Ibid.

TABLE 3.1. *Parliamentary Reelection Rates, 1987–2005*

Election Year	Reelected Parliamentarians (%)
1987	40
1990	21
1995	42
2000	26
2005	19

is more valuable to individual candidates than the selling or trading of services captured through informal influence over the state sector.

Elections are perceived as a relatively fair and even-handed way for distributing these sought-after benefits and opportunities. Individuals that lose any particular election always have a chance to gather their resources and mount a campaign in the future. This means that the Egyptian political elite see their interaction with the authoritarian leadership as an iterated game; there is little incentive to dismantle a system today that could offer you important opportunities tomorrow. As a result, Egyptian politicians tend to have a long time horizon. Many have attempted comebacks years after an unsuccessful run. In addition, as the nature of the Egyptian economy has changed over time, the tacit bargain between the rent-seeking elite and the regime has changed as well. Whereas parliamentarians used to have a greater role providing services in their districts, increasingly they are rewarded with opportunities for graft rather than with the ability to distribute services or jobs. In a sense, this has made the value of a parliamentary seat more valuable over time as the opportunities for graft are only limited by regime and public tolerance.

If my arguments are valid, then we would expect evidence to support at least two empirical regularities. First, we should see relatively high turnover of parliamentarians, because the existence of permanent or semipermanent seats in parliament would imply that some members of the political elite would be perpetually outside of the system of benefits. High incumbency rates would signal a system of benefit by appointment. Low incumbency rates would be consistent with my theory. Second, if the value of a parliamentary seat has gone up over time as a result of the changing economic environment, then we should also expect to see a decline in incumbency since the introduction of structural adjustment as more potential candidates seek to "capture" the benefits associated with being in office.

I have collected parliamentary lists from 1984 until the present, calculated reelection rates, and found that incumbency rates have been relatively low during this period and appear to be dropping over time (see Table 3.1).[25] The highest recorded incumbent reelection rate was 42 percent in 1995, and the

[25] It is significant that structural adjustment in Egypt intensified in the mid-1990s.

lowest was 19 percent in 2005. An important exception to this trend was the 1990 election, which was boycotted by the opposition. As a result, most of the opposition parliamentarians that had been seated in 1987 were not up for reelection in 1990, a likely reason for the anomalous figure in 1990.

What does the authoritarian leadership get out of this arrangement? First, the autocrat creates a mechanism for the distribution of spoils to members of the rent-seeking elite. Political entrepreneurs voluntarily buy into the authoritarian system and remain tacit supporters of the regime as they pursue resources and wealth. At the same time, this system cleverly passes on the costs of mass mobilization to the political elite at the local level. In Egypt, it is widely known that political parties do not pay for campaigns of individual candidates.[26] In el-Abnoudy's documentary film on female candidates in Egypt (1996), NDP candidates state that the party gives them no funds to run their campaigns. In order to win, therefore, candidates fund their campaigns entirely through their own personal and family resources. Mass mobilization of voters at the local level leads to considerable economic redistribution during election years as a result of transfers from the political elite to the masses via vote-buying schemes that are described more fully in Chapter 6. A voting system based on patronage is acceptable, and perhaps even desirable, from the perspective of the authoritarian regime.[27] Parliamentary candidates solve the regime's problem of mass mobilization. Finally, this system is self-limiting in that the more valuable it is to hold office, the more competitive parliamentary elections become. This necessitates higher levels of campaign expenditure (i.e., redistribution via vote buying) to win office. In sum, competitive parliamentary elections solve a number of important problems for the authoritarian leadership in Egypt, including distribution of spoils to political elite and local-level political mobilization.

3.2.2   Performance-Based Promotion Strategies

Existing studies describe a number of objectives authoritarians may have for the shuffling of party cadre. Migdal writes that "the powers of appointment and removal from office in state leaders' hands have proved an important tool in preventing state agencies or state-sponsored political parties from becoming threatening conglomerates of power" (1988, 214). Barkey argues that the leadership of the Ottoman Empire engineered a system in which the military and bureaucratic elite were regularly rotated to make them unwilling to challenge its authority: "the patrimonial state performed its task of elite control and shuffling so that elites were constrained by their lack of autonomy, and their dependence on the state for office, awards, and status and brought into a

---

[26] NDP candidates may, however, enjoy the right to use state facilities and are granted permits for rallies, etc., that opposition candidates may not enjoy. Also, see Shehata (2008).

[27] Clientelism tends to be highly labor intensive; with a large population and high unemployment, the cost of labor is relatively low in Egypt, making clientelist practices fairly cost-effective.

seemingly natural competition" (1994, 40). Using a game theoretic framework and evidence from Mughal India, Debs (2007) finds that agents of an authoritarian ruler are shuffled from one assignment to another so that no alliance might emerge between the agent and the local population.

A key to maintaining continued support from party bureaucrats involves the creation of a system of rotation that honors norms of consistency and fairness of treatment for party members, thus avoiding unnecessary conflict within the party. In her article on authoritarian elections and parties, Geddes (2005) argues that elections create "routine ways of choosing lower level officials in order to reduce conflict among supporters." Because this function of elections is not the focus of her article, she does not elaborate on that idea or provide evidence for the existence of such patterns. In this section, I pick up where Geddes leaves off and argue that such a pattern of behavior exists in Egypt as election performance for party members at the provincial level provides important information about competence, connections, and commitment. Although these individuals are not seeking elected political office themselves, their ability to mobilize voters and achieve a favorable outcome for party candidates with a minimum of fraud and coercion reflects important characteristics, including capability and loyalty. In this way, the party is able to dismiss those individuals a) who are underperforming due to poor competence or b) whose loyalty to the party is in question. Elections reveal important information that can then be used to improve the overall performance of the hegemonic party and increase the internal stability of the regime.[28]

How does this informational benefit of elections work? Executive and party authority is organized hierarchically in Egypt, with provincial governors appointed by the president as the highest executive authority in the governorate and provincial secretaries as the head of the local party organization for each governorate.[29] These individuals are typically strongly rooted in their local areas and are not generally assigned to other regions.[30] Together with governorate-level security officials, the governor and provincial secretary provide information to the candidate selection committee about local

---

[28] Egorov and Sonin (2006) have suggested that there is a trade-off between loyalty and competence in high-level agents (viziers) selected by authoritarian rulers. In their model, as the level of competence goes up for a vizier, the probability of betrayal also goes up. Unlike Egorov and Sonin, I do not make this assumption; one reason for the distinction is that the value placed on loyalty for a trusted vizier is much higher than the value one would place on the loyalty of a midlevel party or bureaucratic leader. It is not entirely clear, either, that this trade-off exists for high-level advisors. For example, consider the decision of Arab monarchs to hire their family members as the heads of important technocratic positions; very often, royal family members have the best educational training (i.e., highest levels of competence), suggesting that competence may be endogenous to loyalty in some cases.

[29] I use the terms "province" and "governorate" interchangeably in reference to the Egyptian *muḥāfaẓat*. There existed twenty-six governorates at the time these data were generated. The number of governorates in Egypt was increased by two in 2008 and an additional one in 2009.

[30] Interview with Mohammed Kamal, NDP Policies Secretariat and Professor of Political Science, Cairo University, May 3, 2006.

parliamentary hopefuls. In addition, these individuals play key roles in managing parliamentary elections within their geographic area to ensure that candidates associated with the ruling party enjoy strong performance.[31]

In the months after parliamentary elections, the government typically announces an overhaul of leadership positions across different levels of both the executive and the party. A number of factors go into these decisions, including the performance of provincial-level officials during the recently completed election.[32] High-level sources within the hegemonic party, for example, are quoted in a major pan-Arab newspaper as saying that the party would be replacing provincial officers who did not perform well in the previous elections.[33] State-appointed village mayors (*'umda* – singular)[34] and members of the security services[35] were also sacked for insufficient effort and support in favor of party candidates.[36] During the 1995 election, city executives in Gharbia were threatened by the governor that they would lose their jobs if NDP candidates were not supported (el-Borei 1995, 42–3).

What constitutes satisfactory performance for an official appointed by the regime? For a provincial governor or party secretary, popular mobilization for NDP candidates during elections is highly important.[37] Newspaper reports during the 2000 parliamentary election suggest that the party's particularly bad performance in the governorate of Suez led to the expectation that the provincial secretary would not continue in his position.[38] This individual was subsequently removed from his job.[39]

Poor performance of the party in a particular area may be the result of incompetence on the part of a provincial secretary or governor, but there have also been allegations of secret alliances between regime agents and Islamist candidates, suggesting that disloyalty may be a factor in addition to incompetence.[40] How would disloyalty play out in such a situation? Sometimes conflicts arise between careerism and economic opportunity. A provincial-level official might hoodwink powers at the center regarding the relative popularity or

---

[31] This is not to say that provincial officials do not also have other roles. For example, governors are also held responsible for maintaining internal stability within their respective governorates and effectively quelling other forms of dissent.

[32] In some ways, Egypt resembles Ichino's "tournament party," in that local actors compete with one another to become the agent for a particular location (2005); the difference, however, is that there are not multiple agents operating simultaneously, as in the Nigerian example.

[33] *Al-Sharq Al-Awsat*, February 11, 2001.

[34] Ibid.

[35] Interview with Sherif Wali, Shura Council member, May 24, 2007.

[36] Owen points out that, during Egypt's liberal period (1923–1952), the party in power would typically replace village mayors who were thought to favor opponents with men loyal to their own cause (2004, 132–3).

[37] Interview with Gamal al-Batran, NDP Secretary General, Haram District Giza Governorate, July 19, 2005.

[38] *Al-Sharq Al-Awsat*, November 2, 2000.

[39] *Al-Ahram*, February 27, 2001.

[40] *Al-Sharq Al-Awsat*, November 24, 2000.

reputation of a potential parliamentary candidate in exchange for cash payment.[41] In one such case, a provincial secretary was fired for having lied to a central committee of the NDP.[42]

Analysis of data I have collected regarding turnover of governors and provincial secretaries in Egypt's governorates following the 2005 parliamentary elections suggests that provincial secretaries and governors whose governorates witnessed increases in Muslim Brotherhood voteshare between 2000 and 2005 were more likely to be dismissed from their positions. In my analysis, I control for the inherent difficulty of the job.[43] This variable is constructed by dividing the number of Brotherhood candidates in a particular governorate by the percentage of Egypt's total population residing in that governorate. The idea is that this variable captures the difficulty of garnering NDP voteshare in any particular area. A high-level NDP official conveyed that, under certain circumstances, the party does not expect success, depending on the difficulty of the assignment.[44] For example, in 2005, the Muslim Brotherhood did well in districts across Alexandria; appointed officials were not removed, however, because regime insiders in Cairo realized that it would be impossible to keep the Muslim Brotherhood from winning in this area.[45] I also control for whether the governorate is located on the Sinai Peninsula, where rotation is determined on the basis of security factors rather than election results.[46]

The statistical model I run to analyze these data is a probit, where the dependent variable is a one if the governor or provincial secretary retained his post and a zero if he did not. The analysis suggests that both provincial secretaries and governors were less likely to retain their posts when the Muslim Brotherhood saw large increases in representation in the areas under their control. The result for provincial secretaries is significant at the 0.85 level, and the result for governors is significant at the 0.9 level. These results (displayed in Table 3.2) suggest that governors who saw no increase in Muslim Brotherhood seats in their governorate had a 75 percent chance of retaining their positions, whereas officials who saw a 25 percent increase in their governorate had a 50 percent chance of keeping their posts. Those who saw a 50 percent increase in Muslim Brotherhood representation on their watch only had a 20 percent chance of retaining their positions. I find a similar result for provincial secretaries.

[41] Interview with Gehad Auda, NDP Media Secretariat and Professor of Political Science, Helwan University, May 23, 2007.
[42] Interview with Moheb Zaki, Ibn Khaldun Center for Development Studies, May 23, 2007.
[43] This statement is comparable to saying that it is much more difficult for a Republican to get elected mayor of San Francisco than a Democrat. Should the Republican Party punish the local official who fails in this regard? She was dealt a much tougher assignment and had a low probability of success from the start. Similarly, there are certain areas that may have been predisposed to support the Muslim Brotherhood.
[44] Interview with 'Ali al-Din Hilal, former Minister of Youth and Professor of Political Science, Cairo University, April 30, 2007.
[45] Interview with Sherif Wali, Shura Council member, May 24, 2007.
[46] The NDP has never lost a seat in either North or South Sinai, and security considerations are of utmost importance in this part of the country as a result of proximity to both Israel and Gaza.

TABLE 3.2. *Probit Regression Results (Dependent Variable Is Official Retaining Post)*

	Provincial Secretary	Governor
Constant	−0.208	−0.399
	(0.500)	(0.487)
MB candidates/population	0.510	0.932
	(0.441)	(0.443)
Percentage increase in MB representation	−0.034	−0.041
	(0.023)	(0.024)
Sinai governorates	(dropped)	−0.661
		(1.277)
Pseudo R^2	0.07	0.15
Observations	24	26

Note: Standard errors are shown in parentheses.

These results indicate that the regime uses elections to make determinations about promotions and job security within the NDP.[47] Why is this important? Elections provide the means by which competent and loyal party apparatchik can be selected and promoted through the organization's pyramidal system. The expectations of party and regime officials are fairly clear: large gains for the opposition are seen as a basis upon which to fire or demote. Elections act as a tool for the regime, therefore, to resolve disputes between various political elite, whether they be party apparatchik hoping to maintain their status within the party structure or locally influential elite seeking the benefits of a parliamentary seat.

3.3   CONCLUSIONS

Competitive parliamentary elections serve a variety of purposes for the authoritarian regime in Egypt that go beyond the conventional explanation that elections are used to confer legitimacy. When these elections were first introduced in the 1970s, then-president Sadat was responding in large part to the emergence of right-wing trends within the political elite. Economic opening had created a class of what some have called "parasitic capitalists," who sought ties to the state to improve their economic fortunes (Beattie 1991). The hegemonic party that emerged from this period – the NDP – acted as a "steering committee of Egypt's private sector" by serving as its conduit for getting access to state largesse (Bianchi 1989, 15–16). However, parliamentary elections have

---

[47] In a different context, security considerations may dominate. For example, in April 2008, immediately following the municipal elections, which were competitive only within the hegemonic party, provincial governors were reshuffled with an emphasis on putting into place individuals with strong backgrounds in security. Again, competence is revealed through the governor's ability to handle domestic political concerns. See *Al-Ahram Weekly*, April 24–30, 2008, for more details.

also provided an arena of competition for those capitalist interests during the Mubarak era. Individual political entrepreneurs seek a parliamentary seat to enjoy both the legitimate and illegitimate benefits afforded by holding office. This is largely in line with Ayubi's argument that businessmen and opportunists exploit the party and the regime's parliamentary façade (1989, 17). Corruption is tolerated by the regime because it ensures the long-term loyalty of this influential class. I have also shown that elections provide important information to the authoritarian regime regarding the competence of party apparatchik. This information allows the authoritarian leadership to make promotions on a nonarbitrary basis.

In these ways, elections are a kind of market mechanism, helping to resolve disputes between various groups and individuals operating within Egypt's broad class of political elite. The existence of a relatively even-handed mechanism for providing benefits keeps the regime's coalition invested in the authoritarian system. This suggests that a certain consistency to the rules of the game is important for handling elite expectations in the context of authoritarian regimes. There is little doubt that the majority of these individuals would do worse under a democratic system in which increased accountability would limit opportunities for graft and corruption. As a result, the electoral formula has thus far proven effective for the authoritarian leadership in Egypt. Scholars have long raised questions about the sustainability of systems dependent on the type of crony capitalism we find in Egypt. Haber (2002, xvi) argues that crony capitalism is economically inefficient, with the implication that the equilibrium that we see is ultimately also self-undermining. Elite-supported political change is unlikely unless the costs to the rent-seeking elite associated with maintaining systematic corruption exceed the benefits currently accruing to the coalition.

4

The Politics of Infrastructure Provision

One of the most important decisions facing the governments of both developed and developing countries involves how to distribute critical infrastructure resources given a country's budget constraint. In the developing world, improvements to basic infrastructure can make a profound difference in the health and well-being of populations and can particularly improve the lives and educational opportunities for girls and women who often (quite literally) carry the burden of poor infrastructure. Recent scholarly works have attempted to examine some of the *political* determinants of local economic development in a number of countries, including China, India, Japan, Mexico, and Peru (Schady 2000; Diaz-Cayeros et al. 2003; Parikh and Weingast 2003; Chhibber and Nooruddin 2004; Scheiner 2006; Magaloni 2006; Tsai 2007; Diaz-Cayeros, Estevez, and Magaloni 2007). These studies are informed by competing theories about how an incumbent should distribute selective resources, such as infrastructure and other public goods. Cox and McCubbins (1986) argue that incumbents may be risk-averse and as a result prefer to make transfers to core supporters. Lindbeck and Weibull (1987) suggest that transfers should instead go to swing voters. Dixit and Londregan (1996) contend that the choice between favoring swing voters or core supporters depends on a number of factors. For Bueno de Mesquita et al. (2003), leaders who need to reward a growing coalition of supporters will do so through the provision of public goods.[1] In this chapter, I examine the politics of public goods provision in Egypt with an eye toward answering the following question: Is there a link between support for the opposition and future levels of infrastructure investment in an area? In other words, does a "punishment regime" exist in Egypt?

---

[1] Public goods provision takes place for other reasons as well. Smith (2008) argues that, when confronted with a revolutionary threat, leaders will sometimes increase public goods provision so that citizens will have less incentive to rebel.

I show that governorates that supported opposition candidates in Egypt's first competitive parliamentary election under Mubarak did see smaller improvements to important public infrastructure coverage over the decade that followed.[2] I also test two hypotheses regarding *how* political influence is linked to the allocation of infrastructure investment and find that, even after controlling for the party status of parliamentary representatives, voteshare for the opposition in this key election is still a strong predictor of future infrastructure improvement. As the two areas of infrastructure improvement that I examine – water and sewerage – were largely improved at the discretion of the central government during the period under study, this suggests that areas that expressed a preference for the opposition were penalized for their unwillingness to support the hegemonic party. This finding relates to theories emphasizing the informational role elections have in authoritarian regimes; electoral results can present a fairly accurate map of areas of support and opposition that can be used by autocrats for the disbursal of discretionary funds. The results of my analysis for Egypt are supportive of core-voter models, where the incumbent elite reward loyal constituencies. Consistent with the broader themes of this project, elections are, again, seen as playing an important role in the distribution of scarce resources. This chapter concludes with a discussion of the changing nature of infrastructure provision in Egypt today, particularly the privatization of infrastructure development and the role of popular protest in extracting concessions from the government.

4.1 THE CROSS-NATIONAL LITERATURE

A rich and growing literature examines the politics of economic development within a variety of developing countries and, particularly, disparities in infrastructure and other investment as a function of election results.[3] Schady (2000), in his study of a large-scale development project in Peru, finds that investment was directed to provinces in which the marginal political effect was likely to be

[2] Competitive parliamentary elections took place in Egypt in the late nineteenth and early twentieth centuries. The parliamentary elections of 1984 – whose results are analyzed here – are the first highly competitive, multiparty parliamentary elections to take place in Egypt since the Free Officers' Coup in 1952.

[3] The most commonly articulated theories about the allocation of discretionary funds that do not rely primarily on election results emphasize the importance of ethnic or other group identification in the provision of public goods. For example, one competing hypothesis is that ethnic divisions explain the level of public goods provided. Alesina, Baqir, and Eastenly (1999) argue that politicians are less likely to provide public goods in areas where they rely on the political support of an ethnically based constituency because public goods would be shared among ethnic groups. Other scholars have argued that norms regarding community obligations create modes of informal accountability. Tsai (2007) argues that fiscal decentralization in China has given village governments more responsibility in administering public goods and that the quality of local governance is determined by village social networks in which solidary groups offer moral standing as an incentive for local officials to perform well. Although plausible, I do not test these hypotheses in the context of this project.

largest. Reed (2001) argues that, in Japan, the long-ruling Liberal Democratic Party (LDP) used its budgetary discretion to distribute funds both strategically (i.e., to close districts) and also vengefully. Scheiner emphasizes the strong incentives local politicians have to ally with the ruling party in order to get access to development and other resources for their districts (2006, 90). An implication of this argument is that areas that do not support the ruling party will be denied this type of investment. Scheiner (2006) further offers examples of regions that were punished for supporting parties other than the LDP. The literature on distribution of revenue in India suggests that, until the late 1980s, the hegemonic party established a punishment regime for districts that failed to offer support to the existing political cartel (Parikh and Weingast 2003). This conclusion mirrors the findings of Diaz-Cayeros et al. (2003), who provide evidence of a punishment regime in Mexico under the PRI. Magaloni (2006) finds evidence in favor of allocations for marginal districts; however, Diaz-Cayeros et al. (2007) – using a more complete set of empirical tests – show that the PRI primarily targeted benefits to its core constituencies under the PRONOSOL development program. El-Meehy (2009) argues that, in Egypt, the Social Fund for Development (SFD) penalizes areas with a history of supporting the opposition Muslim Brotherhood by denying those communities development program funding. Other than El-Meehy's investigation of the SFD, no other study that I am aware of has addressed the politicization of discretionary public goods spending in Egypt.

4.2 PUBLIC INFRASTRUCTURE PROVISION

Who is responsible for the provision of public goods in Egypt? Although there has been a general decline in the provision of these goods by the government over time, as described in Chapter 2, two areas where the government has traditionally remained, and, to a large extent, still remains, primarily responsible involve the provision of water and sewerage infrastructure. Part of the reason for this is practical: it is very difficult for individuals to connect to the state water or sewerage grid without cooperation from the government, given the cost and technical difficulty of such an effort. Water and sewerage, therefore, differ from other types of goods, such as electricity or Internet access, where individuals are better able to more easily connect illegally. The services that the government provides also tend to be focused on primary infrastructure rather than smaller scale goods.[4]

Water and sewerage infrastructure development make a useful subject for study because they are described by local government officials as the top two priorities for infrastructure development.[5] Ateyat el-Abnoudy's 1981 documentary "Seas of Thirst" (*Biḥār al-'Aṭash*), for example, highlights the hardships encountered by women in one village who do not have access to piped water.

---

[4] Interview with Moheb Zaki, Ibn Khaldun Center for Development Studies, November 16, 2005.
[5] Interview with 'Abd al-Muhsin Shalabi, President, Local Council Haram Giza, July 19, 2005.

The central government also frequently reminds the public of the state's role in infrastructure provision, calling it the country's "national project."[6]

Financial resources for infrastructure development in Egypt come from the central government and are subsequently disbursed to the governorates (Adams 1993). In Egypt, there is a strong sense that budget decisions are highly centralized and discretionary. Governorates have considerable local executive power but have virtually no own-source revenue; they are dependent on the central government for all budget allocations (Sims 2003). According to one former parliamentarian, the central government maintains a list of infrastructure development priorities based on area need, but political considerations can get certain areas moved up or down on that list.[7]

A variety of ethnographic studies also point to citizen reliance on government for the provision of these basic public goods. One researcher describes the process for getting water and sewerage infrastructure in one area in considerable depth. Taher (1986) writes that about one-third of the buildings in the urban district under study had no water or sewage pipes. Most frequently, local women had to carry jugs of water from the public taps or neighbors' taps, often for a fee. In the absence of public sewerage infrastructure, sewage was disposed via trucked septic tanks. Neighborhood residents paid a fee for this service, and, as a result, there was a strong preference for publicly provided water and sewerage infrastructure. Government representatives told neighborhood residents that there was not enough money for all areas to get water and sewage pipes, and residents would often petition governorate officials, though it could be years before such requests were answered. Other ethnographic works also point to reliance on the state – particularly at the governorate level – for the provision of basic infrastructure both in the Nile Delta (Weyland 1993) as well as in more urban areas (Elyachar 2005).

4.3 POLITICAL GEOGRAPHY OF INVESTMENT

It is widely accepted by both scholars of Egyptian politics as well as everyday citizens and voters that patronage plays a highly important role in the Egyptian political system. This chapter is concerned with understanding the extent to which political factors, particularly electoral support for opposition party candidates, impact critical infrastructure investment in the context of Egypt's resource-constrained environment. Using census data on the accessibility of publicly provided sewerage and water infrastructure across Egypt's governorates, I show that infrastructure improvements were made in a systematic way consistent with the idea of a "punishment regime," even after controlling for important covariates like urban–rural status as well as previous level of infrastructure coverage.

---

[6] *Al-Ahram Weekly,* July 26–August 1, 2007.
[7] Interview with former parliamentarian, May 26, 2007.

There are two primary ways by which a punishment regime like this might work, both of which are supported in the primary source and ethnographic literatures. The first is through bias against representatives who are not members of the hegemonic party; because parliamentarians have historically worked to influence disbursement of resources to their regions through lobbying of the central government, one might expect to see areas with non-NDP representatives suffering from smaller infrastructure improvements. The second mechanism is related to the informational quality of elections; the central government might learn, through election results, where areas of core support lie and then funnel development resources to these areas. From an empirical perspective, even after controlling for the party status of parliamentary representatives, voteshare for the opposition in the first parliamentary election under Mubarak is still a strong predictor of future infrastructure improvement, suggesting support for the informational theory.

The empirical tests that I conduct use data from Egypt's first highly competitive multiparty election since the 1952 coup – which took place in 1984 – as an important source of information revelation. These data serve as a key independent variable and are then used to predict change in the availability of publicly provided water and sewerage infrastructure between 1986 and 1996 (i.e., the first difference) as collected and reported in Egyptian census documents. Because the central government makes disbursements for funds for infrastructure investment to governorates, I use Egypt's governorates as the units of analysis. I also include a variety of covariates in the analysis, including the party status of representatives as well as the previous levels of infrastructure development.

4.3.1   The 1984 Parliamentary Election

The 1984 election was the first major multiparty parliamentary electoral contest to take place in Egypt since the Free Officers' Coup in 1952.[8] The freedom surrounding the election was taken by most as an indication of political liberalization permitted by the regime. Opposition candidates performed well, garnering up to 50 percent of the vote in some areas. Other districts remained staunchly proregime, offering most or all of their voteshare to the NDP. An alliance of the "New" Wafd (*Hizb al-Wafd al-Jadīd*) and the Muslim Brotherhood made the greatest inroads. The Wafd had been electorally popular in the pre-1952 era. As it reemerged in the 1980s, the Wafd sought the electoral support of small businessmen who lacked close ties to the regime (Post 1987). The Muslim Brotherhood, as a result of strict laws governing the creation of parties, did not have legal political party status. By allying with the Wafd, the Muslim Brotherhood was able to participate in the elections despite the constraints of a proportional representation electoral system that favored the participation of parties over independent candidates. The Wafd leadership also believed that it

---

[8] The 1976 and 1979 took place with competition between government-created "proto-parties" and independents.

would benefit from the alliance. The electoral laws in place at that time required a party to receive a minimum of 8 percent voteshare in order to receive any seats in parliament, and Wafd leaders may have been concerned about the party's ability to reach that mark with Brotherhood voters (el-Mikaway 1999, 82). In the election, the Wafd and Brotherhood together garnered 15 percent of the vote nationwide. The Labor (*Ḥizb al-'Amal al-Ishtirākī*) and Tagammu' (*Ḥizb al-Tagammu' al-Taqaddumī al-Waḥdāwī*) parties received 7 percent and 4 percent of the vote, respectively.

In the run-up to the election, there was a great deal of ambiguity regarding the country's political direction (Owen 1983). One reason for this was that elections had not been so freely contested in Egypt for more than thirty years (Hendriks 1985). In other words, there was uncertainty regarding the political preferences of citizens as well as the geographic distribution of those preferences. In addition, the 1984 elections were held under a proportional representation system with an 8 percent minimum threshold that had not previously been used in Egypt; voters were not used to selecting a party slate as previously they had chosen individual candidates. Analysts have observed that regime leaders were surprised by the success of the opposition (Brownlee 2007, 125), and, as such, the 1984 elections represented an important shock – and source of information revelation – to the Egyptian political system. The unexpected success of the Brotherhood prompted the regime to more closely examine the group's activities (Campagna 1996).

4.3.2   Description of Variables

In order to test hypotheses related to how electoral information was used by the central government in the discretionary disbursement of infrastructure development resources, I have collected data on a series of variables.

Dependent Variables. There are two dependent variables in this analysis. The first is the change in the percentage of residential buildings in a governorate that have piped public water between 1986 and 1996. The second is the change in the percentage of residential buildings in a governorate that were connected to the public sewerage network between 1986 and 1996. In order to mitigate problems associated with omitted variable bias, the dependent variable is the change in the percentage coverage between 1986 and 1996 – in other words, the first difference. Data for these dependent variables are maintained by the Central Agency for Public Mobilization and Statistics (CAPMAS), the official statistical agency in Egypt that collects, processes, analyzes, and disseminates all official statistical data, including those from the Egyptian census.[9]

---

[9] Census data collection is an important activity of the Egyptian government and the primary task of CAPMAS. For example, the 2006 census cost LE 170 million and took two years to prepare. Refusal of participation in the census could result in fines and jail sentences. See *Egypt Today*, May 2007, for details on how the census is conducted.

The use of governorates rather than electoral districts as the unit of analysis represents a degree of aggregation. In 1984, there were forty-eight electoral districts in Egypt, whereas there were only twenty-six governorates. Although fourteen governorates were represented by a single district, in the other twelve cases, a single governorate – like Cairo, for example – was divided into multiple districts. Variation in voteshare between governorates was considerably greater than variation within governorates, suggesting a minimization of bias as a result of this aggregation.[10]

Independent Variables. There are four primary independent variables used in this analysis: (a) the existing level of infrastructure coverage, (b) urban–rural status, (c) Brotherhood–Wafd voteshare in the 1984 election, and (d) percentage of non-NDP parliamentary representatives between 1984 and 1995.

Existing Infrastructure: Like many other developing countries, the regime in Egypt has long employed a public discourse regarding the importance of extending public infrastructure to all of the country's citizens. Rational distribution of infrastructure resources would suggest that underserved areas would be most eligible for upgrading and improving their infrastructure. For example, Schady (2000) finds that Peru's state development program favored poor provinces, thus serving a redistributive function. In order to control for this effect, the empirical tests conducted include a variable that measures the 1986 level of public infrastructure coverage. This variable might also be thought of as a proxy for the relative wealth or development of an area, allowing a degree of control for other types of heterogeneity.

Urban–Rural Status: Lipton (1977) argues that power structures in developing countries are often characterized by urban bias and the overriding concern for cheap food in cities. Bates (1981) describes the way governments in Africa have intervened and diverted resources from the rural sector to other sectors of society. Evidence from a variety of sources suggests that forms of urban bias are relevant in Egypt as well. In particular, economic development in Egypt has been uneven, with urban areas often enjoying more benefits than rural areas. For example, Egyptian economists have also found that infrastructure and municipal services are significantly better in urban versus rural areas.[11] This theme also appears in the local press, where articles indicate that the provision of services to cities has improved while infrastructure has been allowed to deteriorate in other areas.[12] Local politicians contend that the central government takes a particular interest in developing Cairo, for instance, in comparison with outlying areas.[13]

---

[10] The number of electoral districts increased to 222 following electoral system reform prior to the 1990 election.

[11] Interview with Gamal Siyam, Professor of Agricultural Economics, Cairo University, October 22, 2005.

[12] *Egyptian Gazette*, March 22, 2007.

[13] Interview with 'Abd al-Muhsin Shalabi, President, Local Council Haram Giza, July 19, 2005.

TABLE 4.1. *Logit Regression Results
(Dependent Variable Is Bread Shortage)*

	Bread Shortages
Constant	0.555
	(0.543)
Urban area	−1.328
	(0.542)
Observations	103
Log likelihood	−67.616

Note: Standard errors are shown in parentheses.

Investment in human capital also appears to favor urban over rural students. According to one study, average expenditure per pupil was more than four times higher in urban versus rural areas.[14] Urban areas also benefit from superior provision of subsidized foodstuffs, such as cut-rate bread, sugar, and cooking oil. In a survey of more than 100 local leaders selected from across Egypt to participate in a 1997 Egypt Integrated Household Survey (EIHS), local leaders from urban areas did not report shortages of subsidized oil and sugar. Both urban and rural areas reported shortages in subsidized bread, but such incidents were much higher in rural areas. Using data from the EIHS, a logit regression – where the dependent variable is one if the local leader reported there were subsidized bread shortages and zero otherwise and the independent variable is whether the area was classified as urban – suggests (as presented in Table 4.1) that urban areas are less likely to suffer shortages of subsidized bread. This result is significant at the 0.99 level.

Brotherhood–Wafd Representation and Voteshare: Egypt is an electoral authoritarian regime where the primary political opposition group – the Muslim Brotherhood – has at times competed fiercely with regime candidates for votes during elections. However, is there a link between support for the Muslim Brotherhood and public infrastructure investment? A variety of anecdotal and ethnographic sources suggest that voting for the opposition might hurt an area's prospects for future infrastructure investment.

For example, in one ethnographic study of village politics, the researcher reports that locals believed that "the government's candidate would be the one most capable of helping them get what they want from the local authorities" (el-Karanshawy 1997, 16). Kassem finds that only candidates representing the NDP had direct access to state resources (1999, 128). Singerman quotes a member of parliament who says "only the party with authority can serve the people. . . . if I ask for something from the bureaucracy, my demands will be met and theirs [the opposition's] will not" (1995, 255). Similarly, Wickham writes that "Egyptians typically vote for the NDP not out of support for its platform

[14] *Al-Ahram Weekly*, September 21–27, 2000.

but as a means to secure access to government resources" (2002, 89). She also finds that "as an arm of the state, the NDP was far better equipped than any of the opposition parties were to reward loyal constituents" (Wickham 2002, 91). NDP bureaucrats also contend that their party's candidates are better at providing infrastructure as a result of their superior connections to the government.[15] During the 1995 campaign, one government official stated that land and facilities in the village would be developed only if the NDP candidate won (el-Borei 1995, 42). In a separate incident during the same campaign season, a provincial governor stated that all demands made by towns that helped NDP candidates win would be fulfilled (el-Borei 1995, 38).

Related accounts have emerged regarding how districts that support the opposition do not enjoy the same levels of infrastructure development as those that support the NDP. During the 1995 parliamentary campaign, a government official held a meeting and announced that constituencies would be deprived of all services and facilities if the NDP candidates did not win the elections (el-Borei 1995, 41). Independent newspaper reports suggest that residents of a district in Giza believe that the central government penalized them for voting out an NDP member by failing to install water lines to the district; neighboring areas and all of the areas surrounding them were served, whereas pipes to be used in their district were left lying by the roadside.[16] According to Moheb Zaki, when the NDP loses in a district, nothing "gets done" for five years.[17] Similarly, Hassan Abu Taleb argues that there is a tendency to punish villages that support the opposition, but that a talented or well-connected opposition parliamentarian can exert influence under some circumstances.[18] In one district, constituents felt that the central government did not invest in their infrastructure development projects because they had voted for an opposition candidate (Koehler 2008, 980).

Another possible explanation is that NDP parliamentarians are, on average, able to negotiate the bureaucratic system more effectively than the opposition.[19] According to one Muslim Brotherhood parliamentarian, the regime tells "government offices not to deal with us – and even those government officials who know us very well fear to help us because they can be punished."[20] Certain

---

[15] Interview with Makram Hilal, Secretary General of the NDP for Giza, October 25, 2005.

[16] *Al-Masry Al-Youm*, August 1, 2007.

[17] Interview with Moheb Zaki, Ibn Khaldun Center for Development Studies, May 31, 2005.

[18] Interview with Hassan Abu Taleb, Al-Ahram Center for Strategic and Political Studies, April 5, 2005. Muslim Brotherhood parliamentarian 'Ali Fatah al-Bab has argued that sometimes parliamentarians representing the Muslim Brotherhood can actually be more effective than those from the NDP because Brotherhood parliamentarians are not afraid to put pressure on the government. Interview with 'Ali Fatah al-Bab, Muslim Brotherhood parliamentarian, September 25, 2005.

[19] Interview with Samer Soliman, Assistant Professor of Political Science, American University in Cairo, June 5, 2005.

[20] *Wall Street Journal*, May 15, 2009.

areas that are known to be anti-NDP – like Port Said – may also be "bumped down" in priority for infrastructure development, forcing them to wait longer for a budget allocation.[21]

Explanations for why areas that supported the opposition enjoyed lower levels of infrastructure provision tend to fall into one of two categories. The first is that the parliamentarians representing the NDP enjoy better connections with the government and, as a result, are able to negotiate a higher level of state resource provision for their areas. The second explanation is that the government is at best indifferent and at worst vindictive regarding the infrastructure development of areas represented by opposition parliamentarians.

The first mechanism is operationalized here as the percentage of non-NDP representation for each governorate from 1984 to 1995. This calculation is accomplished by counting the number of non-NDP parliamentarians in each governorate and dividing it by the total number of parliamentarians for each governorate.[22] Then I calculate a weighted average based on the number of years the parliamentarians served. The second mechanism is operationalized in a straightforward manner. For governorates that were represented by a single electoral district, the variable is simply the percentage of voteshare for the Brotherhood–Wafd alliance in 1984; for governorates with multiple electoral districts in 1984, average voteshare for the Brotherhood–Wafd alliance across these districts in the governorate is used. Although these two measures are correlated at about the 0.6 level, they are not identical. Differences between the two are introduced at multiple levels, including as a result of the 8 percent minimum threshold requirement in 1984 as well as the fact that there have been parliamentarians representing parties other than the NDP and the Brotherhood–Wafd alliance during the period under study. From the discussion of these two mechanisms and the mechanisms associated with the two control variables presented, consider four hypotheses for empirical testing.

HYPOTHESIS 4A: *Areas that were not previously receiving infrastructure will get infrastructure (rational distribution effect).*

HYPOTHESIS 4B: *Urban areas will benefit more than rural areas (urban bias effect).*

HYPOTHESIS 4C: *Areas with NDP MPs will receive more improvement to their infrastructure than areas with non-NDP MPs (political efficacy effect).*

HYPOTHESIS 4D: *Areas with high voteshare for the opposition alliance in 1984 will receive less infrastructure development (punishment regime effect).*

[21] Interview with Shura Council member, May 24, 2007.
[22] NDP members that ran as independents and then rejoined the party once in parliament are coded as NDP members.

4.3.3   Empirical Tests and Results

Using census data on sewerage and water accessibility across Egypt's governorates, we are able to determine which areas saw the greatest increases or decreases in coverage between 1986 and 1996.[23] The statistical model employed is as follows:

$$Y_{1996} - Y_{1986} = \beta_0 + \beta_1 Y_{1986} + \beta_2 X_2 + \beta_3 X_3 + \beta_4 X_4 + \varepsilon \qquad (4.1)$$

Y represents the percentage of residences that have publicly provided infrastructure, where water and sewerage infrastructure are analyzed separately. X_2 is whether or not the governorate is an urban governorate; X_3 is the governorate's average voteshare for the Brotherhood–Wafd alliance; and X_4 is the average representation of non-NDP parliamentarians in a governorate for the period 1984–1995.

The statistical results indicate that a higher level of sewerage or water coverage in 1986 was associated with a lower likelihood of receiving water or sewerage improvements in 1996, suggesting that the government favored development of underdeveloped areas after controlling for cities. The sign and statistical significance of this variable also suggests that it may be difficult to create large improvements in infrastructure to areas that are already fairly well covered. The results also indicate that urban areas were systematically improved over rural areas. This may be because it is easier to extend these services to urban areas or because urban areas are visited by tourists and other visitors, and thus have to be maintained for reputational reasons. Finally, as suggested previously, the regime may also engage in forms of urban bias that are fairly typical to the developing world.

After controlling for these two factors, it is also the case that areas that voted for the opposition were less likely to see improvements to their sewerage and water coverage in the ten years following the election. As described previously, there are two possible reasons for this. The first is that individual parliamentarians from parties other than the NDP are less effective at lobbying for infrastructure improvements. The second is that the central government is less likely to favor areas that supported the opposition in the election. When a variable for each is independently analyzed with prior infrastructure level and urban status, voteshare for the Brotherhood–Wafd alliance in 1984 is a stronger predictor of diminished social service provision than the percentage of non-NDP representatives in that governorate. When each variable is analyzed individually, in both cases, the variable carries a negative sign (as expected), but only the variable on voteshare is statistically significant at conventional levels (at the 0.92 level for sewerage and at the 0.99 level for water). When both voteshare and non-NDP representation are included in the same regression, non-NDP representation remains statistically insignificant. On the other hand, the coefficients on voteshare for the Brotherhood–Wafd alliance increase in size and

---

[23] 1986 and 1996 are chosen because both were years in which Egypt conducted its census.

TABLE 4.2. *Linear Regression Results (Dependent Variable Is Public Goods Provision)*

	Water	Sewerage	Water	Sewerage	Water	Sewerage
Constant	19.290	3.20	17.737	−4.640	18.342	3.245
	(10.128)	(5.701)	(11.554)	(5.693)	(10.299)	(5.741)
Percentage Wafd/MB voteshare in 1984	−0.750	−0.856			−0.916	−1.073
	(0.277)	(0.292)			(0.354)	(0.387)
Percentage non-NDP Representation in Parliament			−0.206	−0.270	0.192	0.244
			(0.223)	(0.246)	(0.251)	(0.284)
Previous coverage	−0.276	−1.028	−0.340	−0.966	−0.275	−1.065
	(0.152)	(0.123)	(0.169)	(0.143)	(0.153)	(0.131)
Urban	29.152	29.368	20.894	18.182	27.331	28.372
	(7.953)	(9.40)	(8.972)	(10.207)	(8.374)	(9.668)
R^2	0.44	0.79	0.28	0.73	0.46	0.80
Observations	26	26	26	26	26	26

Note: Standard errors are shown in parentheses.

remain statistically significant at the 0.88 level for sewerage and at the 0.98 level for water. In other words, even after controlling for the level of non-NDP representation in a governorate, voteshare for the Brotherhood–Wafd alliance in 1984 remains a strong predictor of diminished social service provision in the period to follow. This suggests that there is a discretionary aspect to infrastructure spending in Egypt that goes beyond the challenges faced by non-NDP representatives in negotiating infrastructure improvement.

The statistical results presented in Table 4.2 can be substantively interpreted as follows: governorates with high levels of support for the Brotherhood–Wafd alliance (i.e., voteshare of 50 percent) saw 30 percent less water infrastructure development than governorates that saw low levels of support for the Brotherhood–Wafd alliance (i.e., voteshare of 0 percent). This result is consistent for both rural and urban governorates. A similar result is found for sewerage infrastructure where governorates that were highly supportive of the 1984 opposition alliance saw 20 percent less infrastructure development than governorates that exhibited no support for the alliance.

4.4 CONCLUSIONS

A view began to emerge in Egypt during the 1980s and 1990s that suggested that voting for opposition candidates might reduce a district's access to public funding for infrastructural development. This view is supported by statistical analysis of census data. Even after controlling for the party affiliation of a governorate's parliamentarians, voteshare for the Brotherhood–Wafd alliance in Egypt's key parliamentary election in 1984 has a powerful statistical impact

on an area's prospects for water and sewerage development in the decade that
followed.

Looking forward, the Egyptian political scene has undergone considerable
change, particularly with regard to the way that services are provided via
parliamentary channels. As one NDP insider put it, following the structural
adjustment of the 1990s, the government scarcely provides services to anyone,
even areas supportive of the NDP.[24] According to one ruling party representative, parliamentarians have had to work harder than ever before to extract
any kind of development assistance from the government.[25] By 2000, there
began to emerge what might be called the "super-MP," parliamentarians who
used their personal wealth to pay ministries to build infrastructure in their
districts.[26] According to one former parliamentarian, by offering to pay for
some portion of the project cost, a super-MP might get a project for his or her
district moved to the top of the list of development priorities.[27]

Beginning most prominently in the summer of 2007, a second major trend
emerged regarding the politics of infrastructure development in Egypt. Villagers
began protesting the lack of clean water in a number of areas.[28] Protesting
residents of one village in Kafr al-Sheikh complained that they had been buying
water in plastic containers or collecting it from polluted sources for years.[29]
Villagers in Minya complained that they had been drinking directly from the
polluted Nile in the absence of clean water.[30] In many cases, demonstrators
refused to yield to what they considered threats from the security forces to
pressure them to break up their protests.[31] In response, President Mubarak
instructed the government to make additional funds available to speed up
the implementation of drinking water projects nationwide,[32] and the Minister
of Housing visited some of the protesting villages.[33] Although it is unclear
whether protest will ultimately prove to be an effective strategy for achieving
an improvement to poor infrastructure provision, government officials seem
increasingly to only move to improve infrastructure under extreme criticism or
the threat of a strike.[34]

---

[24] Interview with NDP official, May 1, 2007.
[25] Interview with Shura Council member, May 24, 2007.
[26] Ibid.
[27] Interview with former parliamentarian, May 26, 2007.
[28] *Al-Masry Al-Youm*, July 18, 2007.
[29] *Egyptian Gazette*, July 17, 2007.
[30] *Al-Masry Al-Youm*, July 28, 2007.
[31] *Al-Masry Al-Youm*, July 17, 2007.
[32] *Egyptian Gazette*, July 19, 2007.
[33] *Al-Masry Al-Youm*, August 2, 2007.
[34] *Al-Masry Al-Youm*, July 16, 2007.

5

Electoral Budget Cycles and Economic Opportunism

Do authoritarian regimes manipulate fiscal and monetary policy in the run-up to elections? Whereas most of the academic literature on electoral budget cycles has focused on democratic countries (with mixed empirical results), researchers are now turning their attention to the existence of electoral budget cycles in autocratic countries, whose highly centralized processes for economic policy making and fewer independent economic institutions make them prime candidates to exhibit such patterns. This chapter investigates the existence of opportunistic electoral budget cycles in Egypt. Although most research on electoral budget cycles focuses exclusively on econometric analysis of economic data, this chapter also includes a detailed discussion of the specific mechanisms used by the regime to court citizens. This information reveals particular patterns and strategies for orchestrating economic incentives.

In Egypt, the main budgetary manipulations take place to benefit state employees, farmers, and the urban poor. These preelectoral economic changes provide small improvements in salaries and services to a fairly broad swath of the populace to create the impression of gradual improvement in economic conditions for these beneficiaries. From an econometric perspective, Egypt's electoral budget cycle is apparent in five areas: a) inflation is higher in election years, b) calorie consumption is higher in election years, c) total reserves drop in the six months prior to the election, d) claims against the government increase following elections, and e) exchange rate devaluations tend to take place after elections.

5.1 ELECTORAL BUDGET CYCLES UNDER AUTHORITARIANISM

Since the seminal contributions of Nordhaus (1975) and Tufte (1978), a rich empirical and theoretical literature has developed surrounding the existence of electoral budget cycles. This literature has attempted to explain how governments use expansionary fiscal and monetary policy tools in the run-up to elections and the subsequent effects that these actions have on inflation and other outcomes. Theoretic models of this phenomenon have evolved over time as a result of an increasing emphasis on rational choice theory. Whereas early models assumed that myopic voters viewed economic policies in a retrospective fashion, fully rationalized models of these cycles have focused on how economic policy can signal incumbent competence (Rogoff and Silbert 1988; Rogoff 1990; Lohmann 1998). Both theoretical perspectives lead to the expectation that politicians will prime the economy to favor their reelection prospects if given the opportunity and that this will have observable implications on indicators like inflation and budget deficits.

Empirical evidence for electoral budget cycles has been mixed, in both industrialized and developing countries.[1] For example, Ames (1987) found considerable evidence for the existence of electoral budget cycles in Latin American countries, whether authoritarian or democratic. Remmer (1993), on the other hand, finds evidence for postelection acceleration of inflation and exchange rate depreciation, rather than the more traditional expectations of preelectoral priming. Persson and Tabellini (2002) find that tax decreases take place before elections in a sample of sixty democracies.

Implicit in models of electoral budget cycles is the idea of voters holding their politicians accountable for poor economic performance. Yet, some of the strongest recent evidence for electoral budget cycles has been found in authoritarian or semiauthoritarian countries. Block (2002) finds evidence for fiscal and monetary manipulation in a mixed panel of forty-four sub-Saharan African countries. Schady (2000) shows that the Peruvian Social Fund (FONCODES) significantly increased its expenditures before the national election. Grier and Grier (2000) and Gonzalez (2002) find evidence of cycles in Mexico during the period 1958–1997.[2] Magaloni (2006) finds evidence of increased government spending around the time of elections in Mexico. In addition, Shi and Svensson (2002b) find preelectoral increases in the budget deficit in a wide sample of democracies and nondemocracies. Pepinsky (2007) shows that Malaysian fiscal expenditure increases before elections and argues that the logic of electoral budget cycles is particularly well-suited to authoritarian regimes, despite the fact that these regimes have little risk of losing the electoral contests at stake. These findings suggest that authoritarian rulers may manipulate the economy in many of the same ways that democratically elected leaders hope to, though with a significant advantage – authoritarians are seldom subject to the same number of veto players as found in democracies.

This chapter describes the mechanisms by which electoral budget cycles exist in Egypt and the constituencies that are specifically targeted. The econometric

---

[1] There are a number of possible reasons for the lack of empirical support for these theories. Schultz (1995) has argued that manipulation of the economy can be costly and the need to manipulate may vary from election to election. This would suggest that the study of electoral budget cycles needs to be more context-specific.

[2] Whereas Block (2002) refers to the countries in his sample as "nascent democracies" because of the existence of competitive or semicompetitive legislative elections, many do not offer the possibility for a freely elected head of state on a consistent basis.

findings in this chapter are consistent with some of the predictions of both rational and traditional opportunistic business cycle theory.

5.2 ECONOMIC DECISION MAKING

Egypt is a presidential regime in which both informal and formal political institutions dictate that the president is the dominant political and governmental authority, and any important policy or project must have the president's blessing. In addition, previous president Anwar Sadat empowered the president with the ability to issue laws by decree on all economic matters.[3]

More broadly, the executive branch consists of the president and the cabinet. The cabinet is headed by the prime minister, who serves at the discretion of the president, and is composed mainly of technocrats with academic backgrounds. Essentially, the president is responsible for making policy, and the members of the cabinet implement these policies. In this way, the cabinet is part of the "Egyptian bureaucracy which executes the decisions taken at the apex of the authority pyramid" (Fahmy 2002, 46). Although the president may delegate decision making to a trusted economic advisor on the more technical aspects of economic policy, the president, together with his ministerial council, determine economic policy and supervise its execution. Special interest groups made up of businessmen may exert influence on the process through elite advisors to the president (Sadowski 1991). The legislature plays a minimal oversight role because the president has the power to initiate and propose laws, approve them, or return them to the People's Assembly for reconsideration.[4]

Fiscal and monetary policy authority, therefore, is highly centralized in the executive branch with the president and his cabal of experts essentially free to act without restriction. The regime is not accountable to any domestic oversight agencies or an independent central bank, though international financial institutions do influence domestic economic policy.

5.3 ELECTIONS AND ECONOMIC MANIPULATION

The regime has an established pattern of economic manipulation that precedes Mubarak. Changes to public sector compensation has been historically subject to political considerations. By the mid-1960s, there already existed more than 200 different types of bonuses and exceptional allowances that might be offered

---

[3] Under certain circumstances, international financial institutions, like the IMF, can influence Egyptian economic policy. However, the authoritarian leadership implements IMF prescriptions with a considerable degree of flexibility and latitude.

[4] The ability of lower levels of the bureaucracy to implement the policy set forward by the executive branch may be limited. By the time orders from Cairo descend to the local level, implementation and interpretation of the directive can vary (Sadowski 1991, 89–90). For the purposes of electorally timed economic interventions, the policies are generally implemented in a straightforward manner (across-the-board bonus for public sector employees), or the announcement of the economic change precedes the election with the actual implementation to follow.

to public sector employees (Ayubi 1980, 374). Hinnebusch describes Sadat's announcement of a ten-day bonus for government employees and pensioners just prior to an election as "a classic bit of patronage politics" (1988a, 173). Waterbury writes: "Authoritarian regimes, no less than democratic polities, buy incumbency through strategically timed giveaways. In Egypt the tactic followed has always been to give publicly and take away indirectly. The giveaway is a one-shot affair, while the indirect take is permanent.... Sadat was thoroughly at home with the giveaway. Because his incumbency was so closely associated with rapid inflation, he had little choice" (1983, 228). These giveaways included strategically timed minimum wage hikes, tax exemptions, and salary bonuses (Waterbury 1983, 228–9).

As elections became routinized under Mubarak, the timing of increases to bonuses and pensions became routine as well, closely following the electoral calendar. Increasingly, election years became focal points for government increases to giveaways.[5] Singerman describes how bonuses, benefits from pensions, and pay raises could be distributed for political purposes; she writes: "since the President announces these bonuses and implicitly claims responsibility for them, he is seen as the culprit or the benefactor, depending on the size of the bonus" (Singerman 1995, 260). In other words, the size of pay changes are attributed directly to the regime and by implication to the party of the regime. El-Meehy (2009) has also shown how Egypt's SFD – a subsidy program similar to Mexico's PROGRESA program – increased the total volume of loans and beneficiaries to suit political imperatives.

Because presidential elections were uncontested until 2005, electoral budget cycles prior to then centered around lower-house parliamentary elections in which the NDP competes for seats with opposition parties and independent candidates.[6] Upper-house and municipal council elections have remained competitive only within the party, decreasing the need for election-related giveaways.

5.3.1   Courting the Public Sector

Following the 1952 coup, Egypt's public bureaucracy began to grow rapidly and extensively. The regime's expansion into industrial activities, welfare services, and free education was particularly apparent (Ayubi 1980, 6). Under

---

[5] This is not to say that parliamentary election season is the only time when pay increases and increases to bonuses take place. Indeed, May Day is another occasion upon which public sector workers have come to expect a raise. May Day 2008, for example, saw a 30 percent increase in public sector worker salaries, in part to compensate for higher world food prices. See *Al-Masry Al-Youm*, May 1, 2008, for more details.

[6] Presidential "elections" prior to 2005 consisted of an up–down referendum on Mubarak. The amendment to Article 76 of the Egyptian constitution in May 2005 allowed for direct, multi-candidate presidential elections for the first time, although under conditions that stack the deck heavily in favor of the NDP candidate. For more on this change, see Blaydes 2005.

TABLE 5.1. *Public Sector Employment across Egyptian Governorates, 2001*

Governorate	Government Employment (%)	Governorate	Government Employment (%)
Cairo	38.3	Beni Suef	25.1
Alexandria	38.1	Fayoum	18.9
Port Said	45.8	Minya	21.7
Suez	45.9	Assiout	25.2
Damietta	24.8	Suhag	23.0
Dakahlia	28.3	Qena	27.3
Sharkia	29.4	Aswan	37.8
Kaliyoubia	34.5	Luxor	32.1
Kafr al-Sheikh	22.8	Red Sea	31.5
Gharbia	34.1	Al-Wadi al-Gedid	59.7
Menoufia	32.9	Matrouh	20.3
Behera	24.1	North Sinai	37.3
Ismailia	38.1	South Sinai	35.6
Giza	30.9		

Nasser, elements of the public bureaucracy gained a reputation for good performance, particularly those engineers and public servants involved in the building of the High Dam at Aswan. Over time, however, the Egyptian bureaucracy grew to an enormous size and became widely known as unproductive. Beginning with Nasser, the public bureaucracy began to employ the bulk of Egyptian university graduates, many of whom were forced to hold second jobs after fulfilling their minimal public sector obligations.[7] This practice largely continues. Although most bureaucrats can no longer can support their families on their government salaries alone, a public sector job often offers security from dismissal that is highly valued.

Table 5.1 shows the public sector and bureaucratic employment figures for each of Egypt's twenty-six governorates in 2001.[8] Individual electoral districts exhibit considerable variation with regard to state employment, but in sum, it is clear that the state is the single largest formal sector employer in Egypt and typically employs between one-fifth and one-half of workers in areas across the country. This suggests that state employees, and their dependents, are an important political constituency in the country and the constituency that is perhaps the most susceptible to government economic manipulation. The following section describes the specific mechanisms by which the regime courts these public sector employees.

---

[7] The guarantee of public sector employment for university graduates was introduced in 1961 and extended in 1964 to include vocational and technical school graduates (Handoussa and El Oraby 2004).

[8] Two additional governorates were added in 2008. An additional one was added in 2009.

Bonuses ('ilāwāt). The most commonly used and flexible instrument at the disposal of the government is the *'ilāwa*, or bonus, given periodically to public sector employees. In addition to annual bonuses that are given to public sector employees, there are also exceptional bonuses that are occasionally offered. Bonuses and the other nonsalary forms of remuneration are not used to reward individual performance, but rather as a means for increasing the average wage (Handoussa and El Oraby 2004).[9]

The regime has long increased *'ilāwāt* (plural) in the run-up to elections. In 1984, the baseline annual bonus was increased by 33 percent from LE 75 to LE 100.[10] Later that year, the government announced an additional LE 5 exceptional bonus for government employees.[11] It was also announced that public sector employees would receive the same bonuses as government employees and, soon thereafter, armed forces employees would as well.[12] Prior to the 1990 parliamentary elections, the public sector's quarterly bonus increased by 5 percent, and it was announced that college graduates who were supposed to receive public sector jobs would get "credit" toward retirement for the years that they spent working in nongovernment jobs.[13] Before the 1995 elections, the government announced a 10 percent increase in government workers' bonuses,[14] and the war production industry received an increase as well.[15] Parity between the private and public was also assured.[16] In 2000, public sector companies and ministries announced bonuses for their employees prior to parliamentary elections.[17] The year 2005 – another parliamentary election year – saw a number of announcements regarding increases to public sector bonuses as the election season approached. For example, an annual bonus of 15 percent of salary for all public sector employees and retirees was announced, and the government promised that, after five years, the bonus amount would become part of the base salary.[18] In addition, Minister of Finance Yusuf Butrus-Ghali also announced a 15 percent exceptional bonus (*'ilāwa khāṣṣa*) that would benefit 1.8 million public sector employees.[19]

---

[9] In fact, supplemental payments, like bonuses, represent the principal sources of income for some government employees, constituting up to 83 percent of total salary (Handoussa and El Oraby 2004).

[10] *Al-Ahram*, January 29, 1984.

[11] *Al-Ahram*, March 12, 1984.

[12] *Al-Ahram*, March 10, 1984; *Al-Ahram*, April 13, 1984.

[13] *Al-Ahram*, November 13, 1990. This is significant because it credits these individuals toward their retirement as potential public sector employees, should they one day get a job in the government.

[14] *Al-Ahram*, June 12, 1995.

[15] *Al-Ahram*, July 31, 1995.

[16] *Al-Ahram*, June 4, 1995.

[17] For example, sectoral bonuses prior to the 2000 parliamentary elections went to employees of the public electricity company (*Al-Ahram*, October 8, 2000) and the public petrol company (*Al-Ahram*, November 15, 2000).

[18] *Al-Ahram*, March 19, 2005.

[19] *Al-Ahram*, April 28, 2005, with additional details May 5, 2005.

Retirement Pensions (ma'āshāt). The government also uses its power to upgrade and improve retirement services and benefits for former public sector employees. In the months prior to the 1984 elections, for example, it announced that any public sector employee who retired after 1974 would receive a 20 percent increase in their retirement benefits, and those who retired prior to 1974 would receive a 10 percent increase.[20] In addition, the required number of months of civil service needed to receive certain benefits was reduced from 180 (15 years) to 120 (10 years), and everyone who retired in 1984 would receive the benefits of an additional year of civil service credit.[21] Prior to the 1995 elections, a cost of living increase was approved for all retirement benefit holders.[22] In 2005, the government announced that retirement funds would be put into a special account, and the government began to run articles about the increased number of families covered by these benefits and the total dollars spent on retirement benefits.[23] Retirement benefits were increased from LE 60 to LE 80 per month with an additional bonus of LE 20 per month per student in the family.[24] Widows, who previously had received the retirement benefits of their deceased husbands until they remarried, were given funds after they married again.[25] Finally, a special bonus for retirees was announced; this covered both public sector retirees and retirees from the armed forces.[26]

Other. In addition to bonuses and retirement benefits, there are numerous other means by which the government can influence public sector employees, especially through incentive and overtime pay for particular sectors.[27] Prior to the 1984 parliamentary elections, special incentives were offered to members of the teachers syndicate; overtime compensation (*badalāt*) cost the government LE 21 million for 400,000 public school teachers.[28] In addition, 15–25 percent incentive pay (*ḥawāfiz*) was offered for workers in government ministries.[29] In 1987, post office employees were offered incentive pay as well.[30] In 1995, just prior to parliamentary elections, the government announced that base salaries for public sector employees could never be reduced.[31] In the run-up to the 2000 parliamentary elections, Ministry of Religious Endowments (*awqāf*) employees received 25 percent of their salaries

---

[20] *Al-Ahram*, March 5, 1984.

[21] *Al-Ahram*, March 14, 1984; *Al-Ahram*, March 23, 1984.

[22] *Al-Ahram*, July 28, 1995.

[23] *Al-Ahram*, March 24, 2005; *Al-Ahram*, April 26, 2005; *Al-Ahram*, May 11, 2005; *Al-Ahram*, May 16, 2005.

[24] *Al-Ahram*, May 11, 2005; *Al-Ahram*, June 15, 2005.

[25] *Al-Ahram*, May 27, 2005.

[26] *Al-Ahram*, June 13, 2005.

[27] Sectoral benefits may be provided either through a particular ministry or through a syndicate, associations for a particular professional groups.

[28] *Al-Ahram*, April 29, 1984; *Al-Ahram*, April 30, 1984.

[29] *Al-Ahram*, May 15, 1984.

[30] *Al-Ahram*, March 22, 1987.

[31] *Al-Ahram*, September 18, 1995.

as stipend (*mukāfāh*), and some public sector employees were bumped up on the civil service scale to higher grades.[32] Prior to the 2005 elections, Mubarak announced that the government would double the salaries of low-ranking civil servants and increase the salaries of higher-ranking government employees by 75 percent.[33]

One way to think about these outlays is that they are actually payments for abstention or as disincentives to support opposition candidates. Public sector employees – many of whom fit the sociodemographic profile of Muslim Brotherhood supporters – feel less dissatisfied with their financial status when they receive these benefits. They are also reminded that, as bureaucrats or public sector workers, their livelihoods are tied to the state and that the security of their jobs may be in question under a different form of government.

5.3.2 Agricultural Sector Incentives

Economic incentives during an election year are not limited to public sector employees. Rural Egyptians in the agricultural sector, for example, also receive strategically timed giveaways. These giveaways fall into three main categories. The first is through improved benefits by way of the farmers' syndicate, the professional association in rural areas that provides members with insurance and retirement benefits. The second is through debt forgiveness and increased loan capacity from Egypt's Principal Bank for Development and Agricultural Credit (PBDAC). The PBDAC, a development bank financed by the Egyptian government, was created by former president Nasser to provide farmers and rural households with financial services. PBDAC has branch offices in almost every community in Egypt and serves as the village bank in most of rural Egypt.[34] In rural villages, the PBDAC channels subsidized agricultural inputs and is "virtually the only source of agricultural credit" (Springborg 1989, 162). In 2005, there were about 1,200 village banks with 3.5 million clients.[35] Given the pervasiveness of the PBDAC in rural Egypt, enhanced services by the bank are of significant benefit to the rural sector. The third means by which the regime uses economic incentives to influence votes in rural Egypt involves eased restrictions on specific crop production. In many areas in Egypt, cultivation of water-intensive crops may be limited or prohibited with severe fines and penalty of imprisonment for those who violate the restrictions. For example, rice production is not permitted in certain governorates because growing rice involves significant water resources. Farmers face fines of LE 600 per feddan

---

[32] *Al-Ahram*, August 6, 2000; *Al-Ahram*, November 28, 2000.

[33] *Egyptian Gazette*, September 2, 2005.

[34] PBDAC provides start-up loans for activities such as poultry raising and vegetable trading. Microloans are typically valued up to 1,500 LE, and the term of the loan is generally one year with up to a seven-month grace period. For more information, see the United Nations Capital Development Fund report on Egypt.

[35] Interview with Mahmud Nur, PBDAC, July 12, 2005.

for violating these restrictions.[36] Prior to elections, the regime may "forgive" farmers who cultivate restricted crops.

In the countryside, the agricultural bureaucracy can be used to provide political "sticks and carrots" (Springborg 1989, 162). For example, prior to the 1987 parliamentary elections, the PBDAC announced that 50 percent of debt held by farmers would be forgiven and that the PBDAC would increase the funds available for low-interest loans from LE 200 million to LE 500 million.[37] In 2000, the Ministry of Agriculture announced that individuals who illegally cultivated rice would not be fined or put in prison.[38] Just prior to the 2005 parliamentary election, *Al-Ahram* ran a front-page article with cheering farmers who had been given an opportunity to reschedule their debt to the PBDAC at a reduced interest rate.[39] These strategically timed giveaways to the rural sector are generally accompanied by announced spending increases to help the regime's third mass constituency – the urban poor.

5.3.3 Assistance to the Urban Poor

The authoritarian regime in Egypt has reason to fear the urban poor. In 1977, following the announcement that subsidies would be lifted on some goods, riots broke out, leading to numerous deaths; these riots changed the perception of Egyptians as quietist. In recent years, the Egyptian "street" has proven that it is increasingly willing to protest vocally regarding certain issues, particularly related to economic conditions. As a result, the urban poor are an important constituency, and the regime has made repeated attempts to assure them that subsidies will not be further eliminated and additional funds and benefits will be forthcoming.[40] The allocation of subsidies and "stomach fillers" is seen as a key to the government's control strategy.[41] Regime incentives offered to this group typically involve increased benefits for low-income families, unemployed youth, and, in recent years, better insurance coverage. In addition, the regime uses the services of the Nasser Bank – a state assistance bank aimed at urban Egyptians.[42] The urban poor have been an increasingly important constituency since the 1990s, as Egypt's participation in an IMF-sponsored structural adjustment program left many individuals formerly dependent on government employment without public sector jobs.

---

[36] USDA Foreign Agriculture Service, Egypt Grain and Feed Annual Report 2006.

[37] *Al-Ahram*, March 26, 1987; *Al-Ahram*, March 30, 1987.

[38] *Al-Ahram*, September 26, 2000.

[39] *Al-Ahram*, November 7, 2005.

[40] Subsidies have a long and complicated history in Egypt. In 1980, the food subsidy system included eighteen goods. Over time, the system was carefully downsized to include bread, wheat flour, sugar, and cooking oil (Ali and Adams 1996).

[41] Interview with Karima Korayem, Professor of Economics, Al-Azhar University, April 20, 2005.

[42] The Nasser Bank was established in 1972 and, as of 2002, it had LE 350 million, 90 branches, and 500 zakat branches (*Al-Ahram*, November 10, 2002). The Nasser Bank gives loans to people who want to engage in small-scale entrepreneurial activity.

Prior to the 1990 parliamentary elections, the regime promoted its youth program (*mashrū' al-shabāb*), through which college grads who were promised public sector employment became eligible for cut-rate loans in lieu of jobs at the end of their university educations.[43] This program was aimed largely at unemployed young men in urban areas. Just prior to the election, it was announced that the size of these loans would be increased from LE 1,000 to LE 3,000.[44] In the run-up to the 1995 parliamentary elections, the regime promoted special tax breaks for small enterprise in which businesses developed as part of the youth program would not have to pay taxes for ten years and would also enjoy some tariff breaks on imported goods.[45] During this period, the regime also promoted new poverty alleviation schemes for low-income families.[46] Coverage under health insurance became an increasingly important issue as well, with the regime promising more money to be dedicated to insurance coverage for students and promises to provide insurance coverage for all public sector employees and retirees.[47] The 2000 parliamentary election season also witnessed promises concerning health insurance coverage, particularly a widening of government programs to cover insurance for all children.[48] In addition, it was announced that LE 600 million would be spent on social security payments to low-income families who would be receiving between LE 50 and 70 per month.[49] The Nasser Bank also made extra funds available and announced that individuals seeking loans to prepare for weddings and to buy apartments would receive between LE 4,000 and LE 10,000.[50] Prior to Egypt's election season in 2005, professional syndicates promised to find a way to insure all currently uninsured syndicate members, and the government promised to investigate the possibility of universal health coverage for all citizens.[51] Finally, the minister of finance assured citizens that subsidies on gasoline would remain in place, and this was followed by a later announcement that all subsidies on goods and services would remain.[52]

5.3.4   Exchange Rate Policy

During the 1980s, Egypt maintained a complex system of multiple exchange rates. As part of the country's structural adjustment–related reforms, the Central Bank began the process of unifying these exchange rates in the late 1980s and allowed a managed peg by 1991 through which the government

[43] Under Nasser and Sadat, public sector employment was promised to all college graduates.
[44] *Al-Ahram*, November 18, 1990.
[45] *Al-Ahram*, July 13, 1995.
[46] *Al-Ahram*, October 17, 1995.
[47] *Al-Ahram*, September 29, 1995; *Al-Ahram*, November 2, 1995.
[48] *Al-Ahram*, October 27, 2000; *Al-Ahram*, November 16, 2000.
[49] *Al-Ahram*, June 13, 2000; *Al-Ahram*, July 27, 2000.
[50] *Al-Ahram*, May 30, 2000; *Al-Ahram*, June 7, 2000.
[51] *Al-Ahram*, April 4, 2005; *Al-Ahram*, April 25, 2005.
[52] *Al-Ahram*, May 5, 2005; *Al-Ahram*, November 19, 2005.

allowed the Egyptian pound to trade within a narrow band.[53] This move largely eliminated the need for an unofficial parallel market until the late 1990s, when a black market began to emerge again. In January 2003, the Egyptian pound was allowed to float, though the currency is still managed by the regime to maintain a rate considered politically acceptable.

Various commentators have argued that Egypt's exchange rate policy is subject to political considerations. Editorials in major opposition newspapers have discussed the politicization of Egyptian exchange rate policy.[54] In fact, commentators on the Egyptian economy have speculated that exchange rates are susceptible to election calendars (Dowell 1999). Schamis and Way (2003) argue more generally that choice of exchange rate system – fixed or floating – is decided opportunistically based on an electoral calendar.

For example, the government slowly devalued the exchange rate during the first half of 2001, in the six months following the parliamentary elections. By the time the government was finished with its devaluation, the Central Bank of Egypt confirmed that the pound was approximately 22 percent less valuable than in August 2000, just before the election.[55] The Chief Executive Officer of HSBC Bank Egypt said, "I think that it is the right move although it should have taken place six months or 12 months before, however better late than never." Sfakianakis (2002) concurs, arguing that the devaluation of the pound in 2001 was overdue. The next section shows that the government routinely delays devaluations until after elections.

5.4 INCOME REDISTRIBUTION AND VOTE BUYING

Numerous informants, newspaper articles, and books report that candidates running for parliament give money and other benefits to their constituents in the run-up to elections. These wealth transfers take place among candidates, family heads, and individuals and can appear in many different forms.

In the Egyptian novel *The Yacoubian Building*, a character running for parliament secretly channels tens of thousands of pounds to poor families in his constituency; following his victory, he distributes the meat of three butchered cows to the same families (al-Aswany 2004, 123). A magazine article describes the pile of free shoes given to supporters of an opposition candidate running for parliament while a candidate from the regime's NDP passed out job applications for prestigious public sector employment opportunities (Ehab 2005). Candidates give away everything from CDs, pens, mobile phones, meat, and even payment of phone bills.[56] In a political cartoon by Sa'd al-Deeb, citizens beat a candidate with sticks, complaining that the TV sets that they

---

[53] *Daily Star*, July 21, 2003.
[54] *Al-Usbu'*, August 13, 2001; *Al-Wafd*, December 1, 2003; *Al-Araby*, August 17, 2003; *Al-Araby*, December 28, 2003.
[55] *Washington Times*, International Reports, Egypt, 2001.
[56] *Al-Ahram Weekly*, November 10–16, 2005.

received in exchange for their votes were black and white instead of color.[57] In 2005, typical vote buying cost between LE 20 and 500 per vote.[58]

The trading of food for votes is a popular strategy employed by candidates. Candidates often pay for communal suppers in a village guest house to drum up support (Kassem 1999, 153). During the 2000 campaign, supermarkets saw their sugar sales suffer when candidates distributed free bags of sugar to supporters.[59] In 2005, when campaigning fell during Ramadan, candidates sponsored free meals at tables set up in poor neighborhoods and even delivered meals to homes for families that were concerned about the embarrassment of being seen at a free meal table.[60] In addition, sacks of foodstuffs emblazoned with candidate logos were delivered to potential voters.[61] Families were also given vouchers to claim a free chicken in some districts.[62] Some districts have also seen fast food provided to potential voters. In Cairo and Giza, for example, 400,000 ready meals were distributed to voters on the first day of parliamentary elections.[63] Finally, a political cartoon shows a parliamentary candidate being interviewed by a newspaper reporter and saying that his philosophy is to give constituents food in return for their votes.[64] The empirical section investigates one implication of this qualitative observation.

Elections represent an important opportunity for citizens to renegotiate the payment they receive in exchange for supporting local candidates. During the by-election in 2007 for the seat vacated by Shahinaz al-Nagger – a tourism sector tycoon who married, and subsequently divorced, steel magnate Ahmed 'Ezz – candidates were seen throughout the district offering everything from meat, blankets, and even refrigerators to local voters.[65] According to one voter, "this is a festive season for the poor . . . once these people win the election, they make themselves scarce and that is why the poor get the utmost from them now."[66] Independent election monitors and journalists said vote buying during the by-election was "rampant and that candidates were forced to pay between LE 100 to LE 150 per vote."[67] Voters were disappointed in 2008 when the regime cracked down on Muslim Brotherhood candidates in the run-up to the municipal council elections because a strong Brotherhood showing would increase the amount needed to buy off voters.[68]

---

[57] *Egyptian Gazette*, November 21, 2005.
[58] *Egyptian Gazette*, November 27, 2005.
[59] *Al-Ahram Weekly*, October 19–25, 2000.
[60] *Egyptian Gazette*, October 9, 2005.
[61] Ibid.
[62] *Egyptian Gazette*, October 18, 2005.
[63] *Al-Goumhuria*, November 10, 2005.
[64] *Al-Akhbar*, October 17, 2005.
[65] *Egyptian Gazette*, December 24, 2007.
[66] Ibid.
[67] *Al-Ahram Weekly*, January 3–9, 2008.
[68] *Egyptian Gazette*, March 5, 2008.

5.5 POSTELECTION AND NONELECTION YEAR TRENDS

In June 2007 – two years after lower-house elections – more than 25,000 small-scale farmers in the Delta were fined for growing rice in violation of state agricultural policies.[69] Nonpayment of the fine resulted in a prison sentence.[70] The harsh treatment of peasants stands in contrast to the blanket amnesty for illegal rice cultivation that had been offered in the run-up to parliamentary elections.

5.5.1 Postelection Economic Changes

Announcement of price increases and economic austerity measures often take place just months after the end of the parliamentary election season. For example, just two months after the December 2005 parliamentary election, Egyptian newspapers reported that public bus fares, previously between LE 0.25 and 0.50, would be raised to LE 1. The public bus system transports millions of Egyptians to work every day, 5 million a day in Cairo alone.[71] Low-income commuters, many of whom are public sector employees, say that the fare price hikes are part of a larger government effort to decrease subsidies.[72] Newspaper reports suggest that the price increases were scheduled to have been submitted to Parliament months before the election but were delayed until after the election. In March 2006, the government unveiled a plan for scaling back subsidies more broadly; in particular, the number of beneficiaries would be reduced and, for some traditional subsidies, would be replaced by less appealing bank loans.[73] Only weeks later, the state-owned telecom monopolist announced increases to fees that led to a 50 percent increase in the price of service.[74] Editorialists questioned why price increases would come at such a time, just after Egypt Telecom had announced huge profits for 2005.[75] To propose public transportation fare increases, telephone service hikes, or subsidy cuts during the election campaigns of 2005 would have been politically difficult.

Similar trends can be observed in the weeks and months following other parliamentary election contests. Just weeks after the 1990 parliamentary contest concluded in December, the price of cigarettes increased.[76] A political cartoon that ran shortly after the 1990 election shows a man raising a sign that says "Prices," and the caption below the cartoon reads "No Restraint."[77] By April

---

[69] *Egyptian Gazette*, June 28, 2007.
[70] Ibid.
[71] *Egyptian Gazette*, February 16, 2006.
[72] Ibid.
[73] *Egyptian Mail*, March 4, 2006.
[74] *Egyptian Gazette*, March 22, 2006; *Al-Ahram Weekly*, March 30–April 5, 2006.
[75] *Al-Gomhuria*, March 28, 2006.
[76] *Egyptian Gazette*, January 27, 1991.
[77] *Egyptian Gazette*, February 11, 1991.

1991, Egypt had signed a new agreement with the IMF that increased domestic energy prices and lowered consumer subsidies.[78] Retailers also said that the government allowed private and public sector soft drink producers to increase their prices by 20–25 percent.[79] Following the 1995 parliamentary elections, 2,500 buildings and 5,000 families in the Haram district were displaced for a public infrastructure project, shocking residents who had been promised prior to the election that no more homes would be demolished for the project.[80] Press reports also indicate an increase in inflationary pressure[81] and government steps to increase the pace of privatization.[82] Just months after the 1995 election, specific plans for the expanded privatization program were unveiled, which would include the sale of industrial companies, banks, and department store chains.[83]

5.5.2   Failure to Make Promised Payments

The failure to make promised bonus and other payments has been the source of considerable tension between workers and both state-owned and private industry, particulary since the 2005 elections.[84] According to a study by economists Doha Abdelhamid and Laila al-Baradei, professors at the American University in Cairo and Cairo University, respectively, bonuses are only dispensed to government employees ahead of elections.[85] For example, in 2007 – a year without lower-house elections – protests over nonpayment of bonuses and incentive pay were common. One of the key grievances of the striking textile workers at Mahalla al-Kubra involved bonuses that were promised but not paid (Beinin 2007). Six hundred workers at the Tanta Flax and Oil Company held a sit-in to protest nonpayment of their monthly incentives.[86] In Alexandria, nurses and lab technicians staged a sit-in to protest nonpayment of a 40 percent incentive over the last two years.[87] In 2008, also a nonelection year, female workers at Wabariyat Spinning in Gharbia held a sit-in to pressure management to follow through on promised bonuses and allowances.[88] More than 6,000 workers at Al-Nasr Company for Clothes and Textiles declared a strike to protest nonpayment of a 30 percent bonus previously announced by President Mubarak.[89] The education minister announced a cancellation of

---

[78] *Egyptian Gazette*, April 8, 1991.

[79] Ibid.

[80] *Egyptian Gazette*, January 31, 1996.

[81] *Al-Ahram Al-Iqtisadi*, January 8, 1996.

[82] *Al-Ahram Al-Iqtisadi*, February 26, 1996.

[83] *Egyptian Gazette*, February 15, 1996.

[84] In many cases, private companies are required to meet increases stipulated by the state. The extent to which these requirements are enforced differs in election and nonelection years.

[85] *Al-Ahram Weekly*, July 24–30, 2008.

[86] *Al-Masry Al-Youm*, October 1, 2007.

[87] *Al-Masry Al-Youm*, September 7, 2007.

[88] *Al-Masry Al-Youm*, April 15, 2008.

[89] *Al-Masry Al-Youm*, July 2, 2008.

bonuses for nonteaching school staff employees in violation of a previous presidential decree.[90] Employees at the Banha University hospital staged a sit-in after failing to receive a bonus of half a month's pay that had been previously approved.[91] Railway maintenance workers protested after being denied promised bonuses and incentive pay.[92] Workers also protested nonpayment of salaries[93] and salary cuts,[94] both actions that tend not to occur in the run-up to parliamentary elections.

5.6 DATA AND RESULTS

The qualitative data described suggest a pattern consistent with an electoral budget cycle in Egypt, but there are also a number of other observable implications that should be evident if such cycles exist. The first is that we would expect inflation to be higher in the months before and perhaps after elections as voters benefit from government giveaways. We might also expect that financial claims against the government would increase in the months around the election, and the government may draw down its reserve base to fund spending. We should expect that exchange rate devaluations take place after, rather than before, elections. Finally, if income is redistributed in election years from (often wealthy) candidates vying for seats in parliament to voters, we would expect that voters live "better" in election years than nonelection years.

5.6.1 Description of Variables

This section examines five variables that might indicate the existence of an electoral budget cycle in Egypt.

Dependent Variables. One important indicator of the existence of an electoral budget cycle is a rate of inflation that varies with the political calendar. As in many countries, inflation is a highly politicized indicator, changes in which attract considerable attention as a bellwether of economic health and consumer strength. In general, consumer price inflation (CPI) is measured by examining prices of a weighted basket of representative goods and services. In Egypt, however, many analysts have become increasingly skeptical of using the CPI as a basis for analyzing inflation. For example, economists have argued that the way consumer price levels are determined in Egypt is flawed, pointing out that 40 percent of the items included in the Egyptian basket of goods as determined by CAPMAS are items immune to any price change and that the representative

[90] *Al-Masry Al-Youm*, July 1, 2008; *Egyptian Gazette*, July 2, 2008.
[91] *Al-Masry Al-Youm*, September 5, 2008.
[92] *Al-Masry Al-Youm*, August 18, 2008.
[93] *Al-Masry Al-Youm*, January 14, 2008.
[94] *Egyptian Gazette*, September 9, 2007.

basket of goods is outdated (Lindsey 2003).[95] Regular Egyptians concur with
the assessment of economists, arguing that reported inflation (as measured
by the CPI) wrongly estimates price changes in Egypt (al-Shawarby 2008). In
addition, opposition newspapers have argued that the government manipulates
the rate of CPI to hide the truth about rising prices.[96] Hibbs (1987) and others
have also suggested that the CPI is problematic because it does not allow for
shifts in consumption from goods with rising relative prices to goods with
falling relative prices while maintaining consumer satisfaction.

Rather than using the traditional CPI data as published by the Egyptian
government, inflation is calculated based on the GDP deflator, which provides
a much broader price index than the CPI. Changes in consumption patterns or
the introduction of new goods and services are automatically reflected in the
deflator. Finally, these data are less vulnerable to manipulation by the regime
if it seeks to underestimate price increases in the country for political reasons.
This data is at the yearly level, and the variable used in analysis is percentage
increase in the GDP deflator, conventionally known as inflation as measured
by the GDP deflator.

The remaining dependent variables in the analysis are measured in conventional ways. The other variable measured yearly is average daily calorie
consumption. These data are provided by the UN Food and Agriculture Organization (FAO).[97] This variable ranges from 2,997 to 3,349 calories per person
per day. From 1981 until present, the progression in calorie growth has been
upward, but not steadily so. Because this variable is a level that increases incrementally every year, we can convert it to percentage change increase in calorie
consumption to mitigate problems of autocorrelation from one year to the
next. Yearly percentage change also emphasizes the increase in consumption.

In order to determine whether the Egyptian government is digging into its
reserve base in order to finance election year expenditures, this chapter also tests
the election effect on Egypt's total reserves. This variable is essentially Egypt's
foreign exchange reserves (the deposits held by national banks in "hard" cur-
rencies like the $US) plus gold or other holdings. In Egypt, total reserves
are almost entirely driven by the foreign currency holdings. These data are

---

[95] A 2005 IMF report flagged a number of issues related to the accuracy and reliability of Egypt's
CPI, including the selection of unrepresentative outlets for retail activity and a tendency to
overweight subsidized items and items with controlled prices, such as rents (al-Shawarby 2008).

[96] *Al-Wafd*, July 17, 2003; *Al-Ahaly*, July 30, 2003.

[97] Food consumption data are taken from the FAO food balance sheets and are some of the most
important data collected by the organization as these data provide the basis for UN estimation of
global and national undernourishment assessments (FAO 2001). Food balance sheets measure
food consumption from a supply perspective. The total quantity of all primary and processed
food commodities are added to the total quantity imported of each and adjusted to any change
in stocks that may have occurred since the beginning of the reference period. The data also take
into account food that is exported and attempt to quantify the type and quantity of food that
is wasted, lost, or put to other use (i.e., as animal feed or seed). See Blaydes and Kayser 2007
for more details on this measure.

compiled monthly by the IMF. Because the variable is a level that changes incrementally, in this analysis, it has been converted into percentage change increase. Also, this makes interpretation more straightforward because the percentage change in reserves is the quantity of interest rather than the sheer level of reserves.

Another way to test the election year effect is to examine whether the claims on the government increase with the proximity of the election. Claims on the government and other public entities comprise direct credit, most prominently financing of the government budget deficit or loans made to state enterprises. This can also take the form of government bonds held by banks.[98] These data are from the IMF and are measured monthly. Both reserves and claims on the government are avenues for financing spending and could, therefore, be affected as part of an electoral budget cycle.

The final variable is the exchange rate as published by the IMF, measured monthly. The dependent variable used in the statistical analysis is the difference between the exchange rate period t and period $t - 1$. This mitigates problems of autocorrelation and eases interpretation of the results.

Independent Variable. The key independent variable in this analysis is related to the year or months surrounding the election. For the yearly variables, this variable is coded one in election years and zero in all other years. Parliamentary elections in Egypt have not always occurred at the same time of year; elections took place in the spring during the 1980s and in the late fall since then.[99] This analysis also codes for postelection year. For the analysis of the monthly data, I examine the six months before and after election. For the monthly analysis, this analysis also includes month-dummy variables to control for any potential seasonal effects.

5.6.2 Empirical Strategy

All of the data used in the analysis are time series of either monthly or yearly data from 1981 to 2005. Analysis is conducted using two models for time series analysis. The first is the AR(1) model, which assumes a first-order autoregressive disturbance. A first-order autoregressive disturbance occurs when the disturbance in one time period is correlated with the disturbance in the previous time period, plus a spherical disturbance. The empirical literature in econometric analysis of time series is overwhelmingly dominated by this model, for

---

[98] Prior to 1992, Egypt offered housing, treasury, and national development bonds. Since then, a wider range of instruments has been offered.

[99] The respective dates for each of the elections since Mubarak came to office were May 1984, April 1987, November/December 1990, November/December 1995, October/November 2000, and November/December 2005. Elections since the 1990s have taken place in multiple stages across different parts of the country.

both statistical and practical reasons (Greene 2000, 531). This model can be represented by the following equations:

$$y_t = x_t\beta + \varepsilon_t, \tag{5.1}$$

$$\varepsilon_t = \rho\varepsilon_{t-1} + \mu_t, \tag{5.2}$$

where μ_t is independent and identically distributed.

Here, we supplement the AR(1) model with a lagged dependent variable (LDV) model, which is much more common in the political science literature and less common in econometrics. The LDV model is often employed to rid a model of autocorrelation. Keele and Kelly (2005) have argued that specification-induced autocorrelation can be eliminated when dynamics are captured with an LDV, making the LDV model an appropriate fix in many cases. The LDV model can be represented by the following equation:

$$y_t = x_t\beta + \alpha_t y_{t-1} + \varepsilon_t, \tag{5.3}$$

where, if we assume that ε_t is independent and identically distributed, ordinary least squares with an LDV is consistent, though biased. The results for each of the five variables are presented with each of these two models.[100]

5.6.3   Results

Each of the dependent variables is tested in two ways: with the AR(1) model and the LDV model. Inflation increased 6 percent according to the AR(1) model and 7 percent according to the LDV model in the year of the election (see Table 5.2). The election result is highly statistically significant in both models. Although each regression was run with a postelection variable, this variable did not prove to be statistically significant in any of the specifications with the yearly data and so is not reported with these results. This differs from other studies of electoral budget cycles in which inflation generally occurs in the period directly following the election and suggests that election spending in Egypt takes place before the election. In addition, this result may be capturing some postelection inflation because elections in the 1980s took place in the first half of the year.[101] This finding is consistent with the expectation of Egyptian economists who have argued that government moves to increase salaries and retirement benefits have highly inflationary effects.[102] Political cartoonists like Mustafa Hussein have described this phenomenon in satire. One cartoon shows an Egyptian (with the face of a skeleton) being interviewed by a reporter where

[100] Following Achen (2000), each of the regressions was run without the LDV, and all results were similarly signed with comparable levels of significance.
[101] To ensure that stationarity was not a concern, the same results were found when the dependent variable was the difference of the inflation rate. This precaution was probably not necessary because inflation itself is already a difference.
[102] *Al-Masry al-Yowm*, August 31, 2005; see Helmy 2008 for more on government spending as a determinant of Egyptian inflation.

TABLE 5.2. *Regression Results (Dependent Variables Are Economic Outcomes [Yearly Data])*

| Dependent Variable | AR(1) | | LDV | |
	Inflation	Calorie Consumption	Inflation	Calorie Consumption
Constant	7.909	0.290	3.382	0.250
	(2.689)	(0.217)	(2.158)	(0.250)
Election	6.281	0.918	7.213	1.044
	(1.897)	(0.508)	(2.693)	(0.440)
Lagged DV			0.528	−0.162
			(0.164)	(0.188)
R^2	0.31	0.13	0.47	0.30
Durbin–Watson (transformed)	2.23	1.72		
Observations	23	21	22	20

Note: Standard errors are shown in parentheses.

he says "Prices? Heaven knows what will happen to prices. But what can we do? We are still alive, aren't we?"[103]

The other dependent variable measured at the yearly level is per capita daily calorie consumption. Both the AR(1) and the LDV models suggest about a 1 percent increase in daily calorie consumption in election years. This effect is equivalent to approximately 30 additional calories per day per person in Egypt in the years in which elections take place.[104] If one follows the qualitative literature on elections in Egypt, it would appear that this calorie consumption may have been even higher in the months directly before the election as parliamentary candidates sought to buy votes with money and other handouts. This result is also robust for the dependent variable when measured as a difference of the percentage change.[105]

Electorally related changes in the level of total reserves would suggest government manipulation of the economy (see Table 5.3). The empirical analysis shows that total reserves are between 4 and 4.5 percent lower in the six months prior to the election, according to the AR(1) and LDV models, respectively.[106]

[103] *Egyptian Gazette*, October 18, 2005.
[104] This effect is strengthened with the inclusion of a variable measuring growth of the economy to about a 1.5 percent increase in calorie consumption per Egyptian per day in the year of the election.
[105] Qualitative evidence would suggest that this phenomenon is probably not unique to Egypt. For example, Stokes (2005) describes soup kitchens in Argentina that spring up in the months prior to elections.
[106] Because the 1987 election took place with a truncated campaign period, the preelection variable is only coded for the two months prior to the election. The reason for the shortened election period was elections were forced by a constitutional crisis that developed in late 1986 due to the lack of individual candidacy in the 1984 election. The government called the election

These results also hold for foreign exchange reserves. These results are statistically significant at the 0.05 and 0.01 levels, respectively.[107]

The effect of elections on claims against the government or loans to state enterprises made to finance the government budget deficit have also been considered. Claims against the government increase by about 5.5 percent in the six months following elections. This result is statistically significant at the 0.05 level and similar for both the AR(1) and the LDV models.

Finally, the analysis indicates that currency devaluations are more likely to occur in the six months after an election. This effect is statistically significant at the 0.1 level. In both the AR(1) and LDV models, the Egyptian currency appears to be about 0.04 lower. The currency has ranged between 0.7 and 6 pounds to the $US during the past 25 years. Together, these statistical findings correspond with the qualitative evidence that I have presented on the existence of electorally related manipulations of the economy.

These results conform to some of the predictions of both traditional and rational expectations models of opportunistic business cycles. Both models expect that inflation increases in the period before each election, and, in Egypt, this increase was in the 6–7 percent range for the period prior to parliamentary elections. Evidence regarding the financing of preelectoral giveaways suggests that these manipulations are short term, consistent with the rational model; in the six months prior to the election, reserves are drawn down to support spending, and borrowing appears on the books in the six months after the election. The effects do not appear to begin earlier or linger beyond that time frame as suggested by more traditional models. Neither model makes particular predictions regarding exchange rate devaluations (a likely result of the fact that these models were developed for countries with floating rates), although exchange rate devaluations are more likely in the six months after an election, consistent with the experience of some Latin American countries in Remmer's sample (1993). Finally, the hypothesis that citizens actually live "better" in election years as a result of income redistribution that takes place at both the national and local level is supported by a finding here that Egyptians consume 30 additional calories per day in the year of an election. Qualitative evidence suggests that this increase is probably even higher in the particular weeks and months leading up to the election. Although none of these factors are inconsistent with the traditional model of opportunistic business cycles, the short-term nature of the financing and other effects more strongly support the recently developed, rationalized models.

---

to preempt a likely decision by Egypt's judiciary (Ayubi 1989). The campaign lasted about seven weeks (Post 1987). The court decision that led to the calling of the 1990 parliamentary election was made on July 8, 1990, about six months before parliamentary elections took place.

[107] For the monthly analysis, I also include month-dummy variables to control for any potential seasonal affects. These results are suppressed in the table.

TABLE 5.3. *Regression Results (Dependent Variables Are Economic Outcomes [Monthly Data])*

	AR(1)			LDV		
	Total Reserves	Claims on Government	Exchange Rate	Total Reserves	Claims on Government	Exchange Rate
Constant	−0.784	−1.953	0.006	−0.501	−1.768	0.006
	(1.846)	(2.429)	(0.022)	(1.819)	(2.503)	(0.022)
Six Pre	−4.156	0.906	0.027	−4.619	0.885	0.025
	(1.602)	(2.444)	(0.024)	(1.912)	(2.474)	(0.023)
Six Post	1.548	5.456	0.039	1.806	5.643	0.036
	(1.545)	(2.391)	(0.023)	(1.860)	(2.502)	(0.021)
Lagged dv				−0.215	−0.009	0.099
				(0.088)	(0.079)	(0.061)
R^2	0.06	0.07	0.04	0.08	0.07	0.05
Durbin–Watson (transformed)	1.57	1.70	2.01			
Observations	266	252	280	264	250	279

Note: Standard errors are shown in parentheses.

5.7 CONCLUSIONS

Do authoritarian regimes manipulate economic policy in the run-up to elections? Implicit in traditional models of electoral budget cycles is the idea that voters hold their politicians accountable for poor economic performance in democratic societies. We find here, however, that authoritarian rulers manipulate the economy in many of the same ways that democratically elected leaders hope to, although with a significant advantage – authoritarians are seldom subject to the same institutional norms of independent economic policy making found in democracies. In this chapter, we investigated the existence of opportunistic electoral budget cycles in Egypt during more than twenty-five years of electoral authoritarianism under Hosni Mubarak and describe the specific mechanisms by which the regime courts three important constituencies: public sector employees, farmers, and the urban poor. Quantitative analysis suggests that these budget manipulations have a number of tangible effects, including election-year inflation, a preelection drain on reserves, and a higher level of per capita calorie consumption in election years. Whereas some of these factors – like economic redistribution via calories – may represent a net positive for Egypt's citizens, others aspects of these cycles suggest inefficiencies and costs. In particular, inflation, the growth of claims against the government, and a drawdown of reserves all represent quasi parameters of the equilibrium that I have described with the potential to undermine stability.

Therefore, even in authoritarian regimes, elections matter; in part, they matter because of the electoral budget cycle that these contests induce. Whereas empirical support for the existence of electoral budget cycles is mixed in democratic countries, increasingly the strongest statistical evidence for the phenomenon has been in authoritarian regimes. Here, we see that both the qualitative evidence and the empirical analysis suggest the existence of a robust electoral budget cycle in Egypt. In particular, time-series analysis demonstrates that inflation and calorie consumption both increase in election years. Government spending is financed by drawing down the country's reserve base and increasing the level of outstanding credit owed by the government. In addition, the regime delays exchange rate devaluations until after elections. On the qualitative side, electoral opportunism revolves around transfers made to three key constituencies: government employees, the rural sector, and the urban poor. Finally, in addition to the national-level manipulation, there is also a massive redistribution that takes place on the individual level as parliamentary candidates offer side payments to voters. Although these effects are short term, they do imply that elections matter enough to authoritarians that manipulation is a worthwhile endeavor. Elections represent a time of potential vulnerability for authoritarian leaders, and it is rational to expect they would engage in actions at their disposal to increase the voteshare of the ruling party.

The question of why elections matter is the subject of subsequent sections of this book, although it seems clear that authoritarians need to build coalitions to maintain power in ways similar to what we observe in democratic polities.

They use public expenditure and other preelection policies to target particular constituencies. Reliance on such strategies, however, has implications for the durability of authoritarianism and the possibility of democratic transition in Egypt. As long as redistribution is taking place at a level that satisfies most of the regime's most important constituencies, then the likelihood of revolution remains low. The ability of the regime to increase giveaways in the future is an open question, however. Although Egypt enjoys significant external rents as a foreign aid recipient, budgetary constraints combined with a rapidly growing population portend difficulty in the future. Therefore, although this chapter has suggested that attempts to manipulate economic conditions prior to elections are not exclusive to regime type, the stakes for success in authoritarian regimes may be even higher.

6

Vote Buying, Turnout, and Spoiled Ballots

Authoritarian elections are as varied as the regimes that hold them. Within a single nondemocratic country, elections can take place at various levels of competitiveness and mobilizing different constituencies. And although authoritarian elections rarely offer the opportunity to change the existing regime, these elections can have politically important results. Even acts of voter abstention or ballot nullification can provide meaningful signals of discontent and voter preference. Studies of voting in the Soviet Union, for example, suggest that nonvoting was seen as an act of protest in which relatively well-educated individuals consciously decided to ignore mandatory voting laws or spoil their ballots in a country where there was no real choice between candidates (Karklins 1986; Roeder 1989). In China, voters participating in local elections tend to be individuals seeking to punish corrupt bureaucrats (Shi 1999). In Brazil, under military rule, compulsory voting led to high turnout, but blank and spoiled ballots have been interpreted as an indication of dissatisfaction with authoritarian governance (Powers and Roberts 1995). In all of these cases, voters had political beliefs and preferences that led them to engage in the act (or nonact) of voting, and the submission of a valid or spoiled ballot often was a representation of preference. These examples also suggest that, in a wide range of authoritarian countries, there are avenues of limited political expression, some of which include voter choice, and perhaps even forms of accountability.

Egypt holds elections for a variety of offices. At the parliamentary level, electoral races are highly competitive as official party candidates from the hegemonic regime party – the NDP – compete with NDP independents, candidates from legally established opposition parties, and members of the popular opposition group – the Muslim Brotherhood. In addition, the regime holds municipal elections that are competitive primarily within the ruling party cadre. Finally, Egypt had its first multicandidate presidential election in 2005. Although it was clear from the start that incumbent president Hosni Mubarak would win the election, two prominent opponents did provide the potential for individuals to express their opposition to the regime.

Here, we consider the incentives associated with voter turnout and behavior in Egyptian elections. Although some percentage of voters cast their ballots on the basis of ideological concerns, the majority of Egyptian voters expect to receive material or other compensation for their votes.[1] In line with a series of formal works that argue how certain constituencies are likely to be more responsive to targeted rewards than others (Dixit and Londregan 1996; Calvo and Murillo 2004; Stokes 2005), I expect the poor to be more responsive to vote buying because they benefit more from consumption goods. In addition, I find that regime pressure also makes the poor more likely to turn out, particularly in Egypt's first multicandidate presidential election, in which widespread vote buying was more difficult to organize. In most circumstances, therefore, voting in Egypt has a highly rational basis. Using data on voter turnout for the 2000 and 2005 Egyptian parliamentary elections, the 2002 municipal council elections, and the 2005 presidential elections, I find that, in Egypt, illiterates are roughly twice as likely to vote compared with their literate counterparts. This finding complements previous studies focusing on Latin America by investigating the ties between poverty and turnout. Rather than relying on survey data, however, to establish this relationship, I use district-level turnout and literacy figures as well as statistical techniques appropriate for estimating the impact of literacy on voter turnout.

The second empirical finding of this chapter involves patterns of spoiled ballots. I find that the relationship between ballot nullification and literacy is nonmonotonic; spoiled ballots are common in districts with both extremely low and high levels of literacy and are rare in middling districts. Whereas spoiled ballots in districts with high illiteracy rates are probably explained by individual error during the voting process, high levels of ballot nullification in literate areas suggest the existence of a protest effect. Elections, then, offer the opportunity for voters to express their distaste either for the political system or for candidates who choose to engage in vote buying.

6.1 THEORETICAL CONSIDERATIONS

The majority of voters in Egypt make their voting decision based on clientelistic considerations. Clientelism is generally defined as a relationship between parties of unequal status that involves some form of exchange. Huntington and Nelson have written:

> In traditional societies, patron–client relations provide a means for the vertical mobilization of lower-status individuals by established elites.... The introduction of competitive elections gives the client one additional resource – the vote – which he can use to repay his patron for other benefits (1976, 55).

[1] A number of important works consider the question of electoral support for the Muslim Brotherhood, the largest recipient of ideology votes in Egypt. See Wickham (2002) and Masoud (2008b) for more on this literature.

"Other benefits" generally refers to some form of vote buying, although it may not involve cash, but rather goods or services rendered on the part of the patron in exchange for the client's vote.

The clients in these vertical relationships tend to be members of lower classes. Poor voters are more susceptible to clientelistic practices than wealthy voters because the marginal benefit of the consumption good is greater for them than for the wealthy. This is not to say that the poor do not have preferences. In fact, they may prefer one candidate over the other, but the marginal benefit of voting based on preference may be less than the marginal benefit of voting based on cash or other reward.[2] Calvo and Murillo (2004) argue that patronage provides different returns to economically advantaged or disadvantaged voters; in other words, patronage targeted at the poor is more efficient than patronage targeted at the middle or upper classes. Stokes (2005) – modeling the interaction between voters and a political machine as a repeated prisoners' dilemma – shows that machines target the poor, for whom the payoff of even a small reward outweighs the expressive value of voting for one's preferred party. The implication is that, in many developing countries, voter mobilization has become synonymous with building an organizational network for the purposes of vote buying. Nichter (2008) argues that turnout buying is an alternative to vote buying; by rewarding unmobilized supporters for showing up at the polls, parties are able to activate their passive constituencies. These formal treatments of the issue are consistent with the idea that there is a diminishing marginal utility of income.

A preponderance of the empirical work on this subject has focused on Latin America, including the evidence presented in Calvo and Murillo (2004) and Stokes (2005) as well as the narrative account of Auyero (2004). Brusco, Nazareno, and Stokes (2004), using the same data as Stokes (2005), argue that vote buying is an effective strategy for mobilizing electoral support among low-income individuals in Argentina. They arrive at this conclusion based on evidence from surveys conducted that were augmented with qualitative research and in-depth interviews. Not surprisingly, the percentage of individuals who admitted to receiving payment for votes appears to be far lower than both the authors' expectations regarding the widespread nature of vote buying as well as other, more qualitative, accounts of the subject. Only 7 percent of their sample admitted to receiving goods in exchange for votes (Brusco et al. 2004).[3]

---

[2] It may also be possible that poor, illiterate voters are indeed less ideologically committed because they may not have been exposed to campaign and other literature to the same extent as literate voters. This is a subject in need of further empirical investigation.

[3] Other notable studies of vote buying in Latin America include a poll undertaken by Transparency International, which reveals that 7 percent of voters were offered money for their votes in a Brazilian municipal election (Pfeiffer 2004) and Desposato's observation that poor areas of Brazil witness more vote buying than wealthy areas (2006). Estimates for vote buying in Mexico range from 5 to 26 percent (Pfeiffer 2004). A 1999 Gallup poll in Argentina found that 24 percent of those interviewed knew someone who sold his or her vote, and low-income individuals are thought to be most susceptible to vote-buying schemes (Pfeiffer 2004).

The previous literature, therefore, raises some important empirical questions. First, is survey data a reliable tool for examining this question? Individuals may be reluctant to admit to engaging in an act that is both illegal and socially undesirable. Second, does this phenomenon travel beyond the borders of Latin America, an empirical focus of much of the work on this subject? My project builds on the important contributions of Stokes (2005) and others by testing some of the key hypotheses in the literature relating patronage to turnout on nonsurvey data (i.e., behavioral rather than self-reported data). I also provide a narrative discussion of how vote buying takes place outside of the context of Latin America by considering the case of Egypt. The qualitative evidence I present suggests that vote buying and clientelistic voting are pervasive in Egypt and operate in ways consistent with the previous literature on Latin American clientelism.

The second major area that this research addresses is the issue of why individuals engage in a political act that has almost no probability of influencing an election. Riker and Ordeshook (1968) suggest that people vote because they overestimate the minuscule chance that they will be decisive or they get some large direct benefits from the act of voting. For Egyptian voters that are part of clientelistic networks, turnout is not paradoxical. Goods and services are exchanged for votes in a fairly straightforward manner. The literature on the turnout paradox is, however, relevant for our understanding of voters who engage in intentional ballot nullification. This chapter considers the following question: do we observe individuals intentionally spoiling their ballots even when this action can only be pivotal under the rarest of circumstances (i.e., the ballot they have spoiled would have broken a tie between two candidates)? The risks associated with engaging in ballot nullification – although small – do exist; ballot spoiling is technically illegal in Egypt, and vote brokers threaten to punish individuals who engage in this act. I find that rates of ballot nullification in Egypt follow a specific empirical pattern that suggests the intention to nullify. Although specifically identifying the psychological or other mechanism leading to this finding is beyond the scope of this project, some scholars have argued that individuals sometimes engage in political acts to say something about who they are more than to earn a specific payoff (Schuessler 2000).

6.2 VOTER CALCULUS IN PARLIAMENTARY ELECTIONS

Voters who have jumped through the appropriate hoops to ensure their eligibility to vote face a number of possible options on election day. For those who believe the costs of voting will exceed the benefits that they might receive or who are not part of clientelistic networks, staying at home may be the logical choice. Some voters who turn out will make their selection on ideological grounds. Although some Egyptian politicians ably provide public goods to their constituents and earn votes without forced reciprocity, in many cases, voters receive constituency services with the expectation that a vote will follow.

The agents of various candidates, known locally as brokers (sing. *simsār*, pl. *samāsir*), enforce these arrangements through a series of monitoring techniques.

Zaki writes that political participation through patron–client relationships is "extremely widespread" in Egypt (1995, 99). This is consistent with accounts of Egyptian elections even prior to the Mubarak period (Hinnebusch 1988a, 172). In addition, political parties – with the exception of the Muslim Brotherhood – tend not to run on ideological platforms. As a result, "votes are not cast on the basis of political issues or party platforms but as a choice between competing personalities within a context of patron-client relations" (Zaki 1995, 101). This is even echoed in editorials run by *Al-Ahram* – the semi-official government newspaper.[4]

6.2.1 Direct Exchange on Election Day

The most obvious case of vote buying – direct exchange of cash for votes on the day of the election – is well documented by Egyptian journalists, academics, and human rights organizations.[5] Researcher 'Amr al-Shoubaki has argued that, although candidates for parliament used to focus their efforts on district service provision, increasingly, candidates have won seats through direct vote buying.[6] The opposition press reports that partisan affiliation matters very little in parliamentary elections compared with the power of financial exchange.[7] One monitoring group recorded vote buying on the part of independent and NDP candidates for between LE 20 and LE 500 during the 2005 parliamentary elections.[8] Press reports suggest that some individuals may have earned as much as LE 700 for their votes.[9] Vote buying is also common in urban squatter settlements, where citizens report having no contact with the government except during the parliamentary election season when candidates pay cash or goods for votes (Fahmy 2004). Interestingly, some poor voters defend the integrity of the system of cash exchange, arguing that it is "fair."[10] According to one voter in southern Cairo, "the candidate wants the Parliament's seat and we want

---

[4] *Al-Ahram*, December 19, 2005.

[5] Whereas this section describes voter choice in parliamentary elections, municipal elections in Egypt operate in largely the same manner, although primarily within the ruling NDP. For example, according to one politician, there might be 15 municipal council seats at stake with more than 200 candidates seeking those seats. Because the vast majority of those candidates represent the same political party, voting decisions are made on a clientelist basis rather than based on programmatic concerns. Interview with former parliamentarian, May 1, 2006.

[6] "Legislative Elections in Egypt: Indicators and Consequences," Al-Ahram Center for Political and Strategic Studies, Issue 46, December 2005.

[7] *Al-Wafd*, December 13, 2005.

[8] Independent Committee on Election Monitoring (ICEM) Monitoring the Third Phase of the Parliamentary Election Preliminary Report, December 2, 2005.

[9] *Egyptian Gazette*, March 5, 2008.

[10] Ibid.

money."[11] Al-Sawy, Moussa, and Ibrahim (2005) attribute vote buying to the low levels of income and bad economic conditions in Egypt.[12]

A front-page article in Egypt's independent newspaper *Al-Masry Al-Youm* with the controversial headline "Who Pays More...?!" ran the day after the re-vote of the first round of parliamentary elections.[13] The article focused on rampant vote buying that took place during this re-vote phase of the election.[14] The pictures that accompanied the article spoke volumes about the nature of vote buying in Egyptian parliamentary elections. In one, the caption reads "a candidate's assistant distributes cash to voters." A second picture shows a man holding up five bills; it is unclear whether he is a vote seller or a vote buyer. The caption reads "for every vote (there) is a price." A third photo of an outstretched arm holding bills has the caption "a shower of banknotes came down on eight governorates yesterday." A final picture shows a well-dressed professional man marking the ballot of an older, working-class man. The caption reads "a picture from inside a polling station...vote outside of the curtained ballot area or help?!" In addition, the voter appears to be holding a banknote. The implication is clearly that observers cannot be sure whether that older man is simply seeking help to vote for his chosen candidate or if the politico inside the polling station is making the choice for him. The content of the article goes on to say that vote buying and the influence of hired thugs (*baltaga*) dominated the election.[15]

So how do vote buyers ensure that the people they pay vote for their candidate? In the 1980s, vote buyers used to split a bill in half and promise to

---

[11] Ibid.

[12] Although most of the individuals who sell their votes are poor, this is not meant to suggest that the poor have no interest in programmatic issues. Rather, it reflects the need to act based on a short-term economic imperative. Poor or illiterate voters often exhibit considerable savvy and have been known to auction their votes to the highest bidder. Interview with Saad Eddin Ibrahim, Ibn Khaldun Center for Development Studies, September 27, 2005.

[13] *Al-Masry Al-Youm*, November 16, 2005.

[14] When a candidate receives a plurality of votes in the first round, rather than a majority, there is a re-vote with the highest vote getters.

[15] It is worth noting that, in addition to positive inducements for voting, there are also reports of the use of hired thugs to force voters to choose particular candidates. Following the first round of parliamentary elections, in which citizens of eight Egyptian governorates voted, the independent daily *Al-Masry Al-Youm* ran a front-page article describing the influence of the hired thugs (*baltaga*) in these districts. The article – which ran on November 10, 2005 – said that state security forces imposed a form of "passive neutrality" that allowed these hired thugs to dominate the scene, and violations in individual districts are discussed in the article as well, particularly in the districts of Sayeda Zeinab and Helwan. Egyptian sociologist Saad Eddin Ibrahim called the police's unwillingness to stop the thuggery "negative neutrality" (*Al-Ahram Weekly*, November 17–23, 2005), and even Makram Mohammed Ahmed – a well-known, state-affiliated journalist – said that the absence of government action to deter bullying marred the process (*Al-Ahram*, November 20, 2005.). Al-Sawy et al. write that, although thugs are used to force voters to support a certain candidate, they are also used to prevent supporters of other candidates from voting at all (2005, 73–5). It is not clear whether the newspaper articles references were referring to the former or latter phenomenon or both.

give the person the other half of the bill upon completion of voting.[16] In recent years, new mechanisms have been developed to ensure that the vote broker gets a vote for his chosen candidate. With the advent of the camera phone, voters now capture their voting in a photo to show to the vote buyer upon leaving the polling station.[17] Al-Sawy et al. describe what is known as the "revolving ballot" strategy (2005, 9). At the beginning of the day, a voter leaves the polling station without having voted. This ballot is then filled out by the vote broker and handed to the vote seller. The vote seller submits this ballot in the polling station and returns a blank ballot to the vote broker. The vote seller is paid after coming out of the station with this blank ballot. This process is then repeated throughout the day (al-Sawy et al. 2005, 9–11). In this way, the vote buyer always fills out the ballot without fear that the voter will have a chance to make his own choice.[18] In addition, one article reports that NDP candidates even exploited special-needs women whose votes were bought and then closely monitored by vote brokers because the handicapped could be accompanied into the polling station.[19]

6.2.2   Preelection Exchange

In addition to the exchange of cash for votes on election day, parliamentary candidates also cultivate support with goods and services in the weeks and months leading up to the election. Because these income and other transfers take place unofficially, documentation of this phenomenon tends to be from personal interviews, newspaper accounts, and other sources. It has been reported that candidates running for parliament distribute everything from free shoes to mobile phones to even job applications for public sector employment. During one parliamentary election campaign, the minister of housing was running for office and promised subsidized apartments for individual slum dwellers in a bid to secure their votes; aids of the minister also distributed free water containers to people who did not have access to running water (Fahmy 2004). In addition to goods transfers that take place, individuals running for parliament can also negotiate for the votes of families and even entire villages by securing the release of men arrested on suspicion of being involved with insurgent activity.[20]

   The 2005 parliamentary elections were characterized by vote buying both on the day of the election and in the months and weeks prior. In the hotly contested

---

[16] *Egyptian Gazette*, November 27, 2005.

[17] Ibid.

[18] Another more subtle way of undermining the perceived sanctity of the secret ballot involves the way balloting is portrayed on state television. For example, during the 2005 electoral season, President Mubarak was shown marking his ballot without the use of a curtain for privacy.

[19] *Sawt al-Umma*, November 14, 2005.

[20] For more details, see former Brigadier General Hamdi al-Batran's exposé of regime activity in the Egyptian countryside, *Yaumiyāt Ḍābiṭ fī al-Aryāf* (The Diary of an Officer in the Countryside), pages 24 and 92.

district of Kasr al-Nile, press reports suggested that candidate Hisham Khalil spent upwards of LE 10 million on his campaign.[21] In Manial, the campaign manager for candidate and wealthy hotelier Shahinaz al-Naggar describes the personal payment of monthly stipends for 500 families in her constituency, at between LE 20 and 50 per family (Blaydes and el-Tarouty 2008). The trading of food for votes is also a popular strategy employed by candidates. Sacks of dried fruit (*yamish*) and other foodstuffs are distributed in the election season.[22] Vouchers for chickens are also offered; the willing voter must also submit a copy of his or her electoral card to be eligible for these items.[23] School fees and trips to Mecca or seaside resorts are also provided as well as payment for expensive medical surgeries.[24] Beneficiaries of these benefits prior to election day are also subjected to the "revolving ballot" or other monitoring mechanisms (al-Sawy et al. 2005).

6.2.3 Longer-Term Familial and Clientelistic Relationships

In many cases, particularly in the Egyptian countryside, individuals are involved in longer-term clientelistic or familial relationships with political candidates. Voters often support candidates from the same family, clan, or tribe, believing these individuals will be more likely to offer patronage goods (Masoud 2008b; Shehata 2008). For example, NDP stalwart Kamal al-Shazli ran for reelection in 2005 in his home district in the governorate of Menoufiya; he is thought to be the longest serving parliamentarian in any parliament in the world. A newspaper article describes some keys to his long-term electoral success. "'He (al-Shazli) got my children good jobs and is always there for the people of this district'.... It was a story repeated by a great many voters, who said they supported al-Shazli because of his ability to provide their communities with jobs and other services."[25] In fact, it is rumored that the majority of police officers stationed all over the country originally hail from al-Shazli's district.

Kassem writes that "personal assurances of support sought by electoral candidates are largely conditional upon the downward flow of patronage, most of which can realistically be channeled only from the center" (1999, 127). Singerman also paints a compelling picture of patronage relations based on her field work in Cairo during the 1980s. She argues that parliamentarians who provided access to public housing units for constituents were rewarded with the political support of those families at election time (Singerman 1995, 256). Voting by family bloc is also common. For example, in Springborg's description

[21] *Al-Ghad*, November 23, 2005.
[22] *Egyptian Gazette*, October 18, 2005.
[23] Ibid.
[24] Ibid.
[25] *Al-Ahram Weekly*, November 10–16, 2005.

of Sayed Marei's electoral strategy in the post-1976 era, Springborg writes that Marei's electoral success rested on a coalition of four families who formed the basis for a clientelist network (1982, 113).[26] In areas of upper Egypt where tribal affiliations are particularly strong, individuals vote for candidates from their tribe with the expectation of receiving some of the spoils of office (Nielsen 2004).

There are some indications, however, that these longer-term, clientelistic relationships are beginning to break down. Springborg has argued that modernization has eroded traditional patron–client relationships in Egypt (1988, 156). 'Amr al-Shoubaki has written that, at the time of the 1976 Egyptian elections, parliamentarians offered services – like paving roads, building schools, and helping people find jobs – to voters in their constituencies.[27] During this period, a parliamentary representative served as an intermediary between the people and the state, distributing public services and state money (Bin Nefisa and Arafat 2005, 121). As parliamentarians become increasingly incapable of providing services, business tycoons – who can either dip into their own pockets for payment of these expenses or turn to vote buying with cash – have come to play an important role in the parliament.[28] Al-Shoubaki argues that parliamentarians have found ministers increasingly unwilling to fulfill demands for their districts.[29]

Budgets have grown tighter over the years, and ministries are simply less capable of meeting these demands. This is the result of a variety of factors, including increasing economic liberalization, IMF-imposed structural adjustment, or government lack of revenue. As state services were eliminated as a result of structural adjustment, citizens came to accept the replacement of these services with market-mediated interactions, which had the effect of transforming "relationships into a cash nexus" (Elyachar 2005, 194). Elyachar has characterized this as the emergence of a *"biznis"* culture (i.e., business culture) that has come to pervade all segments of Egyptian society (2005, 165). The result has been a significant increase in the importance of cash transfers – versus services – rendered at election time as well as the development of new forms of clientelism that are less reliant on public funds and resources and more reliant on the financial capabilities of individual candidates who use their own private resources to woo voters (Bin Nefisa and Arafat 2005, 184–5).[30] As the relationship between voters and patrons has changed, opportunities for political expression have emerged.

---

[26] Others have argued that patron–client exchange is a societal microstructure. In particular, Reeves (1990) writes that ritualized exchange is part of the cultural schema in many parts of Egypt.

[27] "Legislative Elections in Egypt: Indicators and Consequences," Al-Ahram Center for Political and Strategic Studies, Issue 46, December 2005.

[28] Ibid.

[29] Ibid.

[30] This description is consistent with other studies that describe the way neoliberalism has revived clientelism in places like Argentina. See Brusco et al. 2004.

6.2.4 Intentional and Unintentional Ballot Nullification

Once a vote has been bought, there are two possible choices for the vote seller: he or she can go through with the transaction as promised or can double-cross the vote buyer. For some percentage of voters, however, even if they seek to fulfill their end of the tacit contract, they may make an error in voting. This is particularly the case for illiterate voters who are more likely to make mistakes in filling out or casting their ballots.

The literature on ballot nullification is particularly well developed in the context of Brazil, where voting is compulsory. Powers and Roberts (1995) describe a number of Brazilian studies that show that invalid voting increases in poor neighborhoods versus rich neighborhoods, and their own statistical work finds that literacy is inversely related to spoiled ballots. This phenomenon is most likely explained by voter error. This is not the whole story, however. Vote sellers may also intentionally nullify their ballots. This can happen in two primary ways. Voters can take a preprepared ballot and in the privacy of the voting booth either a) defile the ballot or b) check more than the appropriate number of names.

Intentional ballot nullification may occur for a number of reasons. First, the voter may nullify his ballot as a protest to the political system or the quality of the candidates from which they have to choose. According to one voter, "I went to disable my vote because I'm not convinced by any of the candidates, and I didn't like any of the agendas presented, and candidates themselves are not convinced with their own agendas."[31] Another voter spoiled a ballot because he did not agree with recent changes to the constitution.[32]

A voter might also spoil his or her ballot in order to deceive the vote buyer as well as the candidate for whom the vote buyer is working. The vote spoiler may actually have a preference for one candidate or the other and feel that by spoiling his or her ballot they are at least not helping the candidate they oppose; in this way, vote spoilers may be trying to influence the outcome of the election and double-cross the vote seller (al-Sawy et al. 2005, 11–12). According to one NDP member, this is a game of trust where the vote buyer cannot know for sure that the voter has not spoiled the ballot; in order to discourage this, the vote buyer can threaten to punish ballot spoilers by creating negative rumors about the individual or trying to run him out of the neighborhood should the double-cross be discovered.[33] As a result, ballot spoiling is not a widespread phenomenon,[34] and the threat of sanction may partially explain why it is not a dominant strategy for those who sell their votes. Another reason is that defacing or ruining a ballot is a criminal offense punishable by a six-month term in prison, although this is rarely enforced.

[31] Election Day Coverage: Quiet Marks Egypt's Landmark Election, International Journalists Network.
[32] Ibid.
[33] Interview with NDP official, May 1, 2006.
[34] Ibid.

Under these circumstances, we might expect two trends to emerge with regard to ballot spoiling in Egypt. First, as has been discovered with studies of this type in Brazil, illiterate areas should have relatively high levels of spoiled ballots as a result of errors in balloting. In addition, we might expect to find some evidence of intentional ballot nullification in areas where individuals either a) have a strong desire to express their dislike of the political system or policies or b) believe the expressive value of ballot spoiling exceeds the potential cost of being caught engaging in such act.

6.3 VOTER CALCULUS FOR THE 2005 PRESIDENTIAL ELECTION

The most significant recent development in Egyptian politics has been the introduction of a constitutional amendment allowing for the direct election of the president from a multicandidate, multiparty field. Although the institutional design of the amendment stacks the deck heavily in favor of the ruling party, Egypt did hold its first multicandidate presidential election in September 2005.[35] Until 2005, the NDP-dominated parliament would nominate a single candidate – Mubarak – and voters had to check either "yes" or "no" on the ballot in the style of a referendum. In the 2005 contest, however, Mubarak ran against candidates Ayman Nour of the Ghad Party and No'man Gom'a of the Wafd Party, among others.

Although it was clear from the start that Mubarak would emerge victorious from the contest, turnout was of paramount importance to the regime, given a desire to make the process appear legitimate.[36] Public officials, like NDP stalwart Safwat al-Sherif, publicly emphasized the importance of high turnout,[37] and Mubarak himself was constantly urging Egyptians to turn out to vote on his campaign stops.[38] Mubarak campaign officials during the election period also believed that high turnout would strongly favor the incumbent.[39]

Yet, achieving a high level of turnout in the presidential race posed a challenge to Mubarak and his campaign advisors. Whereas vote buying was a viable strategy for parliamentary candidates at the district level (because thousands of individual office-seekers would bear the costs), at the national level a different approach was needed. Paid voting was not as common as in parliamentary elections, though after the election, Nour held a press conference where he held up an envelope with a ballot marked "Mubarak" and LE 20. Gom'a – the other main challenger – also accused the regime of forcing government employees to vote for Mubarak.

---

[35] See Blaydes 2005 for more details on the institutional design of this amendment.

[36] Two days before the election, *Al-Masry Al-Youm* reported that government agencies had already begun to prepare the banners congratulating Mubarak's victory (September 5, 2005).

[37] *Al-Ahram*, July 23, 2005.

[38] *Egyptian Gazette*, August 28, 2005.

[39] Interview with Mohammed Kamal, NDP Policies Secretariat and Professor of Political Science, Cairo University, July 31, 2005.

In addition to these illegal strategies, the regime had to use a number of other legal or semi-legal strategies to induce turnout; in other words, many voters were actually "choosing" the authoritarian ruler. In particular, the regime found ways to ensure that Egypt's poor turned out to vote, and, in many cases, cast their ballots for Mubarak out of fear or a lack of knowledge regarding the other candidates. These mechanisms included the threat of economic sanction and the (ab)use of state-supported religious institutions and media. Each is described more fully in the sections to follow.

6.3.1 Threat of Economic Sanction

A number of countries in the developed and developing world have compulsory voting. Whereas in countries like Brazil, compulsory voting is taken quite seriously (Powers and Roberts 1995), in Egypt, compulsory voting has been used in a strategic manner by the regime at certain points in time and to intimidate poor voters or members of particular constituencies, but is otherwise rarely enforced.[40] For example, although compulsory voting has not historically been enforced in Egyptian parliamentary elections, there was a great deal of uncertainty regarding this issue in the run-up to Egypt's first presidential election. In an election where standard vote-buying techniques would have fallen entirely on the budget of the regime and party (rather than individual parliamentary candidates), regime and party representatives created the impression that economic sanction would be enforced for individuals who failed to turn out and vote.

An article in the independent newspaper *Al-Masry Al-Youm* reported that the LE 100 sanction called for in the compulsory voting law was a significant factor in driving up voter turnout.[41] According to one journalist, the regime stretched its abilities to the maximum to ensure a high turnout. The article describes how in one district loudspeakers blared, "O People of Al-Daba'h! Go to the polling station to cast your vote in the presidential elections. Failing to go exposes you to (pay) a fine of LE 120!"[42] In addition, imams of the main mosques (using mosque loudspeakers) called on people to vote, so as not to anger Allah.[43] The same article reports in this district that "All village mayors were summoned last night (Tuesday) for a meeting at the police station (*al-markaz*) with NDP officials and others from the governors office. Orders were clear: 'Any low turnout means losing your jobs.'"[44]

---

[40] Issue 39 of the Egyptian constitution called for a LE 20 fine for nonvoting in 1976. This amount was increased over the years to LE 100.

[41] *Al-Masry Al-Youm*, September 12, 2005.

[42] Khaled Mamdouh, *Turnout ... Mubarak's Greatest Challenge*, http:www.IslamOnline.net, September 7, 2005.

[43] Ibid.

[44] Ibid.; mayors, or village chiefs, used to be elected in Egypt but are currently appointed by the Ministry of Interior.

Another journalist describes the situation in Kafr Sha'ban, a small village in northeastern Egypt, where loudspeakers mounted on the local mosques exclaimed, "Oh people of Kafr Sha'ban, if you do not come to vote, you will be fined immediately and on the spot LE 105 in cash."[45] After these announcements were made, villagers, many of whom were dressed in traditional clothes, arrived to vote, uncertain of the candidates or procedures and stating that the fine would be too much for them to bear.[46] The journalist notes that, when one elderly man asked to vote, a local NDP representative said, "Go in and choose the president or the crescent sign."[47] The same article reports that a civil servant manning the polling station said that the calls from the mosques came at the order of the state-appointed village chief (*'umda*).[48] A woman is quoted as saying, "We are so poor, and we are scared that the village chieftain will fine us LE 100 . . . [we] had to vote for the president. They told me at the door to pick the crescent sign. So I did. We do not want trouble and he will win anyway."[49]

This suggests that the compulsory voting law was used as a threat targeting the underprivileged and illiterate population.

6.3.2   Biased Media Coverage

In Egypt, the major media outlets are owned and operated by the state. Flagship dailies like *Al-Ahram* and *Al-Ahkbar* have tried to cultivate an impression of neutrality and professionalism. However, within Egypt's educated classes, it is common knowledge that there exists an implicit bias in the reporting of the state-owned press.[50]

When the announcement was made that Egypt would be holding its first multicandidate presidential election in the fall of 2005, there were immediate concerns that biased media coverage would provide an unfair benefit to Mubarak. The government responded by legislating that government-owned media would apply a strict equality of time for candidates. Nevertheless, subsequent reports have shown that Egypt's state-owned media remained biased for the incumbent both in terms of the amount of coverage as well as the tone of the coverage provided.[51] The state media strongly encouraged potential voters

---

[45] Emad Mekay, "Choose the Crescent or Be Fined," *Interpress News Service*, September 8, 2005.
[46] Ibid.
[47] Ibid.; because of the high illiteracy rate in Egypt's rural areas, candidates are represented by symbols like the palm tree or the crescent to make it easier for voters who cannot read to find their names on the ballot.
[48] Ibid.
[49] Ibid.
[50] Even Salama Ahmed Salama, famous for his long-running column in *Al-Ahram*, conceded in an interview with *Al-Masry Al-Youm* that *Al-Ahram* is a mouthpiece for the NDP and a defender of regime interests (*Al-Masry Al-Youm*, July 8, 2006).
[51] Independent Committee for Elections Monitoring, Final Report on the Egyptian Presidential Election, September 2005.

to turn out, and the television and radio airwaves carried countless Mubarak campaign advertisements.

The Independent Committee for Elections Monitoring (ICEM) studied media coverage during the official campaign period from August 17 to September 4. Although some independent newspapers were found to be impartial, *Al-Ahram* – the newspaper of record in Egypt – was not. According to the ICEM report, Mubarak received front-page coverage for 83 percent of the campaign period versus his nearest competitor, who received front-page coverage just 8 percent of the time.[52] Photo coverage was even more unequal between Mubarak and his competitors.[53] Coverage of Mubarak was also found to be more positive.[54] This bias in coverage was discussed in the opposition press.[55]

How does media bias affect voter choice and turnout? Hinnebusch writes that the government-controlled media is a potent instrument for influencing the masses (1988a, 227). Similarly, opposition activists in Egypt believe that government-generated mass propaganda continues to be an important pillar of support for the NDP.[56] Terrestrial television is state-run, and this is the television that poor voters are most likely to see. They may also be less equipped to resist government propaganda. Geddes and Zaller (1989) argue that those with high levels of political awareness are able to resist regime-issued propaganda, whereas those who are exposed to such messages but do not have high levels of political awareness are more likely to follow government dictates. Radio in Egypt is state-dominated as well. The middle class and wealthy have access to satellite television. Those who are sufficiently educated are also able to read the opposition press and are more likely to have access to foreign media.

6.3.3 State-Affiliated Religious Institutions

Since the early 1960s, the Egyptian government has sought the publicly announced approval from Al-Azhar – the highest authority of Islam in Egypt – to legitimate the government's most controversial foreign and domestic policy decisions. Al-Azhar is traditionally known to be Egypt's most respected and influential center for Islamic study. After Egypt negotiated a peace agreement with Israel at Camp David in 1979, Anwar Sadat asked Al-Azhar to publicly recognize the legitimacy of an agreement that most Egyptians opposed. Upon entering the U.S.-led coalition against Saddam Hussein in the Gulf War, Hosni Mubarak used Al-Azhar to assure the Egyptian public that the war effort was acceptable under the dictates of Islam. The Egyptian regime also sought the

---

[52] Ibid

[53] Ibid.

[54] Ibid.

[55] *Al-Wafd*, September 7, 2005.

[56] Interview with Gouda 'Abd al-Khalek, Professor of Economics, Cairo University and Tagammu' Party activist, May 8, 2005.

approval of Al-Azhar to justify a crackdown on Islamist insurgents.[57] These were politically significant policy choices that were highly controversial; religious sanction helped to make the regime's actions more palatable to the general public.

In the run-up to the presidential election, the regime publicized in the state-run media statements by religious figures about the importance of voting.[58] For example, an article that ran in *Al-Ahram* summarizing the religious pronouncements made during the presidential election campaign reported that major Islamic religious scholars agreed that participation in the election was highly important and considered a vital duty.[59] Some went as far as to characterize nonvoting as un-Islamic. These figures included Sheikh Tantawi of Al-Azhar as well the the former head of Al-Azhar University, members of the Islamic research group associated with Al-Azhar, and the chairman of the council of Islamic studies.[60] This trend of using religious figures to provide support to the regime exists at lower levels in the religious hierarchy as well. According to one press report, Ahmed 'Ezz, an influential NDP figure, provides monthly salaries to hundreds of imams in addition to inspectors and directors of the Ministry of Endowments in a bid to maintain support of the NDP at election time.[61] Imams are reported to receive LE 150 per month, whereas inspectors and directors receive LE 300 and LE 500 per month, respectively.[62]

In addition to seeking the public support of Islamic religious figures, the influential head of the Coptic Christian church in Egypt – Pope Shenouda – went beyond encouraging turnout and endorsed President Mubarak.[63] In addition, Mubarak was endorsed by the Coptic leader of Alexandria and seventy-one Coptic bishops and archbishops.[64] It has also been reported that a large percentage of Egypt's 2,500 Coptic priests are members of the NDP.[65] This suggests support for the conclusion that Shenouda's backing of the president and the NDP has been institutionalized across the church hierarchy (Tadros 2009). An interview with a high-level regime official suggests that Shenouda was promised

---

[57] Al-Azhar also enjoyed financial benefits as a result of this relationship. In return for acquiescence on these and other controversial policies, the government channeled money to Al-Azhar. The funds allowed Al-Azhar to develop a nationwide program for primary and secondary religious education. It also permitted Al-Azhar to build and maintain thousands of mosques and religious schools throughout sub-Saharan Africa and Southeast Asia.

[58] So who is most affected by these religious pronouncements? Similar to the Geddes and Zaller (1989) argument that those with high levels of political awareness may be able to resist these types of messages, it is likely that individuals who are exposed to these dictates, yet not sufficiently sophisticated as to resist them, may be susceptible to these types of influences.

[59] *Al-Ahram*, September 11, 2005.

[60] Ibid.

[61] *Al-Masry Al-Youm*, February 3, 2009.

[62] Ibid.

[63] *Al-Ahram*, September 11, 2005.

[64] *Al-Ahram*, September 6, 2005.

[65] Ibid.

government approval to crack down on a dissident faction of the Coptic church in exchange for his strong public support of the president.[66]

6.4 EMPIRICAL TESTS

Parliamentary elections in Egypt, then, are characterized by vote buying and clientelistic networks of exchange of goods and services for political support. The votes of the poor and illiterate are generally the "cheapest" to buy as the marginal benefit or payoff for selling a vote is higher for the underprivileged segments of the population. This suggests that members of the underprivileged class turn out at disproportionately high rates in Egyptian parliamentary elections. Efforts to turn out voters in Egypt's first presidential election targeted the same voters by different means. Threats of economic sanction for nonvoting affect the poor disproportionately, and the underprivileged are more suspectable to the messages advertised by the state to support Mubarak.

6.4.1 The Effect of Literacy on Turnout

One observable implication of the arguments presented is that Egypt's underprivileged – who are disproportionately susceptible to vote buying and state influence – turn out to vote at higher rates than the rich. In order to test this implication, I have compiled data provided to the United National Development Program (UNDP) by the Egyptian Ministry of Planning on both literacy and voter turnout for the 2000 parliamentary elections and the 2002 municipal council elections. These data are reported at the level of the local administrative unit. For the 2005 election, I have matched the most recent data on literacy from the UNDP at the level of various administrative units with data on turnout levels for electoral districts as reported by the Egyptian government on a state-sponsored Web site (the data have subsequently been removed from this location). Although district lines and local administrative units are often not a precise match, there is no compelling reason to believe that data on literacy would be biased in any particular direction through this process.[67] Finally, for the 2005 presidential election, the government did not release turnout data on the local level. The most reliable data on turnout in this election was collected by the ICEM – a collection of independent NGOs that stationed monitors at almost 30 percent of Egypt's 10,000 polling stations. The data on turnout for the presidential election is presented at the governorate level.[68]

Regarding the primary independent variable in the study – literacy – approximately 65 percent of Egyptians are literate, although there is considerable

---

[66] Interview with NDP member, September 2, 2005.

[67] For urban areas, I used the administrative unit known as the *ḥayy*, whereas I used the *markaz* and *qism* for rural and desert areas, respectively.

[68] Governorates in Egypt are similar to states in the United States. At the time of the 2005 election, there were twenty-six governorates in Egypt.

TABLE 6.1. *Average Turnout for Four Egyptian Elections*

Election	Turnout across Local Units (%)
2000 Parliamentary	25
2002 Municipal Council	45
2005 Presidential	24
2005 Parliamentary	25

variation across regions of the country. In fact, district literacy rates range from about 20 percent to more than 90 percent, depending on the area.

Literacy status tends to be a blunt, but effective, measure of socioeconomic status. The ability to read is something that individuals are highly unlikely to lie about because it can be so easily verified on the spot. In fact, respondents may even anticipate having to sign or fill out a document if they claim that they are literate. These factors have led other researchers favor of the percentage of the population that is literate over other indicators of socio-economic status (Sims 2003).

Table 6.1 summarizes the percentage turnout for each of the four elections used in my data analysis.[69] Overall levels of turnout in Egyptian elections are low. Possible explanations for low turnout include widespread cynicism about the efficacy of political participation, lack of confidence in the fairness of procedures, and the weakness of party platforms.[70] Nonetheless, considering the low policy stakes involved with these elections, the fact that one-quarter of registered voters do turn out is a nontrivial phenomenon. Although the regime has a record of overstating political participation, it does so more frequently for Shura council elections[71] and referendum turnout figures than for recent elections of the lower house. Egyptian political analysts have also argued that turnout figures have become more accurate since 2000 when the Egyptian judiciary began monitoring elections (Soliman 2006).

Empirical Strategy. The data are aggregated at the level of the local administrative unit, electoral district, or governorate, but the mechanisms proposed refer to the actions undertaken by individual citizens making the decision of whether or not they will turn out to vote. Problems such as this are generally called "ecological inference" problems. In order to analyze these data, I use Gary King's ecological inference estimation strategy, which allows quantities of interest (like the proportion of literates or illiterates who vote) to vary over districts, while at the same time incorporating the logical bounds for these values (1997). Table 6.2 shows the marginals, or information that we currently have at the local level, regarding literacy and turnout. T_i is the level of turnout in district i, and X_i is the percentage of literates in that district. My goal is to infer

[69] These turnout figures are the average across the local units and are not weighted by population.
[70] See Wickham 2002, 85; *Al-Ahram*, August 28, 2005; *Al-Ahram*, December 19, 2005.
[71] See Springborg 1989, 163, for more details.

TABLE 6.2. *Ecological Inference Problem for Turnout*

	Vote	No Vote	
<u>l</u>iterate	β_i^l	$1 - \beta_i^l$	X_i
<u>il</u>literate	β_i^{il}	$1 - \beta_i^{il}$	$1 - X_i$
	T_i	$1 - T_i$	

the quantities of interest within the cells. These quantities of interest include β_i^{il}, the fraction of illiterates who vote in district i, and β_i^l, the fraction of literates who vote in district i. Applying King's ecological inference model to these data yields estimates of these and other quantities of interest.[72] In addition to the EI (ecological inference) results, I also report the results of Goodman's regression, which assumes that the quantities of interest are constant over districts.

Results. The results of this analysis, presented in Table 6.3, suggest that illiterates turned out at more than twice and sometimes at three times the rate of literates in the 2000 and 2005 parliamentary, 2002 municipal council, and 2005 presidential elections. The largest discrepancy between literate and illiterate turnout was in the presidential election, where, according to the statistical analysis, 11 percent of literates voted and 33 percent of illiterates voted. In the 2000 parliamentary elections, 15 percent of literates and 39 percent of illiterates voted; in the 2005 parliamentary race, 18 percent of literates and 37 percent of illiterates voted, according to the estimation.[73] These results are also robust within rural and urban subsets of the data.[74] For example, in the 2000 election, rural illiterate and urban illiterate turnout exceeded rural literate and urban literate turnout by 9 and 14 points, respectively. Although these figures are not intended to be definitive, they are highly suggestive and provide evidence that Egypt's underclasses make up a large percentage of voters within both urban and rural settings.[75]

[72] The results in this section were estimated by using King's *EzI* statistical package.
[73] Egyptian parliamentary elections are held in three separate rounds, an accommodation introduced to allow monitoring by the judiciary. The first round of the election was not seriously marred by government security service intervention, whereas the second and third rounds witnessed violence and government intervention at many polling stations. As a result, I also separately estimated the 2005 results for the first round only and found very similar results to the estimates based on the entire sample (first round: 17 percent for literate voters and 37 percent turnout for illiterate voters). In other words, the relationship between turnout and literacy did not differ meaningfully over different rounds of the election.
[74] Because EI does not allow for the use of control variables, dividing and reanalyzing the data for specific subgroups are a next-best option.
[75] Egyptian municipal elections also exhibit a similar pattern with illiterates almost three times as likely to vote as literates in the 2002 election. Vote buying is common in these elections as well (interview with Mohammed al-Batran, former member of the People's Assembly and Shura Council, May 1, 2006).

TABLE 6.3. *Ecological Inference Results (Dependent Variable Is Turnout)*

	2000 Parliamentary		2002 Municipal		2005 Presidential		2005 Parliamentary	
	Literate	Illiterate	Literate	Illiterate	Literate	Illiterate	Literate	Illiterate
EI	0.148	0.387	0.273	0.743	0.111	0.327	0.182	0.368
	(0.010)	(0.015)	(0.008)	(0.013)	(0.023)	(0.050)	(0.002)	(0.004)
Goodman's regression	0.160	0.375	0.252	0.762	0.139	0.440	0.186	0.384
	(0.011)	(0.012)	(0.027)	(0.041)	(0.067)	(0.136)	(0.015)	(0.024)

Note: Model standard errors are shown in parentheses.

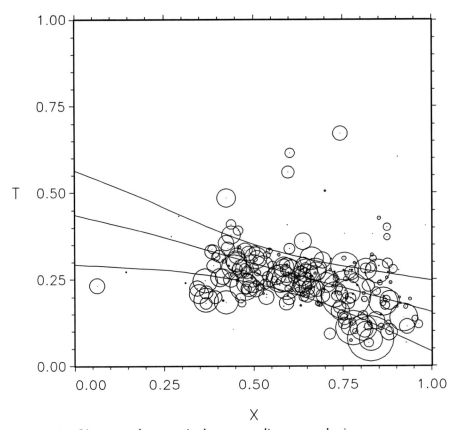

FIGURE 6.1. Literacy and turnout in the 2000 parliamentary elections.

Figure 6.1 is a scatterplot of the relationship between literacy (*X*) and turnout (*T*) from the 2000 parliamentary elections with the maximum likelihood results of the EI model superimposed. Literacy is on the x-axis, and percentage turnout is on the y-axis. The size of each circle is proportional to the district population. The solid line is the expected value of turnout given the level of literacy, and dashed lines are an 80 percent confidence interval around the expected value. The figure suggests that, as literacy increases, turnout decreases across Egyptian electoral districts. Figure 6.2 offers the same information for the 2005 parliamentary elections. Again, literacy is on the x-axis, and percentage turnout is on the y-axis.

The use of Gary King's EI program is not without controversy. Scholars have argued that, if the strict assumptions of the estimation procedure have not been met, then the program is inappropriate and may lead to wrong inferences. In particular, Cho and Gaines (2004) argue that three conditions must be met: a) the data must be informative, b) there should not be evidence of aggregation bias, and c) estimation should only be attempted in the presence of a strong microtheory. Let me consider each of these factors in turn. First, what does

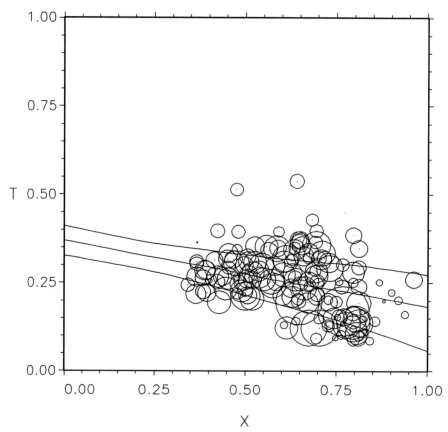

FIGURE 6.2. Literacy and turnout in the 2005 parliamentary elections.

it mean for the data to be informative? Cho and Gaines (2004) write that tomography plots of the data should intersect at a single point or in the same vicinity. Visual inspection of the tomography plots for these data suggest that the lines do intersect in a common area. King (1997) suggests that the data are more informative when there is considerable variation in the explanatory variable. As mentioned previously, there is considerable variation in the level of literacy in Egypt, which ranges from about 20 to more than 90 percent across districts. The next condition put forth by Cho and Gaines (2004) is that the aggregation process did not introduce bias. In other words, literates living among literates cannot be shown to behave differently than literates living among illiterates, and illiterates living among literates do not behave differently than illiterates living among illiterates. Visual inspection of the relationship between literacy and the estimated β^l and β^{il} values suggests that no strong aggregation bias exists.[76] Finally, Cho and Gaines (2004) write that there

[76] All tomography and bias plots are available upon request from the author.

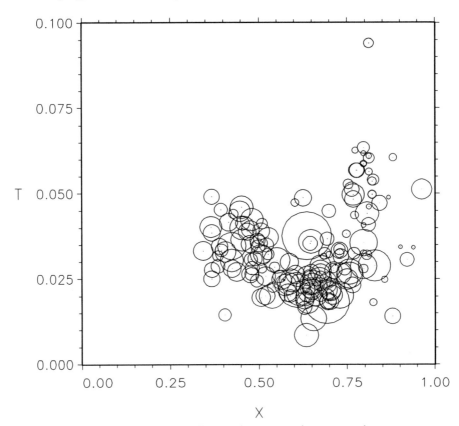

FIGURE 6.3. Literacy and spoiled ballots in the 2005 parliamentary elections.

needs to be a strong microtheory of individual behavior. Details about the microtheory have been presented in the previous sections of this chapter.

6.4.2   Differential Rates of Ballot Nullification

What is the relationship, if any, between literacy rates and spoiled balloting across Egyptian electoral districts and governorates? The dependent variables in this section are the percentage of spoiled ballots out of total ballots cast during each of the 2005 parliamentary and presidential elections. Between 1 and 10 percent of ballots were considered spoiled ballots in the 2005 parliamentary election, depending on the district, with a mean of about 3 percent across districts. For the presidential election, between 1.5 and 5 percent of ballots were spoiled, depending on the governorate, with a mean of about 2.6 percent.

Figure 6.3 is a plot of the relationship between spoiled ballots and literacy across Egyptian electoral districts in the 2005 parliamentary election. Literacy

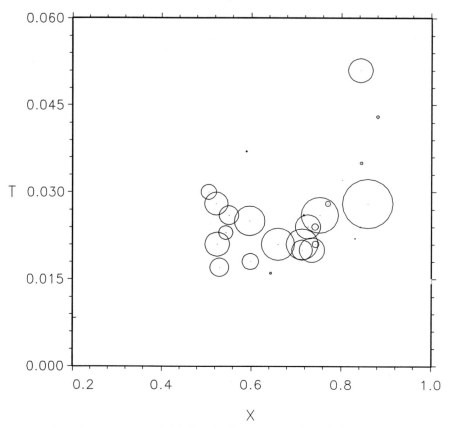

FIGURE 6.4. Literacy and spoiled ballots in the 2005 presidential elections.

is on the x-axis, and percentage of spoiled ballots is on the y-axis.[77] The most striking feature of this plot is the U-shaped relationship between literacy and spoiled balloting. For areas with levels of literacy less than 60 percent, as literacy increases, spoiled balloting decreases, fairly distinctively. For literacy rates of 60 percent and higher, however, there appears to be a positive relationship between literacy and spoiled balloting. A very similar pattern emerges in Figure 6.4, which shows the relationship between literacy and ballot nullification for the 2005 presidential election. Literacy is on the x-axis, and percentage of spoiled ballots is on the y-axis.[78] Spoiled ballots decline with literacy until literacy rates reach approximately 70 percent. Governorates with literacy rates of between 70 and 90 percent see an increase in ballot nullification.

What explains this result? Consistent with previous studies, a likely explanation is that some percentage of illiterate individuals spoil their ballots

[77] Note y-axis scale spans from 0 to 10 percent.
[78] Note y-axis scale spans from 0 to 6 percent.

TABLE 6.4. *Ecological Inference Problem for Spoiled Balloting*

	Spoil	No Spoil	Subtotal (Turnout)	No Vote	
literate	λ_i^l	$1 - \lambda_i^l$	β_i^l	$1 - \beta_i^l$	X_i
illiterate	λ_i^{il}	$1 - \lambda_i^{il}$	β_i^{il}	$1 - \beta_i^{il}$	$1 - X_i$
	S_i		T_i	$1 - T_i$	

unintentionally as a result of voter error. In addition to that, however, we need to address the question of what explains high levels of ballot nullification in highly literate areas. I interpret this result as evidence of a protest vote, or intentional ballot nullification consistent with the qualitative accounts described previously.

Table 6.4 illustrates the ecological inference problem for spoiled balloting. There are three possible outcomes. Voters may turn out to vote and (intentionally or unintentionally) spoil their ballots. Alternatively, they may turn out to vote and submit a valid ballot. Finally, they may choose to stay at home and not turn out at all. λ represents the rate of invalid balloting, and S is the observed total number of spoiled ballots. The nonmonotonic nature of the relationship between literacy and ballot spoiling suggests a complicated statistical relationship that may not be well suited for the use of King's EI method. In particular, diagnostic tests indicate the presence of aggregation bias in these data. As a result, these data are presented without statistical analysis and serve simply as observational evidence for the existence of expressive political behavior among Egyptian voters. As techniques for analyzing data of this type improve, we may, in the future, reanalyze the data to determine the more specific relationship between literacy and ballot spoiling.

6.5 CONCLUSIONS

In Ateyat al-Abnoudy's 1996 documentary, *Days of Democracy*, the filmmaker speaks to everyday Egyptians who describe the use of money to buy votes and how poverty often forces people to sell their votes to local strongmen. The goal of this chapter is not to suggest that the poor or illiterate in Egypt are not politically aware. Indeed, many of the voters in al-Abnoudy's film exhibited considerable political acumen. The ideological predilections of poor voters often take a backseat, however, to more pressing economic concerns. Thus, whereas some voters cast their ballots on an ideological basis, the majority of Egyptian voters expect to receive a direct material benefit for their vote. Although voter turnout is associated with higher levels of education in democratic countries, I find that, in Egypt, illiterates are twice as likely to vote as those who can read. This is because the votes of illiterates tend to be "cheaper" to purchase by political entrepreneurs, and illiterates are also more vulnerable to intimidation by state authorities. This finding is largely consistent with Egyptian commentators, such as Hassan Abu Taleb, who argue that political life in Egypt is dominated by two classes of individuals – the wealthy minority of political elite who buy votes and the poor majority of citizens who sell their votes to the highest bidder.[79] In this chapter, the correlation between literacy and spoiled ballots was also examined, and we find a nonmonotonic relationship; namely, districts with many illiterate voters and very few illiterate voters tend to have the largest percentage of spoiled ballots. This suggests that, in addition to balloting error, some percentage of Egyptians are engaging in forms of political expression through ballot nullification. For citizens who engage in acts of ballot nullification, voting provides an opportunity to hoodwink corrupt vote buyers and to send a signal about distaste for the political system or common practices.

Some Egyptian intellectuals are concerned about the normative implications of voter participation by a largely illiterate electorate. Zaki has argued that this type of participation is harmful to Egypt's political development given the likelihood that these voters will be manipulated (1995, 106). I would argue, however, that even imperfect elections replete with vote buying and clientelistic manipulation still force political elite to court citizens in their districts. Exchange of political support for money, goods, and services represents a net gain for voters who are able to extract some resources out of their elected officials. In addition, having the choice to vote, and perhaps even more important, the choice to spoil one's ballot after selling a vote, provides citizens with some degree of agency. Hermet argues that withholding one's vote is a challenge to power (Hermet and Roouquie 1978, 12), and poor voter turnout may hurt the regime's attempt to institutionalize a succession mechanism through contested presidential elections.[80]

[79] *Al-Ahram*, November 19, 2005.
[80] *Al-Wafd*, October 11, 2005.

7

Elections and Elite Corruption

Why do political entrepreneurs run for parliamentary seats when parliament has almost no influence over policy? Aside from the prestige associated with holding public office, a parliamentary seat offers innumerable opportunities. Serving in parliament can act as a stepping stone to cabinet positions or promotions within the party. But to what end? Ultimately, policy decisions are made at the top, so for those interested in policy change, this is an ineffective route to political influence.

It is common knowledge, however, that holding office can personally enrich an individual, both in developed and developing countries, and that rent seeking (and seizing) can serve as significant motivation to compete for political office. In this chapter, I make three points about rent seeking and the electoral connection in Egypt. First, I argue that Egyptian legislators enjoy a myriad of licit and illicit money-making opportunities. Perhaps most important among these involve laws and norms establishing unusually high guarantees of parliamentary immunity. Although the formal institution of parliamentary immunity – or the granting of protection from prosecution for their actions as parliamentarians – has historically been used to protect legislators from civil actions for libel or defamation, some countries have developed informal norms that allow parliamentarians to engage in corrupt and illegal activities with impunity. In Egypt, a desire to enjoy the benefits of parliamentary immunity, or rather the norms that have come to be associated with immunity, has become a major motivation for legislative office seeking in Egypt. Second, I show that parliamentary rent-seeking opportunities have become more numerous over time, first with the move from socialist to "open door" economic policies and again with economic liberalization and privatization associated with Egypt's structural adjustment program. Finally, I argue that the guarantee of parliamentary immunity can be thought of as a tacit arrangement between the regime and the rent-seeking elite, where corruption on the part of the elite is tolerated in exchange for active or passive political support of the ruling regime. Press freedom is allowed, in part, to monitor the activities of the nonruling elite and serves a "fire alarm" function. Corruption also represents a particularly effective way to bind the rent-seeking elite to the regime because investing members of the elite in below-board activities makes these individuals vulnerable to charges of economic and other crimes under either the current regime or some future democratic or authoritarian government.

7.1 WHY RUN FOR OFFICE? ELECTIONS AND RENT-SEEKING

Formally, the bicameral legislature in Egypt consists of the People's Assembly (*Majlis al-Sha'b*) and the Advisory, or Shura, Council (*Majlis al-Shūrā*). The People's Assembly is the lower house of parliament, and the Shura Council is the upper house. The People's Assembly has 454 seats, 444 of which are elected by popular vote. The remaining 10 seats are appointed by the president. Members of the People's Assembly serve five-year terms, and half of the members must hold the occupation of either worker or peasant.[1] Established in 1980, the Shura Council was endowed with only limited policy-making authority (Bianchi 1989, 86). Of the 264 seats, two-thirds are elected by popular vote, with the remaining one-third appointed by the president. Members of the Shura Council serve six-year terms. Presidential appointees have historically been well-regarded women and Christians or representatives of important occupational groups or national institutions (Bianchi 1989, 86).

Political commentators have written that, in Egypt, "the parliament has very little, if any, independent political power" and that "the irrelevance of parliament to the decisionmaking process is highlighted by the fact that not once has it submitted and passed a bill that was not *a priori* fully endorsed by the government" (Zaki 1998, 134). Why then do political entrepreneurs run for office and spend vast amounts of capital on campaigning when legislative institutions have so little influence on policy? Egyptian legislators are highly circumscribed in their ability to influence policy, and a large percentage of office seekers in Egypt run for parliament with the goal of gaining access to state resources, some with the intention of engaging in corruption under the protection offered by parliamentary immunity.

7.1.1 Ability to Influence Policy Highly Circumscribed

Although the Egyptian legislature enjoys broad policy-making authority in principle, in practice the president controls a compliant majority in parliament that readily translates his legislative requests into formal laws. The president has a number of options for pushing through his policy agenda; for example, when parliament is not in session, the president is permitted by law to issue decrees that act as legislation. The president enjoys veto power over parliamentary enactments, and he enjoys the right to dismiss parliament at will. In addition,

---

[1] There is considerable flexibility, however, in how these terms are interpreted.

the president is the head of the regime's hegemonic party, which dominates parliament.

The legislature has exhibited some limited power to investigate charges of corruption brought against members of the executive branch. The People's Assembly can request the formation of investigative committees to look into the activities of ministers who have been brought up on criminal charges. In addition, it retains the right to question a cabinet member in an accusatory manner on issues involving poor management or corruption. The People's Assembly also enjoys the right to send a formal request for further explanation of any issue to the cabinet. It is often members of the opposition parties who take advantage of these narrow institutional opportunities to challenge the executive branch. Despite these limited powers, however, the executive branch clearly dominates the legislature. Not only does the executive branch draft most bills, the party of the president, the NDP, enjoys a strong hand in running the legislature. The Egyptian parliament, therefore, is weak in relation to the executive branch and largely serves as rubber stamp for government policies.

With the ability to influence policy so circumscribed, many candidates seek office to achieve personal benefit, either professionally, financially, or both. Although opposition parliamentarians, particularly those representing the Muslim Brotherhood, may seek office as a means of personal advancement or to improve the lot of their constituents, their formal influence is largely limited to submitting interpellations of cabinet members and drawing attention to issues of interest through their prominence. Because policy decisions in Egypt are made at the very highest levels of government, it is unlikely that even the most competent of political entrepreneurs would be able to influence policy by these means.[2]

7.1.2 Licit and Illicit Rent-Seeking Opportunities in Parliament

Despite the lack of policy-making power afforded parliamentarians, the large number of individuals seeking parliamentary seats and their considerable willingness to spend money to win those seats suggests that parliament holds other benefits. Winning a parliamentary seat as a member of the NDP, and the Arab Socialist Union before it, has offered opportunities for upward mobility for successful candidates.[3] El-Karanshawy (1997, 9) relates the story of how an

---

[2] Even the growing cadre of businessmen in parliament generally ignore policy promotion in favor of rent seeking. According to Zaki, businessmen in parliament are often accused of seeking ways to circumvent the implementation of existing regulations that hinder their personal rent-seeking opportunities (1998, 136). This has led some to argue that businessmen in parliament do not represent a programmatically coherent political force, but rather individuals pursuing their own economic interests. See the *Arab Strategic Report*, Volume IX, No. 106, October 2003.

[3] This is not to say that winning a parliamentary seat is the only strategy that a rent-seeking individual might pursue. Chapter 3 discusses avenues of upward mobility within the NDP in which high-level party positions also offer opportunities for personal enrichment.

ambitious party activist was able to win office and over time become a businessman and millionaire. Hinnebusch finds that a parliamentary seat might be "seen as a base from which to cultivate strategic connections in the power elite and to build or consolidate roles as brokers and patrons in their constituencies" (1988a, 180). Ismail argues that seeking a seat offers the opportunity for a formal seat of authority with the goal of joining the commercial bourgeoisie (2006, 51). As these authors suggest, opportunities to amass personal wealth are an important benefit of winning public office in Egypt. And, although not all parliamentary candidates are in search of personal enrichment when entering electoral politics, the conventional wisdom remains that this is an important, if not primary, motivation for the vast majority.

Some of the financial benefits of holding a parliamentary seat arise as a result of access to high-level bureaucrats or inside government information. Advance knowledge of public land sales or state-sector privatization give parliamentarians an edge over others who might benefit financially from such opportunities. Parliamentarians also have access to cabinet ministers and governors as a result of weekly "MP hours" set aside by these high-level administrators. During weekly MP hours, parliamentarians have an opportunity to seek building and work permits, export subsidies, authorization to open new business ventures, pilgrimage visas, and allocation of land in previously undeveloped zones. Translating access to rights and permits into rents, however, is largely a below-board activity. Parliamentarians make money in one of three ways. They can charge fees for the rights and permits, which are then sold to a third party. Alternatively, the parliamentarian can become a partner in a business venture that benefits from the privileged access. Finally, the legislator can use the rights, permits or export subsidies himself or for a business that he wholly owns. One increasingly common avenue for enrichment occurs when a parliamentarian receives a newly zoned piece of real estate, often at a cut rate, which he then resells at a much higher price down the line.[4]

Parliamentarians enjoy other benefits of the job. For example, in Egypt, businessmen see a seat in parliament as "an easy and speedy way to get bank loans."[5] Parliamentarians are often able to secure loans without collateral[6] and are able to avoid the types of approvals and guarantees required of other credit seekers. Other reports suggest that parliamentarians enjoy an edge in the scramble for contracts with the government.[7] One fortunate parliamentarian was given control over the distribution of apartments in a public housing project (Singerman 1995, 258), a benefit that provides the possibility for considerable economic dividends. Another was able to grow his business by evading payment on customs duties and taxes (Singerman 1995, 257).

[4] See *Al-Masry Al-Youm*, September 6, 2008, for more details about the land dealings of three prominent parliamentarians.
[5] *Al-Ahram Weekly*, September 28–October 4, 1995.
[6] Interview with member of NDP Policies Secretariat, May 23, 2007.
[7] *Egyptian Gazette*, February 5, 2007.

Successful businessmen increasingly seek seats in parliament to ensure continued growth of their financial ventures.[8] The rich seek to protect their interests by securing opportunities for influence in parliament, as one expert put it, to "cover your candle" (*dārī 'alā shamaàtak*) in order to keep it burning.[9] Being a member of parliament allows one to do just that, protect existing business interests and cultivate new opportunities.[10] According to 'Amr Hashim Rabi, "it is a fact that most of the businessmen who joined parliament in recent years did so in order to further their businesses."[11] Rabi' also argues that, when businessmen spend huge amounts of money on election campaigns, they expect a return for that investment.[12] This has led eminent journalist Salama Ahmed Salama to argue that Egypt's elite have committed a form of treason against society by succumbing to the temptation of financial gain.[13]

The opposition daily, *Al-Wafd*, has been particularly strident in its criticism of profiteering from positions in parliament.[14] An article about the so-called "business" (i.e., *bîznîs*) deputies describes how these individuals exploit parliamentary membership to conclude deals with the government and compares the dealings of these legislators with those of the mafia.[15] Another article accuses the government of turning a blind eye to parliamentary corruption, allowing parliamentarians to accumulate huge sums of wealth outside of Egypt as a result of their shady business dealings.[16] The sudden wealth accumulated by parliamentarians is a subject of considerable suspicion.[17] In fact, the cultivation of competition between business interests for parliamentary seats has been described as a conscious strategy of the NDP,[18] where the party has become a refuge for outlaws.[19] This has led some analysts to describe the NDP as a "a legion of pure opportunists" (Beattie 1991) and as the "steering committee of Egypt's private sector... serving as its conduit for state largesse" (Bianchi 1989, 15).

My objective is not to caricature all parliamentary candidates as fitting a particular mold. Rather this characterization of the modal candidate is meant to reflect the attitudes and opinions expressed by Egyptian editorialists, scholars,

---

[8] A related development has been the emergence of what might be called the "super-MP" or members of parliament who have enjoyed tremendous economic success and are able to exploit crony capitalist relationships with government agencies. Interview with Sherif Wali, Shura Council member, May 24, 2007.

[9] Interview with Moheb Zaki, Ibn Khaldun Center for Development Studies, May 23, 2007.

[10] Interview with Egyptian Foreign Ministry official, May 22, 2007.

[11] *Al-Ahram Weekly*, February 8–14, 2007.

[12] Ibid.

[13] *Egyptian Gazette*, February 5, 2007.

[14] Like many opposition newspapers in Egypt, even the regular reporting in *Al-Wafd* takes on an editorial flavor.

[15] *Al-Wafd*, March 10, 2006.

[16] *Al-Wafd*, July 11, 2006.

[17] *Al-Wafd*, June 19, 2005.

[18] *Al-Wafd*, November 24, 2005.

[19] *Al-Wafd*, September 30, 2005.

and ordinary citizens. There is no doubt that some parliamentary candidates are primarily interested in improving the well-being of their constituencies rather than their own wealth creation or personal aggrandizement. This appears to be particularly true for individuals who run in opposition to the existing power structure. And certainly motivations for seeking office are complicated. Even within the NDP, individual parliamentarians may be highly committed to the economic development of their districts; this commitment does not rule out the desire to *also* accumulate personal or family wealth often out of a need to pay back debts accumulated during a parliamentary campaign. Although the desire to improve conditions in one's home constituency is no doubt a significant motivation, or at least partial motivation, for office seeking, the conventional wisdom suggests that this desire exists in conjunction with or even subordinate to the desire for wealth accumulation.

The financial benefits of holding a parliamentary seat are also highly corre-lated with a desire for social prestige. According to one study, the pursuit of personal economic interests and the gaining of social prestige are both impor-tant factors leading individuals to seek parliamentary seats (el-Menoufi and al-Sawi 2004, 13–14). Yet increasingly, social prestige in Egypt is associated with personal wealth; whereas personal status used to be determined by fam-ily reputation, prestige in Egypt is increasingly determined by financial influ-ence.[20] This suggests that the distinction between parliamentary office seeking for wealth or prestige may be an artificial one.

7.2 PARLIAMENTARY IMMUNITY AND ABUSES OF IMMUNITY

For parliamentarians interested in making money in ways that go beyond the legal and accepted informal perquisites of holding office, the protection of par-liamentary immunity offers a number of potential avenues for such behavior.[21] Many businessmen seek to be members of parliament just to enjoy parliamen-tary immunity to help them in their business ventures (el-Menoufi and al-Sawi 2004, 12; Shehata 2008). The increasing importance of parliamentary immu-nity has heightened competition for votes over time (Soliman 2006). In addi-tion, structural adjustment has led to a shrinking of ministry budgets; whereas parliamentarians used to rely on ministers to offer them benefits or jobs that could be sold or bartered, increasingly, immunity is the primary draw.[22] This is not to say that abuses of parliamentary immunity have not long-existed.

[20] Interview with Gehad Auda, NDP Media Secretariat and Professor of Political Science, Helwan University, May 23, 2007.
[21] This is even more true for cabinet ministers who also serve in parliament. It is not uncommon – and not prohibited – for cabinet ministers to run for office. As ministries in Egypt generally operate as the private fiefdoms of their ministers, this creates even more rent-seeking opportuni-ties. In addition, there do not exist well-established institutional strategies for bringing ministers up on charges of malfeasance. See *Al-Wafd*, May 25, 2006, and *Al-Wafd*, May 31, 2006. Leg-islative institutions like the interpellation and request to form a fact-finding committee are used with this objective with only limited effectiveness.
[22] Interview with Sherif Wali, Shura Council member, May 24, 2007.

Heikal, writing of Egypt in the 1970s and early 1980s, describes one deputy who amassed millions selling drugs and another who was caught smuggling drugs (1983, 128–9). The importance of immunity has increased over time, and this has become clear as professionals of all kinds in Egypt have largely morphed into businessmen (Sonbol 2000, 158); for example, a parliamentarian whose official profession reads university professor may run a for-profit educational institute as well as a manufacturing business on the side.[23]

7.2.1 Parliamentary Immunity

In countries with established rules regarding parliamentary immunity, members of the legislature are granted protection from prosecution under a variety of circumstances particular to each country. Parliamentary immunity was originally created to protect legislators from abuses of power by monarchs. The institution continued as a way to shield representatives from false accusations and trumped-up legal charges (Wigley 2003). In democracies, parliamentary immunity is intended to allow representatives to reflect the positions of their constituents even when these positions may depart from wider popular sentiment (Wigley 2003).

Although parliamentary immunity has been interpreted somewhat differently from state to state, in countries descendent from the British system, parliamentarians are only protected for acts related to legislative activity. Parliamentarians in Westminster-system countries commonly enjoy what is known as "privilege of freedom of speech or parliamentary non-accountability."[24] For example, a legislator would be protected from accusations of slander and libel for speeches made on the floor while discussing legislation. In the United States, all nonlegislative acts, whether performed inside or outside of the chamber, are vulnerable to legal examination (Wigley 2003). The law is interpreted similarly in the UK, India, South Africa, New Zealand, Ireland, Australia, Canada, and the Netherlands (Wigley 2003).

France and countries that have taken the French system as a basis for their constitution offer parliamentarians even more protection than is afforded to former commonwealth countries. In addition to protection from libel charges, for parliamentarians in these systems, there are often severe restrictions regarding the ability of the police to arrest, detain, or otherwise charge them for crimes. In order for prosecution against a parliamentarian to proceed, a court, or often the parliament itself, has to lift immunity. This is known as parliamentary inviolability.[25] In France, for example, members of parliament cannot be arrested until stringent administrative hurdles are met or unless the parliamentarian was actually seen committing the crime (*flagrante delicto*). In other words, parliamentarians are protected for both legislative and nonlegislative

---

[23] This suggests that commonly published figures of the increasing number of businessmen in parliament significantly underestimate the business interests of parliamentarians.

[24] Inter-Parliamentary Union, 2006.

[25] Ibid.

acts (Wigley 2003). Although parliamentarians are not criminally responsible for their official acts, they are technically responsible for their acts as private citizens.

These strong limitations on the types of actions that can be taken against parliamentarians have led to abuse in some countries. In France, parliamentary immunity is controversial. Corrupt businessmen may try to win office to protect themselves from prosecution, and past presidents may seek lifelong parliamentary positions for protection from past corruption scandals. Controversy surrounding parliamentary inviolability has been even more pronounced in developing countries, which often favor the perception that parliamentarians are "above the law."[26] In developing countries with weak institutions, abuses are common (USAID 2006). In Ukraine, a former government official accused of laundering at least $114 million ran for and won a parliamentary seat in 1998. In Armenia, there is a widespread perception that a "large minority of members are in the National Assembly primarily to protect corrupt business interests" (USAID 2006). In Turkey, lifting parliamentary immunity has been touted as an anticorruption measure; it is rumored that parliamentary careers have been launched specifically to avoid fraud charges.[27] In Russia, a parliamentarian enjoys "immunity for the duration of his duties" and cannot face charges, be arrested, detained, or questioned unless caught red-handed.[28] For example, when a state prosecutor attempted to criminally charge a parliamentarian who ran a large-scale pyramid scheme, it took multiple attempts and considerable political wrangling in the Duma to finally have his immunity lifted.[29]

The French-based model is more prevalent than the British system worldwide, and the Egyptian constitution is based heavily on the French system. Although, in principle, the French model of parliamentary immunity could provide appropriate levels of protection for legislators, even in a democratic setting there is the potential for abuse. When translated into an autocratic setting, the French model of parliamentary immunity has become a cover for elite corruption. In Egypt, rent-seeking behavior on the part of parliamentarians has made corruption endemic to an entire class of political elite. It is difficult to strip parliamentarians of their immunity without the tacit approval of the ruling regime, so many legislators know that they will be protected by either their colleagues or the ruling elite if they commit crimes.

7.2.2   Abuses of Immunity

Although the abuse of immunity is considered a highly vulgar way to make financial gains,[30] numerous sources suggest that it is common practice in

---

[26] Ibid.
[27] *Southeast European Times*, July 21, 2005.
[28] *Perspective* 10(1), September, 1999.
[29] Ibid.
[30] Interview with 'Ali al-Din Hilal, Minister of Youth and Professor of Political Science, Cairo University, April 30, 2007.

Mubarak's Egypt. The opposition press has argued that what is known about abuses of immunity represents just a small fraction of actual infractions.[31] The abuses of immunity undertaken by parliamentarians include everything from relatively minor infractions, like forgery, to large-scale fraud and embezzlement rings.[32] In the early 1990s, parliamentarians who were members of the NDP became embroiled in a scandal known popularly as the "drug deputies." These parliamentarians were accused of running illicit narcotics rings. One study suggests that, between 1993 and 2002, Egyptians spent billions on illegal drugs, including hashish and heroin.[33] This suggests that the sale of illicit drugs is an extremely lucrative business for which parliamentary immunity may be particularly appealing.

Deputies have also been found illegally selling permits for the annual pilgrimage to Mecca as well as for bouncing thousands in checks (Langohr 2000). Two parliamentarians from Fayoum were stripped of immunity for forging documents and illegally selling public assets.[34] More than 1,000 rioters in Kaliyoubia attacked the home of a parliamentarian for having connections to a pyramid scheme that defrauded locals out of more than $50 million.[35] Parliamentarians have been reported to have imported expensive vehicles without paying customs duties (which, in some cases, may exceed LE 1 million) only to replace their standard license plates with new ones indicating their parliamentary status, leaving them free to engage in egregious traffic violations.[36] One parliamentarian was even accused of hiring thugs to forcefully evict residents of an apartment building he had purchased and shooting at the building's residents with a firearm.[37]

In a particularly notorious case, Ibrahim Nafi' – Shura Council member and former editor-in-chief of *Al-Ahram* – came under investigation for alleged financial fraud.[38] Mustafa Bakri – editor-in-chief of the independent weekly newspaper *Al-Usbu'* – published documents suggesting that Nafi' had illegally profited from his position as editor; in addition to his LE 2 million/month salary and commissions, Bakri alleges that Nafi' supplemented his income by embezzling hundreds of millions of US dollars, during his term as editor of the paper and chairman of the board of directors of the Al-Ahram Institute.[39] His net worth in 1978 was LE 3,100 when he began working for Al-Ahram.[40]

In an incident widely known as the "shoe" scandal, independent parliamentarian Tal'at Sadat accused the chairman of the planning and budget committee, Ahmed 'Ezz, of stock market manipulations, suspect real estate deals, and

[31] *Al-Wafd*, February 19, 2004.
[32] *Al-Wafd*, March 10, 2005.
[33] *Egyptian Gazette*, February 3, 2008.
[34] *Al-Ahram Weekly*, May 30–June 5, 2002.
[35] *Daily News Egypt*, December 14, 2007; *Egyptian Gazette*, December 16, 2007.
[36] *Egyptian Gazette*, April 14, 2008.
[37] *Al-Ahram Weekly*, August 12–18, 1999.
[38] *Al Ahram Weekly*, March 23–29, 2006; *Al-Masry Al-Youm*, July 14, 2006.
[39] MEMRI Special Dispatch Series, No. 1125, March 24; *Egypt Today*, July 2006.
[40] Ibid.

incredible wealth accumulation in a very short period of time.[41] This incident is known as the "shoe" scandal because it is rumored that Sadat removed one of his shoes to hit 'Ezz with during a verbal altercation. It is alleged that steel magnate 'Ezz earned more than LE 1 billion as a result of engineered stock market fluctuations on a day known as "Black Tuesday," when the Cairo and Alexandria stock exchanges lost 7.5 percent of their value; it is also alleged that 'Ezz purchased state-owned land for LE 5 per feddan, only to resell it for LE 1,500 per feddan.[42] 'Ezz – a topic of considerable discussion in the opposition press – is also suspected of promoting a restrictive press law that would jail journalists for questioning the financial integrity of public officials.[43] Controversy surrounding 'Ezz reemerged in late 2007 when the price of steel increased sharply, and he was accused of monopolistic practices.[44]

In 2007, another scandal erupted when Hani Sorour – a member of parliament and CEO of a major medical supply company – was accused of selling 300,000 contaminated blood bags to the Ministry of Health.[45] Negative publicity surrounding the scandal led to a 90 percent decline in blood donations.[46] According to technical reports, the bags suffered from a number of defects, including high alkalinity, and at least 28 patients who used the bags were poisoned.[47] The People's Assembly eventually stripped Sorour of parliamentary immunity; he was accused of exploiting his parliamentary and NDP membership to bribe the Ministry of Health into accepting his company's blood bags even though officials knew the bags did not meet international standards.[48] Investigations have uncovered that Sorour bribed officials with foreign trips to attend medical conferences and that, in return, officials allowed Sorour's company to win tenders to provide faulty equipment.[49]

Moheb Zaki's study of the Egyptian business elite offers important insights into the motivations of businessmen who seek office and is one of the few academic studies that address the issue of parliamentary immunity and corruption. He writes:

> The spectacle of businessmen running for parliament spending millions of pounds on their campaign, and sometimes resorting to gang violence against

---

[41] *Al-Masry Al-Youm*, May 31, 2006; Sadat is the nephew of late President Anwar al-Sadat.
[42] *Al-Ahram Weekly*, June 8–14, 2006.
[43] *Al-Ahram Weekly*, July 20–26, 2006.
[44] The civil society group Citizens against High Cost of Living prepared a mock trial of 'Ezz over what has been described as his monopolization of steel. In addition, independent parliamentarians have requested 'Ezz be investigated by the Minister of Trade and Industry. In response, the Ministry of Trade and Industry established a hotline for consumer complaints regarding steel pricing. See *Al-Masry Al-Youm*, January 6, 2008; *Al-Masry Al-Youm*, May 26, 2008; *Egyptian Gazette*, May 27, 2008; *Al-Ahram Weekly*, May 29–June 4, 2008.
[45] *Al-Ahram Weekly*, January 25–31, 2007.
[46] Ibid.
[47] *Al-Ahram Weekly*, October 18–24, 2007; *Al-Masry Al-Youm*, June 5, 2007.
[48] *Al-Ahram Weekly*, February 8–14, 2007.
[49] *Al-Masry Al-Youm*, June 6, 2007; *Al-Masry Al-Youm*, January 7, 2008.

their competitors, suggests dubious motives for wanting to get into parliament. The question is why do these candidates want political power so badly?[50]

The response of one informant:

Elections have become turbulent, violent, and corrupt, and many of those running for parliament are merely seeking the immunity which is accorded to its members in order to enrich themselves through corrupt means.[51]

Many believe that corrupt businessmen run for office for the purpose of avoiding future prosecution for illegal offenses they previously committed or plan to commit. A construction magnate who had been imprisoned for forgery won a seat in a major Cairo suburb.[52] Businessman Ibrahim Kamel was stripped of parliamentary immunity three times for various offenses, yet sought office again in 1995.[53] Rashad 'Othman – previously convicted of drug trafficking, smuggling, and expropriating state lands – sought a seat in an Alexandria district by-election.[54]

Financial Sector Scandals. In a series of corruption convictions known as the "loan deputies" scandal, five members of parliament were sentenced to jail for taking millions in "sweetheart" loans.[55] Charges against the parliamentarians included misappropriation of funds and facilitating the illegal acquisition of public funds.[56] The parliamentarians had established front companies to launder millions in illegal loans.[57] Stripped of their immunity in 1996, the loan deputies were not sentenced until June 2000[58] with a higher court finally confirming the judgment in July 2002.[59]

There is little doubt that many of the individuals involved in this scandal sought political office for the express purpose of amassing personal wealth via illegal channels. Even the formal court ruling stated, "It is unjust to describe these criminals as genuine members of parliament. They got into parliament for the purpose of obtaining parliamentary immunity to be able to exploit the people's money in banks."[60] How typical is this type of behavior? One official is quoted as saying that the "loan deputies" scandal revealed just the tip of the iceberg in financial sector corruption.[61]

In another financial sector scandal, the chairman of the parliament's economic affairs committee, 'Abdallah Tayel, was sentenced to a decade in jail for

[50] Zaki 1998, 148.
[51] Ibid.
[52] *Al-Ahram Weekly*, January 24–30, 2002.
[53] *Al-Ahram Weekly*, September 28–October 4, 1995.
[54] Ibid.
[55] *Middle East Report*, November 7, 2000; *Al-Ahram Weekly*, August 8–14, 2002.
[56] *Al-Ahram Weekly*, June 29–July 5, 2000.
[57] Ibid.
[58] Ibid.
[59] *Al-Ahram Weekly*, January 23–29, 2003.
[60] *Al-Ahram Weekly*, August 8–14 2002.
[61] Ibid.

forgery and embezzlement, among other crimes.[62] Tayel – rumored to be a close associate of NDP heavyweight Kamal al-Shazli – is said to have received millions in loans without collateral; Tayel was the executive manager of the bank in question at the time.[63] It is also believed that Tayel created false banking documentation to cover up his activities.[64] What was so particularly disconcerting about the Tayel case is the close association between Tayel and the ruling regime. It was said that Tayel was "hand-picked" by the NDP to serve as chairman of the economic affairs committee; there was also speculation that Tayel was in line to become the next governor of Egypt's central bank.[65]

Another NDP parliamentarian, 'Abd al-Wahhab Quta, was also implicated in the Tayel scandal. It was alleged that Quta paid back a dollar-denominated loan at an exchange rate more favorable than the official rate.[66] Quta, who became the deputy chairman of the economic affairs committee in 1996, was also reported to be a close affiliate of al-Shazli.[67] Tayel tried to cover up his illicit activity, and, eventually, his parliamentary immunity was lifted.[68] In a particularly harshly worded editorial published during the "loan deputies" scandal, commentator Salama Ahmed Salama wrote:

> The gravest aspect of the case, I believe, is the political cover provided by the National Democratic Party to a number of its deputies, propelling them to key positions in the economy and in the banking sector. Wielding uncontested power, they used their parliamentary immunity to plunder bank funds, almost causing total economic collapse. The security forces compounded the situation by allowing nine of those convicted to flee the country.[69]

In a subsequent section of this project, I will argue that the formal political institution of parliamentary immunity has been distorted to create a tacit alliance between the regime and the rent-seeking elite.

The Red Sea Ferry Tragedy. In a particularly tragic case involving high-level corruption, more than 1,000 Egyptians perished when a ferry boat owned by parliamentarian Mamdouh Isma'il sank in the Red Sea while traveling between Saudi Arabia and the Egyptian coast. Subsequent reports on the causes of the disaster have suggested that negligence sank the vessel. In particular, a committee formed by the Ministry of Transportation found that Isma'il and his shipping company failed to inform the port authority about the sinking, did not comply with safety measures, and even ordered a second ship owned by

---

[62] *Al-Ahram Weekly*, September 18–24, 2003.
[63] Ibid.
[64] *Al-Ahram Weekly*, January 23–29, 2003.
[65] *Al-Ahram Weekly*, September 26–October 2, 2002.
[66] *Al-Ahram Weekly*, January 23–29, 2003.
[67] *Al-Ahram Weekly*, February 6–12, 2003.
[68] Ibid.
[69] *Al-Ahram Weekly*, July 6–12, 2000.

his company that was in the vicinity of the accident not to stop and help passengers.[70] Furthermore, the ship's maritime certificate prohibited it from undertaking the route it was on when it sank, and lifeboats from the ship were not deemed seaworthy.[71] A committee made up of foreign experts accused Isma'il of "gross negligence" and for exceeding the acceptable number of passengers on board.[72] A report prepared by the government, however, did not blame Isma'il for the tragedy but rather portrayed the disaster as "an act of fate."[73] Citing this particular report, authorities did not charge Isma'il with manslaughter but rather of a lesser offense.

Under parliamentary rules, no legal action can be taken against members of the Shura Council unless a request to lift immunity has been submitted and approved. Although the ferry sinking occurred on February 3, 2006, the Shura Council did not lift Isma'il's immunity for more than a month.[74] During this period, Isma'il fled the country. Opposition newspapers argued that, by not stripping Isma'il of his immunity immediately, he was able to flee prosecution.[75] Even commentators and editorialists in state-owned papers criticized government protection of Isma'il. In a harshly worded editorial that ran in a state-owned daily, columnist Mohammed Foda wrote, "In my career as a journalist, I have not seen a citizen commit a crime and the government not only sit by silently but actually go as far as to even pamper the perpetrator as has happened with Mamdouh Isma'il."[76]

Ultimately, Isma'il was required to transfer LE 330 million (about $57 million) into a compensation fund for victims of the incident. In return, the Socialist Prosecutor General lifted a freeze on the assets of Isma'il and his family as well as removed them from the list of people unable to travel outside of Egypt.[77] Compensation was to be paid out in the amount of LE 300,000 for the family of each person who perished and LE 50,000 for each survivor of the disaster.[78] The size of the total compensation award gives some indication of the potential profits parliamentarians may enjoy as a result of their corrupt activities. Isma'il was eventually acquitted by a misdemeanor court of all charges in connection with the sinking of the ferry[79]; however, in March 2009, that ruling was overturned and he was sentenced, in absentia, to seven years in prison.

A number of opposition parliamentarians have said that they believe Isma'il's close association with Zakariyya 'Azmi, President Mubarak's chief of staff,

---

[70] *Al-Ahram Weekly*, June 1–7, 2006; *Al-Ahram Weekly*, July 6–12, 2006.
[71] Ibid.
[72] Ibid.
[73] *Al-Ahram Weekly*, June 1–7, 2006.
[74] *Al Ahram Weekly*, March 23–29, 2006.
[75] Ibid.
[76] *Al-Messa*, May 23, 2006.
[77] *Al-Goumhuria*, June 7, 2006.
[78] Ibid.
[79] *Al-Masry Al-Youm*, July 28, 2008.

was the decisive factor allowing for the delay in lifting of Isma'il's parliamentary immunity.[80] Opposition parliamentarians also credit 'Azmi for Isma'il's appointment to the Shura Council.[81] Opposition papers report that Isma'il's ferry service had enjoyed a monopoly on transport between Egypt and Saudi Arabia thanks to his relationship with 'Azmi and connections to the transport ministry.[82] It also has been reported that Isma'il holds dual Egyptian–British citizenship,[83] even though dual citizenship for parliamentarians is prohibited by law; Britain has a policy of not extraditing its own nationals.[84] Nabil 'Abd al-Fattah – the deputy director of Al-Ahram Center for Political and Strategic Studies – has said that "Egyptian businessmen make sure to acquire another nationality, so they can easily flee in case they encounter some sort of crisis in Egypt."[85]

7.3 INCREASING BUSINESS INFLUENCE IN PARLIAMENT

Egyptian economic policy has made the offer of parliamentary immunity even more enticing.[86] First, Sadat's open-door economic policy (*infitāh*) led Egypt toward a more market-based economy. It was during this time that "fat cats" emerged who showed a penchant for exploiting deficiencies in the financial regulation and tax collection systems (Beattie 2000, 150). According to journalist Mohammed Heikal, *infitāh* had a tremendous effect on the economic structure of Egyptian society. In 1975, there were 500 millionaires living in Egypt; by 1981, that number had risen to 17,000 and the country became polarized between the emerging economic elite and the rest of the population (Heikal 1983, 86–8).[87] Zaki argues that, although it is impossible to provide quantifiable evidence to this effect, press and anecdotal reporting both suggest that corruption has been on the increase since the mid-1970s, at all levels of society (1995, 228). Moustafa concurs, arguing that corruption was exacerbated by *infitāh* as the new economic policies "increased the opportunities for graft exponentially" (2007, 5). This "parasitical" class is seen as lavishly consumerist (Zaalouk 1989).

[80] *Al Ahram Weekly*, March 23–29, 2006.
[81] Ibid.
[82] *Al-Wafd*, May 26, 2006.
[83] *Al-Ahram Weekly*, June 1–7, 2006.
[84] *Al-Wafd*, June 12, 2006.
[85] *Al-Ahram Weekly*, June 1–7, 2006.
[86] In addition, changes to Egypt's formal political institutions beginning in the late 1980s have made independent candidates more viable, and this change has benefited businessmen. The 1984 election was held under a party-list PR system; this system was generally believed to hurt businessmen who often ran as independent candidates. The 1987 election was a parallel system that used party lists and some single-member districts. Egypt's Supreme Constitutional Court ruled that this system discriminated against independents, and, in 1990, candidates competed under the two-round system.
[87] Heikal estimates that the "fat cats" and their hangers-on numbered about 150,000 during this period (1983, 88).

The introduction of structural adjustment and other neoliberal reforms in the late 1980s and 1990s also offered openings for rent seeking. The privatization of public companies, for example, provides opportunities for personal gain through bribes and market manipulations (Weyland 1998). Although it would be incorrect to say that economic liberalization as part of structural adjustment reorganized Egypt into a complete market economy, structural adjustment transformed aspects of the relationships between state and societal actors (Elyachar 2005) as well as the overlapping economic interests of business elite and the state (Zaki 1998).

The 2000 elections saw an increase in both the total amount spent on campaigning as well as the sheer number of candidates seeking office (Hamdy 2002). There was also an increase in the number of self-declared businessmen who won seats in parliament (Boutaleb 2002, 23), although, as mentioned previously, this probably still underestimates the number of individuals with strong business interests seeking office. Estimates suggest that candidate expenditure in 2000 was LE 10 billion compared with LE 4 billion in 1995 (Ouda et al. 2002, 66). In the 2005 parliamentary elections, the influence of business was more strongly felt than in any previous election. The NDP candidate list in 2005 included twenty-five press-designated business "tycoons," including Ahmed 'Ezz, associated with the previously described "shoe" scandal, and 'Abd al-Wahhab Quta, the deputy who was implicated in the Tayel banking scandal.[88] In 2005, businessmen spent millions to secure seats in parliament, coming to control more than 50 percent of the legislature.[89] Although historically, candidates were expected to have long-term ties in a community, increasingly it is possible for wealthy businessmen to become carpetbaggers, moving into a district and winning office.

7.4 ALLIANCE BETWEEN THE REGIME AND RENT-SEEKING ELITE

In Egypt, the formal institution of parliamentary immunity and the informal norms that have developed around it represent an important part of a tacit alliance between the regime and the rent-seeking elite.[90] According to Zaki, this relationship has emerged as a "natural" alliance in society.[91] Although a third of the Shura Council and ten seats in the People's Assembly are appointed, thousands of political entrepreneurs vie for 176 seats in the Shura Council and an additional 444 seats in the People's Assembly via the electoral process. Elections provide political cover by which access to rent-seeking opportunities are distributed in Egypt.

What are the terms of this tacit contract between the ruling regime and the rent-seeking elite, and what happens when these terms are broken? A relatively

---

[88] *Al-Ahram Weekly*, October 6–12, 2005.
[89] *Al-Ahram Weekly*, December 8–14, 2005.
[90] Greenwood (2008) has described the tacit alliance between merchants and authoritarian regimes in the broader Arab world.
[91] Interview with Moheb Zaki, Ibn Khaldun Center for Development Studies, May 23, 2007.

free opposition press serves as a "fire alarm" to alert the regime leadership to excess corruption; at the same time, however, some members of the rent-seeking elite continue pushing the regime to provide more protection from such investigations. In addition, those individuals that break the terms of the contract (whether this means stealing too much from the public, too sloppily, or failing to give regime insiders a large enough cut) risk losing their immunity.

7.4.1 Corruption and Complicity

In *The Yacoubian Building*, a work of fiction first published in 2002, parliamentarian Hagg 'Azzam becomes rich by selling drugs and using informal connections to acquire a franchise to sell foreign cars. When Hagg 'Azzam balks at what he deems as too high a share of his profits that are required to go to the "big man," code for the Egyptian president, 'Azzam is blackmailed by the Egyptian security services, who have evidence of his illicit activities. The story of Hagg 'Azzam illustrates how complicity in corruption might serve as one way to bind members of the rent-seeking elite to the regime. Why is the informal institutionalization of corruption a particularly effective strategy? By investing members of the rent-seeking elite in corrupt activities, this also makes these individuals vulnerable to charges of economic crimes either under the current regime or under some future democratic or authoritarian government. By offering corruption as a perk of office holding, current and former parliamentarians who engage in marginal or illicit activity find it harder to defect against the autocratic regime, which has an extensive apparatus for collecting information on their dealings.

State-sanctioned corruption has served as a cornerstone of regime stability in a number of developing countries. The case of Mexico is illustrative. Blum has argued that corruption was a historically long-lived and even structural aspect of the authoritarian regime that "contributed to the overall stability of Mexico's political and economic systems" (1997a, 68). Rather than being a question of a "few bad apples," Blum finds that "corruption and complicity in corruption appear to have been carefully organized" with the following objectives: to "integrate the political elite, reward loyalty to the president, and provide real and lasting means to punish those who buck the informal system" (1997b, 37). Lupsha and Pimentel (1997) argue that organized crime interests in Mexico are seen as "cash cows" to be exploited by political authorities, where corrupt and illegal activities are brought under an informal system of taxation. They argue that similar processes have taken place in authoritarian regimes in Russia, Pakistan, and Burma (Lupsha and Pimentel 1997). Darden (2001) finds that, in the Ukraine, the executive branch has used extensive surveillance of the corrupt economic activities of the elite as a mechanism of presidential control. Encouraged and condoned to engage in corruption, members of the elite were then rendered vulnerable to blackmail by the president. In this way, elite compliance was ensured (Darden 2001). According to Darden (2001), "the mere threat of exposure and prosecution serves to keep the elite firmly under control."[92]

Early on in his presidency, Mubarak undertook a short-lived anticorruption campaign that made it clear that very few members of the elite were free from corruption (Sadowski 1991, 129–30). Fearful of alienating a key support base, these trials quickly came to an end (Sadowski 1991), although Springborg argues that Mubarak maintains the information he needs to move against selected political targets at his discretion (1989, 36). Egypt – like many other governments in the contemporary Arab world – can be described as a *mukhābarāt* state, or a state with a pervasive and professionalized intelligence service. Information provided by the intelligence services and a relatively free press, as described in the following section, provide details on the illicit rent-seeking activities of the elite to the ruling regime.

Given the widespread nature of corruption, what happens when members of the elite want to withdraw their support from the existing regime? Helmke (2002) finds that judges in Argentina began to strategically defect once governments began to lose power, and there was an expectation that some other leadership would follow. Fearful of sanction under a new regime, judges sought to distance themselves from the government that had appointed them. One might imagine that a similar phenomenon could take place in the Egyptian context except for the fact that the existing regime has damning information regarding economic transgressions for much of the existing elite. In this context, institutionalized corruption creates a type of complicity that is highly useful to the autocrat. As the cost of defection rises, the existing regime is stabilized.

7.4.2 Press Freedoms and Restrictions: Fire Alarms and Protection

This discussion would be incomplete without attention to the issue of press freedom and the way the opposition press alerts the regime to lower-level corruption, as well as how certain types of press restrictions exist to protect corrupt interests. Increasingly, press restrictions serve to protect the highest levels of government, in particular, the president, his family, and his closest associates, from charges of corruption. Allegations of corruption targeted at parliamentarians and other officials are deterred, but only to a limited extent, and may be used by regime insiders as a form of "fire alarm," alerting them to excessive profiting (or profiting without providing a sufficient "cut" up the chain) by members of the rent-seeking elite.[93]

---

[92] Nalepa (2010) makes a complementary argument with implications for transitional justice. She finds that, in Eastern Europe, anti-Communist activists were reluctant to seek punishment of Communist Party leadership when the activists themselves had "skeletons in the closet" from the pretransition period.

[93] Egorov, Guriev, and Sonin (2006) argue that, in the absence of competitive elections, an autocratic ruler has to gather information from either a centralized secret service agency or a decentralized source like the media. In Egypt, we see the authoritarian regime using elections, secret police, and the media to serve this function.

Although tightly controlled under Nasser and for most of Sadat's time in office, the press has enjoyed considerable freedom under Mubarak. Freedom of expression is generally allowed but is highly tenuous in nature (Zaki 1995, 70). For example, direct criticism of the president and his immediate family is not tolerated, and individuals who have crossed this informal redline have been punished by the ruling elite. On the other hand, criticism of the prime minister, the cabinet, most aspects of the bureaucracy, as well as government policy (on nonsensitive issues), and performance is largely sanctioned. Ossama al-Ghazali Harb – editor of *Al-Siyassa Al-Dawliya* and Shura Council member – believes that press freedom does not represent a major threat to the regime given the high levels of illiteracy in society and the limited circulation of newspapers.[94]

Press freedom offers other important benefits to an authoritarian leadership like the one in Egypt. In a highly compelling account, Rosberg (1995) addresses the puzzle of why the Egyptian state would submit itself to the rule of law, which limits its discretionary power. He shows that one reason why the judiciary was allowed to reemerge as a powerful actor was to create a system for monitoring the bureaucracy. In many ways, a relatively free press serves a similar purpose. Because it is potentially costly for an authoritarian elite to monitor the economic activity of key members of society, a vigilant press can serve a similar role, informing high-level officials of who is making money and how. Press articles provide information and leverage to the ruling elite acting as a "fire alarm" (McCubbins and Schwartz 1984). If a particular deputy is benefiting excessively from his post or taking advantage of immunity beyond accepted norms, the ruling elite can learn of this behavior from the press. In addition, if one assumes that high-level regime insiders get a "cut" of profits based on corrupt activities, as is widely believed to be the case in Egypt, investigations appearing in the opposition press may provide these high-level individuals with leverage in negotiations for profit sharing. Corruption becomes self-limiting because parliamentarians benefiting excessively may also be reined in by public outcry when scandals are reported in newspapers.[95]

This type of fire alarm function is not limited to the press and judiciary in Egypt, nor is it limited just to Egypt out of the broader set of authoritarian regimes. The regime – starting with Nasser – has historically had an elaborate system for receiving complaints; by 1966, there were complaints offices for each ministry, public authority, and governorate, and in one year, 650 complaints offices received 627,000 complaints (Ayubi 1980, 285). Interpellations in parliament can also serve a similar function. Hinnebusch writes that, even under Sadat, the creation of a special investigatory committee in parliament could be useful for the autocrat: "if kept within bounds, oversight activity was by no means without utility to the president: it represented an instrument

---

[94] Interview with Ossama al-Ghazali Harb, Editor and Shura Council member, May 3, 2006.
[95] This effect may be mitigated by the existence of corrupt journalists who blackmail politicians and businessmen for cash or advertising revenue. See *Egypt Today*, July 2006, for more on this point.

for controlling his bureaucracy and a safety valve for the venting and per-haps redress of grievances which might needlessly arouse public discontent" (Hinnebusch 1988a, 179). Rather, members of the opposition in both par-liament and the opposition press are "whistle blowers, using their extensive networks of connections within the private and public sectors to collect infor-mation on the wheelings and dealings of prominent members of the *infitāḥ* class and their allies in the state" (Springborg 1989, 36).[96]

Although formal institutions in Egypt are supposed to maintain responsi-bility for investigating and limiting government corruption, bad practices are frequently being exposed in the press rather than via government investigations (Ayubi 1980, 283). For example, lawmakers are supposed to submit a financial statement regarding their personal wealth, but this is not strictly enforced.[97] Instead, opposition papers are best known for investigative reports critical of public officials as well as stories about corruption scandals. The independent daily *Al-Masry Al-Youm* has published a series of anticorruption articles for instance, including editorials that highlight the links between Egypt's politi-cal and business elites. Opposition papers like *Al-Wafd* and *Al-Ahaly* publish articles exposing corruption in virtually every issue. For example, opposition daily *Al-Ahrar* published a report that revealed the extravagance of particular governors in refurbishing their offices,[98] providing information to the regime leadership about the activities of subordinates that may have been otherwise overlooked.

Articles about corruption on the part of public officials – other than the pres-ident and his closest associates – are generally tolerated. For example, when *Al-Ahrar* published a series of articles on a major construction scandal in the 1970s, this was tolerated, whereas *Al-Ahaly* was shut down after publishing information on scandals regarding the president's close associates (Hinnebusch 1988a, 182). Journalists and editors that publish articles about parliamentar-ians or public officials do expose themselves to the possibility of slander and libel lawsuits. Those who choose to write articles about highly sensitive issues, like Mubarak family corruption and the succession of Gamal Mubarak, have, in some cases, been abducted and beaten.[99]

In 2006, there was considerable debate over the status of an amendment to the press law that governs freedom of expression. The debate revolved around two issues: a) the right of journalists to criticize public officials, such as the president, and b) the right of journalists to report on the financial dealings of public officials, such as parliamentarians. Ahmed 'Ezz led a campaign to enforce

---

[96] Other authoritarian rulers have created similar fire alarm institutions to monitor their subor-dinates. For example, Saddam Hussein used to have an open phone line several hours a week for receiving public complaints (Marr 2004, 151), and King Hussein of Jordan was known to personally answer radio help lines.
[97] *Al-Masry Al-Youm*, January 19, 2008.
[98] *Egyptian Gazette*, June 4, 2007.
[99] "Mubarak's War on Egyptian Liberals," *Civil Society*, January 2005.

prison terms for journalists investigating the financial activities of public figures.[100] 'Ezz had been closely scrutinized by journalists for activities related to his iron and steel factories.[101] The 'Ezz campaign – in particular – led to an outcry from journalists.[102] The slogan "Viva corruption . . . down with freedom of the press," was used during a protest of journalists. In addition, some twenty-five opposition and independent newspapers did not print on June 9, 2006, in protest of the draft law; the opposition daily *Al-Wafd* called this the "June 9 Revolution."[103] Independent daily *Al-Masry Al-Youm* ran a series of articles on the connection between press restrictions and corruption following the one-day strike.[104] The secretary general of the Federation of Arab Journalists called press restrictions part of an alliance (*taḥāluf*) between corrupt officials and the ruling regime.[105] NDP parliamentarian Hisham Khalil defended 'Ezz's campaign to criminalize investigation into public officials' financial matters by arguing that it would prevent rumor mongering.[106]

In a last-minute intervention, Mubarak eliminated the amendment on prison terms for journalists who reported on the financial dealings of public officials, but maintained them for journalists who "insulted" top officials, such as the president. Parliamentarians – reportedly angry about media coverage of their activities – wanted greater protection from personal attacks in the newspapers but were embarrassed when the president failed to support their initiative.[107] This is consistent with the June 2006 court case involving prominent opposition editor Ibrahim 'Issa. A local court sentenced 'Issa, editor of *Al-Destour*, to one year in prison for "insulting the president."[108] The article in question discussed a lawsuit that had been filed against President Mubarak, his wife, their son Gamal, and high-level officials for squandering government resources and foreign aid as well as creating a system of hereditary succession.[109] Two years earlier, Mubarak had promised to amend the press law so that journalists could not be imprisoned for what they wrote. By allowing journalists to report on financial matters involving parliamentarians, but continuing to make insulting the president a criminal offense, the regime maintained existing redlines protecting the president and his family while allowing the fire alarm function to persist.

The year 2007 saw a series of jail sentences and fines imposed on journalists who were deemed to have damaged Egypt's reputation or threatened the

---

[100] *Al-Ahram Weekly*, July 13–19, 2006; *Al-Masry Al-Youm* also reported, on July 10, 2006, of a "secret" meeting between 'Ezz and eighty-five deputies regarding legislation about financial disclosures.
[101] Ibid.
[102] Sawt Al-Umma, quoted in the *Christian Science Monitor*, July 10, 2006.
[103] *Al-Wafd*, June 10, 2006.
[104] *Al-Masry Al-Youm*, June 10, 2006.
[105] *Al-Masry Al-Youm*, July 10, 2006.
[106] *Al-Jazeera*, June 15, 2006.
[107] Interview with Shura Council member, May 24, 2007.
[108] *Human Rights Watch*, "Egypt: Jailing Journalists Strikes at Press Freedom Editor, Reporter Sentenced for 'Insulting President,'" June 28, 2006.
[109] *Christian Science Monitor*, July 10, 2006.

national interest by insulting the president directly.[110] An *Al-Jazeera* reporter documenting prison abuse was sentenced to six months in prison and a fine of LE 20,000. A court sentenced the editors of four opposition newspapers to prison for insults against the president, his son, and other high-ranking officials.[111] Grand Sheikh Tantawi of Al-Azhar offered his support for the crackdown on journalists, appearing on public television to promote the flogging of these journalists.[112] Ibrahim 'Issa became the subject of additional controversy in 2008. A misdemeanor court sentenced 'Issa to six months in prison for publishing rumors speculating about the health of the president.[113]

7.4.3 Lifting Parliamentary Immunity

Under what circumstances is parliamentary immunity lifted? According to the constitution, except in cases of *flagrante delicto*, no member of the People's Assembly shall be subject to criminal prosecution without the permission of the Assembly. Parliamentary immunity may be lifted when the relevant parliamentary committee approves a submitted request for the removal of immunity or at the discretion of the speaker of the People's Assembly, when parliament is not in session. The Assembly must be notified of the measures taken in its first subsequent session. Following the request to lift immunity, two-thirds of the assembly must vote to lift immunity. Informally, however, immunity is lifted when the relevant individuals within the regime give the go-ahead. As one regime insider put it, those who get nabbed for corruption and lose their immunity have "overplayed their hand."[114]

This occurs under a variety of circumstances. When 'Abd al-Azim al-Hamzawi was found to have murdered his former business partner, 'Ali al-Sayyid al-Badawi, his immunity was lifted.[115] Here, the egregious nature of the crime led the parliament to lift immunity. In other circumstances, the corruption of a parliamentarian can become too much of a political liability for the ruling elite. Mamduh Isma'il – the parliamentarian and friend of the regime who was shown to be negligent in the Red Sea ferry incident – fell into this category. The extreme loss of life (more than 1,000 dead), as well as the poor handling of the crisis by his company, led to a massive public outcry for justice. Although Isma'il's immunity was eventually lifted, the government did not seek manslaughter charges against him, even though many believe that such charges were warranted. Immunity may also be lifted when the body of evidence against certain parliamentarians is such that the government cannot deny wrongdoing has occurred and it would appear incompetent not to take

---

[110] Atef al-Sa'dawi, "Where Is the Egyptian Press Heading?" *Arab Press Network*, February 26, 2008.
[111] *Al-Arabiya*, September 13, 2007; *Egyptian Gazette*, September 14, 2007.
[112] *Al-Ahram Weekly*, October 18–24, 2007.
[113] *Al-Masry Al-Youm*, March 27, 2008.
[114] Interview with Egyptian Foreign Ministry official, May 22, 2007.
[115] *Egyptian Gazette*, January 14, 2008.

some action. As Mohammed Heikal put it, sometimes a person's "activities created too offensive a smell in the nostrils of too many people for him to be any longer immune" (1983, 196).[116]

Whereas these occurrences are relatively public events, there are also sometimes reasons behind the scenes for lifting immunity. For example, it may come to the attention of the ruling regime that a particular individual has benefited too much from his immunity without giving a sufficiently large cut to high-level officials within the regime. If a parliamentarian is discovered holding back on these payments or earning more than he has reported, the ruling elite could green-light proceedings to lift immunity. The lifting of parliamentary immunity has also been threatened against political opponents, particularly members of the opposition Muslim Brotherhood.[117]

This does not preclude the possibility that parliamentarians may try to protect one another against threats of lifting immunity. Kienle reports that members of parliament are typically reluctant to lift the immunity of their colleagues (2001, 64). Delays in formal corruption investigations are known to last months and sometimes years (Zaki 1998, 149). In one case, committee members claimed to have been poorly positioned to judge whether relevant documents were genuine or false out of a desire to avoid having to make a decision about lifting immunity.[118] In fact, it is not unusual for the prosecutor general to make a request for immunity to be lifted only to have that request thrown out by the parliamentary committee for lack of evidence.[119] Committee members have also held sit-ins to protect their fellow members.[120] In other cases, lifting immunity can take months, and, even after immunity is lifted, very little happens by way of prosecution[121] as a result of a slow court system[122] or lack of political will to prosecute.[123]

7.5 CONCLUSIONS

Elite corruption is considered an open secret of Egyptian political life. *Al-Akhbar*'s daily columnist, Ahmed Ragab, wrote a particulary critical editorial where he suggested that Egyptians live in a land of corruption, a "Fasadestan"

---

[116] At the same time, there does exist some ambiguity concerning just how far is too far with regard to corruption. The absence of clear limits creates a degree of uncertainty on the part of a parliamentarian that also benefits the ruling regime. Without knowing the precise location of the redlines, members of the rent-seeking elite are likely to be more conservative in their corruption than if they knew precisely what types of activities might serve as a trigger. Thanks to Kevin Kohler for pointing this out.

[117] *Al-Sharq Al-Awsat*, May 8, 2005.

[118] *Al-Ahram Weekly*, August 5–11, 1999.

[119] Interview with Moheb Zaki, Ibn Khaldun Center for Development Studies, May 23, 2007.

[120] *Al-Ahram Weekly*, August 5–11, 1999.

[121] *Al-Usbū'*, December 4, 2006.

[122] Interview with Gasser 'Abd al-Raziq, Egyptian Organization for Human Rights, April 30, 2006.

[123] *Egyptian Gazette*, March 6, 2007.

(*fasād* is corruption in Arabic).[124] An editorialist for *Al-Masry Al-Youm* argued that the force of corruption in Egypt has become stronger than the regime itself.[125] Parliamentarians were called "liars" who have "milked the country dry."[126]

I have argued that elections serve as a façade for a tacit alliance between the regime and the rent-seeking elite. At the core of this alliance is the distribution of opportunities for both privileged access in parliament and corruption via the institution of parliamentary immunity. This is in contrast to existing theories that argue that shared control over policy in legislatures is the primary mechanism for elite cooptation (Gandhi and Przeworski 2001; 2006). A relatively free and adversarial press is not inconsistent with the persistence of authoritarianism; although criticism of the president, his family, and close associates is not permitted, investigations regarding the economic activities and corruption of the rent-seeking elite may serve a fire-alarm function for the regime.

The argument raises the following question: does the regime pay a long-run price in terms of stability for creating a system that relies on the "immunization of capitalists"[127] through institutionalized corruption? Gupta, Davoodi, and Alonso-Terme (2002) find that "high and rising corruption increases both income inequality and poverty." Corruption also erodes support for a political system, suggesting that corruption itself carries important political costs (Seligson 2002). Concerns about corruption, inequality, and poverty are raised consistently in the Egyptian press. Editorialist Mohammed Baghdadi writes that Egypt contains two peoples living in a single country: the poor, who suffer from chronic poverty, and the über-wealthy, who distance themselves from the masses.[128] A key quasi parameter of the institutional equilibrium that I describe in Egypt involves the negative externalities associated with corruption. The negative factors associated with institutionalized corruption – such as loss of support for the political system and income inequality – could reach a critical level such that the equilibrium is no longer self-enforcing. Given the depth and extent of corruption in Egypt, this is a source of potential instability for the existing regime.

---

[124] *Al-Akhbar*, March 5, 2006.
[125] *Al-Masry Al-Youm*, July 10, 2006.
[126] *Al-Ahram Weekly*, August 28–September 3, 2008.
[127] *Al-Wafd*, April 9, 2006.
[128] *Al-Masry Al-Youm*, August 5, 2007.

8

Elections and the Muslim Brotherhood

The Society of Muslim Brothers was founded in 1928 as a religious organization created for the promotion of Muslim values and the building of mosques and Islamic schools. The focus of the group was "not limited to the establishment of a charitable group or association for the undertaking of social services, but was a broader and more comprehensive organization to reach society in its entirety" (al-Bishri 1983). The goal, therefore, was not to create a Muslim state, per se, but rather to Islamize Egyptian society in a way that reflected a reform of the political, economic, and social life of the country (Mitchell 1969; el-Ghobashy 2005). The contemporary Muslim Brotherhood defies classification as it combines aspects of a religious movement, social movement, charitable association, and political party.[1]

There are a number of excellent books and studies that have focused on the history, ideology, and tactics of the Muslim Brotherhood over time. This chapter is meant to serve as a complement to these studies by specifically focusing on a few narrow aspects of Brotherhood activity that are particularly related to the issue of electoral participation. My primary objective is to discuss Muslim Brotherhood electoral participation with an eye toward answering three questions: Why does the Muslim Brotherhood participate in parliamentary elections that are, as I have argued, key to maintaining the stability of the authoritarian regime? What are the electoral bases of Muslim Brotherhood support? And, how does the Brotherhood convince individuals to vote for candidates representing the group?

This chapter arrives at a number of conclusions. The first is that the Brotherhood participates in Egyptian electoral politics to establish itself as the primary opposition to the existing authoritarian regime in a way that does not challenge the short-term existence of the regime itself. The Brotherhood has capitalized on growing support for Islamist ideology in Egyptian society and attracts supporters who are ideologically like-minded as well as those that are

---

[1] International Crisis Group report, *Islamism in North Africa II: Egypt's Opportunity*, April 2004.

antiregime and favorably inclined toward the Brotherhood's charitable work and "clean hands" reputation. In order to attract individual voters, the Brotherhood engages in a number of strategies at election time. The most important of these strategies involves the use of person-to-person recruitment of voters and maintenance of a well-run, centralized organizational structure. The Brotherhood is also effective at signaling its electoral strength in ways that convince sympathetic voters, who may be on the fence about turning out, that Brotherhood candidates have a chance to win.

8.1 ISLAMIST ELECTORAL PARTICIPATION IN EGYPT

Why does the Muslim Brotherhood participate in electoral politics? In this section, I argue that the Brotherhood has a very long time horizon with respect to its political role in Egypt; elections are seen as an opportunity for the organization to establish itself as the most viable opposition group in the country without posing a direct challenge to the short-term existence of the regime. Before discussing this argument more fully, first I provide a brief summary of regime relations with the Brotherhood since Nasser.

8.1.1 Historical Background

The Muslim Brotherhood has a long and complicated relationship with the current Egyptian regime. In 1954, following a failed assassination attempt on his life, Nasser launched a series of violent purges in an attempt to suppress the Muslim Brotherhood, which had been implicated in the attempt. Following a second major roundup in 1965, a number of Muslim Brothers were hanged, including Sayyid Qutb, a leader credited with being one of the founding fathers of the modern radical Islamic movement. Thousands more were imprisoned and tortured.

The Brotherhood emerged from this experience with a new outlook on the use of violence as well as updated strategies for managing relations with the existing regime. In particular, the group saw a move away from the ideas of Qutb toward a "cautious reinterpretation" of the ideas of the groups' founder Hassan al-Banna (el-Ghobashy 2005, 375). This new approach, coupled with Sadat's desire to open the political system, led to a more relaxed environment for the Brotherhood in the 1970s. Sadat also encouraged the growth of Islamist organizations out of a desire to counterbalance leftist holdovers from Nasser's rule.

Kepel (1985) describes 1977 as a watershed year for regime–Brotherhood relations. Before the onset of the peace process, relations between the regime and the Brotherhood were cordial, but "mutual tolerance soured" following Sadat's trip to Jerusalem (Kepel 1985, 71). In September 1981 – just four weeks before his assassination – Sadat engaged in a massive crackdown that led to the imprisonment of more than 1,600 individuals, including a number of Islamist activists. Following release from detention, the group sought a way to carry out its activities without challenging existing laws; elections were seen as an exceptionally good opportunity for achieving this objective (el-Ghobashy 2005, 378).

The political opening introduced by Sadat was expanded under Mubarak, and the Muslim Brotherhood participated in parliamentary elections in alliance with existing political parties. During the 1980s, the Brotherhood emerged as the primary opposition to the hegemonic NDP in parliamentary elections. Despite that, the 1980s were a relatively peaceful period for regime–Brotherhood interactions during which the group established a presence in both parliament and syndicates (Campana 1996). As confrontation increased between the regime and more radical Islamist organizations – like *al-Gamā'a al-Islāmiya* – relations became increasingly difficult for the regime and the Brotherhood as well. During the 1990s, the Muslim Brotherhood was subject to cycles of crackdown as regime policy conflated moderate and extremist Islamist groups. A process of political deliberalization took place during the 1990s (Kienle 2001) during which the Brotherhood was not able to effectively contest parliamentary elections. In January 1995, Brotherhood leaders – charged with plotting to overthrow the regime – were arrested in the most far-reaching crackdown since the 1950s (el-Ghobashy 2005, 384). An unsuccessful assassination attempt against Mubarak in Ethiopia later that year further exacerbated Islamist–regime tension.

This trend of political deliberalization reversed with the 2000 People's Assembly elections and in 2005, when the Brotherhood was able to win about 20 percent of lower-house seats. Since 2005, the Muslim Brotherhood parliamentary bloc has emerged as one of the most vocal critics of the authoritarian regime. The Muslim Brotherhood is among the most important nonstate political actors operating in contemporary Egypt. The group's current role reflects what el-Ghobashy has described as a metamorphosis, where the Brotherhood has "morphed from a highly secretive, hierarchical, antidemocratic organization led by anointed elders into a modern, multivocal political association steered by educated, savvy professionals not unlike activists of the same age in rival Egyptian political parties" (2005, 374).

8.1.2   Electoral Participation as an Opportunity

The Brotherhood has been described as extremely cautious and calculating by Egyptian judge and scholar Tariq al-Bishri[2] and, at the same time, highly flexible and adaptable by Islamist expert Dia' Rashwan.[3] Brotherhood participation in elections can be similarly characterized; the group is careful about the way it contests power and has demonstrated an ability to shift and adapt in the face of changing constraints. Analysts have suggested that one example of this flexibility is the growing and public acceptance of democratic principles

[2] *Al-Ahram Weekly*, December 28, 2006–January 3, 2007.
[3] *Al-Sharq Al-Awsat*, October 13, 2006.

on the part of the Muslim Brotherhood.[4] Egyptian Islamists, having learned from the experiences of their more militant predecessors, have – for pragmatic reasons – come to almost universally support political change via democratic channels.[5] Democracy promotion, therefore, has become a critical part of the Brotherhood's political strategy.

The Brotherhood's decision to participate in multiparty politics was not a trivial one, nor has it been in other Muslim countries. For example, Jordanian Islamists have questioned whether a minority presence in parliament is beneficial as it does not enable the implementation of Islamic law (Schwedler 2006, 156). According to Schwedler:

> The question for the movement at that time was whether participation would likely bring sufficient gains to justify the costs – symbolic as well as material – of working through formal political channels and within a pluralist context (2006, 156).

Over time, however, the need to justify participation in elections evaporated (Schwedler 2006, 166). Instead, Islamist activists focused on the oversight opportunities made possible by participation in parliamentary institutions (Schwedler 2006).

In Egypt, participation in elections was controversial given the fact that electoral institutions are closely associated with the West and Western political practice (Tal 2005, 49). Tal argues, however, that it was the "tactical pragmatism" of the group that allowed for a changing view toward electoral institutions; in particular, Hassan al-Banna argued that electoral participation would further the goal of *da'wa*, or religious outreach (Tal 2005, 49). According to Rutherford (2006, 724), the Brotherhood views free elections as the only legitimate method for selecting a leader where leaders are required to consult with the people via a process of *shura*, or consultation. This is consistent with Islamic constitutionalists, who argue that a parliament is the most effective institution for enabling the public to participate in the drafting of laws in those areas not covered under Islamic law (Rutherford 2006, 716).[6] As a result, the Brotherhood has promoted the view that electoral success – through mobilization of the public – should translate into a parliamentary majority and right to form a new government (Rutherford 2008, 177).

Cook (2003, 4) argues that elections present other opportunities for Islamist groups, like the Muslim Brotherhood, to advance their objectives. For example, elections provide a platform for publicity. The ability to "disseminate its message and influence the rulers of Egypt" has been cited as an important benefit of electoral participation (M. Hafez 2003, 49). As a result, the Brotherhood sees electoral campaigns as an "ideal apparatus for promulgating its

---

[4] Michael Fournie, "Al-Wasat and the Destiny of Moderate Islamists in Egypt," *Civil Society*, September 2005.

[5] Ibid.

[6] According to Rutherford, beginning in the mid-1990s, the Brotherhood became the de facto advocates for Islamic constitutionalists, such as Yusuf al-Qaradawi (2008, 129).

message" (Abed-Kotob 1995, 331). It provides a direct and regular channel of communication with the public that assists in promoting the group's long-term objectives (Abed-Kotob 1995).

Contesting elections also signals that the Brotherhood is a future competitor for political leadership in Egypt. As a result, the Muslim Brotherhood fields candidates in a variety of elections, including for leadership of university groups and professional syndicates, not just parliamentary contests.[7] Further, winning elections may provide additional political space to provide services. Muslim Brotherhood parliamentarians seem to also enjoy some protection from government harassment as a result of their parliamentary immunity, though the regime has shown a penchant for lifting the immunity of political opponents. Other practical benefits include additional mobility in terms of foreign travel and an enhanced ability to meet with foreign diplomats.

While in parliament, members of the Brotherhood's parliamentary bloc have been able to draw attention to bad government policy or corruption through the use of parliamentary interpellations. M. Hafez (2003, 50) finds that the Brotherhood also uses its presence in parliament to root out opponents to its platform. Masoud (2008c) argues that social movements, like the Brotherhood, "must weigh the payoffs of participation relative to those of other available strategies" before deciding how to proceed. Masoud (2008c) finds that, in the Egyptian case, "parliament provides important non-policy goods – from opportunities to propagandize, to access to resources, to a chance to score publicity points against the regime" by engaging in forms of parliamentary oversight.

The group has also gone to great lengths to convince both the regime and the public that it is not currently planning a revolution or overthrow of the existing order. 'Abd al-Mun'im Abu al-Fotouh – in an interview with *Al-Sharq Al-Awsat* – has said that the Brotherhood seeks to promote the advancement of the Egyptian people through peaceful political participation and continued stability; he also said that overthrowing the regime is not a priority of the group at this stage.[8] In an interview, group leader Mohammed Mahdi Akef has also said that the Muslim Brotherhood is not even primarily concerned with displacing the ruling NDP.[9] The Brotherhood also tries to avoid overt confrontation with the regime (Wickham 2002, 225). In the run-up to the 2008 municipal council elections, the Brotherhood's Supreme Guide stated that the group's plan to participate was "not meant as a challenge or a show of strength, but rather it is an attempt to stimulate participation in the country's political life."[10] These statements reflect the Brotherhood's long time horizon with respect to its political role in Egyptian society. According to one Muslim Brotherhood parliamentarian, "the years of Mubarak's rule are just a few drops in the ocean of the life of this nation.... for example, the Soviet Union was

---

[7] As will be discussed further, the Brotherhood is often barred, however, from important avenues of electoral contestation.

[8] *Al-Sharq Al-Awsat*, June 18, 2005.

[9] *Al-Sharq Al-Awsat*, December 11, 2005.

[10] *Al-Ahram Weekly*, February 28–March 5, 2008.

just seventy years old when it started to collapse. We know that the future is for us" (quoted in Bradley 2008, 60–1).

As a result, some have concluded that the Brotherhood prefers a strategy of cooperation rather than confrontation with the regime.[11] According to one member of the Brotherhood's parliamentary bloc, "the Brotherhood is in favor of political stability in Egypt and does not have plans to incite the people on the street against the regime. . . . the Egyptian street is boiling and still we prefer using parliament as a legal window for expressing our ideas."[12] This suggests that the group's leadership may see electoral success as providing the Brotherhood with an opportunity to reform government from within through a slow, incremental process rather than coming to power via a power grab.

Because the Brotherhood may believe it would prevail in free and fair elections, promoting political reform remains a top priority for the group. According to Hamzawy, 70 percent of the issues raised by the Brotherhood in parliament following the 2005 elections have been related to political reform, whereas only 20 percent were related to accountability and 10 percent to cultural issues.[13] In a 2005 interview, Brotherhood leader 'Essam al-'Erian called on Arab governments to put decisions in the hands of "the people" via fair, competitive processes.[14] Group Supreme Leader Mohammed Mahdi Akef, in an interview with a satellite television personality, has also hinted that the Brotherhood would like to someday field a candidate for the presidency.[15] The Brotherhood realizes that it has much to gain from free and fair elections (Cook 2003, 181). This led Sana Abed-Kotob to conclude:

> Participation in the existing electoral system is thus a major tool used by the Brethren to advance their *da'wa* by sidestepping the many legislative restrictions that otherwise prevent promulgation of their message (1995, 331).

Egypt's semicompetitive elections create opportunities for the group to promote its agenda, create political space for itself and its members, and signal its competence and willingness to play by the rules of the game. The leadership of the group appears to take a long view of Egyptian politics in the belief that the current regime will eventually implode under the weight of its own corruption; it is at this time that the group feels it may be well-positioned to move from opposition in parliament to a more active leadership role. In the meantime, however, the group operates very cautiously and remains fearful of state repression. Hamzawy has argued that, as a result of its fear of repression, the Brotherhood tends to operate within the established norms governing its relationship with the regime.[16]

---

[11] Lecture by 'Amr Hamzawy, "Islamists in Electoral Politics – Priorities and Strategies of the Egyptian Muslim Brotherhood," UCLA International Institute, April 20, 2006.

[12] *Al-Ahram Weekly*, August 30–September 5, 2007.

[13] Lecture by 'Amr Hamzawy, "Islamists in Electoral Politics – Priorities and Strategies of the Egyptian Muslim Brotherhood," UCLA International Institute, April 20, 2006. Also see Masoud 2008a for more on this issue.

[14] *Al-Sharq Al-Awsat*, May 9, 2005.

[15] *Al-Masry Al-Youm*, July 30, 2007.

[16] *Al-Masry Al-Youm*, December 22, 2006.

8.2 SOURCES OF MUSLIM BROTHERHOOD ELECTORAL SUPPORT

How can we account for the electoral success enjoyed by the Muslim Brotherhood? This section considers the context for Brotherhood electoral success as well as the specific factors that trigger turnout for Brotherhood candidates. Taken together, these explanations provide a broad picture of Brotherhood electoral success.

8.2.1 A Context of Rising Support for Islam

Whereas political debate in the Muslim world from the 1950s through the mid-1970s was "conducted largely within a secular frame of reference" (Humphreys 2005, 135), this was to change dramatically, both in Egypt and elsewhere in the Islamic world, beginning in the late 1970s. This change in discourse paralleled the development of what has been called the rise of the "mosque movement." According to Mahmood (2004, 44), "the mosque movement emerged...in response to the perception that religious knowledge, as a means for organizing daily conduct, had become marginalized under modern structures of secular governance." Piety activists increasingly sought to infuse daily life with an Islamic ethical sensibility (Mahmood 2004, 47). Eickelman (2002) argues that the popularity of the mosque movement finds its roots in rising levels of education as literacy makes Islamic texts directly accessible to more Muslims.

There are a number of manifestations of the growth of the mosque movement. For example, religious books – which make up 85 percent of total book sales in Egypt – far outsell books on secular topics.[17] Listening to cassette sermons has been and continues to be a tremendously popular activity in Egypt (Hirschkind 2006). In contemporary Egypt, the piety movement has been responsible for the establishment of mosques, social welfare organizations, Islamic educational establishments, and religious printing presses as well as an increase in personal dialogue and communication on religious topics (Mahmood 2004). Muslim Brotherhood electoral participation under Mubarak comes in the context of these social changes, particularly the growing Islamization of Egyptian society. Hamzawy has argued that this general process of Islamization and growing conservatism has favored the Brotherhood electorally.[18]

8.2.2 Islamic Social Services and Selective Incentives

Wickham (2002, 97) argues that there exists a "parallel Islamic sector" that operates in contemporary Egypt that includes private mosques, Islamic voluntary associations, and Islamic businesses. Though not explicitly related to the Muslim Brotherhood, the Islamic sector provides an important basis of

---

[17] *Egyptian Gazette*, May 25, 2007.
[18] Lecture by 'Amr Hamzawy, "Islamists in Electoral Politics – Priorities and Strategies of the Egyptian Muslim Brotherhood," UCLA International Institute, April 20, 2006.

support for the group. If the Brotherhood provides only some percentage of these services itself, how does it enjoy electoral benefits as a result of these activities? The Brotherhood may benefit from common association with the activities of the network of Islamist social service organizations, for example. The conflation of services provided by the Brotherhood and the broader social service network exists both in the eyes of Egyptian citizens and academics focusing on Egyptian politics.

Private voluntary organizations, many of which are Islamist in orientation, have long sought to meet the basic needs of everyday Egyptians (Sullivan 1994). Clark (2004) finds that hundreds of community-based associations and clinics provide or facilitate the provision of health care to the lower and middle classes in Cairo. Wickham details Islamic organizations opening kindergartens (2002, 128). Tal describes how Islamic organizations opened schools in a neighborhood where only four state-run schools served a population of half a million (2005, 47). These services offer the potential to create a political connection. For example, according to a man whose son had received surgery from an Islamic charitable organization, if someone from that organization asked for his vote, he would gladly offer it to them (Bin Nefisa and Arafat 2005, 186). These efforts have helped to establish a strong bond between the Brotherhood and its electoral base.[19] It is also important to point out that most of these charitable organizations emerged and grew in the context of the withdrawal of the state. The services provided by Islamic charitable groups are not dependent on state funding but rather receive their funds from private sector donations (Bin Nefisa and Arafat 2005).

The selective incentives offered to individuals through Islamic social service networks provide a powerful inducement to get involved.[20] According to Wickham,

> Islamic networks not only provided opportunities for comparatively low risk forms of participation that were sanctioned by the local community but also offered graduates a range of 'selective incentives.' For instance, such networks served as channels for the distribution of goods and services and the exchange of favors and protection. Some of the Islamists I interviewed mentioned that they could turn to peers in the movement for help in securing a job or a visa to work abroad. An individual's participation in Islamist networks also might increase his or her chances of securing work in the Islamic parallel sector or enhance his or her family's access to the funds distributed by mosques or subsidized day-care of health services (2002, 153).

Although individuals may continue their involvement in these networks over the longer term for more ideological reasons, the services provided through these organizations provide a powerful inducement.

---

[19] Nabil 'Abd al-Fattah. 2006. "Why the Muslim Brotherhood succeeded in Egypt's 2005 parliamentary elections," in *Democracy Review*. Cairo: Al-Ahram.

[20] Chong (1991) describes "selective incentives" as the material and social incentives people receive for participating in collective action.

8.2.3   Ideological Appeal and the "Lumpen Intelligentsia"

A primary argument put forth by Wickham (2002) is that the ideology of Islamic political organizations has particular appeal for a class of Egyptians that she describes as the "lumpen intelligentsia." Wickham writes that the lumpen intelligentsia emerged as a product of Nasser's system of free higher education. As more and more individuals attended university, the government became unable to absorb these new labor market entrants. As unemployment among university graduates began to increase, these individuals soured on the existing political system and became increasingly susceptible to Islamist political mobilization (Wickham 2002; Rutherford 2008). For Wickham, Islamic ideology developed in response to a culture of alienation that became common among educated, lower-middle-class youth (2002, 59). Many are educated, yet poor, and came to believe that a moral crisis was the root cause of Egypt's problems (Wickham 2002). Angered by corruption in parliament and bureaucratic inefficiency, these individuals felt personally thwarted by their country's failure to reward merit (Wickham 2002).

Although Wickham cautiously points out that the frustrations of educated youth are not a sufficient condition to explain the rise in support for Islamic organizations (2002, 119), she does find that the lumpen intelligentsia have served as a "premobilized support base" for Islamist parties (2002, 175). In the absence of comprehensive public opinion polls that are not subject to censorship by state authorities, it is difficult to gauge support for Islamist organizations like the Muslim Brotherhood. We do know, however, that unemployment is particularly high among university graduates and postgraduates. According to CAPMAS, in 2007, unemployment among university graduates and postgraduates was 34 percent in rural areas and 66 percent in urban areas.[21] In addition, according to a public opinion poll taken in 2000, 34 percent of respondents felt that a political program focusing on religion was important to them.[22] One observable implication of Wickham's argument is that the Brotherhood performs particularly well in districts that have a large number of individuals who fit the demographic profile she has described.

8.3   CONVINCING INDIVIDUALS TO TURN OUT TO VOTE

Muslim Brotherhood candidates operate in an environment of rising cultural support for Islam where there exists a generalized appreciation for the social services that the Brotherhood and other religious organizations provide. Although it is impossible to know the extent of ideological support for the Brotherhood's stated policies, I do not think that it would be an exaggeration to say that the organization enjoys considerable popularity across various classes of Egyptian society, particularly among educated, yet lower-middle-class individuals.

---

[21] *Al-Masry Al-Youm*, July 14, 2008.
[22] *Al-Ahram*, December 19, 2005.

Despite the support enjoyed by the group among both its activist adherents as well as nonaffiliated individuals, convincing supporters to vote for Brotherhood candidates presents a challenge for a number of reasons. The first is common to voter recruitment in any election: voting is a costly act for which there may be no direct reward.[23] The second is more particular to Egypt: individuals who turn out to vote (particularly for the opposition) may also subject themselves to political violence and humiliation at the hands of the state. How, then, does the Muslim Brotherhood convince individuals to turn out to vote?

Individuals who support the Muslim Brotherhood tend to do so for programmatic reasons. Schuessler (2000), for example, argues that people vote to say something about who they are more than to earn some kind of payoff. In his discussion of Mexico, Greene suggests that activists and opposition party candidates are motivated by the "selective expressive benefits of campaigning for a partisan cause in which they believe" (2007, 120). This may be particularly true for individuals who identify with the Islamic movement and may even believe that there will be a God-given reward for their actions. Grofman (1993) has also argued that there are both rational and nonrational reasons to turn out, and, as a result, we cannot predict the absolute level of turnout without both types of theories. Individuals who vote on an ideological basis, then, face the same type of turnout decision faced by voters in democracies: does an individual voter believe that his or her decision will be pivotal or somehow provide a meaningful signal? Although the likelihood of being pivotal is assumed to be zero for any particular voter, I argue that different factors may influence individuals who may be otherwise predisposed to voting for the Brotherhood to turn out. For example, if political entrepreneurs can send the signal that enough people will support the Islamist candidate, then this gives voters confidence in the possibility of achieving a Brotherhood victory in some particular district. In other words, the Brotherhood engages in a number of behaviors that help to convince supporters that their votes may count.

8.3.1 Well-Organized Structure and Strategies

The Muslim Brotherhood has developed a reputation for running clean, highly organized election campaigns, built on the work of an extensive network of local coordinators and volunteers. The Brotherhood will generally work in a constituency for two to three years before fielding a candidate there.[24] Once operating in a district, the group administers internal questionnaires to determine the capabilities of local political activists.[25] The Brotherhood has also shown a penchant for constantly innovating in terms of strategies for communicating its message. The group maintains a highly sophisticated Internet

---

[23] Vote buying is described in more detail in Chapter 6 of this book.
[24] Interview with Gasser 'Abd al-Raziq, Egyptian Organization of Human Rights, April 30, 2006.
[25] Interview with 'Essam al-'Erian, Muslim Brotherhood Political Committee, April 29, 2007.

site, sponsors local dinners, and holds a variety of marches.[26] According to one press report, the group uses communications experts to help them with electoral campaigns.[27] The Muslim Brotherhood has also been very effective at harnessing the energy of committed volunteers.[28] For example, during the 2005 parliamentary elections, the Brotherhood arranged for volunteers to guard the ballot box at each polling station, with additional volunteers assigned to escort the box to collection stations.[29] According to one Brotherhood leader, three factors have been key for the group's success: preparation, planning, and reliance on "highly qualified and competent" activists.[30]

Nabil 'Abd al-Fattah – a fellow at the Ahram Center for Political and Strategic Studies – offered his insights regarding the organizational strengths of the Brotherhood in a newspaper article that ran directly following the group's success in the 2005 parliamentary elections.[31] He argues that the Brotherhood has demonstrated a "rigid discipline" that has always been one of the group's hallmarks.[32] One aspect of this involves the fact that preparations for the 2005 elections began more than a year in advance and reflected a clearly developed and comprehensive campaign strategy.[33] The group engaged in a close study of sociopolitical maps of the constituencies where it planned to field candidates and set up operation headquarters in those areas that were characterized by sophisticated communications networks.[34] The group prepared first, second, and third tiers of candidates to offset expected government clampdowns and arrests.[35] According to one academic closely tied to the NDP, the security apparatus has good knowledge of the first and second tiers but generally does not know the third layer of the Brotherhood leadership.[36]

8.3.2   Person-to-Person Contact

In a 2005 press interview, influential Muslim Brotherhood representative 'Essam al-'Erian said that the Brotherhood has the ability to deploy an army of 25,000 volunteers to mobilize voters door-to-door and even solicit feedback regarding why voters did not support Brotherhood candidates.[37] This strategy of individualized voter recruitment has become a defining characteristic of the organization. Wickham argues that this type of recruitment, which builds on

[26] *Nahdat Masr*, October 30, 2005.
[27] *Nahdat Masr*, November 19, 2005.
[28] *Al-Ahram Weekly*, December 1–7, 2005.
[29] Glain, Stephen. "How far will Egypt's Islamists go?" *Boston Review*, May/June 2006.
[30] *Al-Ahram Weekly*, December 1–7, 2005.
[31] *Al-Ahram Weekly*, December 29, 2005–January 4, 2006.
[32] Ibid.
[33] Ibid.
[34] Ibid.
[35] Ibid.
[36] Interview with 'Ali al-Din Hilal, former Minister of Youth and Professor of Political Science Cairo University, April 30, 2007.
[37] *Al-Ahram Weekly*, December 1–7, 2005.

preexisting social ties, is an important way the Brotherhood disseminates its message (2002, 130–1). She writes, "Islamic ideological outreach was typically a personal, even intimate process, rooted in face-to-face human relationships" (Wickham 2002, 134). The Brotherhood's Deputy Supreme Guide Mohammed Habib has stated that, in light of police crackdowns, person-to-person contact has emerged as an important strategy; "rather than plastering districts with religious posters and slogans Brotherhood candidates will establish direct contact with voters through visiting their homes and canvassing with families one at a time."[38] In addition to recruiting in private homes, Muslim Brotherhood recruitment takes place year round at a variety of locations, including clubs, mosques, universities, and professional syndicates.

According to one Brotherhood spokesman, women have become some of the most important political activists within this volunteer network, particularly given their effectiveness as recruiters of other women.[39] Women, unlike men, are able to make social calls to the homes of other women. In both rural and urban areas, women associated with the Brotherhood go from house to house aiding poor women and recruiting voters.[40] Press reports also suggest that female supporters of the Brotherhood have been very effective at pressuring other women to vote for Muslim Brotherhood candidates.[41] Part of the reason for the effectiveness of these recruiters is reported to be based on the intensive training and direction received by these women. According to one article, well-trained female recruiters take a list of names and make personal visits to local families to encourage turnout and support for Brotherhood candidates.[42] These reports are consistent with academic accounts, which also suggest that female voters supporting the Muslim Brotherhood play a critical – although perhaps less visible – role in the electoral success of the organization (el-Ghobashy 2005).[43]

8.3.3 Creating Common Knowledge

The Muslim Brotherhood provides a number of signals to demonstrate its strength in a district prior to an election. Why is signaling support in the run-up to an election so important? Scholars of American politics have shown that, when the probability that an individual's vote will affect the result of an election increases, turnout increases as well.[44] Egyptian political analyst 'Amr al-Shoubaki has argued that this same type of dynamic might also be relevant in the Egyptian context; he says that Egyptian voters are also more

---

[38] *Al-Ahram Weekly*, June 7–13, 2007.
[39] Interview with 'Essam al-'Erian, Muslim Brotherhood Political Committee, April 29, 2007.
[40] Interview with Sherif Wali, Shura Council member, May 24, 2007.
[41] *Ruz al-Youssef*, November 22, 2005.
[42] *Al-Destour*, December 7, 2005.
[43] For a more in-depth discussion of the role female Brotherhood activists play in Egyptian parliamentary elections, see Blaydes and el-Tarouty 2009.
[44] See Blais 2000 (58) for a summary of these studies.

likely to go to the polls when they believe that their vote makes a difference.[45] In a context of widespread affinity for the Muslim Brotherhood, encouraging turnout, then, is of critical importance for the group's success. In this section, I discuss three broad ways that the Brotherhood signals strength prior to elections. Although I cannot ascertain the group's intentionality with regard to these activities, together they suggest a pattern of signaling to the electorate. The first includes the use of large-scale public marches, rallies, and parades that provide information regarding the preferences of other voters in an area. Second, the Brotherhood carefully selects the districts in which it runs based on certain social and other characteristics; the fact that the Brotherhood has chosen to run in a district itself represents a signal that the group is strong in that area. Finally, events that occur on the day of the election can make a difference in terms of encouraging turnout. I discuss each factor in turn.

The massive marches organized by the Brotherhood in the run-up to the 2005 election served as an effective form of advertising for the group (Soliman 2006). Led by large numbers of children and women holding banners stating "Islam Is the Solution" and "Together for Reform" (Soliman 2006), these marches provided important signals of Brotherhood electoral strength. In the months prior to the 2005 parliamentary election, the Brotherhood organized dozens of protests in which more than 140,000 people participated in 15 governorates.[46] These marches took place without prior government approval, and information about the marches was disseminated during Friday prayers at local mosques.[47] The marches were peaceful, and costs associated with organizing the efforts were paid for by the Brotherhood.[48] Despite the peaceful nature of the marches, Brotherhood activists were arrested in a number of governorates,[49] leading to demonstrations demanding the release of detainees.[50] The Brotherhood performed well electorally in areas where demonstrations took place, such as Minya, Alexandria, and Kafr al-Shaykh, although the direction of the causal arrow is, of course, an open question. The strong performance of the Brotherhood in areas that had previously witnessed marches is at least empirically consistent with the idea that marches provide signals of strength that might induce individuals who were otherwise on the fence about voting to turn out to vote their ideological preferences.

One of the most important components of the Muslim Brotherhood's campaign strategy is to limit the electoral districts in which it fields candidates. Although the stated reason for this is to avoid provoking the NDP and the government more broadly,[51] the strategy has an important other consequence. By running candidates in only the districts where it believes that it has a good

[45] *Al-Ahram Weekly*, December 29, 2005–January 4, 2006.
[46] *Al-Ahram Weekly*, March 15–21, 2007.
[47] *Al-Wafd*, July 15, 2005.
[48] *Al-Wafd*, May 27, 2005.
[49] *Al-Sharq Al-Awsat*, May 7, 2005; May 19, 2005; May 20, 2005; May 23, 2005.
[50] *Al-Sharq Al-Awsat*, July 6, 2005.
[51] *Al-Ahram Weekly*, December 29, 2005–January 4, 2006.

chance of winning, the very fact that the Brotherhood is choosing to run a candidate in a particular area signals to voters in that district that their region has a high concentration of Brotherhood supporters. One observable implication of this strategy is that the districts in which the Brotherhood chooses to run candidates share certain demographic or other characteristics that are associated with core areas of strength for the organization. I test this implication in another section of this chapter.

Even on the day of the election, certain activities of the group can help to create common knowledge about the Brotherhood's popularity. Hussein 'Abd al-Raziq – Secretary General of the Tagammu' party – argues that the large number of Muslim Brotherhood supporters in front of the polling stations arouses the emotions of other voters and gives them the feeling of the power of the Muslim Brotherhood candidates in that district.[52] According to one human rights lawyer who participated in election monitoring during the 2005 election, there tend to be very strong external cues regarding who is voting for whom.[53] In addition, the Brotherhood sends supporters to pray in front of polling stations.[54] The presence of a large number of veiled women in front of a polling station, or even bearded men, signals the strength of the Islamist candidate in that area and may encourage others to turn out to vote. Blaydes and el-Tarouty (2009) argue that the effort of Islamist women to rally in support of Brotherhood candidates is symbolically important. The willingness of Islamist women to make personal sacrifices to support Brotherhood candidates creates a strong emotional pull for other Brotherhood sympathizers to support the cause. One of the most widely publicized images from the 2005 parliamentary elections was one of a veiled woman climbing a ladder over a wall to get to a polling station so that she could vote[55]; this is a powerful image that sends a strong signal, particularly about the intensity of support that exists for the organization and its candidates. Witnessing the courageous acts of female Brotherhood supporters may similarly encourage higher levels of male participation, particularly given the patriarchal tendencies that exists in Egypt.

8.4 THE GOVERNMENT RESPONSE

What has been the government's response to the electoral participation of the Muslim Brotherhood, and how has this response changed over time? According to one analyst and former military official, the regime is not adequately attuned to the dangers associated with the Brotherhood's success.[56] Other members of the party appear quite concerned about the group's potential to challenge the regime, believing that the Brotherhood may use Mubarak's passing as an

---

[52] *Al-Ahrar*, November 19, 2005.
[53] Personal communication with Mohammed al-Sawi, human rights attorney and election monitor, January 10, 2007.
[54] Interview with Moheb Zaki, Ibn Khaldun Center for Development Studies, April 30, 2006.
[55] *Al-Masry Al-Youm*, December 10, 2005.
[56] Interview with Said Kadry, Al-Ahram Center for Political and Strategic Studies, April 29, 2007.

opportunity to seize power.[57] Springborg has written that "the regime without question perceives its major enemy to be the Islamic activists. . . . while not capable of overthrowing the system single handedly, they could serve as the mobilizational nucleus of a mass movement" (1989, 174). 'Amr Hamzawy has argued that there also exists the possibility of forging a political pact between the regime and the Brotherhood, involving an alternation of power.[58] The regime has a complicated relationship with the Brotherhood, which fluctuates from highly adversarial to what appears to be mildly cooperative at other times.

8.4.1   Constant Manipulation of the Rules of the Game

One of the regime's most important strategies for dealing with the Brotherhood involves a manipulation of both the formal and informal rules of the political game. This desire to keep the Brotherhood "off-balance" is believed to help the regime maintain control of the political scene. For example, during the 1980s, a mainstay of Mubarak strategy was the "old colonial device of dividing the opposition" between militant and moderate types (Sadowski 1991). According to Sadowski, "Mubarak sought to temper the demands of these Islamist 'legalists' by offering them a measure of power in exchange for their renunciation of revolutionary tactics" (1991, 130).[59] Albrecht and Wegner describe a similar process whereby radical groups were heavily repressed while moderate Islamists were offered the opportunity to participate in formal political institutions (2006, 125). On the other hand, during the 1990s, the regime showed a tendency to indiscriminately repress both reformist and militant elements of the Islamist movement. This conflation of moderates and radicals limited electoral opportunities for the Muslim Brotherhood in the 1990s, but, following the announcement of *al-Gamā'a al-Islāmiya's* nonviolence initiative in 1997 and subsequent ideological reorientation of the radical movement, the Brotherhood was allowed more room to maneuver in the 2000 and 2005 electoral campaigns.

The arrest of students associated with what appeared to be paramilitary training[60] at Al-Azhar University in December 2006 led to another shift in regime–Brotherhood relations.[61] In fact, the incident triggered a harsh regime response[62] that was probably exacerbated by the Brotherhood's strong

---

[57] Interview with Sherif Wali, Shura Council member, May 24, 2007.

[58] Lecture by 'Amr Hamzawy, "Islamists in Electoral Politics – Priorities and Strategies of the Egyptian Muslim Brotherhood," UCLA International Institute, April 20, 2006.

[59] Although both moderates and militants seek to establish an Islamic state, the Brotherhood has taken a gradualist approach to political transformation rather than change through the use of violence (Wickham 2002, 114).

[60] Muslim Brotherhood students staged a martial arts display dressed in black "ninja" outfits and masks, similar to the uniforms worn by members of Palestinian Islamist militias.

[61] *Al-Usbu'*, December 18, 2006.

[62] Khalil al-Anani, "Egypt: The regime, the Brotherhood, and labor plains of the Fourth Republic." *Arab Reform Bulletin*, March 2007.

electoral showing in 2005. The regime response included both a "constitutional reform program to undercut future political activity by the Brotherhood" as well as repression that fell within the existing legal purview.[63] For example, in January 2007, the Egyptian authorities arrested sixteen leaders of the Brotherhood and seized the financial assets of twenty-nine additional Brotherhood leaders and associated businessmen.[64] Muslim Brotherhood Deputy Supreme Guide Khayrat al-Shater and several other members were accused of money laundering and membership in an illegal organization.[65] Eventually, a military court sentenced al-Shater to seven years in prison, and others received similar sentences.[66]

In addition, the regime engaged in various types of repression and discrimination against Brotherhood candidates in the run-up to both the Shura Council elections in 2007 and the municipal council elections in 2008. In 2007, Brotherhood candidates were blocked from using religious slogans that had historically been an important part of the group's electoral campaigns. Prosecutors in a number of governorates ordered the imprisonment of Brotherhood members for posting election advertisements of a religious nature during the 2007 Shura Council elections.[67] Cairo police also arrested dozens of members of the Brotherhood for using religious slogans during the campaign.[68] On the eve of the nominations deadline, additional arrests took place as Brotherhood members were charged with hanging banners bearing religious slogans.[69] Interior ministry officials were accused of preventing Shura Council candidates from registering their intention to run for office,[70] barring up to 30 percent of candidates from applying.[71]

In the run-up to the municipal council elections scheduled to be held in the spring of 2008, sources within the Brotherhood said that they expected 20 percent of the Brotherhood's members to seek council positions, amounting to 40,000 candidates vying for 52,000 seats nationwide.[72] The authorities prevented candidates from submitting required paperwork; in some cases, thugs barred Brotherhood candidates from entering government offices, and, in other cases, bureaucrats refused to accept the paperwork.[73] According to one Brotherhood spokesman, preventing candidates from running represented an emerging strategy for the regime.[74] Eventually, more than 90 percent of Islamist

[63] Ibid.
[64] *Al-Jazeera, Mā Warā'a al-Khabar* (Beyond the Headlines), January 31, 2007.
[65] *Al-Ahram Weekly*, February 8–14, 2007.
[66] *Al-Masry Al-Youm*, April 16, 2008.
[67] *Al-Masry Al-Youm*, May 24, 2007; June 8, 2007.
[68] *Al-Masry Al-Youm*, June 8, 2007.
[69] *Al-Masry Al-Youm*, May 22, 2007.
[70] *Al-Masry Al-Youm*, May 17, 2007.
[71] *Al-Masry Al-Youm*, May 21, 2007.
[72] *Al-Ahram Weekly*, February 28–March 5, 2008.
[73] *Egyptian Gazette*, March 11, 2008.
[74] Ibid.

candidates were prevented from registering to run,[75] leading the Brotherhood to announce that it would boycott the elections.[76]

8.4.2 Intimidation and Electoral Irregularities

A number of barriers are erected to opposition turnout, particularly hindering the turnout of voters who support the Muslim Brotherhood. Whereas some of these take the form of electoral fraud and other types of irregularity, others involve the use of force and intimidation.

Before polling even begins, it can be difficult to register to vote as acquiring a voting card involves a trip to the police station or civil status authority, a fact that might intimidate some opposition voters. In a loosely fictionalized version of his experiences as a high-ranking police officer posted in upper Egypt, Hamdi al-Batran writes in *Yaumīyāt Ḍābiṭ fīl Aryāf* that, even though election lists are required to be displayed in a public place, the officers laugh and whisper when citizens dare to venture to the police station to check their names or object to something on the list (1997, 94). Voter lists are controlled by the Ministry of Interior, and it has been suggested that these lists are periodically purged of opposition supporters.[77]

Brotherhood supporters have also been a target of attacks by hired thugs who seek to intimidate voters.[78] According to press reports, in one district, a gang of machete-wielding thugs attacked Brotherhood organizers outside polling stations.[79] Thugs do not operate only during election time, but they seem particularly active during this time.[80] Following the first round of parliamentary elections in 2005, the independent daily *Al-Masry Al-Youm* ran a front-page article describing the influence of the hired thugs in a number of districts.[81] The article says that voting was characterized by numerous infractions and violations committed by both the candidates of the NDP as well as independents. Candidate militias are said to have blockaded polling stations while state security forces imposed a form of "passive neutrality" that allowed these hired thugs to dominate the scene.[82] Thugs are particularly deployed to help candidates who are important within the party, like sitting ministers.[83]

In addition to various forms of intimidation, Muslim Brotherhood candidates in many cases are also victims of hegemonic party or regime-orchestrated fraud and electoral irregularities.[84] For example, candidates are permitted proxies to represent them inside the polling station and during vote counting. In

[75] *Egyptian Gazette*, March 14, 2008.
[76] *Al-Masry Al-Youm*, April 8, 2008.
[77] *Al-Ahram Weekly*, September 8–14, 2005.
[78] *Al-Ahram Weekly*, December 1–7, 2005.
[79] Ibid.
[80] According to Ismail, in 1998, there were 130,000 thugs in Greater Cairo (2006, 139).
[81] *Al-Masry Al-Youm*, November 10, 2005.
[82] Ibid.
[83] *Al-Destour*, November 23, 2005.
[84] According to el-Karanshawy, fraud is usually only attempted in close contests (1997, 21).

some cases, these individuals have not been allowed to undertake their duties.[85] In other cases, ballot boxes were stuffed before polling even began.[86] Polling stations are sometimes opened only briefly, limiting the number of voters who are allowed to enter and cast their ballots.[87] In one of the most notorious incidents of electoral fraud, a legal officer named Noha al-Zayni, who was charged with monitoring the electoral contest in Damanhour, released the details surrounding electoral fraud in that district to the independent daily *Al-Masry Al-Youm*. Her article was reprinted for three consecutive days to meet demand (el-Amrani 2005). It became widely known that the popular Muslim Brotherhood candidate – Gamal Heshmet – outpolled Mustafa al-Fekki, former information secretary and chairman of parliamentary foreign affairs committee, although al-Fekki was declared the winner of the race. Despite that, Heshmet discouraged his supporters from protesting the fraud too intensely.[88] These, and other examples, are used as evidence by those who argue that Egyptian elections are meaningless because they are "rigged." On the contrary, there does not actually exist a contradiction between those who say that the elections are rigged and my contention that elections are highly competitive. Both trends exist simultaneously. For a number of districts, forms of rigging take place in a bid to limit the electoral advance of the Muslim Brotherhood. For the majority of districts, however, contests between NDP and NDP independent and, very often, NDP-affiliated and independent or opposition candidates are conducted without regime-orchestrated fraud.

8.4.3 Elections and Repression

The qualitative discussion suggests that one of the ways the regime hurts the Brotherhood is by engaging in forms of repression in the run-up to parliamentary elections. The empirical generalizability of that finding is investigated here through a quantitative analysis of the relationship between elections and arrests.

The dataset used in this analysis was constructed using the raw events data coded by the Virtual Research Associates (VRA) reader, a software tool that parses the lead sentence of Reuters news reports. These data have been made available by Gary King and Will Lowe, who tested the quality of events data compiled by human coders versus by the computer software and found that the computer coding outperformed the human coders (2003). In their analysis, King and Lowe argue that huge quantities of data available in journalist accounts of world events remain underused in the study of international relations (2003). In order to encourage the use of the events data coded by the VRA reader, they made publicly available 3.7 million dyadic events as

---

[85] *Al-Ahram Weekly*, December 7–13, 1995; November 2–8, 2000.
[86] *Al-Ahram Weekly*, December 7–13, 1995; *Al-Masry Al-Youm*, June 28, 2007.
[87] *Al-Ahram Weekly*, December 1–7, 2005.
[88] *Al-Destour*, November 23, 2005.

reported by Reuters, covering the entire world for the years 1991–2004.[89] The data describe the source of some action as well as the target in a condensed format; if the government of country A sends humanitarian aid to an NGO in country B, this might be summarized with country A and government as the source actors, country B and the NGO as the target actors, and the sending of aid as the action. Although the dataset was clearly designed to aid in the analysis of international conflict and cooperation, one of the underemphasized by-products of this effort was that within-country interactions were coded as well. For example, the dataset also includes the government of country A providing humanitarian aid to an NGO *that is also in country A*. The applications, therefore, are potentially of interest to students of comparative politics who are not interested explicitly in typical interstate dyadic relationships.

For this analysis, two variables have been created based on the raw output of the VRA reader. The first is the number of arrests of members of religious or political organizations that took place in Egypt per month for the years 1990 through 2004. This serves as the dependent variable for the analysis. A variable that describes all violence committed by any armed civilian or insurgent group or individual will serve as a control variable in the analysis.[90] Finally, a dummy variable captures whether a parliamentary election took place in that month.

Two factors drive the choice of the autoregressive Poisson model for the analysis of the effect of elections on arrests: a) the discrete nature of the dependent variable and b) the serial correlation found in the data. In order to deal with these two important issues, I analyze the data using a procedure that estimates a Poisson model allowing for autocorrelation.[91]

The results of the analysis – as presented in Table 8.1 – suggest that arrests increase in the month of the election (Model 1).[92] Additional autoregressive terms do not change the coefficient on the key variable. This relationship is also robust to the inclusion of a lag on the number of extremists attacks (Model 2) as one might think that, if extremists increased the number of attacks they committed prior to an election, this would impact the number of arrests that occur.[93] This empirical finding confirms the qualitative wisdom that arrests increase in the weeks prior to parliamentary elections and that this increase exists even after controlling for the level of extremist activity.

---

[89] The complete raw dataset is available at http://www.gking.harvard.edu.

[90] I define violence as a shooting, abduction, assassination, hostage-taking, car bombing, bombing, physical assault, or clash.

[91] The command arpois in Stata estimates a Poisson model allowing for autocorrelation and overdispersion (Schwartz et al. 1996). This procedure has been extensively used to analyze time series regression for counts. Two alternative specifications to consider have been developed by Brandt et al. (2000) and Brandt and Williams (2000).

[92] This result only considers the arrests up to and prior to the day of the election and, therefore, does not reflect arrests during or following the elections.

[93] Rather than a lag, I also estimate this model for attacks in the same month and find the same result on the election variable.

TABLE 8.1. *Autoregressive Poisson Model (Dependent Variable Is Repression [1990–2004])*

	Model 1	Model 2
Constant	1.584	1.416
	(0.054)	(0.068)
Election	0.569	0.649
	(0.279)	(0.273)
Lag attacks		0.024
		(0.005)
ρ_1	0.333	0.216
	(0.072)	(0.077)
Observations	179	178
Adjusted R^2	0.15	0.20

Note: Standard errors are shown in parentheses.

8.5   WHERE DO THEY RUN, WHERE DO THEY WIN?

According to Hinnebusch, electoral outcomes in Egypt are determined by two factors: government intervention and the personal resources of candidates (1988a, 171). For members of the NDP, personal resources can be equated primarily with the financial wealth needed to buy support via political patronage (Hinnebusch 1988a). For members of the Muslim Brotherhood, however, variation across districts in terms of electoral success may be a function of differences in the appeal of the ideological message for a heterogenous voter pool. Wickham (2002) has argued that educated but underemployed Egyptians, whom she calls the lumpen intelligentsia, are an important pillar of support for the Islamist political movement. In this section, I investigate this hypothesis through regression analysis of data from the 2005 parliamentary elections. The success of Brotherhood candidates in these elections cannot be separated from the question of where the group chooses to run candidates, however. Because of the purposeful selection of districts in which to compete, I employ a selection model that considers the question of how the Brotherhood performs in two stages. The statistical analysis uses a variety of covariates to predict where the Brotherhood will run; the second stage considers where the group wins after taking into consideration where they have decided to run. This model, therefore, is an appropriate statistical estimator of the process at work given the fact that the selection mechanism has to be considered explicitly to answer the question of electoral success.[94]

---

[94] Masoud (2010) also investigates the question of whom the Brotherhood mobilizes in electoral campaigns by examining the districts in which the group runs. Masoud considers a wider variety of socioeconomic indicators than I use here and argues that the Brotherhood has a "middle class" core of supporters. A distinction between the tests run here and those found in Masoud (2010) is that I employ a selection model that considers both where the group runs as well as where it is electorally successful in a single statistical model.

The Brotherhood selects districts to run where it feels that it is strong; a primary goal for the organization is to show that they are popular.[95] In line with Wickham's hypothesis about sources of support for the group, we would then expect that the Brotherhood would run candidates in districts that had relatively high rates of literacy, suggesting an educated population yet relatively low levels of per capita wealth after controlling for literacy. The analysis, therefore, includes variables for percentage literate and the log of per capita GDP (i.e., income).[96] I also include a variable for whether or not the district lies in an urban or rural governorate as some might argue that the rise of the lumpen intelligentsia is a largely urban phenomenon.[97]

The second stage of the analysis investigates where the Brotherhood is successful, after considering where it has selected to run. The dependent variable, therefore, is a one if the Muslim Brotherhood won a seat in that district and a zero if it did not. The key variables of interest here are, again, literacy, income, and urban status with additional variables to consider whether the district competed in the first, second, or third round of parliamentary elections. The electoral round is significant here because it allows consideration of the effect of repression. The first stage of the election, which took place in eight Egyptian governorates, did not witness significant and systematic repression of the Brotherhood and its candidates. According to press reports, voters were allowed unfettered access to polling stations in this phase.[98] During the second stage, the security services began to try to "slow down" the progress of the Brotherhood by detaining some of the group's leading campaigners.[99] The third stage was characterized by severe repression, including the detention of

---

[95] Interview with Moheb Zaki, Ibn Khaldun Center for Development Studies, May 23, 2007. This view is also found in Masoud (2010), whose interviews with Muslim Brotherhood activists suggest that the group chooses to run where it believes it has the "best shot of winning."

[96] I have matched data on literacy and income from the UNDP at the level of various administrative units with data on Brotherhood candidacy and victories provided to me directly by the Muslim Brotherhood. Although district lines and local administrative units are not a precise match in all cases, there is no reason to believe that any error introduced through this process would be systematic. For urban areas, I used the administrative unit known as the *ḥayy* to match districts to administrative areas, and I used the *markaz* and *qism* for rural and desert areas, respectively.

[97] Although the Brotherhood has historically had strong bases of support in urban areas, increasingly the group is moving beyond areas of traditional strength into Egypt's rural communities. The conventional wisdom is that peasants respect the Muslim Brotherhood but do not follow the group (Brown 1990, 164). The nature of Brotherhood political support has evolved since the 2005 elections. According to one press report, since 2008, the Brotherhood has shifted with an increasing focus on developing support in rural areas. See *Al-Ahram Weekly*, October 23–29, 2008. Door-to-door recruitment of political support appears to have been a highly effective strategy in rural areas where Brotherhood activities have taken on an almost "missionary" quality, leading one NDP parliamentarian to comment that the Brotherhood may in the future become more powerful in rural areas than urban areas (interview with Sherif Wali, Shura Council member, May 24, 2007).

[98] *Al-Ahram Weekly*, December 8–14, 2005.

[99] Ibid.

TABLE 8.2. *Heckman Selection Model (Dependent Variables Are Brotherhood Candidacy and Victory)*

Second stage: elected candidates	
Constant	5.446
	(3.878)
Literacy	0.018
	(0.016)
Income	−0.759
	(0.653)
Urban	0.108
	(0.817)
Round 2	0.073
	(0.246)
Round 3	−0.853
	(0.519)
First stage: district selection	
Constant	2.534
	(2.181)
Literacy	0.011
	(0.007)
Income	−0.434
	(0.283)
Urban	0.412
	(0.241)
Observations (censored obs.)	444(295)

Note: Standard errors are shown in parentheses.

hundreds of Brotherhood members; the police also closed polling stations and cordoned off streets.[100] If the Brotherhood's electoral fortunes are a function of both its intrinsic appeal to various sociodemographic groups as well as the nature of government repression, we should expect that variables for each of the three rounds would explain some of the variation in Brotherhood electoral success.

Because the dependent variable in the second stage is binary, a standard Heckman model would not be appropriate; instead, I employ a modified selection model with a probit estimator. The model results are presented in Table 8.2. The results suggest a number of interesting patterns. First, we can see that literacy is positively associated with where the Brotherhood chooses to run candidates, whereas income is negatively associated with Brotherhood candidacy. These two variables are statistically significant at the 0.89 and 0.88 levels, respectively. This finding is broadly supportive of Wickham's hypothesis

[100] Ibid.; see el-Amrani (2005) for more details on the differential levels of repression across rounds of the elections.

that the Islamist movement seeks its support among the educated but under-employed. The finding also controls for the fact that the Brotherhood has a sta-tistically significant proclivity for running in urban areas. These results suggest that the Brotherhood chooses to run candidates in districts that share certain demographic characteristics that are associated with core areas of strength for their organization.

The second stage of the analysis considers those factors that predict Broth-erhood electoral victories once we have taken into account the process leading the Brotherhood to select certain districts for candidacy. Literacy and income still both have the predicted sign but decline in statistical significance. The effect of being located in an urban governorate can no longer be meaningfully distin-guished from zero. Whether the district fell into the first, second, or third round of the election becomes meaningful, however. The first round is the omitted category. As expected, the third round – which witnessed the greatest regime repression of the Brotherhood – is negatively associated with the group's elec-toral success at the 0.9 level. The first round – where Brotherhood supporters were allowed virtually unfettered access to the polls – is positively associated with Brotherhood victory, whereas the second round has no discernable effect.

8.6 CONCLUSIONS

This chapter has tried to answer a series of questions regarding the electoral participation of the Muslim Brotherhood in Egypt. This section argues that the Brotherhood participates in competitive elections – despite the benefits and information that these contests provide to the regime leadership – because the group sees participation as consistent with its long-term objectives. These objectives include promoting its message, participating in parliamentary insti-tutions, and encouraging democratic practices that the group expects to be the primary beneficiary of in some future political game. Second, this chap-ter argues that there are both structural factors involved as well as particular strategies employed to convince individuals to turn out. These structural fac-tors include a context of rising support for Islamic ideology more broadly as well as the widespread nature of Islamic social services. Brotherhood strategies of person-to-person mobilization and the many ways that the group provides common knowledge about its popularity also convince fence-sitters to turn out to vote. Finally, empirical analysis shows that, during the 2005 parliamentary election, the Brotherhood ran candidates in districts with a similar sociodemo-graphic profile but after controlling for this, typically won when subject to the least state repression.

9

Liberal Intellectuals and the Demand
for Democratic Change

A series of influential models argue that the reason the rich fear democratization is because democracy entails economic redistribution that favors the preferences of the median voter, who is likely to be poor (Meltzer and Richard 1981; Boix 2003; Acemoglu and Robinson 2006). Similarly, Ziblatt (2008) finds that the existence of an unequal distribution of immobile assets, such as land, is also a major impediment to democratization. Landowners and holders of capital are not, however, the only constituencies concerned about the preferences of the median voter. In Egypt, an additional dynamic is at play where democratic change not only impacts pecuniary redistributive stakes but also the distribution of civil rights and liberties, particularly for liberal intellectuals and artists. Intellectual and artistic elite – who have been key actors in democratic transitions around the world – are fearful of democracy because they believe that the cultural preferences of the median voter may limit their ability to pursue their creative work and livelihood.[1] These fears become particularly heightened as a result of competitive multiparty elections in which the Muslim Brotherhood has enjoyed electoral success. Brotherhood electoral strength has an important demonstration effect, signaling the political prowess of the group to liberal intellectuals.[2] By looking down the game tree, so to speak, intellectuals and artists may see a smaller payoff for democracy than their counterparts in Latin America, Eastern Europe, or East Asia. This may have reduced incentives to dissent among these important opinion makers. The same logic applies to Egypt's Coptic Christian minority, as well as liberal feminist groups.

---

[1] My discussion of intellectuals and artists refers primarily to liberal intellectuals and artists who work in a Western tradition rather than Islamic intellectuals, who may be focused on religious subjects, and Islamic artists, like calligraphers and architects, who work in an explicitly Islamic tradition.

[2] A similar dynamic may be at work for a different target audience. Saad Eddin Ibrahim, and others, have argued that Mubarak has exploited what he calls "Islamophobia" to silence criticism of Egypt by the United States and other Western countries who have been alarmed by Islamist electoral success. See *Washington Post*, August 21, 2007.

This argument suggests that multiple constituencies may fear policy preferences of the median voter, not just the wealthy. The economically redistributive aspects of democracy, then, may be coupled with concern about the distribution of rights over creative output and minority and women's civil liberties. It is important to point out that this is not because these intellectuals are less democratically inclined than their counterparts in other parts of the world. Rather, Egyptian intellectuals find democratic transition less appealing because the results of a free election hold the possibility of bringing to power Islamist parties that have a history of censoring important intellectual outputs, such as philosophy, art, and literature.[3] This complements Kalyvas (2000), who argues that military incumbents and secular democrats can ally in their distaste for electoral victory by religious parties in emerging democracies.[4]

Which groups, then, have the incentive to challenge the authoritarian regime more forcefully? An observable implication of my argument is that we should *not* see artists and intellectuals organizing the most effective protests in Egypt, but, rather, this challenge should come from other sectors of society. Information collected on protest behavior in Egypt indicates that labor groups, university students, bedouin, and peasants – often with significant economic grievances – lead most protests with antiregime undertones in Egypt. These groups are also most likely to lead an effective grassroots, antiauthoritarian movement in Egypt, potentially in alliance with Islamist groups, in the future because the preferences of these activists are not necessarily at ideological odds with Islamist organizations.[5] This is not to say that mobilization against the regime is forthcoming or even likely. The goal of this chapter is simply to describe which societal groups might have the greatest incentive to mobilize given the uncertainty over the preferences of the winner of a first free election in Egypt.

---

[3] Bradley (2008) and Masoud (2008b; 2010) call into question the popularity of Egypt's Muslim Brotherhood and the group's ability to win a freely contested election because the Brotherhood's recent parliamentary victories were won by a small plurality in most districts. Although persuasive, it seems that there continues to exist a great deal of uncertainty regarding the popularity of the Muslim Brotherhood, and most accounts seem to suggest that the group enjoys broad support.

[4] A number of scholars have made arguments that the policy incompatibilities separating the opposition have led to a dominant party system in more democratic contexts. Riker (1976) has argued that, in India, the central ideological location of the Congress Party made it difficult to create an ends-against-the-center coalition. Sartori (1976) provides a similar argument generalized for other cases. Magaloni (2006) finds that opposition coordination failure played a significant role in sustaining the dominance of the PRI in Mexico. She writes that "while opposition parties and voters held similar views on the political dimension, showing the potential to form a united political front against the PRI, on the economic dimension they truly differed" (Magaloni 2006, 192).

[5] Certainly none of these groups are monolithic, and there are very strong democracy advocates within each of the groups that I describe. Many activists in the Kefaya movement, which emerged beginning in 2004, for example, represent some of these groups. There has been some discussion, however, about the effectiveness of groups like Kefaya in mobilizing the masses and providing a genuine challenge to the authoritarian regime.

9.1   RELUCTANT DEMOCRATS?

To what extent are Egyptian liberal intellectuals reluctant democrats? Intellectual life in Egypt has a long and storied history with many of the Arab world's greatest artists, playwrights, poets, composers, and film makers of Egyptian descent. Clearly, these individuals do not act in a unitary way; there are courageous democratic activists within Egypt's intellectual and artistic classes. Rather, this chapter describes some of the structural disincentives for democratic activism that have emerged as a result of the political climate in Egypt and the broader Islamic world.

9.1.1   Liberal Intellectuals and Artists as Democracy Agitators

Resistance to authoritarianism is often led by "non-political leaders who symbolize the moral character" of the democratization struggle (Thompson 2005, 188). Artists and intellectuals are frequently among the first to manifest public opposition to authoritarian rule (O'Donnell and Schmitter 1986, 49). In the early twentieth century, for example, intellectuals – together with either bourgeoisie or working-class interests – emerged as critical advocates for democracy (Kurzman 2008).

Why are artists and intellectuals such important social interlocutors? Artists are frequently at the cutting edge of political change, and protest art – given the tremendous power of visual images – has the potential to inspire societal action. The work of artists and intellectuals frequently resonates with a broad constituency, and the critiques offered by playwrights, satirists, musicians, and novelists are often viewed as socially and politically relevant. Intellectuals and artists are also important opinion leaders who have the potential to influence activists. For example, Noel (2007) argues that intellectuals have meaningfully influenced the ideology of party leaders and political cleavages in the United States on issues ranging from support for slavery before the Civil War to attitudes toward abortion.[6] This is consistent with Zaller (1992), who finds that mass opinion is influenced by elite discourse.

Artists and liberal intellectuals have been important symbolic leaders of pro-democracy movements in a number of previous democratic transitions. In Czechoslovakia, playwright Vaclev Havel was a leading figure in the fight against authoritarian government, penning essays on life after authoritarianism and even going on to become president of the postauthoritarian state. Brazilian musician and writer Chico Buarque was arrested in 1968 for his activity against the authoritarian regime, eventually going into exile; one of his songs became the democracy movement's anthem. Chilean intellectuals played a critical role in the defeat of Pinochet, opening the path for democratic elections (Puryear 1994). During Ukraine's Orange Revolution, pop singer and songwriter Ruslana – winner of the 2004 Eurovision Song Contest – was one of many

---

[6] See Noel 2006 for more on this issue.

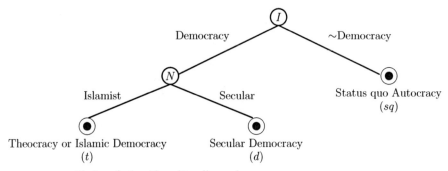

FIGURE 9.1. Choices facing liberal intellectuals.

prominent artists who rallied the crowds, even threatening a hunger strike for the democratic cause. These examples, and countless others, suggest that the actual and symbolic impact of this type of leadership in a pro-democracy movement is an important, and perhaps even critical, aspect of transition. Artists and intellectuals also often serve as important international gatekeepers who are able to generate interest in the transition process of a country abroad.

Historically, intellectuals have been viewed as the class of society most willing to serve the greater good (Kurzman 2008, 13). In fact, there exists an unstated presumption that intellectuals have a certain moral responsibility to oppose authoritarianism; in reality, however, many intellectuals have actively supported totalitarian and other undemocratic rulers (Lilla 2001). In other circumstances, liberal intellectuals and artists have either opted out of discussion of such issues or, in some cases, allowed themselves to be coopted by the regime.

9.1.2 Democratic Reluctance of Artists and Intellectuals

Figure 9.1 depicts the choice node facing Egyptian artists and intellectuals. Assume that the influence of this class of individuals is pivotal in whether or not a country becomes a democracy. The choice is between pushing for democratization or accepting the status quo dictatorship. If the artists and intellectuals push for democratization, a lottery ensues that can lead to either a secular democracy or a theocracy (with or without continued elections).

What might these individuals face under an outcome of theocracy? There exists a great deal of uncertainty in this regard, and the uneasiness of liberals has not been helped by the contradictory statements made by various factions within Egypt's most popular Islamist group, the Muslim Brotherhood.[7] Brown, Hamzawy, and Ottaway (2006) argue that there exist considerable

---

[7] This discussion is consistent with the historical long view in which intellectuals in Muslim societies have viewed the clergy as rivals, openly expressing hostility toward clerics and even cutting clerical staff and salaries given the opportunity (Kurzman 2008, 27, 88).

"gray zones" in the thinking and policies of Islamist movements, in particular regarding the civil and political rights of women and religious minorities. According to Hamzawy, the Brotherhood purposefully maintains areas of policy ambiguity in the following issues: a) the ultimate limits of political pluralism, b) restrictions to personal and civil liberties, c) the status of women, d) the status of religious minorities, e) the relationship between the group's leadership and the rank and file, and f) acceptable uses of violence.[8] Secular, liberal, and leftist intellectuals remain sensitive to areas of ambiguity as well as repeated inconsistencies in Brotherhood public statements.[9] For example, a draft platform for the group issued in 2007 did not reassure liberals and independent intellectuals (Brown and Hamzawy 2008).

The actions of Brotherhood members and supporters have also signaled an uncertainty regarding the acceptance of particular types of creative output. Issues related to culture are central to the activities of Islamist activists given the desire of Islamists to exercise forms of control over social and cultural space (Ismail 2003, 77). Islamist activists have targeted numerous Egyptian actors and directors for films and performances viewed as obscene.[10] In one case, Youssra – one of Egypt's most popular movie stars – was accused of having violated Islamic moral standards (Murphy 2002, 177). Islamist lawyers have launched a series of court cases against moral code "violators," such as movie theater owners (Ismail 2003, 65). Although most morality lawsuits filed by Islamist activists were eventually dismissed, they were nonetheless costly to defendants in terms of time and money (Murphy 2002, 178). These types of challenges not only limit the ability of individuals in the arts to promulgate their creative work but also to pursue their livelihood.

In 2000, students at Al-Azhar University petitioned that the controversial book *A Banquet of Seaweed* by Syrian writer Haider Haider be banned. Brotherhood parliamentarian Gamal Heshmat raised the issue of whether state funds should be spent on a book some considered to be obscene.[11] The culture ministry dismissed the bureaucrat responsible for approving the book (Masoud 2006a).[12] The director of the movie *The Yacoubian Building* said that the Muslim Brotherhood initially complained about the film's content and wanted to have it censored for its portrayal of the Islamist movement; the group eventually decided against pursuing this issue.[13] According to Abu-Lughod, "local westernized elites are singled out as sources of corruption and moral decadence by Islamic groups deploying a populist rhetoric" (1995, 53) – in fact, Islamist activists often target female film and stage stars and

---

[8] Lecture by 'Amr Hamzawy, "Islamists in Electoral Politics – Priorities and Strategies of the Egyptian Muslim Brotherhood," UCLA International Institute, April 20, 2006.
[9] *Al-Ahram Weekly*, December 29, 2005–January 4, 2006.
[10] See Hammond 2007 for details on a number of specific cases.
[11] *Al-Ahram Weekly*, January 18–24, 2001.
[12] Some writers try to preempt criticism by publishing books or articles demonstrating their religious faith at the start of their literary careers (Sagiv 1995, 1).
[13] Lecture by Marwan Hamed, UCLA International Institute, May 13, 2007.

newscasters, pressing them to give up their careers and wear Islamic headcovering. Renowned Egyptian poet ʻAbd al-Muʻti Higazi refused to pay a court fine following a conviction for insulting religious sensibilities; following his refusal, a court announced a date for the sale of Hegazi's home furnishings.[14]

The stakes can sometimes be even higher, particularly for intellectuals who write about Islam, but occasionally also for writers and artists. Egyptian writer Farag Foda, who satirized Islamic fundamentalism in Egypt, was shot dead in his office in 1992. Liberal theologist Nasr Abu Zayd was sued in 1994 for apostasy and forced to divorce his wife on the grounds that a Muslim woman cannot be married to an apostate.[15] Nobel Prize–winning Egyptian novelist Nagib Mahfouz was stabbed outside his Cairo home in 1994 by Islamic extremists who objected to the content of his novels. To some secular Egyptians, Islamist activists are seen as "cultural terrorists" whose activities are a form of fascism (Murphy 2002, 178). These types of incidents are not limited to Egypt, and similar events in other Muslim countries also impact the perspectives of Egyptian artists and intellectuals. A popular Sudanese singer was stabbed and two other artists were wounded by an Islamic activist; press reports suggest that some Islamists in Sudan consider singing and other artistic works as immoral and against religion.[16] Publisher Hamada Imam began receiving death threats after he was incorrectly identified as the author of the book *Love and Sex in the Life of the Prophet* (he is the publisher of the book).[17] Writing about Algeria, Brumberg argues that "caught between illiberal Islamists and autocratic regimes, some of which have actually tolerated or even assisted the former in an effort to silence liberal thinkers, the modernists have faced two unfavorable options: retreat or exile" (2005, 102).

Although the mainstream Muslim Brotherhood was clearly not responsible for these attacks against artists and intellectuals, the organization has not yet convinced these groups that it would serve as an advocate, either. Part of the reason for this is the perceived generational and ideological differences between factions of the Brotherhood with some members offering more progressive attitudes than their counterparts.[18] Even a single spokesman for the group can simultaneously offer relatively progressive views on some issues and less progressive views on others. For example, in an attempt to bring the group's reputation closer to the views of the median Egyptian, Deputy Head Mohammed Habib tried to dispel concerns that the Brotherhood is anti-art by saying that he likes the music of Mohammed ʻAbd al-Wahhab and Umm

---

[14] *Afrol News*, July 31, 2008.
[15] See Najjar 2000 for more details on the Abu Zayd case and tension between Islamic fundamentalists and liberal Muslim intellectuals.
[16] Reuters, November 14, 1994.
[17] *Egyptian Gazette*, February 19, 2008.
[18] There have been calls for key Brotherhood figures to step down from their positions, thereby allowing a younger generation of members to take on leadership positions. See *Al-Masry Al-Youm*, October 26, 2008.

Kulthum.[19] Habib also made statements in 2005 of a less progressive nature, however, suggesting that Copts could not become presidential candidates and that they should have additional taxes imposed upon them (Hamzawy, Ottaway, and Brown 2007). Although a younger member of the Brotherhood leadership, Habib is thought to be more ideologically aligned with the group's old guard.[20] Habib has also made statements that have conflicted with some of the group's more progressive wing, making them look as though they had been "talking out of turn," according to one analyst.[21]

This has left liberal intellectuals in an awkward position (Abaza 2000, 111), and the difficulties facing the Egyptian, and more broadly Arab, intelligentsia has been a subject of considerable hand wringing. The authoritarian state has been and continues to be viewed as "custodian of art" in Egypt (Winegar 2006, 137), where regime support of the arts is seen to "thwart political Islamists, whose ideal polity (artists presume) would ban much of the work they did" (Winegar 2006, 152). As one commentator on *Al-Jazeera* put it, liberals find themselves stuck between dictators on the one hand and Islamist fundamentalists on the other.[22] As a result of the concerns I have outlined, Egypt has witnessed the emergence of an artistic class that operates in the shadow of organized religious groups that have the potential to threaten its livelihood and under the tacit protection of the regime. Winegar finds that artists have significant "suspicion and criticism of dominant Islam and its institutions. . . . artists said that they were against the blind devotion of religion that they believed that these institutions engendered" (2006, 77). This tension manifests itself in a number of ways; for example, an informal ban on nude models at one of Cairo's best-established arts schools has led many fine arts students to feel a deficiency in their technical training.[23] Art students are refusing to enroll in sculpture classes at Egyptian art schools for fear of being targeted by Islamic activists who have accused sculptors of reviving pre-Islamic paganism with their human and animal representations.[24] Winegar also finds that the majority of artists she interviewed for her project were not highly religious, nor did they pray with regularity; rather they were "committed advocates of secularism and were particularly concerned about the rise of Islamist political opposition in Egypt" (Winegar 2006, 76–7). She concludes that this was because artists

> saw their careers threatened by an Islamism that they were sure would make image-making a dangerous, if not illegal, endeavor. Furthermore, because the spirit of inquiry and freedom of expression were cornerstones of their identities

[19] *Al-Sharq Al-Awsat*, July 19, 2005.
[20] 'Amr al-Shoubaki, Future Scenarios for the Muslim Brotherhood, Ahram Center for Political and Strategic Studies, January 2004.
[21] *Al-Ahram Weekly*, December 6–12, 2007.
[22] *Al-Jazeera*, "al-Ittijāh al-Mu'ākis" ("The Opposite Direction"), May 22, 2007.
[23] *Egypt Today*, July 2008.
[24] *Egyptian Gazette*, December 18, 2008.

as artists and intellectuals, they were concerned about the institutionalization of religion, and even more about the convergence of religion and politics (Winegar 2006, 77).

In many cases, intellectuals have chosen exile, silence, or self-censorship over other options.[25] Egyptian economist Galal Amin has argued that, in the current atmosphere, reform-minded individuals have withdrawn from actively pursuing a reformist agenda.[26] Other editorialists find that intellectuals have done more than withdraw and that there, in fact, exists a tacit alliance between intellectuals and the regime.[27] Muslim Brotherhood spokesman 'Essam al-'Erian has countered, arguing that there is a crisis of the liberal elite who have became increasingly alienated from their nation.[28] And with the increasing electoral appeal of Brotherhood candidates, writers, filmmakers, and others in cultural circles continue to express their apprehensions about the preferences of the organization.[29]

State Islamist Institutions. Although the state has thus far been described as a protector of certain types of artistic output in Egypt, the picture is complicated by the fact that criticism of individual artists can come from state entities that enjoy some policy-making authority delegated to them by the regime. As I point out, however, final word on these issues remains with higher levels of government that have, historically, provided a degree of protection for the artistic community. Most frequently this has been manifested in showdowns between the Academy of Islamic Research at Al-Azhar – a quasi-state institution – or lower-level courts and the Ministry of Culture, where the latter maintains the upper hand in resolving disputes. In many ways, attacks from both Islamists as well as conservative bureaucrats highlight for artists and intellectuals their continued vulnerability, even in the absence of Muslim Brotherhood cultural activism.

For example, in the 1990s, the Academy of Islamic Research at Al-Azhar petitioned for the removal of books deemed to be immoral from libraries and bookstores (Kienle 2001, 41). The Academy – although not authorized to undertake this action itself – did make its recommendations in its capacity for oversight of publications related to Islam (Kienle 2001, 109). The recommendations of the Academy have frequently put it in conflict with the Ministry of Culture (Kienle 2001, 112–3).

It is important to point out that the executive branch has retained its ability to make final determinations on issues of artistic output (Kienle 2001, 110). In one instance, when a lawsuit was brought against noted director Yusuf Shahin, a court overturned a ban on one of Shahin's films with the judge

[25] *Al-Hayat*, April 11, 2004; also see al-Khalil 1989.
[26] *Al-Ahram Weekly*, April 17–23, 2008.
[27] *Al-Ahram Weekly*, May 3–9, 2007.
[28] *Al-Hayat*, December 29, 2005.
[29] *Al-Ahram Weekly*, December 29, 2005–January 4, 2006.

finding that only the Ministry of Culture had the authority to call for such a ban (Ismail 2003, 66). Following the Abu Zayd case, a bill codifying *ḥisba* – the doctrine used by Islamists to justify forcibly divorcing Abu Zayd from his wife – was passed that gave the state prosecutor the sole authority to initiate *ḥisba* cases (Ismail 2003, 70). When a prominent judge objected to the removal of his books from the 1992 Cairo book fair, he appealed directly to President Mubarak to intervene in the situation (Kienle 2001, 110). In 2008, Minister of Culture Faruq Hosni challenged a court ruling that ordered withdrawing the 2007 State Prize from an Egyptian poet on the grounds that one of his works was blasphemous.[30]

The challenges to artistic output have come from both outside the state and, in some cases, from within the state, yet the ultimate protection of creative rights rests with the executive branch and the Ministry of Culture. Saad Eddin Ibrahim has suggested that the ruling regime has engaged in a strategy of "spreading panic" among intellectuals and innovators to increase fear of the Muslim Brotherhood.[31] Whether this is a deliberate strategy of the regime or a case of delegation gone awry is unclear.

9.1.3 Similarly Motivated Groups

The logic described also applies to other societal groups, including Coptic Christians and secular feminists. These are groups that, in the aggregate, would not expect to receive a larger benefit from *t* than *sq*.

Coptic Christians. Copts – who are estimated to be about 10 percent of the Egyptian population[32] – are Egypt's largest ethnic minority group. Some members of the Coptic community contend that systemic discrimination has kept Copts out of influential government positions.[33] Copts have also been underrepresented on candidate lists of Egypt's hegemonic party and among the military leadership.[34] The Coptic community has been the target of forms of workplace discrimination and physical violence by Islamist extremists; some have argued that the Egyptian government has been unsympathetic to these concerns. Given these factors, why hasn't the Coptic community been more of a vanguard for political change?

Zaki has argued that the resurgence of Islamic sentiment in Egypt has been accompanied by a "diffused feeling of hostility towards Christians among a broad sector of society."[35] In this climate, ambiguous statements by members

---

[30] *Egyptian Gazette*, April 20, 2008.
[31] Saad Eddin Ibrahim (translated by Blake Hounshell), "The Constitution and the Supreme Court and the Armed Forces," *Civil Society*, September 2006.
[32] 2006 CIA World Factbook.
[33] *Al-Ahram Weekly*, May 17–23, 2007; Moheb Zaki, "The Copts of Egypt: Victims of Discrimination," *Civil Society*, May 2007.
[34] *Al-Wafd*, December 2, 2005.
[35] Moheb Zaki, "The Copts of Egypt: Victims of Discrimination," *Civil Society*, May 2007.

of the Muslim Brotherhood have made the Coptic community fearful of encouraging any political change that might lead to the creation of an Islamist government, even one that was elected democratically. In 2005, former Brotherhood Supreme Guide Mustafa Mashhur reversed a 1995 Brotherhood statement on the equality of Copts as citizens.[36] Habib's 2005 declaration also suggests that Copts might suffer professional and economic discrimination under political leadership of the Brotherhood (Hamzawy et al. 2007). Mohammed Mahdi Akef – General Guide of the Muslim Brotherhood – is reported to have said that a Malaysian Muslim would be preferable to a Christian Egyptian as president of Egypt.[37] This sentiment was echoed in August 2007 when the Brotherhood published a draft political program that expressed the view that only Muslims would be eligible for the Egyptian presidency.[38]

Not surprisingly, Copts have been troubled by the contradiction in public statements of the Brotherhood and the issuing of inflammatory religious pronouncements by individuals associated with the group.[39] George Ishaq, an antiregime activist of Coptic descent, has publicly expressed concerns about the proposed creation of a council of religious scholars tasked with guaranteeing that legislation adopted by the president and parliament conformed with Islamic law.[40] To ease some of these fears, the Muslim Brotherhood has made public statements about the common "fabric" shared by Copts and Muslims.[41] There are also reports of a secret dialogue taking place between the Muslim Brotherhood and Coptic leaders to remove fears in the wake of the Brotherhood's parliamentary successes in 2005.[42] Despite this, members of the Coptic community are likely to maintain some skepticism regarding the commitment to minority rights under a government dominated by the Muslim Brotherhood or other Islamist group. Ibrahim has argued that Egypt has witnessed an increasing polarization between Muslims and Copts, with Christians increasingly taking refuge in the church.[43]

Secular Feminist and Women's Organizations. In countries around the world, secular feminist and women's organizations have played an important role in transition from authoritarian rule to democracy. Friedman (1998) has argued that women mobilized politically under highly repressive authoritarian rulers in many Latin American countries, often playing a central role in the overthrow of those dicators. In countries like Brazil, the fate of the women's movement

---

[36] *Al-Ahram Weekly*, December 29, 2005–January 4, 2006.
[37] International Crisis Group Report, "Egypt's Muslim Brothers: Confrontation or Integration?" Number 76, June 18, 2008, citing an interview in *Ruz al Youssef*, April 9, 2006.
[38] Ibid.
[39] *Al-Ahaly*, November 2–9, 2005.
[40] *Egyptian Gazette*, September 16, 2007.
[41] *Al-Sharq Al-Awsat*, December 11, 2005.
[42] *Al-Sharq Al-Awsat*, December 15, 2005.
[43] Saad Eddin Ibrahim, "The Constitution and the Supreme Court and the Armed Forces," *Civil Society*, September 2006.

was closely linked to the success of the political opposition (Alvarez 1990). Yet women's experiences in Middle Eastern countries "contrast sharply with the Latin American cases, in which women actually put themselves on the front lines of the battle against authoritarian regimes" (Brand 1998, 251). What accounts for the reluctance on the part of secular feminist and women's groups to combat authoritarian regimes like the one in Egypt in a more forceful manner?

Secular feminist and women's groups in Egypt may be unlikely to promote democracy for a number of reasons.[44] First, the current regime – which has its historical antecedents in the 1952 Free Officers' coup – has offered an explicit commitment to public equality for women (Hatem 1992). Egyptian women are equal to men under the law, and women have benefited from state educational and employment opportunities. Zuhur (2003) describes the patriarchal bargain struck by elite women and authoritarian states where these women were permitted to enjoy some access to power in exchange for supporting basic state structures.[45] Second, what types of policies might secular feminists expect under Islamist government? Islamists threatened the life of Egyptian feminist activist and physician Nawal al-Sa'dawi in 1991. Al-Sa'dawi has been taken to court repeatedly for writing a book that is deemed by some as "offensive to God"; one claimant wants the court to annul her Egyptian citizenship.[46] The 2007 Muslim Brotherhood draft program also suggested that a woman could not be president of Egypt.[47] Examples from other Muslim majority countries are also illustrative and may have informed the political choices of Egyptian feminist groups. When a Moroccan woman gathered a million signatures in support of a ban on polygamy and repudiation in Morocco, an influential religious leader issued a *fatwā* calling for her death.[48]

Although a mainstream group like the Egyptian Muslim Brotherhood cannot be held responsible for such threats, Islamists in government have not demonstrated a commitment to secular conceptualizations of women's rights. The Islamist government in Sudan has been considered a serial violator of women's liberties. When Islamists from Jordan's Islamic Action Front were given positions in Jordan's cabinet, they advocated policies that were not consistent with the preferences of most secular feminists, such as a ban on coeducation (Brand 1998, 111). This suggests that secular feminist and women's groups – which

---

[44] This is not to say that Egyptian women have not played an important role in popular protests, particularly protests in reaction to rising prices and inflation. A key distinction to be made is between secular feminist organizations and more mainstream economic protests in which women participate.

[45] A similar dynamic has been described in Tunisia, where Redissi (2009) argues there exists an alliance between the ruling party and liberal women's organizations.

[46] *Egyptian Gazette*, February 19, 2008.

[47] International Crisis Group Report, "Egypt's Muslim Brothers: Confrontation or Integration?" Number 76, June 18, 2008.

[48] Ann Louise Bardach, "Tearing off the Veil: Islamic Fundamentalism's War against Women," *Vanity Fair*, August 1993.

are reported to have played an important role in regime transition in a number of Latin American countries and other contexts – have been reluctant to advocate as strongly in favor of democracy in Egypt. Brand has called into question the role that women's organizations can play as a vanguard for greater democratization in the Middle East (1998, 261), and the mechanism that I describe here may be part of the explanation.

9.2 WHO IS LIKELY TO MOBILIZE AGAINST THE AUTHORITARIAN REGIME?

O'Donnell and Schmitter (1986) write that democratic transition occurs when diverse layers of society come together to support each other's efforts toward democratization. In their conceptualization, these groups include "trade unions, grass-roots movements, religious groups, intellectuals, artists, clergymen, defenders of human rights, and professional associations" (O'Donnell and Schmitter 1986, 53–4). But what happens when these various groups share a desire for democracy but expect to receive very different outcomes depending on the winner of the country's first free election? Thus far, I have argued that liberal intellectuals and artists, Coptic Christians, and secular feminist and women's groups may be reluctant to mobilize against the authoritarian regime in Egypt because they believe that their policy preferences are better served under a status quo authoritarian regime than a democracy under which Islamists have a high probability of winning office. As a result, these groups, which have been critical, if not pivotal, for democratic transition in other contexts, are unlikely to play a similar role in the Egyptian context.

What groups then might mobilize against the authoritarian regime in Egypt? Nascent political parties are often shut down or prevented from organizing (Stacher 2004). Existing opposition parties do not appear to hold much promise for effective mobilization against the government. Opposition parties also suffer from a weakness in their organizational machines (Teti, Gervasio, and Rucci 2006) and are financially fragile, relying heavily on state largesse for funds crucial to their continued survival (Langohr 2004; Masoud 2006b). Albrecht (2005) has argued that Egyptian opposition parties are an integral part of the state's "juggling act" and, as such, ultimately contribute to authoritarian stability rather than challenge the system. Effective mobilizers would have to be actors or groups that have both the capacity to influence change and also expect to do better under a democracy with Islamists in power than under the status quo authoritarian regime. These actors and groups need not be supporters of Islamist policies *per se*, but at the very least should have no strong ideological opposition to the likely programmatic policies of a democratically elected Islamist government. In this section, I ask the following highly speculative question: What groups might make up an effective antiauthoritarian coalition in Egypt?

Although there continue to be some who argue that Egyptians do not engage in social protest as a result of a cultural quietism or complacency, this stereotype overlooks the fact that there have been and continue to be small mutinies taking place across the cities and villages of Egypt on an almost daily basis. Although these acts of protest are often misreported as crime, subversion, or even terrorist activity, very often, political protest is at the core of the activism.[49] Widespread national protests have taken place at various times across Egypt, for example, in reaction to light sentences given to corrupt military leadership following the 1967 loss to Israel, following the announcement that certain food and other subsidies would be lifted in 1977, and after low-level security service personnel were told that their service would be extended by an extra year in 1986. More recently, rural Egyptians have protested new land tenure arrangements that were implemented in late 1997. Ismail writes that, since 1998, citizen confrontations with the police have become increasingly common, with citizens frequently protesting poor provision of public services (2006, 161–2).

Citizen protests, particularly labor strikes, often emerge in response to neoliberal economic reforms (Beinin 2008). This includes protest activity as a result of both the privatization of state sector firms as well as the shrinking of services provided by the Egyptian government. In addition, anti-Israeli demonstrations that began in the fall of 2000 and anti-U.S. protests with the U.S. invasion of Iraq eventually morphed into more generalized antiregime demonstrations. Although occurances of protest are generally short-lived, Ismail characterizes them as both recurrent and widespread (2006, 162).

One implication of the argument that I have put forth is that we would not expect to see extensive antiregime protest on the part of liberal artists and intellectuals, Coptic Christian organizations, or secular feminist groups. Using qualitative data regarding instances of major grassroots mobilization, I show that popular protest against the regime in Egypt more typically involves one or more of the groups described below. A common feature of these groups is that they are less threatened by the prospect of Islamists in government than the liberal intelligentsia, Christians, and feminists.

9.2.1   Islamist-Oriented Intellectuals

What types of intellectuals might provide the leadership for a pro-democracy movement in Egypt? Sonbol writes that Egyptian intellectuals have had the greatest impact on political change when in partnership with Islamists; in particular, she writes that, when Islamic thought is brought together with "demands for human and personal freedoms... combined with a strong belief in social justice and redistribution of wealth," intellectuals can enjoy widespread appeal to the masses (Sonbol 2000, xl). Egyptian political sociologists have suggested that intellectuals can only be effective if they are able to pull along some important mass segment of society.[50]

---

[49] Interview with Gehad Auda, NDP Media Secretariat and Professor of Political Science, Helwan University, May 1, 2007; Bush 2002a.

[50] Interview with Moheb Zaki, Ibn Khaldun Center for Development Studies, May 23, 2007.

Tariq al-Bishri – prominent judge, historian, and left-leaning intellectual – represents the leading example of an Egyptian intellectual who has the ability to employ Islamist ideals of justice for political change. Al-Bishri has insisted on a "need to integrate Islam into the national political formula" (Binder 1988, 246). According to al-Bishri, this would require Islamic thinkers to grant equal political rights to Egypt's Copts (Binder 1988). Al-Bishri has also encouraged the Muslim Brotherhood to increase its levels of cooperation with other civil society groups (Binder 1988). In October 2004, al-Bishri published "A Call for Civil Disobedience," the basic tenets of which were adopted by Kefeya, also known as the Egyptian Movement for Change.[51] Kefeya – an organization of elite activists opposed to the Mubarak presidency and the possibility that power may transfer to Hosni Mubarak's son, Gamal – asked al-Bishri to run as its presidential candidate in the 2005 presidential election, a proposal he turned down.[52] Al-Bishri's outstanding reputation and the respect he enjoys from both Islamists and non-Islamists would make him, or someone with a similar profile, a likely leader of a successful pro-democracy movement in Egypt. This group might include other individuals who focus on Islamic constitutionalism, such as Yusuf al-Qaradawi and Kamal Abu al-Magd. Al-Qaradawi – trained in Islamic law at al-Azhar University – hosts a weekly show on Islamic law on *al-Jazeera*. Abu al-Magd is a prominent lawyer in Egypt and operates both inside and outside of government circles. Rutherford (2006) profiles the positions of these and other similar individuals in considerable detail.

Other leading intellectuals of this type may emerge from Egypt's network of activist judges,[53] university professors,[54] or the leadership of Kefeya, whose members have shown a propensity for effectively crossing ideological barriers (Shorbagy 2007).

9.2.2 Peasants

It has generally been assumed that Middle Eastern, and particularly Egyptian, peasants are politically acquiescent and submissive; both recent and more distant history convey a different impression, however, given the ability of peasants to bring pressure on ruling elites from time to time (Ansari 1986, 12). Brown finds, for example, that a primary weapon of peasants has historically been physical attack, particularly assassinations of local officials and notables (1990, 90). Such acts occur with surprising frequency and often emerge spontaneously, as a result of specific threats to a local community (Brown 1990, 111).

An important source of grievance for Egyptian peasants is related to the changes in land tenure arrangements. Legislation, which was phased in between 1992 and 1997, ended fixed rents for tenants and the right to inherit tenancies

---

[51] *Al-Ahram Weekly*, December 28, 2006–January 3, 2007.
[52] Ibid.
[53] See the writings of Mona el-Ghobashy for more details on the judge's movement.
[54] Faculty members of various political ideologies publicly joined antigovernment protests in 2005 at Cairo and Minya Universities. For more details, see the *Chronicle of Higher Education*, April 29, 2005, p. 39.

in perpetuity (Bush 2002a). Prior to 1992, rent was fixed to land tax rates and tenants could not be evicted unless unable to pay their rent (Saad 2002). As land values increased, landowners found themselves unable to sell their holdings at market value because buyers did not want to be saddled with permanent tenants (Saad 2002). Peasants aggressively resisted implementation of the new legislation (Land Center for Human Rights 2002).[55] Confrontations took place in villages across the country. For example, in 1997, land disputes resulted in the deaths of 100 farmers.[56] To a large degree, the legislation reflected "the prevailing power structure at the national level, and especially the power of the landlords, who were backed by the government, or who were members of the government" (Saad 2002, 106). Villagers turned their anger against security services in 1998, often attacking symbols of government power (Ismail 2006, 162). Seeking to defuse the tension, the government publicized a statement by the Shaykh of Al-Azhar that the tenancy law was consistent with Islamic legal tenents (Bush 2002a). It is not clear that this pronouncement had an effect.[57]

What long-term impact did the change in land tenancy have on the Egyptian peasantry? Bush (2002a) and others have argued that these changes had a very detrimental impact on rural peoples, including more expensive land rents for tenant peasants and higher levels of rural unemployment and poverty (Bush 2002a). Rural debt levels also increased, which evolved into new forms of forced labor (Bush 2002b). Tenants coped in ways that tended to impact the lives of women. For example, women often sold gold and livestock to make ends meet, and girls were frequently kept home from school (Saad 2002).[58]

9.2.3 Bedouin

Egypt's Sinai residents are a geographically marginalized but symbolically important minority group.[59] Suicide bombings in the resort cities of Taba in October 2004 and Sharm al-Sheikh in July 2005 drew attention to the Sinai Bedouin, both as a result of their alleged complicity in the attacks and the numerous articles that have been written about the treatment of Bedouin in the wake of those incidents.

The roots of Bedouin discontent have a long history. The Bedouin have lived under the control of Egyptian State Security since the return of Sinai in 1982. It is reported that the vast majority of government facilities in the Sinai

---

[55] Violence prior to 1997 was fairly limited because many believed that the law would never be fully implemented (Saad 2002).

[56] *Al-Ahram Weekly*, January 24–30, 2008.

[57] Interestingly, peasant movements in Egypt – like elsewhere – use the normative discourse of the existing order to legitimate their demands (Scott 1985, 336–8). For example, protesting peasants often appeal directly to the president to help them solve their problems. See *Al-Masry Al-Youm*, July 3, 2008, for one example.

[58] Processing of milk products often provides a source of extra income for rural women.

[59] The Bedouin are not the only minority group with grievances against the regime. In a provocatively titled editorial, "The Nuba: A Ticking Time Bomb," Ossama Heikal makes the case that long-suffering Nubian citizens of upper Egypt who have been displaced by projects related to the high dam are ripe for political dissent. See *Al-Masry Al-Youm*, June 30, 2007.

are security facilities that are not related to the provision of other services.[60] Seventy percent of Sinai Bedouins reportedly do not trust the government.[61] Poverty and unemployment are widespread; youths report that it feels as though 90 percent of the Bedouin are unemployed.[62] Bedouin are typically barred – for both cultural and security reasons – from lucrative employment positions at coastal resorts in Sinai.[63] The proximity of the Sinai tourism boom has also forced the Bedouin to face the relative poverty of their situation.[64] Left with few alternatives, Bedouin youth often earn money from smuggling and bootlegging.[65]

In the wake of the 2004 and 2005 bombings, state security has engaged in a massive crackdown of Sinai Bedouin. Press reports suggest that thousands have been arrested without charge or trial.[66] Security services employed collective punishment tactics, angering large swathes of the community.[67] In response, the Bedouin have organized protest activities,[68] with some threatening to seek political asylum in Israel.[69] Sinai citizens rioted against government plans to demolish the homes of thousands of families.[70] Sinai residents targeted government offices and infrastructure, including the local NDP headquarters during tension in 2007.[71] Hundreds of Bedouin protested bad living conditions in 2008.[72] In response to Bedouin discontent, the government has sought to buy off Bedouin with land and salary for tribal chiefs.[73] Despite these measures, the Sinai Bedouin remain one of the most economically deprived and marginalized groups in all of Egypt. Heavy-handed government crackdowns have left some Bedouin willing to engage in more militant activity in protest.

9.2.4   University Students

University students have been, and continue to be, among the most influential sources of mobilized political protest in Egypt. For example, university students vocally protested light sentences received by senior military officers who shared some of the responsibility for Egypt's 1967 defeat to Israel. Nasser had created openings for protest on university campuses that had not existed previously

---

[60] *Al-Ahram Weekly*, May 17–23, 2007.
[61] *Al-Ahram Weekly*, May 3–9, 2007.
[62] *Egyptian Gazette*, May 8, 2007.
[63] *Al-Ahram Weekly*, May 17–23, 2007.
[64] Julia Barth-Knowles, "On the Margins: The Roots of Bedouin Militancy," *Civil Society*, November 2006.
[65] *Al-Ahram Weekly*, May 17–23, 2007; *Egyptian Gazette*, May 8, 2007.
[66] *Al-Masry Al-Youm*, June 16, 2007.
[67] *Al-Masry Al-Youm*, May 6, 2007.
[68] *Al-Ahram Weekly*, May 3–9, 2007.
[69] *Egyptian Gazette*, April 30, 2007; *Al-Masry Al-Youm*, May 5, 2007.
[70] *Al-Ahram Weekly*, August 2–8, 2007.
[71] *Al-Masry Al-Youm*, October 10, 2007; *Al-Ahram Weekly*, October 11–17, 2007.
[72] *Al-Masry Al-Youm*, August 4, 2008.
[73] *Egyptian Gazette*, July 4, 2007.

(Wickham 2002, 33). University students mobilized in support of social justice and freedom of expression, against the Israeli military occupation (Wickham 2002, 34), and in opposition to the declining quality of public education and employment prospects.

Mobilization on campuses intensified in 2000 following the start of the Al-Aqsa Intifada. Alexandria University students protested the poor treatment of Palestinians in occupied areas.[74] Similar demonstrations eventually spread to other Egyptian universities.[75] University campuses have also seen increased activism on the part of Islamist student organizations. Students affiliated with the Muslim Brotherhood have enhanced their public presence on university campuses with calls for political reform and social justice.[76] In 2005, thousands of students demonstrated at campuses across Egypt, seeking an end to emergency law.[77]

State intervention in student elections has also led students to mobilize against the state. When Muslim Brotherhood–affiliated candidates were left off candidate lists for student elections at Cairo, 'Ain Shams, and Helwan Universities, students demonstrated in opposition.[78] The activism of university students suggests that campuses continue to be a location of important political activity.

9.2.5 Labor Movements

Although labor has a long history of activism in Egypt (Posusney 1997; Beinin and Lockman 1998), recent labor movement protest has been described as "the longest and strongest wave of worker protest since the end of World War II" (Beinin and el-Hamalawy 2007). There are dozens, if not hundreds, of examples of specific labor protests to describe. Twenty thousand workers at the public sector textile factory at al-Mahalla al-Kubra went on strike in December 2006. Workers in Suez and Mansoura went on strike in protest of low wages and bad treatment by management.[79] Three hundred subway workers went on strike in May 2007.[80] In the Nasr City area of Cairo, 3,000 bus drivers, ticket collectors, and maintenance workers went on strike and 1,500 garbage collectors went on strike to demand the payment of back wages.[81] Two hundred employees picketed in Assiut in protest of failure to renew the contracts for 400 staff members.[82] According to media reports, there were more than 200

---

[74] *Al-Ahram Weekly*, October 5–11, 2000.
[75] Ibid.
[76] *Al-Ahram Weekly*, October 13–19, 2005.
[77] *The Guardian*, April 13, 2005.
[78] *Al-Ahram Weekly*, November 9–15, 2006.
[79] *Al-Masry Al-Youm*, May 20, 2007.
[80] *Al-Masry Al-Youm*, May 16, 2007.
[81] *Al-Ahram Weekly*, May 10–16, 2007.
[82] *Al-Masry Al-Youm*, July 2, 2007.

labor protests in Egypt during 2006.[83] In the first 5 months of 2007, new labor protests were reported on a daily basis (Beinin and el-Hamalawy 2007).

Labor strikes in Egypt have challenged some of the conventional wisdom regarding worker activism. Although protests have typically occurred in a public sector context, increasingly sit-ins and strikes are occurring in both the public and private sectors.[84] In addition, evidence suggests that the workers' movement is more coordinated than in the past.[85] The protests also extend beyond the textile industry to include a variety of sectors of the economy (Beinin and el-Hamalawy 2007). Protests have also taken place outside of the Delta, extending to almost all geographic areas of the country. The conventional wisdom regarding white collar employees of the state is that they have been coopted as a result of their state employment and have too much to lose by engaging in protest behavior. There are some indications that this is no longer the case. When teachers in Egypt's parallel Azhari educational system were excluded from pay increases promised to Ministry of Education teachers, 22,000 Azhar teachers organized a strike and refused to correct exams.[86] Other state sector professionals have also gone on strike, most frequently angry that salaries have not met price increases. These groups include veterinarians,[87] doctors,[88] and university professors.[89]

In September 2007, 5,000 employees at the real estate tax department in Giza demanded reaffiliation with the Ministry of Finance rather than local councils.[90] According to one protest leader, the real estate tax department – which used to be governed by the Ministry of Finance – was put under the authority of local councils in 1974 by a vengeful finance minister who was angered that real estate tax collectors attempted to collect taxes from his father.[91] Protesters insisted that they did not receive compensation commensurate with their work, whereas auditors affiliated with the Ministry of Finance received higher pay for less complicated work.[92] In December 2007, 55,000 real estate tax employees went on strike to protest the differential treatment between themselves and the Ministry of Finance's real estate tax department.[93] The strike continued

[83] Arab Reform Bulletin, Carnegie Endowment for International Peace, May 2007.
[84] *Al-Araby*, September 24, 2006.
[85] *Al-Ahram Weekly*, June 21–27, 2007.
[86] *Al-Masry Al-Youm*, June 27, 2007.
[87] *Al-Masry Al-Youm*, March 14, 2008.
[88] For details see *Al-Masry Al-Youm*, November 26, 2007; *Egyptian Gazette*, February 3, 2008; *Al-Masry Al-Youm*, February 3, 2008; *Al-Ahram Weekly*, May 1–7, 2008; *Egyptian Gazette*, March 7, 2008.
[89] For details, see *Al-Ahram Weekly*, November 22–28, 2007; *Al-Masry Al-Youm*, November 26, 2007; *Al-Masry Al-Youm*, December 5, 2007; *Al-Ahram Weekly*, December 6–12, 2007; *Al-Masry Al-Youm*, February 19, 2008; *Al-Masry Al-Youm*, March 24, 2008; *Egypt Today*, April 2008; *Al-Ahram Weekly*, March 27–April 2, 2008.
[90] *Al-Masry Al-Youm*, September 11, 2007.
[91] Ibid.
[92] *Egyptian Gazette*, December 9, 2007.
[93] *Al-Masry Al-Youm*, December 3, 2007.

for several days, with some workers threatening a hunger strike.[94] In many cases, protesters were joined by their families to emphasize the broader economic strain of their situations.[95] The real estate tax collectors temporarily suspended their sit-in after being promised a bonus of two months' salary each.[96] After months of protest, the real estate tax collectors eventually won wage parity with their Ministry of Finance counterparts (Beinin 2008).

What precipitated the resurgence of labor in Egypt? Labor's distrust of government increased in the 1990s (el-Mikaway 2000). The gradual withdrawal of the state from the social contract established under Nasser had intensified tension between workers and the government. Privatization of state-owned enterprises also led to worker grievance in many cases. The Nasserite newspaper *Al-Araby* describes the most common sources of grievance for workers as denial of health insurance, corrupt company officials, nonpayment of bonuses, failure to apportion a promised percentage of profits to workers, denial of pension payments, violation of labor laws, and poor treatment of workers, including but not limited to verbal abuse and insults.[97] Workers have also gone on strike as a result of salary arrears and failure to pay promised meal allowances.[98] In some cases, workers strike because the deteriorated nature of equipment makes an accident likely[99]; this is particularly the case for workers in the transportation industry, who fear that a train or metro accident might leave them responsible for hundreds of deaths.[100]

In general, laborers have witnessed a deterioration in quality of life for their families.[101] Rising food prices, low salaries, and the government's inability to provide relief for poor citizens spurred worker discontent.[102] Uneven distribution of income in Egypt has also contributed to the protests.[103] Although these strikes have been described as largely apolitical in nature,[104] they are fueled by the government's failure to ensure a social safety net and minimum standard of living for citizens and reflect a more generalized dissatisfaction. Because it is difficult to distinguish bread-and-butter issues of economic redistribution from "politics," per se, it is problematic to characterize these protests as strictly apolitical.

Despite attempts by successive Egyptian presidents to manipulate and control the behavior of workers, corporatist structures have not been able to eliminate strikes, which sometimes take an antigovernment or anti-NDP tone

---

[94] *Al-Masry Al-Youm*, December 9, 2007; *Egyptian Gazette*, December 9, 2007; *Al-Masry Al-Youm*, December 10, 2007; *Al-Masry Al-Youm*, December 11, 2007.

[95] *Al-Masry Al-Youm*, December 8, 2007.

[96] *Al-Masry Al-Youm*, December 14, 2007.

[97] *Al-Araby*, September 24, 2006.

[98] *Al-Araby*, May 6, 2007.

[99] *Al-Araby*, September 24, 2006.

[100] *Al-Masry Al-Youm*, December 7, 2007.

[101] Matthew Devlin, "Workers of Egypt, Unite?" *Civil Society*, May 2007.

[102] *Al-Masry Al-Youm*, February 18, 2008; *Egyptian Gazette*, April 28, 2008.

[103] *Al-Wafd*, June 16, 2007.

[104] *Egyptian Gazette*, May 15, 2007.

(Posusney 1997, 155). The evolution of Egyptian leftism may also create opportunities for Islamist-labor cooperation (el-Hamalawy 2007). The emergence of Muslim Brotherhood parliamentarians like 'Ali Fatah al-Bab, who represents a district on the industrial outskirts of Cairo, also suggests that workers could potentially provide electoral support for Brothers. Although ruling party officials have accused the Muslim Brotherhood of organizing riots in Mahala Al-Kubra,[105] Beinin argues that the Brothers have played little role in the workers' movement (2008).

9.3 CONCLUSIONS

In January 2008, Mubarak played down fears of social instability in Egypt, arguing that "strikes and sit-ins are signs of an increasing margin of freedom."[106] The implication of this statement is that popular protest is actually a positive development, reflecting the strength of the regime through its ability to tolerate dissent. Lorentzen (2006) makes a similar argument with a different causal logic to explain why the occurrence of protests in authoritarian countries may not be a harbinger of regime collapse; he finds that the Chinese government has engaged in a policy of deliberate toleration of economic protest that actually helps the regime in two ways. First, protest allows the government to identify and coopt discontented groups, and, second, it provides a signal of local corruption (Lorentzen 2006). This suggests that, although Egyptian society is quite strong vis-á-vis the state (Sadowski 1991, 90), social protest does not necessarily signal the fall of the existing regime. This chapter has argued that one reason for this might be that, without the symbolic leadership of liberal intellectuals and artists, transition to democracy is highly difficult.

To summarize, this chapter makes two primary arguments. The first is that liberal intellectuals and artists – often a symbolically important vanguard of pro-democracy protests in autocratic countries – are less likely to mobilize in authoritarian Egypt given the uncertainty of these liberals and artists regarding the commitment of Islamists to guarantee personal and artistic freedoms. The threat of Islamist electoral success is used to systematically demobilize this important class of potential activists. This is not to say that these individuals are less democratically inclined than their counterparts in other parts of the world; rather, my argument is that, given the very high stakes associated with mobilization against a regime with considerable repressive capacity, it is not surprising that artists and intellectuals would be apprehensive about the social and political policies that might emerge under democratic government. Islamism is, arguably, the most popular movement in Egypt today, and the vague and often contradictory nature of public statements by the Muslim Brotherhood regarding the group's commitment to issues like artistic freedom and women's

---

[105] *Al-Ahram Weekly*, April 17–23, 2008.
[106] *Egyptian Gazette*, January 15, 2008.

and minority rights give pause to liberal intellectuals and artists. Other potentially important groups, like Coptic Christians and secular feminists, may also be reluctant to organize and participate in pro-democracy protests for similar reasons. The Muslim Brotherhood has responded to this criticism by seeking a renewal of its relationship with intellectuals.[107] Despite these efforts, intellectuals may continue to feel greater security accommodating an authoritarian regime with a secular orientation (Beattie 1991).

The second argument that I have made is that protest behavior – if it is to intensify – is likely to draw on societal groups that are not ideologically fearful of Islamist government, in principle. Many of these groups, like peasants, workers, and university students, are already engaged in acts of protest on a regular basis.[108] A pro-democracy movement in Egypt with the greatest opportunity for success would need to develop a political program that appealed to broad segments of the public as well as the Islamist movement (Ottaway and Carothers 2004). Left-leaning intellectuals with Islamist inclinations, like Tariq al-Bishri, could provide leadership for a broad-based political opposition movement of this type (Abaza 2000, 92).

[107] *Al-Ahram Weekly*, March 15–21, 2007.
[108] And there are some indications that protest behavior can sometimes be effective; for example, villagers who barricaded the main road in their village in Kafr al-Shaykh were able to force the construction of a water pipeline to their village. For more details, see the *Egyptian Gazette*, July 8, 2007.

10

Foreign Pressure and Institutional Change

The distributive implications of authoritarian elections in Egypt extend beyond the internal political dynamics that have thus far been the focus of this book to include Egypt's relationship with external actors, such as the United States. External actors play a critical role in providing financial assistance for the regime. This chapter investigates how elections affect Egypt's relationship with external actors, such as the United States, and why foreign efforts to promote democratization in Egypt have been so unsuccessful. To answer these questions, I develop an agenda-setting model of policy change in authoritarian regimes where foreign actors, such as the United States or international financial institutions (IFIs), serve as veto players along with the ruling elite. I argue that the actions of foreign actors tend to promote the *electoralization* of authoritarian regimes rather than democratization because democratization could end regime dominance. This is because authoritarians are agenda setters and they have the ability to select their preferred point (i.e., the set of institutions) after considering the winset of the foreign actor as a constraint. I discuss this model in the context of electoralization in Egypt with a focus on the amendment to Article 76 of the Egyptian constitution, which created the country's first multicandidate presidential elections in 2005.

10.1 PREVIOUS LITERATURE

This chapter explores the extent to which foreign actors, such as the United States and IFIs, can serve as veto players in a country's domestic policy environment. Although the circumstances under which this occurs are fairly limited, both IFI conditionality and threats to reduce or eliminate foreign assistance on the part of a donor country can grant these actors the power of veto players on particular policy issues.

There are two primary means by which external actors can influence policy change in a host country. The first is through conditionality agreements set by IFIs seeking particular policy changes in return for loans or other assistance.

The second is as a result of political pressure and threats to cut off assistance by individual donor countries, such as the United States. In addition to attempts to influence policy and orientation, there are also a number of less obvious externalities that can arise as a result of foreign assistance. I briefly address the literature on each of these in turn.

10.1.1   Conditionality

Conditionality generally refers to commitments on economic and financial policies that are often a requirement for IFI assistance or borrowing. For example, IMF lending has involved policy conditions since the 1950s; and until the early 1980s, IMF conditionality largely focused on macroeconomic policies designed to ensure that the loan would be used in an effective manner to resolve a country's economic problems.[1] The conditionality associated with IFI lending, however, has been a major source of controversy. Developing countries have complained that conditionality is intrusive and that IFIs fail to tailor conditions to the circumstances of particular countries (Dreher 2002). Perhaps more importantly, policies included in IFI programs often differed dramatically from the policy preferences of the borrowing countries' governments.[2]

10.1.2   Foreign Assistance, Influence, and the Externalities of Aid

The second literature regarding the potential influence of foreign actors involves the use of foreign aid disbursements to influence either specific policies or the pace of political liberalization. Palmer, Wohlander, and Morgan (2002) argue that powerful states seek to change the policy status quo or maintain some favorable status quo through the use of foreign aid or other policies. Alesina and Dollar (2000) find that aid is allocated with regard to the political and strategic considerations of donors. Stone (2002) investigates the question of why the Soviet Union could not control its own satellites. He argues that Soviet officials did not monitor the behavior of satellite countries closely enough to identify infractions (Stone 2002).

Another strand in this literature attempts to explain the extent to which foreign aid impacts democratization in developing countries. The empirical evidence on this subject is mixed. During the Cold War, powerful international actors used aid disbursements to prop up or support strategic allies. Ake (1996) argues that, in sub-Saharan Africa, democracy promotion took a backseat to the allocation of aid to strategic allies. This practice continues to occur, although to a lesser extent than during the Cold War. Based on evidence from

---

[1] IMF Fact Sheet on Conditionality, September 2005.

[2] In related literature, Vreeland (2002) has explored the extent to which domestic institutions influence participation in IMF programs. In particular, he argues that executives facing many veto players are more likely to turn to the IMF, but that the IMF is ultimately more likely to conclude agreements when there are fewer veto players.

sub-Saharan Africa, Dunning (2004) argues that the end of the Cold War reduced the geopolitical criteria for donor aid allocation, allowing forms of aid conditionality to become possible.

In addition to concerns about the political intentions of donor country foreign aid disbursements, there is also reason to believe that any type of aid given to authoritarian regimes helps to strengthen the existing autocrats. Ross (2001) classifies the mechanisms supporting this argument into three categories, which he calls the rentier, repression, and modernization effects.[3] The rentier effect refers to the perverse impact of external rents (like aid), where recipient regimes are less likely to tax their citizenries and hence are less likely to represent them. The external rents also provide wealth that can be spent buying off segments of the population. The repression effect describes the ability of rent-rich states to build up military and security forces that can repress opponents. Finally, the modernization effect refers to the perversity of resource-led growth that is not accompanied by higher education levels and occupational specialization. The perverse externalities of foreign aid are also echoed by development economists (Easterly 2001).

This suggests that foreign aid has the potential to impact a regime in a number of different ways and that the nature of this influence may have changed over time with the end of the Cold War. Although conditionality creates a tension between donor and recipient countries, scholars focusing on the Cold War period see aid as a way to prop up an authoritarian regime. With the end of the Cold War, and the increasing emphasis on democratization and good governance on the part of major donors, there may be reason to believe that aid can play a more effective role in promoting political change.[4]

10.2   CAN AN EXTERNAL ACTOR BE A VETO PLAYER?

Under a variety of circumstances, external actors can serve as veto players in a country's domestic politics. A veto player is defined as the collection of individual or collective actors needed to change a country's policy (Tsebelis 2002). In the context of the United States, the House, the Senate, the president, and potentially the Supreme Court are all veto players; without the agreement of each of these actors, policy change cannot be implemented and the status quo prevails. In authoritarian settings, veto power on most issues is held by the authoritarian ruler, or the small junta or inner circle surrounding him.

10.2.1   Egypt's Domestic Veto Player

Policy in Egypt is generally made at the discretion of a single veto player. An argument could be made regarding whether or not the single veto player in

---

[3] Although Ross (2001) is referring explicitly to the way oil rents help an authoritarian regime, these ideas are largely applicable to foreign aid as well.

[4] Levitsky and Way (2005) argue that countries with high levels of linkage and leverage to the West had intense international democratizing pressures.

Egypt is an individual or collective. The assumption is that, if there is a single veto player, Egyptian President Mubarak makes decisions unilaterally; if it is a collective, then Mubarak and a small group of his inner circle make decisions in group fashion. This distinction is not critically important for the objectives of this chapter except to argue that the agreement of no other political actor within Egypt is generally needed to make policy change.[5]

The power of the executive branch in Egypt has an important historic and institutional basis. Following the 1952 Free Officers' coup, splits existed within the ruling junta between Colonel Gamal 'Abd al-Nasser and General Mohammed Nagib. "The brief period of collective decisions and responsibility under the Free Officer regime lasted barely two years. By November 1954 Nasser was supreme" (Vatikiotis 1992, 424). By 1956, Nasser had taken control from Nagib and others, who favored more of a constitutional government. A new constitution was promulgated that same year and called for a presidential system of government, replacing the parliamentary system of government that was previously in place; the president was given the power to appoint and dismiss ministers (Vatikiotis 1992, 387). The constitution also established a unicameral national assembly, although most major decisions were undertaken by the regime without parliamentary consultation.

According to one historian, during this period of rapid political and economic change, either there was no legislature at all (i.e., after the overthrow of the previous regime until July 1957) or there was "the elected Assembly (which) met from July 1957 to March 1958, but only as a dutiful audience for ministerial and presidential speeches" (Vatikiotis 1992, 402). Further, it is likely that Nasser made many of these decisions in consultation with just a handful of advisors, if any at all:

> It is sure that only a few men had any role in the decision to nationalize (the Suez Canal), but with the passage of time the tendency has been to attribute the decision almost exclusively to Nasser. Those who were in control of the Ministries of Finance and Plan, for instance, claim that they were never consulted on the advisability of the measures (Waterbury 1983, 77).

Although Sadat did allow the formation and limited participation of political parties in Egypt, the net effect of his rule was to increase the constitutional authority of the executive branch. During his years in power, Sadat enjoyed numerous titles, including president of the republic, the chief of state, the head of government, and the supreme commander of the armed forces. In addition, Egypt was in a government-declared state of emergency for much of Sadat's time in office, empowering the president to legislate by decree as prescribed in the constitution (Baker 1990, 60). Baker (1990, 60) writes that the executive

---

[5] It is reasonable to argue that on certain issues – particularly issues related to bread-and-butter economics – the Egyptian public also has the ability to serve as a veto player via a credible threat of protest. The military leadership might also be considered a veto player on issues related to its core interests, although the military as an institution has rarely intervened on policy issues. In general, however, decisions on most policy issues in Egypt are made by the executive branch.

branch enjoyed powers of arrest and detention that allowed the government to eliminate virtually all independent political activity.

Commentators have written that the constitution contained no mechanism for controlling the exercise of these great emergency powers (Baker 1990, 59). Whereas Nasser had allowed some of the Free Officers to construct their own bases of support, Sadat eliminated alternative fiefdoms of power in order to enjoy a position of personal power. Vatikiotis writes:

> Important decisions were made by him in a state of splendid isolation. At the same time, he shifted the political center of gravity from the military establishment to a more varied civilian technocracy. As the armed forces were transformed from the political vanguard of the revolution to a professional force, as they grew in size and professional effectiveness, their political authority diminished.... As for the ASU's fiefdom of power, it was gradually diminished and, by 1978, replaced by political parties, chief among them being Sadat's own National Democratic Party (1992, 438).

In other words, under Sadat, there was greater pluralism of political life, but power was still heavily concentrated in the hands of the president. Although Sadat had previously supported limiting the tenure of the Egyptian president to a maximum of two terms, in 1980, he held a referendum to allow himself to stay in office as president indefinitely. Sadat was assassinated in 1981 by Islamic militants, and Vice President Hosni Mubarak took office immediately. During the first few years of Mubarak's presidency, the regime emphasized political liberalization.

The most important constraint on executive authority in Mubarak's Egypt has come from external actors. Dessouki (1981) finds that Egypt has been "highly susceptible to external influences," particularly given its dependence on the outside world. Among the actors that have had real influence over Egyptian policy are the IMF, the United States, and Saudi Arabia (Dessouki 1981). Indeed, according to Springborg, Egypt's economic dependence on aid donors is the "major constraint, indeed the determinant" of its foreign and domestic policy choices, as a necessary first priority is feeding a growing population dependent on this assistance for sustenance (1988, 139–40). Brownlee argues that "external backers may hold the most potential for gradually limiting executive power while supporting the parties and an embattled civil society" (2002, 53). The United States is frequently singled out by both Egyptian and foreign analysts as the external power with the ability to exert the most meaningful pressure on Egypt.[6] This invites the following question: under what circumstances may external actors actually serve as veto players in a country's domestic policy?

---

[6] Interview with Moheb Zaki, Ibn Khaldun Center for Development Studies, May 23, 2007; interview with Ossama al-Ghazali Harb, August 27, 2009; Andrew Exum and Zack Snyder, "Democracy Demotion in Egypt: Is the United States a Willing Accomplice?" PolicyWatch 1212, March 23, 2007.

10.2.2   International Financial Institutions

Egypt has a long and contentious history of relations with IFIs like the IMF and the World Bank. In 1976, the IMF representative in Cairo sent a memo to the Egyptian cabinet outlining economic reforms that were to include drastic reductions in subsidies (Heikal 1983). The cabinet – alarmed by the scope of the forms – challenged the IMF proposals, though "it quickly became apparent that they (the outlined reforms) were commands rather than recommendation" (Heikal 1983, 90). Riots took place across Egypt in January 1977 in response to the decrease in subsidies. Describing Egypt's relationship with the IMF during this period, Dessouki writes that "Egypt had to concede. She accepted the principle of international supervision over its economic policy as a condition for financial aid from Arab and western sources" (1981, 414).

During the 1980s, Egypt's food bill and associated deficit grew as the regime feared cuts to subsidies would spark additional unrest. By the late 1980s, Egypt could no longer finance its debt. Capital inflows decreased, and GDP growth dropped (Weiss and Wurzel 1998, 23). Zaki writes:

> This crisis signalled strongly that there could be no more postponement of embarking on the IMF program of economic structural reform. In 1991 Egypt took the painful step. The plan was the standard IMF prescription which included, among other things: a reduction in government spending, the grad- ual cutting of subsidies, privatization of the economy, a contraction of gov- ernment intervention in the economy and a much greater reliance on market mechanisms (1995, 164).

IMF conditionality required that Egypt undertake macroeconomic restruc- turing as well as privatization of state-owned enterprises (Weiss and Wurzel 1998, 24–5). These were policies that the ruling elite may have otherwise been reluctant to put into place if they had not been forced to by the IMF. In fact, it has been argued that, in light of the regime's hesitancy to reform, the donor community insisted on strict conditionality (Weiss and Wurzel 1998, 33). This discussion suggests that, at particular times and on certain issues, Egyptian policy decisions are not made purely at the discretion of the country's domestic veto player – the executive branch. During Egypt's period of economic vulner- ability beginning in the late 1980s, it became increasingly clear that the IFIs would have a hand in Egyptian economic policy.

Despite the relative unpopularity of some of these economic reforms, the regime was forced to implement a policy position that differed from its ideal point as a result of IFI conditionality. It is important to point out that priva- tization was accomplished in a way that was consistent with the state's need to "distribute economic wealth to supporting networks of economic actors" (Wurzel 2004, 114). Thus, although the government was hesitant about imple- menting required reforms, ultimately the regime maintained enough control over which firms to privatize and the pace of privatization in order to enjoy some strategic benefit. This has led some to characterize privatization in Egypt as a "political tactic" for sustaining the authoritarian regime rather than as a set of reforms for stimulating free enterprise of markets (Moore 1986, 634).

10.2.3   United States

The other external actor that has had and continues to have the potential to influence Egyptian domestic policy is the United States. As Egypt's patron since the 1970s, the United States has contributed aid money to the Egyptian regime over the last 20 years. The critical role that Egypt has played in the Arab–Israeli peace process has been at the core of the U.S.–Egyptian relationship (Durac 2009).[7] The aid package was initially provided as a "reward" for having been the first Arab country to make peace with Israel; an additional goal was to bring stability to the regime.

How important has U.S. aid been to Egypt? Even at the peak of its influence over Egypt, the Soviet Union never had as many "points of leverage" over Egypt as enjoyed by the United States (Waterbury 1983, 404). Zaki finds that, between 1975 and 1991, American aid amounted to about 10 percent of Egypt's GDP (1995, 183). Mustapha Kamel al-Sayyid estimates this amount to have been more than $25 billion, split between $6.7 billion for commodity imports, $5.9 billion for physical infrastructure, $3.9 billion for food aid, $3.3 billion in cash transfers and technical assistance, and $4.5 billion for services like health care, family planning, education, and agriculture (although this figure does not include additional military aid).[8] One researcher writes that, in the 1980s, "U.S. bilateral aid to Egypt, including commodity and technology transfers, has probably been indispensable for meeting immediate resource needs" (Weinbaum 1986, 2).

United States aid to Egypt has been important in several areas, particularly with regard to food security, development assistance, and support and training for the Egyptian military. Egypt has been one of the world's largest importers of American wheat (Weinbaum 1986, 49). Concessionary food sales made up nearly a quarter of foreign aid in the 1980s. Wheat was used to make the ubiquitous loaves of local bread that are a staple of the Egyptian diet. The price of these loaves was heavily subsidized. Whereas Egypt used to be more dependent on U.S. wheat, increasingly it is turning to less expensive imports from Ukraine and Russia. Nevertheless, Egypt continues to import two-thirds of its food, and U.S. assistance frees up important hard currency sources for the purchase of this important commodity.[9]

In addition to the important food aid and wheat imports, Egypt has been a major beneficiary of development assistance from the United States by way

---

[7] Because of this, the U.S.–Egypt dyad is actually quite unique, potentially limiting the generalizability of the arguments made here.

[8] *Al-Ahram Weekly*, June 21–27, 2001.

[9] Congressional Research Service Issue Brief for Congress, Egypt–United States Relations, updated June 15, 2005.

of the United States Agency for International Development (USAID) (Sullivan 1984). Mitchell (2002) writes that development aid gave the United States a "powerful position of influence within the Egyptian state. USAID conducted what it termed 'cabinet-level dialogue' on macroeconomic policy with the Egyptian government" (Mitchell 2002, 240). The release of USAID funds could also be delayed if particular policy goals were not met. Over time, however, development assistance has been replaced by military assistance, particularly in the form of training and equipment. According to the Congressional Research Service, between 1993 and 1998, Egypt received $815 million per year in Economic Support Funds. Economic aid dropped in annual $40 million increments from $815 million in the 1998 fiscal year to $535 million by 2005. This economic aid was replaced by increasingly important military assistance.[10]

To what extent does U.S. military assistance contribute to the stability of the regime? Frisch (2001) writes that, by 2001, the United States had contributed nearly $28 billion in military aid to Egypt since 1975 – a figure that includes weapon sales, training, and exercises with U.S. forces. 'Abd al-Mon'im Sa'id writes that "the modernization of the Egyptian armed forces in the past two decades has in large measure relied on American military aid."[11] Azarva (2007) concurs, finding that Egypt's arsenal has been improved qualitatively and quantitatively in nearly every military branch thanks to aid. In addition, U.S. military aid has financed Egypt's most expensive and prestigious defense acquisitions and provided support for many of the military's economic and industrial projects. Projects including the Abrams tank manufacturing facility, an armed vehicle coproduction program, and aircraft rebuild facilities – all critical to the interests of military constituencies – have been possible because of this assistance. The United States has also sold or supplied Egypt with armored personnel carriers, Apache helicopters, anti-aircraft missile batteries, and surveillance aircraft (Aly 2006). Frisch (2001) writes that the United States has bolstered the strength of both Egyptian ground and air forces, in part because of the acquisition of 160 U.S.-built F-16 jet fighters.

U.S. military assistance has helped Egypt become the Arab world's leading manufacturer of military equipment with positive spillover into other aspects of the vast military economic machine. Former Field Marshall Abu Ghazala has said that U.S. military assistance was not only a cost-effective means of providing for Egypt's defense, but also important for developing Egypt's defense industrial base (Cook 2003, 179; quoting a May 13, 1988 interview in *Al-Mussawwar*). Military factories produce a myriad of civilian products and are thought to be among the most profitable of state-owned enterprises in Egypt; these factories are likely an important source of economic opportunity for the elite within the armed forces.

United States aid to Egypt has not been without controversy, however. Researchers have pointed out that there exists a tension between the United

---

[10] Ibid.
[11] *Al-Siyasa al-Dawliyya*, October 1998.

States and Egypt regarding this assistance, particularly because the objectives of the aid do not closely coincide with those of Egypt (Sullivan 1984, 3). This tension and the strong influence of the United States on Egyptian policy has not been lost on Egyptian commentators. Opposition journalist Hisham Kassem has said that "US pressure on the Mubarak regime has been the catalyst for most of the change we have seen."[12] Al-Ahram editorialist Salama Ahmed Salama writes that it is no secret that Egypt coordinates its domestic policy with the United States and, despite feigning resistance, has to give into U.S. demands because of aid.[13]

This sentiment is also found in the popular press in Egypt. Moheb Zaki writes that leftist newspapers, such as *Al-Ahaly* and *Al-Araby*, as well as newspapers on the right, "maintain a constant criticism of what they consider Egypt's subservience to the US and the IMF (which they take to be merely an instrument of American hegemony over the region)" (1995, 66). For example, the Egyptian opposition daily *Al-Wafd* published an article in 2005 reporting that Egyptian intellectuals supported No'man Gom'a in his call to end U.S. aid.[14] The article suggests that Egypt has given up its sovereignty in exchange for aid and cites a number of prominent public intellectuals who believe that aid has led to Egypt's subordination and that political independence will only be possible when economic independence has been achieved.[15] An opinion poll of Egyptian elites cited in a separate *Al-Wafd* article found that 62 percent of respondents believed that the relationship between the United States and Egypt was one of subjugation.[16]

Leading Egyptian political scientist Mustapha Kamel al-Sayyid writes, "Some condemn foreign aid in general, viewing it as an expression of a power relationship, with the donor country using the aid to impose its own conception of 'good society' on the recipient country."[17] This "power relationship" has manifested itself in threats to cut aid on the part of the U.S. Congress. When the Mubarak regime arrested and imprisoned Egyptian sociologist Saad Eddin Ibrahim in 2001, Congress threatened to cut Egyptian aid. Ibrahim was eventually released in 2003, likely due to U.S. pressure. The U.S. Congress also threatened to cut aid to Egypt in 2004. Democratic House member David Obey of Wisconsin wanted to tie aid improvements to Egypt's human rights record, particularly in the wake of the Mubarak administration's jailing of Ayman Nour, but this effort was blocked by the Bush administration when Assistant Secretary of State David Welch, among others, lobbied against the measure.[18]

---

[12] *Washington Post*, March 27, 2006.
[13] *Al-Ahram Weekly*, June 15–21, 2006.
[14] *Al-Wafd*, March 20, 2005.
[15] Ibid.
[16] *Al-Wafd*, March 4, 2005.
[17] *Al-Ahram Weekly*, June 21–27, 2001.
[18] *Los Angeles Times*, July 12, 2006.

Some scholars argue that U.S. assistance "effectively subsidizes authoritarianism in Egypt" (Mustafa and Norton 2007, 41).[19] In the absence of alternative sources of profit, assistance, or investment, the Mubarak regime continues to rely on U.S. aid.

10.3 DOMESTIC REGIME AS THE AGENDA SETTER

This section models the relationship between the United States and the ruling elite in Egypt, where both actors serve as veto players on particular policy issues. This section draws on the analysis in Tsebelis (2002).

10.3.1 The Formal Model

In this model there are two veto players: the United States and Egypt (Figure 10.1). Assume that both of them want to achieve their ideal point in a two-dimensional policy space. The two issue dimensions in question are the degree of electoralization within Egypt and political control. Keep in mind that the level of electoralization may or may not be associated with higher levels of political control. Political control refers to the control the authoritarian regime in Egypt exerts over the country rather than the control the United States exerts. The United States wants to have a level of electoralization and political control as represented by the point labeled "US." Assume that Egypt wants a similar degree of electoralization at time $t - 1$, but a higher level of political control. In addition, the indifference curve surrounding Egypt's preferences are ovular rather than circular because the regime is unwilling to give up much political control – in particular, there is not an equal trade-off of electoralization for political control. Egypt's ideal point is represented by the point designated "Egypt." "SQ" represents the status quo.

Assume that there is change in U.S. preference where the United States now desires a higher level of electoralization in Egypt, which shifts its ideal point to the location designated by US_t. Egypt now makes the offer to the United States. Because Egypt has the ability to set the agenda, it will choose point A as the final policy outcome. Why? The United States is indifferent between A and other locations along the indifference curve. If Egypt sets the agenda, it will choose point A because A is the closest point on the U.S. indifference curve to its own ideal point. The authoritarian regime in Egypt increases the level of electoralization while at the same time increasing its level of political control. This is evident from the fact that the line segment connecting SQ–Egypt is longer than that connecting A–Egypt. There is a significant advantage to making proposals. The player who makes the proposal – Egypt – considers

---

[19] It is interesting to also note that Egypt does not have many good alternatives to U.S. aid. Mustafa and Norton (2007) argue that, in November 2006, President Mubarak personally led a large state delegation to China in the hopes of bringing back lucrative economic agreements but returned largely empty-handed.

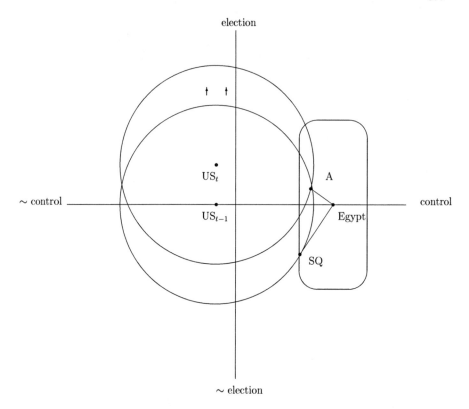

FIGURE 10.1. An agenda-setting model of the United States and Egypt.

the winset of the other veto player – the United States – as its constraint. After considering the winset of the United States, then, Egypt can choose the outcome that it prefers.

   This dynamic helps to provide an explanation for the Egyptian regime's decision to introduce multicandidate presidential elections in 2005. In the run-up to the amendment to Article 76, the Egyptian regime and the United States had different ideal points regarding the degree of electoralization and political control that should be exerted in the country. The Bush administration was heavily promoting its Middle East democracy initiative. In the face of U.S. pressure, the ruling elite in Egypt chose a set of electoral institutions that allowed it to strengthen its hold on power while conceding some ground to the United States on the issue of electoralization.[20]

---

[20] Landolt (2007) argues that U.S. democracy promotion in Egypt has backfired, though for different reasons. Using the development of family-planning NGOs supported by USAID as a case study, she finds that these organizations were eventually subsumed by the Egyptian bureaucracy despite their initial reform-minded orientation.

10.4　ELECTORAL REFORM IN EGYPT: AMENDING ARTICLE 76

What role did the United States play in Egypt's decision to hold its first multi-candidate presidential election in 2005? This project finds that U.S. influence affected the content and timing of this decision, while the Egyptian regime maintained agenda-setting authority that allowed it to select a final policy outcome that favored its domestic political objectives.

10.4.1　Bush's Middle East Democracy Initiative

Following September 11, 2001, the promotion of democracy in the Middle East emerged as an important objective of U.S. foreign policy. This was in contrast to decades of "stability-first foreign policy" in a way that increasingly staked U.S. security on the spread of democracy.[21] The logic of this policy lay in the belief that undemocratic regimes in the Middle East provided the "breeding ground" for terrorists and terrorist organizations. This policy contrasted with previous, largely unconditional, U.S. government support of authoritarian regimes in countries like Egypt and Saudi Arabia (Ottaway and Carothers 2004). Articles in the popular press focused on the fact that most of the nineteen hijackers hailed from these two countries; and, in 2002, a new U.S. aid doctrine was put forth that refocused funding priorities in the Middle East on democracy promotion.[22] Neoconservative elements within the administration came to believe that nondemocratic allies in the region represented unsustainable regimes and that political repression fostered growth of terrorist networks that had the potential to impact U.S. security in ways previously underemphasized. Proponents of democracy promotion in the Middle East often used the argument that meaningful elections in one country would lead to elections in other Arab regimes. Implicit within this ideology was also the belief that America had a "democratizing mission" in the region (Ottaway and Carothers 2004).

The emphasis on Middle East democratization first became evident about a year following September 11, 2001. In December 2002, Richard Haas, National Security Council Senior Director for Near East and South Asian Affairs, made public statements about the importance of U.S. democracy promotion in the Arab world. Secretary of State Colin Powell announced a plan for a U.S.–Mediterranean partnership in that same time period. In a speech at the American Enterprise Institute in February 2003, President Bush described the need to spread democracy in the Middle East. National Security Advisor Condoleezza Rice made public statements about U.S. resolve regarding the transformation of the Middle East, comparing it to the way the United States transformed Europe at the end of World War II. The promotion of Middle East democratization became more evident when weapons of mass destruction were not found in Iraq.

[21] Jeffrey Azarva, "Reneging on Reform: Egypt and Tunisia," *Middle East Outlook*, April 2007.
[22] *Christian Science Monitor*, April 12, 2004.

The rhetorical peak of the Bush democracy initiative came in the early part of 2005. In January 2005, the Iraqi people voted in the country's first postwar legislative elections. The elections were unexpectedly free of violence and declared a major policy success for the Bush administration. In his State of the Union address weeks later, Bush exhorted Egypt, saying that Egypt could "show the way toward democracy in the Middle East."[23] Opposition journalist Hisham Qasim argues that the summit between Mubarak and Bush in April 2004 was the turning point in the bilateral relationship.[24] Qasim says that it was then that Mubarak heard from Bush – for the first time – that Mubarak would have to be popularly elected in a multicandidate competition.[25] Although Mubarak stalled for a while in the hope that Bush would lose the 2004 election, it eventually became clear that Bush's demands would have to be met.[26]

Although it is not possible to know precisely what happened behind closed doors between Mubarak and Bush, or Rice and her interlocutors, international relations theorists argue that public statements were perhaps even more important than private ones in pressuring the Egyptian regime. What makes public threats particularly credible? Fearon (1994) argues that leaders will suffer domestic audience costs if they fail to follow through on foreign threats, demands, or promises. Domestic audience costs, then, can serve as a mechanism for credible commitment (Schultz 1998, 1999). Tomz (2007) – using a series of experiments embedded in public opinion surveys – finds empirical evidence for audience costs. The statements made by Bush in the 2005 State of the Union address as well as formal comments made by Condoleezza Rice in June 2005 that "Egypt should be at the forefront of this great journey" toward a fully free and democratic world suggest that Egypt would be the benchmark for success of U.S. democracy promotion in the region. According to one U.S. Embassy official, Egypt was the most important piece of the puzzle when it came to the Greater Middle East Democracy Initiative, and it was necessary that Egypt show some positive movement.[27] An official in the Egyptian foreign ministry, however, argued that Washington had raised the bar uncomfortably high for the Egyptian regime.[28] Washington's sudden shift of strategy from an emphasis on stability to an "aggressive push for rapid reform and democratization" destabilized the U.S.–Egyptian relationship (Aly 2006, 16).

---

[23] The full passage from the February 2, 2005, State of the Union address is excerpted here: "To promote peace and stability in the broader Middle East, the United States will work with our friends in the region to fight the common threat of terror, while we encourage a higher standard of freedom. Hopeful reform is already taking hold in an arc from Morocco to Jordan to Bahrain. The government of Saudi Arabia can demonstrate its leadership in the region by expanding the role of its people in determining their future. And the great and proud nation of Egypt, which showed the way toward peace in the Middle East, can now show the way toward democracy in the Middle East."

[24] *Washington Post*, March 27, 2006.

[25] Ibid.

[26] Ibid.

[27] Interview with First Secretary, U.S. Embassy, Cairo, April 20, 2007.

[28] Interview with Egyptian Foreign Ministry official, May 22, 2007.

Other administration successes were also becoming evident. The Cedar Revolution in Lebanon – triggered by the assassination of former Prime Minister Rafiq Hariri in February 2005 – provided evidence of the power of popular protest in the Middle East. Bush's emphasis on Middle East democratization was also evident in March of 2005 in an address at the National Defense University. Bush stated that democracy was spreading throughout the Middle East and that freedom would prevail in Lebanon. He declared, "Our duty is now clear. For the sake of our long-term security, all free nations must stand with the forces of democracy and justice that have begun to transform the Middle East.... Across the Middle East, a critical mass of events is taking that region in a hopeful new direction.... [For places that] have seemed frozen in place for decades... at last, clearly and suddenly, the thaw has begun." Saudi Arabia announced that the kingdom would hold its first municipal council elections as well.

On the heels of this growing U.S. pressure, Mubarak announced that the Egyptian constitution would be amended to allow other candidates to run against him in the presidential election. In response, President Bush praised Egypt as a shining example of an emerging democracy in the Middle East. Egypt also received favorable press coverage in Europe as a result of the decision to hold the multicandidate elections. The official response of the European Union was very positive.[29]

10.4.2 Institutionalizing a Dominant Party Succession Scenario

Prior to 2005, electoral contests for the presidency in Egypt consisted of an up–down referendum on Mubarak, following the inevitable renomination of Mubarak on the part of parliament. The amendment to Article 76 of the Egyptian constitution in May 2005 allowed for direct, multicandidate presidential elections for the first time, although under conditions that stacked the deck heavily in favor of the NDP candidate. How was the ruling elite in Egypt able to achieve a policy outcome closer to their own ideal point as a result of U.S. veto player pressure to increase Egypt's level of electoralization? The formal model presented in Figure 10.1 presents a scenario under which, by increasing its level of electoralization, Egypt was actually able to gain a small amount of political control. In other words, by instituting the multicandidate presidential elections, Egypt was able to increase its level of control while at the same time achieving a final policy outcome closer to the ideal point of the United States.

As a result of Egypt's agenda-setting prerogative in its interaction with the United States, the ruling elite were able to design the political institutions surrounding the introduction of multicandidate presidential elections. It is widely believed that multicandidate presidential elections fit into a regime plan at the time to create a viable succession strategy for Hosni Mubarak's son, Gamal,

[29] *Al-Ahram Weekly*, March 3–9, 2005.

head of the NDP Policies Secretariat. Careful institutional design increased the power and potential influence of the regime's single party in future elections, as Egypt sought to move away from personalist and military influences that were more evident under the Free Officers.

Which specific institutional features ensure NDP dominance? First, presidential candidates are nominated from an existing political party only if that party has been in existence for at least 5 years and has achieved at least 5 percent representation in the parliament.[30] The regime's control over which groups are certified as recognized political parties is also significant; unrecognized parties would have to wait years to run, even under the most favorable of circumstances. The amendment also states that the prospective candidate must have occupied a leadership position in the party for a period of at least one year, precluding the possibility of importing a previously unaffiliated figure to run under a particular party label.

Second, independent presidential hopefuls must obtain the endorsement of 250 members from the People's Assembly, the Shura Council, and local councils nationwide. This includes endorsement from a minimum of 65 elected members of the People's Assembly, 25 from the Shura Council, and 10 from the local councils in each of at least 14 provinces. The NDP typically makes up at least three-quarters of the People's Assembly and an even larger percentage of the Shura and local councils. This stipulation effectively gives the NDP the ability to veto any candidate that it views as undesirable.[31]

Finally, the amendment to Article 76 establishes a presidential election commission that is to enjoy "complete independence" in supervising the election process. The independence of this committee has already come into question during the course of the 2005 presidential election. Membership of the commission includes the Chief of the Supreme Constitutional Court and other prominent judges who are believed to be close to the ruling party, as well as "five independent and neutral public figures" to be selected by the NDP-dominated parliament. Decisions of the commission are final, with no possible appeals. This clause of the amendment eliminates the formal jurisdiction that Egypt's larger body of judges previously enjoyed in supervising the elections. Final

---

[30] In 2005, opposition parties were exempt from these rules; without this exemption, no opposition candidate would have been eligible to challenge the NDP candidate, because none of the opposition parties in parliament enjoyed the minimum 5 percent level of representation. The 5-year, 5-percent rule is planned to be enforced beginning with the 2011 presidential election.

[31] This assumes, however, that party discipline exists in what is a very loosely arranged group. Although it is technically possible for an independent to garner signatures from local councils and the People's Assembly, potential candidates will have to expend considerable time and political capital in order to secure the endorsement of these individuals, each of whom will expect to receive some political or other benefit in exchange for their endorsement of the candidate. The real challenge, however, lies in getting the approval of twenty-five members of the Shura Council, particularly given the institutional design of this organization. With its high ratio of appointed to elected officials and reputation for being composed largely of regime and party insiders, this institutional burden virtually precludes the candidacy of any individual that does not receive the tacit approval of the regime.

word on supervision and irregularities is formally moved from the mainstream judiciary to the presidential election commission, which will likely continue to be dominated by regime loyalists.

Do opposition parties have any ability to compete in this framework? The institutional design of the amendment to Article 76 works against Egypt's most potentially competitive presidential candidates. Attempts to work around these institutional hurdles will probably be thwarted by new laws or stipulations, either from the NDP-dominated legislature or by executive decree. These rules all but ensure the hegemony of the NDP, and the establishment of multicandidate presidential elections have established a formal procedure for succession.

10.5 CONCLUSIONS

Following September 11, 2001, the United States sought to change the Middle East through a program of intensive democracy promotion. United States policy makers were increasingly attributing the region's problems to constraints that Arab regimes were imposing on political rights and liberties (Aly 2006). The response the United States received from countries in the region, like Egypt, was defensive.[32] The Egyptian regime was critical of the way the democracy promotion initiative was conceived, viewing the policy as politically naive.[33] Although extensive political reform was not part of Mubarak's vision in 2002, U.S. demands for more competitive elections reached fertile ground in 2005.[34] The Mubarak regime took U.S. pressure to democratize as an opportunity to institutionalize a dominant party succession mechanism.

The Egyptian regime's ability to dictate the terms of U.S. democratization pressure has led some to argue that U.S. pressure on Egypt has done little more than strengthen the authoritarian regime.[35] Heydemann has argued that Arab regimes, like Egypt, have "adapted to pressures for political change by developing strategies to contain and manage demands to democratize" (2007a, 1). Kienle concurs, contending that democracy engineering contributes most commonly to the reconfiguration of authoritarian rule rather than to democratization (2007, 247). Similar conclusions have been reached by al-Sayyid, who has argued that Arab autocrats have been pretending to introduce genuine political reforms while "not conceding a single inch of real power to their serious rivals" (2007, 229), and Durac (2009), who finds that U.S. democracy promotion has had the unintended consequence of "supporting the entrenchment of an authoritarian political order." In this way, regimes have adapted selectively to the demands made upon them, making U.S. gains at best "incremental"

[32] Interview with Sa'id Qadri, Al-Ahram Center for Political and Strategic Studies, April 29, 2007.
[33] Interview with Hatim Sayf al-Nasr, Assistant Foreign Minister for American Affairs, May 2, 2007.
[34] Interview with 'Ali al-Din Hilal, former Minister of Youth and Professor of Political Science, Cairo University, April 30, 2007.
[35] *Al-Arabi*, October 8, 2005.

(Heydemann 2007a, 31). Nonetheless, Egyptian political analysts continue to assert that external pressure is a necessary condition for all meaningful reform steps.[36]

Levitsky and Way (2003) argue that the costs associated with full-blown authoritarianism have increased in recent years with the end of the Cold War. And the Bush administration's Greater Middle East Democracy Initiative raised those costs once again, particularly for Arab autocracies. In this chapter, I have formalized the relationship between a domestic authoritarian regime and an external actor – like the United States – where the external actor has the ability to influence policy outcomes through the use of foreign aid as an instrument of influence. My contention is that it was not coincidental that Mubarak announced the amendment to the Egyptian constitution that allowed for the country's first multicandidate presidential elections shortly thereafter. Although the United States served as a veto player (or an actor whose agreement is needed to change the status quo) on this particular policy dimension, Egypt retained the ability to set the agenda and, as a result, was able to select a set of institutions that actually increased the ruling elite's control over the political system.

There eventually came to be a retreat of the Bush administration strategy and a new emphasis on "gradual measures designed to promote democratic change without unduly challenging the authority of incumbent governments," which came to dominate the U.S. approach (Ottaway and Carothers 2004). This was particularly the case as the United States faced its many other priorities in the region, including "access to oil, cooperation and assistance on counterterrorism, fostering peace between Israel and its neighbors, stemming the proliferation of weapons of mass destruction, and preventing Islamist radicals from seizing power" (Ottaway and Carothers 2004). Fukuyama and McFaul (2007) conclude that Bush's new attention to democracy promotion has not resulted in more people living in freedom. Following the success of the Muslim Brotherhood in Egypt's parliamentary elections, as well as the victory of Hamas in the January 2006 Palestinian elections, a reverse of previous policy was also evident. Although some conservatives have criticized Bush for backing down in his democracy promotion program, this analysis suggests that the ideal points of Egypt and the United States may not be very far from each other.[37]

What, then, might an effective democracy promotion program look like for countries like Egypt? Because authoritarian elections serve as an arena for competition over access to state resources, Lust-Okar argues that democracy promotion in support of elections can be counterproductive (2009a). Rather, effective democracy promotion would seek to limit the resources available to

---

[36] Interview with Moheb Zaki, Ibn Khaldun Center for Development Studies, May 23, 2007; interview with Sa'id Qadri, Al-Ahram Center for Political and Strategic Studies, April 29, 2007.
[37] See the editorials of Max Boot, for example, *Los Angeles Times*, May 10, 2006.

state elites (Lust-Okar 2009a). It is also possible that the potential democratizing impact of multicandidate presidential elections will not be realized until some future period. Once in place, multicandidate presidential elections are unlikely to be rescinded, and, if the ruling party splits over the selection of a nominee, this could create the type of division in the ruling elite that is often a first step toward democratic transition (Przeworski 1991).

Egypt in Comparative Perspective

The Mubarak regime in Egypt is just one of many authoritarian regimes that holds some form of competitive elections. In this chapter, I explore how competitive elections function in a broader set of Arab cases. I find that there exist four primary types of electoral–institutional arrangements across the authoritarian states of the Arab world: a) hegemonic party regimes with high levels of political contestation, b) constitutional monarchies with high levels of contestation, c) single-party regimes with limited electoral competition, and d) nonconstitutional monarchies with low levels of electoral contestation. In terms of the distributive implications of electoral competition, there are a number of similarities between hegemonic party regimes with high levels of contestation – such as Egypt – and constitutional monarchies with political contestation. These similarities exist to a lesser extent in single-party regimes with limited contestation. The goal of this chapter is not to undertake an exhaustive review of other regimes but rather to demonstrate that patterns in the development of authoritarian institutions in Egypt are also found in a wider set of cases.

A primary argument of this project is that electoral competition, even in an authoritarian context, is meaningful for the way that it mediates several types of elite conflict and informs patterns of distribution. Based on these ideas, where and when could we expect to see competitive authoritarian elections emerging in countries of the Arab Middle East? A final section of this chapter considers whether the theories I have put forth regarding Egypt can be used to account for at least some of the variation in authoritarian survival strategies observed across the Arab world. I arrive at some tentative conclusions. In particular, two factors stand out. The first is the relative wealth of citizens in the polity, which, in the Middle East, is largely a function of access to external rents, particularly oil revenue. In countries with high levels of natural resource wealth, authoritarian regimes are less in need of mechanisms to distribute patronage, as individuals are more likely to satisfy their financial needs through government giveaways and state-offered benefits. In other words, when financial scarcity is not as critical an issue for a regime, elections are less necessary as a mechanism for patronage distribution. The second dimension of interest involves the nature of the ruling coalition. Regimes that are ruled by a minority group, whether ethnic, religious, geographic, familial, or otherwise, may already have mechanisms for patronage distribution in place, minimizing the need for elections to serve this role. In such regimes, the size of the elite may be fairly small, easing certain types of patronage distribution. Monarchies also appear to have different incentives for convoking elections when compared with hegemonic and single-party regimes. Clearly, these are not the only relevant factors. A country's historical legacy and other considerations matter for determining levels of electoral contestation.

11.1 HEGEMONIC PARTY REGIMES WITH COMPETITIVE ELECTIONS

There exist and have existed a number of authoritarian regimes in the Middle East that resemble contemporary Egypt in political structure and levels of electoral contestation. For example, since reintroducing multipartyism in 1997, Algeria has held a series of parliamentary elections that allow proregime members of the political elite to compete with one another for seats in parliament while also competing against moderate Islamist candidates. Since its unification in 1990, Yemen – like Egypt – has witnessed political dominance by a strong executive branch that oversees relatively competitive parliamentary elections. Mauritania's Ould Taya introduced competitive legislative elections in the early 1990s that helped to divide patronage spoils within the country's class of political elite. These Middle Eastern autocracies share other characteristics with Egypt, including a relatively undifferentiated elite class, a poor median voter, and a resource-constrained fiscal environment. Exploring the specific dynamics of authoritarian rule, particularly with regard to electoral institutions, provides an illustration of how three regimes with some structural similarities to Egypt use electoral competition.

11.1.1 Mauritania under Ould Taya

An August 2005 military coup ended the more than 20-year rule of Ould Taya in Mauritania – a majority Muslim, largely Arabic-speaking country located in the Maghreb. Taya, army chief and prime minister from 1981 to 1984, came to power in a 1984 coup. Taya thereafter ruled a country that had gained its independence in 1960 and was a single-party state between 1960 and 1978. During this period, the type of authoritarian populism that emerged in Mauritania resembled the political structure of Egypt under Nasser (Seddon 1996, 201). Mauritania's "white" Moors, or Beydane, have historically made up about a third of the total population and dominate all political and economic institutions, promulgating policies that have perpetuated the group's monopoly on power (N'Diaye 2006). Political competition in Mauritania has revolved around struggles for power within this traditional ruling class (Seddon 1996, 198).

Although economic liberalization in Mauritania created financial opportunities for some, in the aggregate, these policies hurt the poor and increased the gap between high and low social classes. IMF-sponsored economic reform began in Mauritania in 1985, and associated programs led to politically unpopular public sector job losses (Seddon 1996). Although a number of programs have been implemented to mitigate the social effects of structural adjustment, these efforts have been largely "unsuccessful in limiting growing unemployment and deteriorating living conditions for a very substantial portion of the Mauritanian population" (Seddon 1996, 205). In particular, economic austerity reduced the ability of the state to fund political clientelism and reward supporters (Ould-Mey 1996), creating an environment of resource scarcity. On the other hand, structural adjustment also generated opportunities for social mobility that allowed a small minority of well-connected businessmen to become very wealthy (Ould-Mey 1996, 209).

In this environment of economic austerity, Mauritania – which has historically been dependent on aid from France – came under increasing pressure from the French to hold multiparty elections (Ould-Mey 1996, 228; Marty 2002). Although there is little doubt that pressure from France influenced Taya's decision to hold these elections, multipartyism suited the country's newly liberalized economic environment (Ould-Mey 1996, 216). Mauritania introduced competitive municipal, legislative, and presidential elections with more than a dozen parties in contention for elected seats. The goal of this process was to strengthen the regime without changing the existing power structure (N'Diaye 2001). Whereas the democratization process has been described as a façade, Mauritanian elections have been characterized by "fierce competition" (Ould-Mey 1996, 215).

As a way to manage these elections, Taya created the Democratic and Social Republican Party (PRDS).[1] The PRDS has been described as a virtual "elephant's belly" (Ould-Mey 1996, 240), as it encompassed so many disparate interests. A coalition of local "notables, tribal chiefs, and businessmen," the PRDS was held together by "clientelism and the promise of access to state resources" (Marty 2002, 96). Elections served as a location where individuals and factions would compete for power and resources. As seen in the Egyptian case, candidates who were not chosen for the official PRDS party list would often run as independents and rejoin the party upon winning their seats (Marty 2002, 103). Although there was never any doubt that the PRDS would dominate elections and related parliamentary institutions, party list candidates had to "fight for every district because of the independent candidature" (Marty 2002, 97).

---

[1] Postindependence Mauritania had a history of single-party structures prior to the creation of the PRDS. See Pazzanita 1996.

Political parties in Mauritania during this period functioned as coalitions of nonprogrammatic interests, differentiated by narrow clientelist interests, not ideological distinctions (Marty 2002, 96). As such, voters turned out to cast ballots for "desired goods" that they could obtain, including government jobs and food assistance (Marty 2002). Turnout rates for these elections have generally ranged between 25 and 40 percent.

The tacit alliance that emerged in the early 1990s was primarily between Mauritania's rent-seeking elite and the ruling regime. The result was significant overlap of the political and commercial elite. The "backbone" of this system was a coalition of tribal and business allies who formed the core of the PRDS (N'Diaye 2006). Electoral competition between candidates from the regime's party, parties affiliated with the regime, and independent candidates friendly to the regime's party helped to mediate conflict within the rent-seeking elite. This led to the creation of parliament as a patronage-sharing, rather than a policy-making, institution; popular perceptions of the legislature reflect this. Citizens in Mauritania have tended to take a very critical view of parliamentarians, the majority of whom are seen as only reaching out to citizens during the election season.[2] Parliamentarians are viewed as being primarily interested in their own personal enrichment. According to one Mauritanian, "the Members of Parliament become richer, take the decisions that seem good to them and forget largely the rest of the population."[3]

Elections in Taya's Mauritania did not diminish the power of the executive branch (Aghrout 2008). Local notables – many of whom sought parliamentary seats – served as middlemen between the state and the general population (Marty 2002). Challenges to the hegemonic party came from independent candidates and other progovernment parties. Intense intra-elite rivalries existed, and the "shuffling" of the political elite took place through elections (Marty 2002). The system of powersharing that emerged was perceived as highly corrupt, and the regime was eventually replaced by a military council with an anticorruption agenda (Zisenwine 2007).[4]

The political structure of Mauritania under Taya resembles the electoral authoritarian system in Egypt under Mubarak in a number of ways. As relatively resource-poor states with a potentially large elite class, elections in both cases channeled intra-elite rivalry over patronage distribution. In both cases, clientelist interests motivated voter turnout rather than party ideology. Since the 2005 coup that ended Taya's rule, Mauritania has undergone a series of tumultuous political changes. Whether an electoral authoritarian equilibrium reemerges in Mauritania is an open question.

---

[2] Public Perception of the Parliament in the Islamic Republic of Mauritania, National Democratic Institute, 2007.

[3] Ibid.

[4] The demise of the electoral authoritarian equilibrium in Mauritania provides potentially interesting lessons for the Mubarak reigme. Chapter 12 describes how corruption, a quasi parameter of this equilibrium, might undermine Egyptian political stability over the long term.

11.1.2   Postunification Yemen under Salih

The Republic of Yemen was created in 1990 from the Yemen Arab Repub-
lic (North Yemen) and the People's Democratic Republic of Yemen (South
Yemen). Upon unification, each of the two states had an established ruling
party. The General People's Congress (GPC) was created in 1982 in North
Yemen four years after 'Ali 'Abdallah Salih came to power in a 1978 coup.
The GPC is believed to have been modeled on Egypt's hegemonic party (Dresch
and Haykel 1995) and shares many characteristics with the ASU and the NDP.
The Yemeni Socialist Party (YSP) was the ruling party in South Yemen prior to
unification. Unification ended single-party rule in each of the two states; over
time, however, the unified Republic of Yemen politically came to resemble the
preunification north (Schwedler 2002).

The first parliamentary elections to take place in a unified Yemen were in
April 1993. The two ruling parties from the former period – the GPC and the
YSP – as well as Islah, a party broadly identified as Islamist, enjoyed the broad-
est electoral support (Carapico 1998, 144). The 1993 elections were competitive, witnessed relatively high turnout, and were characterized by considerable
participation by independent candidates (Carapico 1993). More than 3,000
independent candidates initially registered to compete, and more than 70 percent of those individuals remained in contention on election day (Detalle 1993).
In fact, independent candidates – often GPC or YSP members not selected for
their party slate (Carapico 1998, 148) – won nearly as many votes as candidates from the GPC.[5] Whereas YSP candidates tended to focus on ideological
issues, the most successful independent and GPC candidates were generally
local notables or successful entrepreneurs who spent considerably on lavish
banquets and *qāt* chewing sessions (Detalle 1993).[6] The election – which was
considered by most to have been largely free from fraud – yielded a multiparty
assembly dominated by the GPC, but in which the YSP and Islah won 56 and
62 seats of 301, respectively (Schwedler 2002). A tripartite coalition of these
three parties eventually emerged.

In April 1997, 12 political parties fielding 850 candidates and 3,700 independents competed vigorously for 301 parliamentary seats.[7] The YSP chose
to boycott this election. Many of the independent candidates seeking office
were identified with the GPC (Wedeen 2008, 70) and chose to run in districts
where the GPC and Islah had previously agreed not to compete with each
other (Schwedler 2002). Independents received 28 percent of the vote (Carapico 1998, 149), but most did not maintain their nonpartisan status. A majority
of elected independents announced after the election that they were joining a
political party (usually the GPC).[8] The assembly that emerged was dominated

---

[5] Ahmed Abdul-Kareem Saif, Yemeni Electoral and Party Systems, April 24, 2000, Working Paper.
[6] *Qāt* is a shrub whose leaves are used a stimulant.
[7] National Democratic Institute, 1998, The April 27, 1997 Parliamentary Elections in Yemen.
[8] Ibid.

by the GPC, and successful candidates were most often tribal leaders, merchants, and other local notables with strong links to the GPC.[9]

The April 2003 elections were the third held since Yemen's unification. As in the previous two elections, party candidates competed against independents with party connections. Press reports suggest that vote selling was a common occurrence,[10] particularly among illiterate Yemenis.[11] Election observers witnessed money being given to voters leaving polling stations, and, although privacy was possible in curtained voting booths, voters often intentionally marked their ballots in clear view of others.[12] In some cases, voters worried that, if they took money but did not vote as promised, regime enforcers would discover the double cross and mete out punishment (Wedeen 2008, 129). The GPC won 230 seats, and a number of successful independents rejoined the party after the election.[13] Northern districts – which tend to have higher illiteracy rates – had an average 6.5 percent higher rate of turnout than southern districts, although the south had a higher rate of invalid balloting.[14] In addition, voteshare for Islah declined since the 1997 election.[15]

There are a number of significant parallels in terms of political climate and electoral politics between the Egyptian and Yemeni cases. For example, although irregularities and bias do play a role in Yemeni elections, the results cannot be viewed as a fabrication (Longley 2007), and contests in both Egypt and Yemen reflect important and highly intense forms of political competition. Also, as in Egypt, there is relative freedom of information in Yemen (Carapico 1998, 151; Dresch 2000, 211), and Yemenis from a variety of classes and regions regularly criticize the regime without fear of repercussion (Wedeen 2008, 76). Incumbency rates for sitting parliamentarians tend to be low[16] and comparable to what I have reported for Egypt. Furthermore, rates of turnout and ballot spoiling in Yemen bear important similarities to the Egyptian case where areas with higher literacy have both lower turnout and higher levels of ballot nullification.

Party structures in Egypt and Yemen also bear important similarities. The GPC, like the NDP, was established as an umbrella party largely devoid of an ideological agenda (Carapico 1998, 140); as such, both parties have been able to incorporate a variety of individuals and interest groups. Individuals who vote for GPC candidates tend not to have very strong party identification,

---

[9] Ahmed Abdul-Kareem Saif, Yemeni Electoral and Party Systems, April 24, 2000, Working Paper.

[10] *Al-Sahwa*, April 29, 2003.

[11] *Al-Sahwa*, May 1, 2003.

[12] National Democratic Institute for International Affairs, The April 27, 2003, Parliamentary Elections in the Republic of Yemen.

[13] Ibid.

[14] Ibid.

[15] Part of the reason may be that Islah had lost supporters among the business class to the GPC, as GPC affiliation often helped entrepreneurs run their businesses more smoothly (Longley 2007).

[16] Ahmed Abdul-Kareem Saif, Yemeni Electoral and Party Systems, April 24, 2000, Working Paper.

but instead support GPC or GPC-affiliated candidates due to tribal influence, monetary inducement, or both. Members of the GPC frequently run as independents if they fail to win the party's endorsement.[17] This has led some to argue that parliamentary participation as a GPC member simply means that one follows the instructions handed down by the ruling party and the president.[18] The GPC stands in contrast to its primary electoral competitor Islah, which, like Egypt's Muslim Brotherhood, is a pragmatic and moderate political organization that uses door-to-door canvassing to spread its social and political message.[19]

As Yemen's hegemonic party, the GPC enjoys the ability to chair electoral commissions, manage public airwaves, and dispense jobs and services to win votes (Carapico 2003). State-run media in Yemen tend to favor the hegemonic party,[20] and this influence is particularly effective on illiterate voters.[21] The GPC also uses state facilities as locations for campaign events.[22] Perhaps even more influential is the role of state patronage. The president and ruling party "control the dispensation of patronage," which is largely derived from state coffers (Corstange 2008). According to Carapico (2003), the ruling party threatens to withhold funds from constituencies that fail to support the hegemonic party. Threats of denial of pay and projects are reported in the opposition press, for instance.[23] Development projects are promised for loyal constituencies, a strategy that favors the hegemonic party in electoral contests (Carapico 1998, 142; Wedeen 2008, 200). Sometimes public services that had been delayed for years are supplied just prior the election with an important political message: "vote for the GPC and you will get services, vote for the opposition and you will get nothing" (Longley 2007, 245). The prime minister has visited constituencies in the run-up to the election to discuss the opening of new projects, highlighting the connection between the state and the dominant party.[24] The government has also been known to issue a one-month bonus to all civil servants the day before elections (Longley 2007, 244).[25]

In addition to the state-sponsored clientelistic ties that exist, there also exist more individualized "webs of patronage" (Dresch 2000, 189) that, in many cases, are based on nepotism and corruption (Wedeen 2008, 129). Although

---

[17] *Yemen Observer*, May 20, 2008.
[18] *Yemen Times*, February 27, 2006–March 1, 2006.
[19] National Democratic Institute for International Affairs, The April 27, 2003, Parliamentary Elections in the Republic of Yemen.
[20] *Al-Sahwa*, April 20, 2003.
[21] *Al-Sahwa*, May 3, 2003.
[22] *Al-Sahwa*, May 6, 2003.
[23] *Al-Sahwa*, May 3, 2003.
[24] *Al-Sahwa*, April 22, 2003.
[25] Like in Egypt, civil service salaries in Yemen represent a key connection between citizens and the state. As in Egypt, pay for state-sector positions in Yemen tends to be low, but job security is all but assured (Corstange 2008). When salaries were withheld, the fragile nature of the citizen–state equilibrium becomes apparent (Wedeen 2008, 83).

there exist strict formal restrictions on corruption,[26] according to one Yemeni businessman, corruption exists openly and is supported by parliamentary practices.[27] According to one parliamentarian, political corruption is widespread and the GPC is not serious about combatting graft.[28] Press reports suggest that the Yemeni government suffers from entrenched corruption across all levels of the bureaucracy and that the prevalence of graft is a function of patron–client political relationships.[29] President Salih is described as ruling Yemen based on a "complex web" of highly personalized patron–client ties with elite actors (Longley and al-Iryani 2008). The president and his family are involved in commercial activities, emblematic of a broader pattern of consolidated political and economic interests common throughout the elite classes (Dresch 2000, 201). Although ordinary Yemenis may not have access to wealth-creation opportunities, access to illicit wealth is available to a class of elite actors (Dresch 2000, 204), and those with good connections to the government can live comfortably, even in a country as poor as Yemen (Dresch 2000, 206–7). Islah ministers who entered the ruling coalition in the 1990s encountered a deeply entrenched system of corruption and patronage that served Salih and his network of allies (Schwedler 2002).[30]

Burrowes and Kasper (2007) provide a compelling picture of politics in Yemen, particularly as it relates to the interlocking patronage networks that have come to dominate politics in the country. They argue that Yemen is best described as an oligarchy where a class of elite actors – increasingly Northerners with business interests – compete for and have come to enjoy economic wealth and political power (Burrowes and Kasper 2007, 4–5).[31] They describe the system as something between a kleptocracy and plutocracy, where occupants of key government offices enrich themselves, using their positions as "profit centers" (Burrowes and Kasper 2007). These concerns exist for all levels of government, including the presidency; in particular, there is a common perception that the president steals and "he allows others to steal" (Wedeen 2008, 71).[32] Visible measures of elite corruption include the growing number

[26] Mohammed Abdo Moghram, "Political culture of corruption and the state of corruption in Yemen."

[27] Code of Conduct for Members of Parliament and Conflict of Interest, Yemeni Conference, Arab Region Parliamentarians Against Corruption.

[28] Ibid. As in Egypt, constitutional immunity prevents taking any judicial action against a parliamentarian, including investigation, detention, or imprisonment, without referring the matter first to the parliament.

[29] *Yemen Times*, September 11–14, 2008.

[30] Investigative reporting into corruption is allowed to some extent, but a number of taboo topics remain, including the president, his family and close associates, oil revenues, military budgets, and certain types of corrupt and nepotistic practices. See *Yemen Times*, September 11–14, 2008.

[31] This arrangement became increasingly clear in the late 1980s as the current regime crystallized and the Yemeni state, for the first time, became the principal source of wealth and private gain for members of the rent-seeking elite (Burrowes and Kasper 2007).

[32] A Yemeni comedian released a cassette tape of songs and skits alluding to how corruption has become a part of ordinary life in Yemen. In one vignette, a man known only as "the boss"

of high-end vehicles and villas around the capital; this consumption stands in stark contrast to the declining economic prosperity of the majority of citizens (Burrowes and Kasper 2007). Corruption has allowed a "core group of elite" to grow wealthy while leaving the majority of Yemenis marginalized and discontented (Longley and al-Iryani 2008, 8).

In this way, the Yemeni regime has created an authoritarian system that resembles the political setting in Egypt in a number of important ways. The state is closely associated with the ruling party. Parliamentary elections in both countries are highly competitive. Although violations of electoral laws are common in Egypt and Yemen, the regimes rely less on direct cheating and more on other types of political manipulation. Money and promised patronage are often decisive in Yemeni electoral outcomes (Wedeen 2007, 76), and a similar dynamic has been described in Egypt. Party candidates, independents associated with the ruling party, actual independents, and Islamists all compete for the opportunity to sit in parliament. Both Yemen and Egypt are republics with strong executives. Officials in Yemen's ruling GPC have repeatedly said that they cannot find a candidate to replace President Salih and have urged him to seek a new term.[33]

11.1.3   Algeria under Zeroual and Bouteflika

Elections have taken place in Algeria since the country's independence from France. During the period of single-party rule, candidates sought office after receiving approval from the National Liberation Front (FLN); genuine competition existed within the single-party context (Roberts 1998). The FLN – with its origins as the primary revolutionary group in the struggle against colonial France – has been characterized in the pre-1988 period as a "state machine" (Roberts 1992). Because all candidates represented the single party, the regime was largely indifferent to which specific candidates won office (Roberts 1998). FLN rule during this period tended to be clientelistic, as candidates could not be distinguished from one another on ideological grounds (Bouandel 2003, 6). Elections closely resembled what will be described in a subsequent section of this chapter as single-party regimes with limited contestation.

Although some form of electoral competition has long existed within the Algerian context, it has been the army, not the party, that has remained the principal "locus of power" (Roberts 1992; Volpi 2006). This was particularly evident in the events leading up to the cancellation of Algeria's first multiparty parliamentary elections in 1991. Algeria's first free and fair multiparty municipal elections took place in June 1990, which saw the overwhelming victory of the Islamic Salvation Front (FIS) over the FLN. When the FIS appeared to be on

(i.e., the president) asks employees how they became so corrupt, to which they respond, "We learned it from you." See Gregory D. Johnsen, "The election Yemen was supposed to have," *Middle East Report*, October 3, 2006.

[33] *Daily Star*, June 25, 2006.

the verge of winning an absolute majority of parliamentary seats the following year, however, the elections were canceled by forces within the military. The FIS was banned and its leadership repressed. The upper echelons of the military continue to have an important role in political life.[34]

The authoritarian regime in Algeria eventually began a process of political institutionalization in January 1994 as part of an attempt to rehabilitate itself following the events of 1991 (Bouandel and Zoubir 1998). A proportional representation electoral system was adopted, and the ruling elite created the National Rally for Democracy (RND) to compete with the discredited FLN for parliamentary seats. The RND has been described as a coalition of technocrats,[35] workers, and war veterans (Bouandel and Zoubir 1998). The majority of RND members were previously associated with the FLN, suggesting that candidates from the two parties would compete for the same voters; in fact, the RND has been described as a "party of opportunists who jumped on the bandwagon to seize another opportunity to access state resources" (Bouandel and Zoubir 1998, 16). One objective of the ruling elite was to ensure that progovernment parties (the RND and the FLN) would be able to secure a parliamentary majority (Roberts 1998). The result was political competition between candidates from two progovernment parties, which together came to monopolize representation in the post-1997 period.[36]

Three parliamentary elections occurred in Algeria between 1997 and 2007. The 1997 elections saw more than 7,000 candidates competing on dozens of party and independent candidate lists.[37] In addition to the FLN and the RND, Islamists representing the Movement for a Peaceful Society (MSP) also ran for seats and performed well. Although some irregularities were reported, most who observed the elections agreed that the contest was largely free and fair (Bouandel and Zoubir 1998, 186). The RND received about 34 percent of the total vote and 41 percent of the total number of parliamentary seats. Together with the seats won by the FLN, the two proregime parties controlled a majority in parliament while still allowing for opposition representation.

The FLN rebounded in the 2002 parliamentary elections, doubling its popular vote compared to 1997 and tripling its total number of seats (Roberts

---

[34] Rachid Tlemcani, "Algeria: Bouteflika and civil-military relations." *Arab Reform Bulletin*, June 2007.

[35] International Crisis Group. 2002. Diminishing Returns: Algeria's 2002 Legislative Elections, Middle East Briefing.

[36] Algeria's lower house is directly elected every five years by popular vote. In the upper house, two-thirds of members are selected indirectly at local assemblies, and one-third of members are appointed by the executive. Elections for lower-house seats employ a proportional representation system with closed party lists. See Bouandel (2008) for more details on Algerian electoral institutions.

[37] Algeria's June 5, 1997, Parliamentary Election, National Democratic Institute for International Affairs.

2002). The RND, on the other hand, saw a decline of support.[38] About 5 percent of citizens cast blank or spoiled ballots (Quandt 2002). Independent lists
continued to compete with about two dozen party lists. What accounts for the
decline in support for the RND? The FLN, which still enjoyed historical legitimacy, benefited from the political unpopularity of the RND's implementation
of structural adjustment (Roberts 2002). The 2007 parliamentary elections witnessed 24 parties and 100 independent lists (with a total of more than 12,000
candidates) seeking office (Bouandel 2008). Independent candidates were frequently party supporters who thought they had a better chance of winning on
their own rather then in a low position on a party list (Bouandel 2008). Despite
losing some voters, the FLN retained a plurality and the RND won the second
largest share of seats in parliament (Bouandel 2008).

Werenfels (2004, 2007) describes how Algeria's core political elite were able
to use parallel economic and political openings to their advantage. In particular,
she argues that structural adjustment provided new avenues for rent seeking and
rent distribution at a time when oil resources were contracting; in the process,
this created a new business elite motivated by "personal interest and survival
strategies rather than on attitudes and political agendas" (Werenfels 2007, 6).
Through this process, structural adjustment helped to bring new actors into the
ranks of the elite (Werenfels 2004, 174). Parliament – which generally bowed to
executive prerogatives – saw an inflow of private sector elite in 2002 (Werenfels
2007, 69) and a growing overlap between the legislature and the business community (Werenfels 2004, 180). Candidates were expected to provide money
or goods to voters, and elections were periods of rent allocation (Werenfels
2007, 136–40). Clientelist links between the state and the public through parliamentarians became common via individuals known as "entrepreneurs of
clientelist mediation" (Werenfels 2004, 186). IMF-sponsored reforms created
new opportunities for personal enrichment, allowing the regime to "tighten its
grip on society" by encouraging interlocking economic and political ties among
the elite (Cavatorta 2002).

Volpi (2006) argues that Algeria's pseudo democratic institutions, such as
elections, enhance short-term authoritarian stability, thus staving off longer-
term democratic transition. This occurs in three ways, according to Volpi. First,
by favoring candidates approved by ruling regime, electoral competition largely
takes places within the class of rent-seeking elite. This is similar to the Egyptian
case, despite the fact that the authoritarian elite in Algeria have opted for a
different electoral system. Since reintroducing competitive multiparty electoral
competition in 1997, two proregime parties, which are minimally differentiated in terms of party platform, have dominated parliament. Second, political
debate in Algeria is administered by the regime. In particular, as witnessed
in Egypt, the ruling elite favors the electoral messages of some parties over
others in the local press, although, in both countries, there exists a relatively

[38] International Crisis Group. 2002. *Diminishing Returns: Algeria's 2002 Legislative Elections,
Middle East Briefing.*

free press. Finally, patronage networks are used to influence vote outcomes. In particular, the disbursement of targeted material rewards has been effective at buying electoral support, emphasizing the importance of patron–client relations in Algerian political life (Volpi 2006). Historically, politics in Algeria has revolved around access to rents via patronage networks (Cook 2007, 42–3), and corruption has become endemic (Werenfels 2007), particularly following structural adjustment. Ideology has not played a pivotal part in explaining Algerian political behavior, either historically or more recently (Willis 2002, 17).

Competitive elections then solve important political problems facing the authoritarian regime in Algeria and should be viewed as political institutionalization of authoritarianism rather than democratization (Roberts 1998). The decade following the 1991 democratic moment witnessed an increase in the number of individual and collective actors constituting the politically relevant elite (Werenfels 2004, 173). Given this fact, it became increasingly important for the regime to manage competition within this class, and institutionalized authoritarian elections contributed to this objective. The Algerian political situation during this period can be characterized as a managed and manipulated form of limited pluralism, or "pluralism without enfranchisement" (Roberts 2003, 263, 266). To a large extent, contestation across parties represents intraelite factional competition rather than disagreement on ideological grounds (Roberts 2003, 238). As democratization would threaten the interests and privileges of those drawing profits from their political status (Tahi 1995), it is important to view competitive elections in the context of authoritarian resilience.

11.2 MONARCHIES WITH HIGH LEVELS OF ELECTORAL CONTESTATION

There exist a number of parallels between hegemonic party regimes with high degrees of contestation and monarchies with similarly high levels of electoral competition. According to Herb (2004), there are four constitutional monarchies in the Arab Middle East: Morocco, Jordan, Kuwait, and Bahrain. These states are distinguished from the governments in Oman, Qatar, the United Arab Emirates, and Saudi Arabia despite the fact that countries in the latter category may, in some cases, hold very limited elections (Herb 2004). In constitutional monarchies, constitutions differentiate between monarchical authority exercised by the cabinet and those exercised by the monarch personally (Herb 2004). Although Huntington has argued that monarchies are not able to use modern channels of political participation (1968, 168), examination of the cases of Morocco, Jordan, Kuwait, and Bahrain suggests that this is not the case. Each of these four countries holds regular parliamentary elections that are relatively free and fair and reflect high degrees of contestation between candidates. The biggest difference between the cases described here and the previously defined hegemonic party regimes is that monarchs in Jordan, Morocco,

Bahrain, and Kuwait do not represent a party, and, as a result of their monarchical status – and the historical legitimacy they are able to draw on as a result of their status as "royals" – are able to appear to be above the political fray.[39] Mufti (1999) has argued that, as such, monarchies are uniquely positioned to implement reforms that allow the monarch to appear as a "neutral arbiter between contending forces."

Previous theoretical work also suggests that the role of competitive elections differs depending on authoritarian regime type. In particular, monarchies might have a different incentive structure than other types of authoritarian regimes when it comes to convoking elections. Lust-Okar and Jamal (2002) describe how monarchies with competitive elections differ from authoritarian party states. They argue that the two types of states have divergent preferences because the structure of political power differs across the two types of regimes. Monarchs seek to arbitrate with the goal of dividing political power among competing parties without directly participating in electoral politics (Lust-Okar and Jamal 2002). This suggests that monarchies use elections to split the opposition more than to mediate intraregime disputes. Despite this important distinction, elections in monarchies do appear to have implications for patronage distribution. Lust-Okar (2006) describes how in Jordan, for example, "elections under authoritarianism provide an important arena of competition over access to state resources," particularly from the perspective of constituents who seek jobs and favorable allocation of discretionary funds.

11.2.1   Morocco under Hassan II and Mohammed VI

The Moroccan monarchy has long used a system of patronage to sustain the loyalty of the politically relevant elite (Waterbury 1973). In the 1950s and 1960s, the regime sold colonial lands and nationalized industry to finance the purchase of support; as these resources dissipated, however, the existing political system became threatened (Hammoudi 1997, 33). Within this context, the monarchy introduced elections in 1963 to create a network of rent-seeking elite who would support the regime in exchange for the opportunity to participate in parliament (Hammoudi 1997, 34). According to Hammoudi, this informal alliance continued to persist in Morocco in the decades to follow. The competitive, multiparty system was "from the outset tied to the logic of authoritarianism," as elections served to neutralize the elite through political competition (Zeghal 2008, 157). The parliament became the location where the elite would be compensated, manipulated, integrated, and coopted, providing the regime with the "ideal space to manage and prevent conflicts between different stakeholders" (Zerhouni 2008, 219).

Given the importance of parliament as a location for patronage distribution, there exists considerable competition within the ranks of the elite to get close to the "center" (Hammoudi 1997, 82). As such, competition in electoral

---

[39] See Lust-Okar and Jamal (2002) and Lust-Okar (2005) for more on this point.

contests has been intense; as one parliamentarian put it, candidates "fight to the death in order to get into the parliament," and electoral campaigns are expensive (Sater 2007). Vote buying is common, especially for non-Islamist candidates and parties (Zeghal 2008, 262). The privileges of being a deputy in Morocco, however, make it well worth the cost of campaigns (Benstead 2008), as parliament serves as a key location where individuals defend their interests (Zerhouni 2008, 219). Electoral campaigns are highly visible and elections are relatively free and transparent, although not in a way that produces a more liberal political system (Zeghal 2008, 263). Rather than engaging in outright rigging, the monarchy prefers to use gerrymandering and other strategies for controlling the electoral map (Zeghal 2008, 260). Elections also appear to serve another "crucial function," as they are used by the authoritarian as "regularly generated opinion polls providing information" for regime use (Zeghal 2008, 263–4).

Zeghal argues that elections in Morocco are "the means through which political resources . . . are regularly redistributed" (2008, 263–4). The Moroccan elite support the regime for material reasons, and favors and access are distributed from the center, including from the parliament (Hammoudi 1997, 11–12). In this way, members of the elite became auxiliaries of the *makhzen*, or establishment, as a result of their participation in corrupt activities in institutions like parliament (Zerhouni 2004, 78). Economic reforms, and particularly privatization projects, have been well-suited for the promotion of these types of patron–client networks (Willis 2002, 14).

11.2.2 Jordan under Hussein and 'Abdallah

Like Morocco, Jordan provides another example of an Arab monarchy that has exhibited high levels of electoral competition for parliamentary seats. The regime in Jordan engages in both gerrymandering and manipulation of electoral rules to ensure favorable election outcomes (Lust-Okar 2009b). Regular parliamentary elections have been held since 1989,[40] and candidates for parliament have typically run either as independents or under the auspices of the Islamic Action Front (IAF). In 1989, 38 of 80 newly elected deputies were described as regime loyalists (Mufti 1999). In the 1993 elections, more than 500 candidates competed for 80 seats; almost all of these individuals were independent candidates who campaigned on their ability to deliver services rather than their ideological positions (Baaklini et al. 1999, 157). Jordan's 1997 elections saw the victory of a number of independent candidates who supported the monarchy (Ryan 2002), a trend that continued to a large degree in subsequent elections. In 2007, for example, independents prevailed in the vast majority of districts compared with only 5 percent of seats won by the IAF. Turnout in these elections has typically been higher in rural compared with urban districts (Ryan 2002),

[40] Jordan's parliament was suspended from 1967 until 1989.

and there are relatively low levels of continuity from one parliament to the next (Lust-Okar 2006, 463) – two trends also apparent in the Egyptian context.

Given the limited influence parliament exercises over policy in Jordan, parliamentarians in Jordan serve a primary role as "distributors of rents and patronage through clientelist networks" (Bank and Schlumberger 2004, 48). Candidates fund their own campaigns, drawing primarily on personal resources (Lust-Okar 2009a). Lust-Okar argues that parliamentarians mediate between government and the citizenry in the form of constituency service (2006, 459). Voters in Jordan, therefore, typically cast their ballots for patronage, not for reasons of ideology or policy preferences (Lust-Okar 2006, 460). Very often, these are individuals who are independent candidates and members of their tribe or with whom they have close personal ties (Lust-Okar 2006, 461).

Ryan (2002, 15) draws a connection between Jordan's economic liberalization in the 1980s and the increase in political contestation to follow. Over time, business interests have become politically important (Bank and Schlumberger 2004, 54). Journalist investigations into parliamentary corruption have manifested in increased animosity between journalists and deputies.[41]

11.2.3   Kuwait under the House of Al-Sabah

The primary role for the Kuwaiti parliament has been to provide "tangible benefits" to voters via service candidates who act as intermediaries between their constituencies and the regime (Tetreault 2000, 73). Tetreault argues that the government is a "silent partner in this patron-client system, helping to entrench service candidates by channeling favors through parliamentarians who prove themselves to be the kind of men the government prefers" (2000, 115). In order to win a parliamentary seat, family resources are important, as elections are competitive and vote buying is common (Tetreault 2000, 114, 123). Making the investment in winning a seat can pay off financially; according to Herb (2009), a parliamentary seat offers a quick way to greater wealth. Historically, vote buying was monitored by brokers who would bring their voters into mosques and have them swear to vote as promised (Tetreault 2000). Illiterates (or those who could pass themselves off as illiterates) have been permitted to vote aloud (Tetreault 2000, 124), providing brokers with assurance that the vote seller has followed through on his or her promise. More recently, the standard method for monitoring votes is what Tetreault calls the ballot switch (2000, 124–5), a process very similar to the Egyptian "revolving ballot."

11.3   SINGLE-PARTY REGIMES WITH LIMITED CONTESTATION

There exist, and have existed, a number of single-party regimes in the Arab Middle East in which elections provide only limited opportunities for competitive

---

[41] Against Corruption: The Role of Arab Civil Society in Fighting Corruption. Amman, Jordan: Arab Archives Institute, 2007.

engagement. Like the hegemonic party regimes described previously, the single-party regimes generally have a president at the head of government who also serves as the leader of a party structure. How can we characterize these regimes and the nature of political competition within them? Although electoral contestation is clearly limited, there frequently exist opportunities for real competition, even within such a context. This often takes the form of members of the regime's single party competing with one another or with regime-vetted independents. In this sense, these states differ from Egypt in terms of the intensity of electoral competition more than institutional structure. A common thread in these countries that contrasts with the Egyptian case, however, involves a reluctance on the part of single-party regimes to allow Islamists to participate in these contests. Single-party regimes also tend to be more heavily policed than Egypt. Iraq, Tunisia, and Syria all serve as illustrative examples of regimes that operate or have recently operated in this fashion.

In all three cases, the regime enjoys a broad support elite, but this elite is tiered in a way that structures the routes by which rents are distributed. The core support elite in Tunisia consists of a handful of clans closely related to the ruling family and held together by highly interpersonal ties (Erdle 2004, 214). A second tier of elite related to the security services also maintains close ties to the ruling regime in Tunisia. In Iraq, under Saddam Hussein, family, clan, and village ties helped to define the elite. In Syria, members of the Alawi sect have enjoyed privilege in terms of access to the regime leadership and associated spoils. Although both Syria and Iraq possess some oil rents, the impact of these rents is limited by the fact that both countries have relatively large populations. This is in contrast to Gulf monarchies, for example, that have oil revenues with relatively small domestic populations.

11.3.1 Iraq under Saddam Hussein

By 1973, it became apparent that Saddam Hussein wanted to create a one-party state in Iraq, where the party apparatus would enjoy "centralized control over all key institutions" (Marr 2004, 148). Upon swearing in as president in 1979, Saddam set up the National Assembly, Iraq's first parliamentary body since the overthrow of the monarchy in 1958. The 250-member assembly was to be elected every four years (Marr 2004, 180). Although the vast majority of legislators elected to parliament were Ba'th party members, independents were also able to secure seats. For example, in the 1989 legislative elections, independents were able to win 43 seats to the Ba'th party's 207 seats. Political power remained within the party, and the parliament was a largely symbolic body, neither passing important laws nor debating critical issues. According to one researcher, "yet, despite the obvious impotence of this body, competition between candidates was strong: a seat in Parliament means moving to the capital, media coverage, contacts, and better chances for promotion" (Baram 1989, 462).

Although some competition existed even in this highly constrained context, why didn't Saddam use elections to a greater extent to manage the internal distribution of patronage? There is no doubt that the repressive capacity of the regime and Saddam's personal penchant for cruelty and torture played a role in mitigating any demands for redistribution among the elite; his sadism is legendary, and experts specializing in the psychology of dictators have compared him to Stalin and Hitler in terms of his capacity for "malignant narcissism" (Glad 2002). Another explanation is that the composition of the regime elite under Saddam created channels for personal patronage. In particular, the Ba'th regime oversaw a decline in the political importance of the urban educated classes and a rise of the urban lower classes, particularly individuals who shared Saddam's tribal and geographic background (Baram 1989; 1997). Under Saddam, national political figures were replaced by less-qualified loyalists; the result was political dominance by Tikritis, individuals from Saddam's hometown (Marr 1988; Baram 1989). Individuals who shared Saddam's tribal and geographic origins were used as the president's personal bodyguards as well as in military and security service positions (Baram 1997). For serving in sensitive and critical security positions, these regime loyalists with close clan ties enjoyed personal financial rewards, and the president provided their villages with new roads, electricity, and water systems (Baram 1997).

11.3.2   Tunisia under Ben 'Ali

In the period between its independence from France in 1956 and the 1987 coup deposing long-time president Habib Bourguiba, Tunisian politics was dominated by a single party (Murphy 1999, 4). Under Bourguiba, the president served as the country's chief patron, using personalism more than intimidation to maintain his political dominance (Alexander 1997). Choice for voters was limited largely to candidates who all came from within the single party (Murphy 1999, 61).

Bourguiba's successor, Zine al-'Abidine Ben 'Ali, was new to ruling party politics and lacked the well-cultivated patronage networks that had been crucial to Bourguiba's success (Alexander 1997). Relative to Bourguiba, Ben 'Ali "did not have the political resources to referee and manipulate effectively an ongoing competition between powerful politicians and the social actors they rallied to their camps" (Alexander 1997). To meet this challenge, Ben 'Ali pursued a two-pronged approach. On the one hand, he introduced party-level political competition. Although this contestation did not pose a challenge to the social control of the regime, it did entrench forms of patronage through electoral channels that shored up the regime. Ben 'Ali simultaneously created nonelectoral channels of rent distribution that operated through clan ties and the security apparatus from which he hailed. This patronage served the needs of Ben 'Ali's most critical and loyal allies. Both the development of Tunisian electoral institutions and the cultivation of security and clan patronage networks are discussed.

The Democratic Constitutional Rally (RCD) – the party developed by Ben 'Ali – came to serve as an important institution for patronage distribution (Murphy 2001a, 150). In 1988, Ben 'Ali negotiated a national pact that included regularized electoral competition between political parties (Murphy 2001a, 153; Dillman 2003). Despite some initial optimism about Ben 'Ali's reformist intentions, two factors made it clear that this optimism was misplaced. The first was Ben 'Ali's refusal to legalize the Islamist Nahda Party; the second was that the RCD won every seat in the 1989 legislative elections (Alexander 1997). Islamists running as independents received about 14 percent of the popular vote (Dillman 2003) but no seats in parliament (Halliday 1990). Revision of the electoral law allowed a small percentage of seats to go the opposition (Alexander 1997), and, in 1994, the opposition was able to win fifteen seats (Sadiki 2002). The RCD continued to dominate electoral politics in Tunisia without having to resort to electoral fraud (Willis 2002). In 1999, the party won more than 90 percent of ballots to the national assembly (Willis 2002). Parliamentary elections in this context have been controlled by those individuals best able to distribute state patronage (King 2003, 43).

At the level of elites, state largesse has been distributed based on proximity to the president. How does one gain access to the president? Aside from a small Jewish community, Tunisians are almost universally Arab, Sunni Muslims suggesting that patronage distribution could not be determined by sectarian membership. Proximity to the palace appears to be two-tiered. The regime's inner circle included "all those people related to or affiliated with the president and his wife, especially hailing from five clans: the brothers and sisters of Ben 'Ali himself; the brothers and sisters of his second wife, Leila Trabelsi; and the families married to his three daughters – the Chiboubs, Mabrouks, and Zarrouks" (Erdle 2004, 214). According to Murphy (2001b), Ben 'Ali's extended family has "assumed control of major economic interests in the country," encouraging the growth of nepotism and clan links as channels of patronage distribution (Sadiki 2002, 69). In 1997, an underground document circulated that described the "families that pillage Tunisia," complete with details about illegal appropriation of land and abuses of power committed by the clans associated with Ben 'Ali (Sadiki 2002). A book entitled *La Régente de Carthage* (*The Regent of Carthage*) by French journalists Nicolas Beau and Catherine Graciet describes the inner workings of the patronage networks of Tunisia with a focus on how Leila Trabelsi, the wife of Ben 'Ali, personally facilitates corruption on the part of these clans. According to one account, the Trebelsi clan came from modest origins but has been able to accumulate tremendous assets, "including the only private radio station in the country, Radio Mosaique; the country's most important airline and hotel company, Carthago Airlines; and important stakes in the wholesale, service, and agribusiness sectors" (King 2007).

In addition to clan ties, Ben 'Ali has also developed a strong foundation of support in the Interior Ministry. According to Erdle (2004), this is where Ben 'Ali finds his dependable and competent support elite. Under Ben 'Ali, the security apparatus expanded and came to be run directly from the presidential palace (Alexander 1997). The security services became a virtual "state within a state," supporting up to 10 percent of the population (Erdle 2004, 214). Patronage in Tunisia, then, appears to be distributed through these two inter-related channels – clan ties to Ben 'Ali and position within the security service apparatus. Although the Mubarak family in Egypt and the families surrounding Mubarak have undoubtedly benefited financially from access to power centers, clan ties do not appear to serve as a dominant avenue for patronage distribution in Egypt.

Neoliberal reforms have not served to undermine the patronage ties described previously. On the contrary, according to some, economic liberalization has actually promoted traditional patronage networks (King 2003, 49). Sadiki argues that there exists a "quasi-tacit contract between state and society whereby economic goods are exchanged for political deference" (2002, 68). Economic liberalization, in this scenario, has fueled Tunisia's economic success, allowing the regime to rely on "the *'ayshīn* (those living comfortably) to reproduce its power base" (Sadiki 2002, 59). In this process, the state and the party become intertwined, and "'electoral democracy' rubber-stamps the selection of intermediaries whose participation entrenches authoritarian corporatism not democratic pluralism" (Sadiki 2002, 72).

What has emerged is a coalition of supporters sustaining the Ben 'Ali regime that has at its core the loyal clans closely associated with the president, the security apparatus from which he was groomed, and, more broadly, elite and popular sectors that have benefited from Tunisia's relative economic prosperity. Electoral competition has its most important distributive implications for this final category of individuals. For members of the privileged clans and the security elite, patronage is offered to those who demonstrate subservience and loyalty (King 2003, 40; 2007). Access to state financial largesse and shelter from formal and informal "taxation" are distributed on a "discretionary basis" (Murphy 2001a, 150) in a system where control of financial resources and budgetary control remains highly centralized (King 2007).

11.3.3   Syria under Hafez and Bashar al-Asad

The Syrian president is surrounded by a cadre of elite advisors who are primarily, but not exclusively, high-level bureaucrats belonging to the 'Alawi sect (Bar 2006).[42] Individuals in the upper echelons of the Syrian bureaucracy enjoy both legal and illegal financial benefits associated with their posts (Perthes 1991, 33–4). Many of the most important of the bureaucratic elite are military generals and security service directors. The army – which exercises what Hinnebusch calls "a priority claim on the economic resources of the country" given continued tension with Israel (1994, 99) – has emerged as an important location for

---

[42] The Syrian state has been described as a "font of patronage" from which those with connections derive important material benefits (Hinnebusch 2001b, 87).

rent distribution. Sheltered and encouraged by the regime, military and security units have been transformed into revenue-generating economic fiefdoms (Zisser 2001, 32). Officers are also the beneficiaries of subsidized housing and smuggling and drug distribution rights (Rubin 2007, 53).

Asad's 'Alawi "barons" are overrepresented in key leadership positions in Syria and are particularly prominent in the military and security services (Hinnebusch 2001b, 70). One often-cited statistic is that, at the time of Hafez al-Asad's death in 2000, 'Alawis held 90 percent of the top posts in military and security sectors, despite the fact that they represented only 12 percent of the population (Zisser 2001, 26; Bar 2006; Rubin 2007, 52). Van Dam (1981, 52) suggests that this has come about as a result of "anti-Sunni sectarian discrimination in the Syria armed forces" and a systematic purge of Sunnis. Sadowski concurs that confessionalism has been a "hallmark" of Asad's rule with 'Alawis commanding virtually all the military-intelligence services (1988, 164).

'Alawi affiliation is an important channel of access to patronage (Sadowski 1988, 168), although not the only one. Alongside the 'Alawi political elite sit a number of privileged families with close ties to the regime (Bar 2006). Many of these families hail from the Sunni merchant class, which is closely tied to 'Alawi centers of power (Hinnebusch 1997). Therefore, while the 'Alawi-dominated state elite enjoy particularized access to patronage rents, the private sector Sunni community has become "embourgeoised" through corrupt activities (Hinnebusch 1997, 250–1) and also enjoys access to political patronage. One avenue for achieving these clientelist benefits has been through participation in parliament. Parliamentary participation has offered Sunni merchants and industrialists access and opportunities to state patronage (Hinnebusch 1994, 108). Economic partnerships with regime insiders are also often the product of parliamentary participation (Rubin 2007, 59).

In 1972, the National Progressive Front (NPF) was established with the Arab Socialist Ba'th as the most important party of the coalition. A small number of seats were reserved for parties other than the Ba'th in the NPF. Parliamentary elections took place in 1973. In addition to the candidates nominated by the NPF, hundreds of candidates ran as individuals. Competition also took place within the NPF. Although there was never any doubt that the NPF would prevail in the elections, voters were offered some choice on the ballot (Picard 1978, 135).[43]

Issues of legitimacy loomed large in terms of the initial motivation for convoking elections. Perthes argues that elections were instituted by Asad in an attempt to "broaden his basis of support and to legitimize his regime by institutionalizing it" (1997, 136). Picard contends that elections were meant to "endow his regime with a legality that it possessed only doubtfully at its origin (1978, 132).

Elections took place at regular intervals after 1973, and, with the exception of the 1981 contest, voting was largely considered to be free (Perthes

---

[43] In 1973, a small number of opposition candidates also contended for seats.

1997, 166).[44] What compelled individuals to run for parliament in the Syrian context? According to Perthes, parliamentary seats served as "a means of patronage" (1997, 167). Deputies used parliament as a locale to broaden their social networks rather than promote policy change or engage in oversight activity (Perthes 1997, 167).

Over time, Asad was able to use electoral institutions to coopt members of the Sunni economic elite. Merchant families sought to improve their economic position by winning public office (Bar 2006, 362). Bar describes the political alliance that emerged from this period as the "symbiosis between the 'Alawite military elite and the Sunni business sector" (2006, 358). Over time, the connection between business interests and independent parliamentary candidacy became more pronounced. This has led commentators like Hinnebusch (1997) to observe that political liberalization had increased bourgeoisie access to government without transfer of real power.

The 1990 legislative elections saw an increase in the size of the assembly with one-third of seats reserved for independents (Perthes 1997, 168). According to Perthes,

> It was clear in advance that the NPF would secure seats for all its candidates and maintain about the same number of deputies as it had presented in the outgoing council. But there was considerable competition among non-NPF candidates. Of course, every candidate had to be approved by authorities. Many candidates had marked views and independent opinions, but none of them represented an anti-regime opposition (1997, 168).

A primary purpose for expanding the assembly was to accommodate Syria's growing business community in the wake of economic reforms implemented in the late 1980s (Perthes 2004b, 93). Indeed, Asad himself acknowledged the direct link between economic and political pluralism (Perthes 1997, 258–9). Businessmen candidates typically performed well in parliamentary elections (Perthes 1992, 16–7), using a variety of patronage-based campaign tactics like hosting banquets and receptions (Perthes 1992, 16). Successful candidates would recoup the cost of their campaigns once in parliament (Perthes 1992).

The first parliamentary elections to take place under Bashar al-Asad's rule were in March 2003 and resembled previous elections in a number of ways. Competition was largely restricted to the slots allotted to independent candidates (Perthes 2004a, 21). In 2007, more than 2,500 candidates ran for seats, largely ignoring ideological issues in their campaigns (Abdel Latif 2007). Most independent candidates represented business interests[45]; independent candidates appearing on various lists, the most prominent of which – al-Sham – represented politically influential merchants (Abdel Latif 2007). According to one press report, businessmen spent so much on their campaigns that independents

---

[44] In particular, parliamentary elections took place in Syria in 1973, 1977, 1981, 1986, 1990, 1994, 1998, 2003, and 2007.

[45] *Al-Nahar*, March 23, 2007.

outside the business sector were unable to successfully compete, and the Syrian authorities were fully aware of vote buying that takes place on behalf of these business candidates.[46] Many of these successful business candidates represented the manufacturing sector.[47] Candidates often sponsored tents that featured food, drink, and smoking to win support from voters.[48] Voting cards could be obtained for about 500 Syrian Pounds (SP) (approximately $10), and the price for a single vote ranged between 1,000 and 3,000 SP (approximately $20–$60).[49]

Sunnis are well represented in the legislature and cabinet; informal power and associated financial resources, however, are dominated by 'Alawis (Zisser 2001, 25). This has led Hinnebusch to suggest that the political "amalgamation" of the 'Alawi political elite and the Sunni business elite has been "delayed by the sectarian barrier" (2001a, 131). This discussion of Syria suggests that first-order access to patronage benefits takes place via sectarian connections as related to proximity to the president. Although not all 'Alawi are beneficiaries of their cosectarians political influence, 'Alawi are disproportionately represented among the regime elite and offered access to clientelist channels. It is the 'Alawi barons who have enjoyed most "privileged access to patronage" (Hinnebusch 2001b, 69) importantly through 'Alawi dominance of the military – a key institution by which patronage is distributed and within which the 'Alawi have enjoyed clear dominance (Sadowski 1988, 164, 173).

For members of the Sunni merchant class, economic liberalization was followed by increased opportunities for political competition, where businessmen on independent lists would compete for access to patronage through position in parliament. Since the introduction of additional independent seats in 1990, members of the Sunni business community were further integrated into formal state institutions (Perthes 2004b, 93). In this way, competitive elections to parliament have primarily been contests between rich businessmen seeking access to state spoils.

11.4 MONARCHIES WITH LIMITED ELECTORAL CONTESTATION

The final category of Middle Eastern autocracies under consideration here is monarchies with extremely limited or no electoral competition. All of the countries in this category – including Saudi Arabia, Libya, Qatar, and Oman – are wealthy, rentier states that derive a large percentage of their wealth from oil revenues. In some cases, very limited elections are held in these countries. For example, Saudi Arabia held municipal council elections in 2004–2005 in which only half the seats were chosen by votes.

---

[46] *Al-Watan*, March 14, 2007.
[47] *Al-Safir*, April 18, 2007.
[48] "Dancing, Smoking, Shisha, and Eating?" *Syrian Elector*, April 20, 2007.
[49] "Monitoring the Syrian Legislative Elections," *Syrian Elector*, April 25, 2007.

According to Gause (1994), the key to understanding domestic political processes in oil monarchies is to look to the "enormous amount of wealth that oil revenues have placed in the hands of the state" since the early 1970s. Tribesmen loyal to the monarch dispense patronage, encouraging the prominence of personal and tribal connections in rent distribution (Gause 1994) rather than other mechanisms. Oil revenues tend to be government-owned, and public sector employment is a second, related, mechanism for rent sharing. Oil wealth led to sedentarization of the population as citizens sought public sector employment (Gause 1994). Regimes subsidized life in other ways as well, including through the provision of free health and education services and utilities. Oil rents in Oman enabled Sultan Qaboos, for example, to put in place a far-reaching allocation state offering employment to both skilled and unskilled workers (Valeri 2007).

The tremendous oil wealth of these countries also allowed regimes to distribute their windfalls to groups without necessarily extracting from existing economic elite. For example, in Saudi Arabia, a new business class was created as a result of the oil boom; according to Gause, this was not accomplished by impoverishing the established commercial elite but rather by bolstering the interests of the new group, and "similar stories can be told of the other Gulf states, where governments have had enough money both to benefit the established merchant families and to encourage new individuals and groups to get into business" (1994, 56–7). This suggests that rent distribution was not taking place in an environment of resource scarcity as is common in the other types of Arab authoritarian regimes described in this chapter.

11.5   WHEN AND WHY COMPETITIVE AUTHORITARIAN ELECTIONS?

The previous section demonstrates that there exists considerable variation in institutional design, even across authoritarian regimes. For example, the manner by which legislatures are selected varies tremendously around the world, with Middle Eastern states exhibiting tremendous heterogeneity in terms of their legislative arrangements (Gandhi 2008, 35). What explains this variation and how do authoritarian regimes come to develop a particular set of institutions? In some cases, there is considerable path dependence; a country with a long history of parliamentary politics and electoral competition will be more likely to continue down such a trajectory. This section offers some tentative conclusions regarding how structural factors, like a natural resource endowment or the nature of the ruling coalition, impact the design of authoritarian institutions.[50] The argument put forth is twofold: a) that states with a relatively large natural resource endowment are less in need of a mechanism for

---

[50] Kamrava (1998) argues that the structural characteristics of various Middle Eastern states can account for differential rates of liberalization. His account, however, focuses primarily on a regime's ability and willingness to use repression, deeming elections as "meaningless."

distribution of rents than their more resource-scarce counterparts, and b) that states with established avenues for rent distribution as a result of the size and cohesion of the ruling regime are less likely to use elections as a distribution mechanism for rents.

In rent-wealthy contexts, the economic resources of the state tend to overwhelm the rent-seeking elite in a way that diminishes the latter's capacity. In minority or clan-ruled states, the strength of the ruling regime's "*'aṣṣabīya*," or group solidarity, diminishes the contribution the rent-seeking elite makes to regime stability.[51] This argument is consistent with the view that authoritarian elections tend to be introduced in countries where the bourgeoisie is strong, particularly as a result of economic liberalization (Ehteshami and Murphy 1996).

11.5.1 Resource Wealth of the State

A critical factor differentiating states across the region involves the availability of access to external rents, particularly rents from oil. In fact, Perthes (2004c) argues that the availability of oil rents remains the most salient feature of the political economy of the Middle East. Can this variation in resource wealth – and the related variation in per capita income across the region – explain, at least in part, the likelihood of autocrats to employ authoritarian elections as a tool of regime maintenance?

The rentier state model suggests that regimes with access to externally accruing rent establish legitimacy on their allocative role and, as such, do not need democratic legitimation to the same extent (Luciani 1987; 2007). Crystal writes that oil revenues undermined political coalitions in a number of Gulf states, and that once rulers had direct access to rents, merchants traded economic largesse for political quiescence (1990, 9). Oil-flush regimes focused on spending money rather than extracting it from their citizenries (Gause 1994, 43). Oil monarchies offered education, medical treatment, subsidized food, housing, and employment to their populations, allowing rulers to establish direct clientelistic ties with tribesmen (Kamrava 1998). Hinnebusch (2007) finds that the rentier monarchy has shown itself to be a durable political model as a result of the economic dependence social classes have on the state.[52] Regimes that operate under conditions of resource scarcity may find elections to be more useful for patronage distribution than rentier states that have the means to distribute resources more freely.[53] The empirical expectation would be that autocracies with relatively wealthy citizenries and greater resource wealth would be *less*

---

[51] The concept of *'aṣṣabīya* was introduced by fourteenth-century philosopher–scholar Ibn Khaldun.

[52] Herb (1999) provides an alternative perspective to rentier state theory, arguing that the way power is shared within the royal family matters more for regime survival than rentier status.

[53] Rentier states may also have lower levels of inequality as a broad swath of the citizenry is afforded access to rent revenues. Acemoglu and Robinson (2006) point out that, in Singapore, with relatively low levels of income inequality and economic prosperity enjoyed by most, there

likely to have competitive authoritarian elections than authoritarian regimes operating under conditions of resource and wealth scarcity.

Although there have been a number of studies that consider the influence of a country's natural resource wealth on its prospects for democracy, previous scholarly works have frequently neglected the important distinction between electoralization and democratization. Empirical work has shown that natural resource wealth hinders the development of democracy (Ross 2001). Another mechanism contributing to this empirical finding may be that countries with a large natural resource base do not need elections to mediate resource distribution because these states have enough rents to distribute to everyone. Gandhi argues that dictators in resource-rich countries counter political threats by distributing rents (2008, 89). In particular, she finds that dictators who can extract rents from mineral or other resources do not need as much cooperation from domestic elites (Gandhi 2008, 81). Gandhi's empirical analysis suggests that the availability of natural resources reduces the need for parliamentary institutions and associated elections (2008, 98–9).

The Arab world represents an ideal setting for considering such a theory, as there is considerable heterogeneity in terms of both the extent to which regimes hold competitive authoritarian elections as well as the relative resource endowment and wealth of citizenries. For example, Sadiki (2000) considers the relationship between per capita GDP and the number of elections held since 1979 in Arab states. Aside from Kuwait, he finds that the wealthy states held virtually no elections, whereas states with poor citizens held many electoral contests. Perthes (2004c) attributes this empirical regularity to the fact that rents enable core elites to establish clientelistic relationships with lower-tier elites, thus mitigating the need for liberalization. Further, when considering variation in liberalization across Gulf states, Perthes writes that, "although the relation between rent income and political competitiveness is neither direct nor mechanical, it cannot be ignored: No one should be surprised that Bahrain, the Gulf monarchy least dependent on oil income, has advanced the furthest in pluralizing its system" (2004c, 302). Gause (1994) argues that rentier states, with their sizable resource endowments, are able to buy off emerging elite groups while at the same time maintaining levels of support for previously important elites.

The case studies presented in this chapter are consistent with the idea that elections are less important for rent distribution in oil-rich states. The level of authoritarian electoral competition is greatest in relatively resource-poor countries, such as Egypt, Yemen, Morocco, and Jordan. The degree of electoral competition that exists in Kuwait poses an interesting challenge to this theoretical expectation. Given the high levels of rent availability and the relative wealth of the citizens of this polity, I would not have predicted that Kuwait would have competitive parliamentary elections, yet it does. There exists a

---

is little pressure to democratize. Dunning (2008) also argues that resource rents reduce the political salience of redistribution.

fairly large body of literature dedicated to describing Kuwaiti "exceptionalism" with regard to its higher-than-expected levels of political competition. Kuwait has a relatively long experience with parliamentary politics, which makes it distinct from many of the other oil-rich Gulf states (Baaklini et al. 1999, 169). The roots of Kuwait's parliamentary experience are believed to lie in the historical relationship between the ruling al-Sabah and a group of elite merchant families (Baaklini et al. 1999, 171). According to one scholar, "it was understood... that the emir would always consult with the merchants on matters of importance to them" (Baaklini et al. 1999, 171). The need to balance merchant families in the early twentieth century led to the creation of representative assemblies.[54] The conventional explanation, therefore, for the emergence of competitive institutions in Kuwait is related to the nature of coalitional politics during the period of Kuwait's state formation prior to the discovery of oil there, when Kuwaiti merchants more powerfully asserted their right to representation than merchants in other states, such as Qatar (Crystal 1990, 173).

More recent explanations incorporate external influences. One suggests that the Kuwaiti government and ruling family were shaken by the experience of the Iraqi invasion, leading the regime to respond to popular demands for accountable government to a greater extent than other similar regimes (Gause 1994, 101). Posusney (2004) has argued that Kuwaiti exceptionalism with regard to electoral competition is related to unusual international pressures following the Gulf War.

11.5.2 Nature of the Ruling Coalition

A second factor that impacts an authoritarian regime's need for mechanisms of patronage distribution relates to the size and nature of the ruling coalition. Given similar levels of resource availability, authoritarian regimes vary in terms of whether or not there exist established clientelist channels or whether elections might usefully serve that purpose. In Egypt, there is a "quantitatively large politically relevant elite" (Abdelnasser 2004, 119) and regional or religious identities are not used, to a great extent, to determine membership in that elite. This is in contrast, for example, to regimes where the autocrat comes from an ethnic minority group, like in Syria.[55] In Syria, the 'Alawi enjoy a position of political privilege and are overrepresented in military and intelligence circles that enjoy a disproportionate percentage of state patronage. Similarly, Tunisia under Ben 'Ali and Iraq under Saddam Hussein both have been ruled by a coalition that enjoyed some natural bounds. In the case of Tunisia, the

---

[54] Michael Herb, "Kuwait." Paper prepared for the USIP – Muslim World Initiative Working Group, October 26, 2005.

[55] Geddes (2004) argues that minimum winning coalition logic can be seen in an authoritarian setting where autocrats have an incentive to reduce the size of the ruling group to limit the number of individuals with whom spoils need to be shared. Characteristics of the ruling coalition, like the minority status of the ruler, can provide a natural basis on which to limit coalition size.

clans related to Ben 'Ali and intelligence elite stand out as being particularly important, whereas, in Iraq, the Tikritis enjoyed privileged status.

A variety of empirical studies have shown that the existence of ethnic fractionalization within a country negatively impacts that country's prospects for both democratization as well as the development of authoritarian institutions associated with competitive elections, such as legislatures. Barro (1999) has shown that more ethnically diverse countries are less likely to liberalize on the Freedom House scale. In her empirical work, Gandhi finds that ethnic divisions are negatively related to the development of institutions associated with competitive elections, such as authoritarian legislatures (2008, 98–99).

11.6 CONCLUSIONS

Arab regimes exhibit considerable variation in terms of electoral competitiveness, and this chapter has sought to situate the Egyptian case within a broader comparative framework. Regimes appear to fall into one of four types with regard to their electoral–institutional arrangements. Hegemonic party regimes with high levels of political contestation bear close resemblance to Egypt in terms of patterns and processes of electoral competitiveness. Constitutional monarchies with high levels of contestation, like Morocco, Jordan, and Kuwait, exhibit similarities to the Egyptian case in terms of voter mobilization and recruitment, but differ from the first category in that the monarch is able to stand above the political fray as a result of his privileged position. Single-party regimes also have important forms of electoral competition, although they are more constrained in their extent and impact. Finally, nonconstitutional monarchies tend to have very low levels of electoral contestation.

At least some of the variation in the level of electoral competitiveness witnessed across Arab regimes seems to be explained by structural characteristics like the natural resource wealth of a state and the nature of the ruling coalition. Rich states, which tend to be ones with oil rents to distribute, are not confronted with conditions of scarcity found in oil-poor states. Authoritarian regimes that are dominated by an ethnic, tribal, regional, or other type of minority group are also less likely to have developed highly competitive parliamentary elections because distribution of patronage to the politically relevant elite may take place through preexisting channels. The Egyptian case, which is the focus of this book, represents an example of a hegemonic party regime with a competitive electoral environment. The Egyptian state is a relatively poor nonmonarchy, and there exists a fairly large politically relevant elite. Other authoritarian regimes with a similar profile, including Algeria and Yemen, bear a number of striking similarities to the Egyptian case in terms of the distributive implications of competitive elections. Parallels to the Egyptian case can also be found, although to a lesser extent, in monarchies with competitive elections and some single-party regimes.

12

Conclusion

In the course of my fieldwork in Egypt, I once directly asked an official affiliated with the NDP why the regime in Egypt continued to hold competitive parliamentary elections given the political risks. Political violence remains a common feature of parliamentary elections, and the regime not infrequently is required to perpetuate fraud and repression to quell the success of Islamist candidates. The party official responded that elections give the regime a new lease on life. Elections, it seems, are a key to the regime's very survival, and a counterfactual claim implicit to this project is that, absent these elections, the regime would not be so durable.

This book has sought to more fully articulate the specific ways in which elections contribute to the durability of the authoritarian regime in Egypt. Whereas existing explanations for the persistence of authoritarianism have described autocracy as an historic by-product of Egypt's natural environment or an outgrowth of the country's religious or cultural tradition, this project instead builds on a growing literature that considers the institutional basis for autocratic persistence in Egypt with a particular focus on how competitive multiparty elections have stabilized aspects of rule under Hosni Mubarak. Although it has been argued that elections inflame state–society tension in authoritarian regimes, this project has found that elections help to solve certain types of problems, particularly problems related to the distribution of scarce resources. Whereas existing arguments in the study of comparative authoritarianism provide important insights into the electoral motivations facing autocrats, I argue that the previous literature on this subject underemphasizes, ignores, or fails to empirically verify a number of important points. I stress the institutional and informational benefits of elections as well as the role elections play in managing public and elite expectations, particularly regarding the distribution of rents. It is a contention of this project that processes related to rent distribution are core to the persistence of the current political system. In this way, I seek to move beyond the common tropes of elections as a source of legitimacy or as primarily an outgrowth of international influence.

It is important to point out that the dynamics that I describe taking place in Egypt are in no way unique to authoritarian or Arab politics. In fact, many of the same political features of the Egyptian system – electoral budget cycles, vote buying of the underprivileged, rent-seeking by the elite, abuse of parliamentary immunity, rewarding of political supporters – take place in a variety of contexts, both historical and contemporary, authoritarian and democratic. This suggests a confluence of political tactics across regime types rather than the exceptionalism of Egyptian or Arab politics.

12.1   ELECTORAL AUTHORITARIANISM AND DISTRIBUTIVE POLITICS

A primary argument of this book is that competitive parliamentary elections lead to a series of distributive outcomes that provide functional benefits for the authoritarian regime in Egypt. Rather than viewing elections as the product of a process of democratization, the competitive nature of electoral competition in Egypt is a strategy of regime maintenance. From a normative perspective, this conclusion raises questions about whether elections actually enjoy the virtues frequently attributed to them.

To describe elections as a strategy of authoritarian maintenance is not intended to exaggerate the regime's capacity for control.[1] On the contrary, it is by delegating distributive decisions to the political marketplace in the form of competitive elections that the regime actually creates a more robust form of social control. Such a political system works well in the context of the contemporary Middle East, where a number of countries, including Egypt, have witnessed a gradual withdrawal of the state after a period of public sector dominance of the economy.[2] Across the region, government agencies have shown a tendency to relinquish day-to-day management of economic affairs and allow market mechanisms to govern the economy (Lawson 2007, 111). This project argues that a similar dynamic has taken place with regard to political outcomes.

The extent to which competitive elections are used as a mechanism for distribution differs across states. In some contexts, the elite support base for a regime consists of a narrow, ethnic clique, a military officer corps, or a clerical leadership. In other authoritarian regimes, such as can be found in the Arabian peninsula, government coffers are deep enough that an entire class of elite, or even society, can be bought off. In Egypt, financial resources have become increasingly strained over time with economic liberalization, and there is no obvious way to narrow the class of individuals who might be eligible for spoils in exchange for their support. Elections serve this purpose in a public, credible way while also providing other functional benefits to the authoritarian leadership.

---

[1] Editoralist Magdy al-Gallad provides an alternative perspective, arguing that the regime maintains total social control through the efforts of political "masterminds." See *Al-Masry Al-Youm*, February 19, 2009.

[2] See Pioppi 2007 for more on this point.

Whereas Rutherford see elections in Egypt as a "symptom of the regime's weakness" (2008, 22), one might counter that elections are actually a manifestation of the regime's strength or capacity. For Koehler (2008), electoral contests renew channels of clientelist inclusion while at the same time enhancing the ruling elite's ability to control political actors and tie them to the state. Similarly, the regime's ability to fragment the opposition through elections helps to secure a stable equilibrium of power (Lust-Okar 2005; Albrecht 2007).

12.2 THE POSSIBILITY OF POLITICAL CHANGE

I have described the institutional arrangement in Egypt as enjoying a type of political stability. In what ways might this equilibrium be undermined?

12.2.1 Undesirable Externalities of Autocratic Elections

Geddes (2005) argues that elections in authoritarian regimes always involve some risk and that, because the mobilization of support that goes along with elections is quite costly, we can infer that they must provide authoritarian leaders with benefits that can outweigh the costs.[3] In this project, I have described the benefits associated with authoritarian elections, particularly as they accrue to the existing regime. What are the risks, however, of electoral authoritarianism? One important category of risk involves the danger associated with fraud and political repression. A second is related to the unexpected repercussions of political expression.

Fraud is a costly strategy for authoritarian regimes, particularly as it undermines many of the reputational, informational, and institutional benefits a regime accrues by holding elections in the first place. Despite these costs, fraud occurs for a variety of reasons. At the level of a presidential contest, one might expect that an authoritarian will almost always employ fraud before relinquishing his hold on power. At the parliamentary level, fraud tends to be employed when either government candidates are not going to win a sufficient percentage of seats or a favored candidate of the regime is in danger of losing a particular electoral contest. In Egypt, there are a number of ways that fraud is employed. In some cases, the security services block opposition voters from entering polling stations; in other cases, the switching of vote counts and stuffing of ballots has occurred.[4] When elections have to be postponed, or canceled, this also creates problems for the authoritarian regime. The way citizens react to fraud of this type is unpredictable. Tension between voters and either the security forces or party affiliates could erupt.

---

[3] Mezey (1983) makes a similar argument regarding authoritarian legislatures.
[4] These violations are carefully detailed in both press reports and al-Sawy et al. (2005), among other sources.

Elections in Egypt have been accompanied by bloodshed that has increased in intensity over time (Teti et al. 2006), and election violence has the potential to create the same kinds of political problems as regime-perpetuated fraud. Fearon (2006) finds that the convention of holding elections can provide a public signal for coordinating rebellion. Although Egyptians have not yet used the occasion of elections to coordinate violence to bring down the existing regime, the potential for such action is possible. In addition to the violence surrounding the elections themselves, the increase in political sensibilities of the citizenry that can be incited by elections may result in the political demands that require regime repression. Although it is impossible to directly link elections to repression of political opponents at some point in the future, it seems plausible that elections play a role in increasing the potential for political activism. Independent newspapers like *Al-Masry Al-Youm* have reported on the poor treatment of political prisoners in Egypt, describing the use of electric shock, hanging of prisoners from wrists and ankles, death threats, sexual abuse, and unfair trials before military and emergency courts.[5] In many cases, these incidents have elicited violent reactions from the towns and villages of the victims.

12.2.2   Quasi Parameters and the Existing Equilibrium

Heydemann argues that authoritarian durability in the Middle East is produced by the extent to which the norms and formal institutions that define existing social pacts are able to adapt to endogenous pressure for change (2007b, 35). Whereas the focus of this project has been empirical and not primarily concerned with predicting future change, there is compelling reason to believe that some of the very conditions endogenous to the equilibrium that I have described may actually undermine its stability over time. Pierson (2004), for example, points out that specific institutional arrangements have multiple effects, only some of which may be related to the original reason why the institution was first introduced. The equilibrium that I have described in this project carries within it a number of self-undermining quasi parameters. For example, electoral budget cycles in Egypt induce inflation, a drawdown of reserves, and economic inefficiencies like the politically motivated postponement of necessary policy changes. Inflation and economic growth are thought to be negatively related, in part because of the way inflation impacts investment decisions. The nonprogrammatic mobilization of voters at election time also has made vote buying a cornerstone of the existing equilibrium. Yet, vote buying has the potential to undermine stability as citizens become frustrated by what they see as regime sanctioning of corrupt behavior.

Income inequality associated with the financial privileges of the rent-seeking elite has the potential to create widespread economic tension between these elite and the masses. At some point in the future, short-term buy-offs may no longer suffice for Egypt's poor. The underprivileged classes have proven

---

[5] *Al-Masry Al-Youm*, May 24, 2007.

to be highly vulnerable to commodity price increases, particularly increases in the price of food. For example, due to a shortage of food stock in 2008, Egypt – which imports 50 percent of its food – saw tremendous increases in food costs.[6] These price increases were accompanied by major civil disruptions, including fights at extremely long bread queues[7] and incidents where the hungry stormed bakeries to steal bread.[8] Poor Egyptians are also acutely aware of other forms of growing income inequality. Editorialist Magdi Mehanna has written that it is increasingly difficult for lower-class Egyptians to be confronted by advertisements common on billboards and in subways for expensive villas with private golf courses and swimming pools, given the abject poverty in which they are living.[9] Demands for economic redistribution continue to resonate strongly within Egypt's lower classes, and the ability of these groups to engage in collective behavior may increase over time.

Regime reliance on corruption as a strategy to bind the rent-seeking elite to the ruling regime is perhaps the quasi parameter with the greatest potential to undermine the long-term stability of the current institutional arrangement.[10] Bicchieri (1993) describes corruption as a stable equilibrium, but one for which the cumulative social costs can drive the system to a catastrophic point at which this equilibrium becomes suddenly unsustainable (Bicchieri and Rovelli 1995).[11] A similar dynamic could be at work in Egypt, where a strong and growing anticorruption movement could cooperate effectively with an Islamist opposition that enjoys a reputation for "clean hands." A government survey of more than 2,000 Egyptians found that the majority of respondents listed "businessmen, especially those with close links to authorities, as the most corrupt group in society."[12] In 2009, Mubarak made a speech to an audience of workers complaining that Egyptian businessmen were exacerbating tensions between themselves and the poor by flaunting their wealth.[13]

Popular organization of anticorruption advocates has become increasingly common. Why is corruption such a big concern for ordinary Egyptians? One member of the Muslim Brotherhood parliamentary bloc has noted that most Egyptians are generally not concerned with ideology because they have too many other things to worry about, particularly the responsibilities they have to

---

[6] *Al-Ahram Weekly*, April 24–30, 2008.
[7] *Al-Jazeera*, March 12, 2008.
[8] *Al-Masry Al-Youm*, August 5, 2007.
[9] *Al-Masry Al-Youm*, July 23, 2007.
[10] There is also the possibility that Egypt's business class, although initially rent seeking, may eventually mutate into what Luciani calls a genuine entrepreneurial class, or bourgeoisie, and that, over the long term, maintaining a crony capitalist system will become untenable (2007, 169).
[11] Pierson argues that scholars need to pay attention to slow-moving dimensions of social life because, in many cases, incremental or cumulative forces need to reach some critical threshold before triggering change (2004, 83).
[12] *Al-Ahram Weekly*, May 21–27, 2009.
[13] *Al-Masry Al-Youm*, April 30, 2009.

their own families.[14] When corruption affects the ability of everyday Egyptians to meet those responsibilities, then we may begin to see an intensification of protest. Consider April–May, 2007, when I happened to be in Egypt. The biggest stories in the news and the ones that were most discussed by the nonelite Egyptians that I spoke with involved rumors that corrupt businessmen were growing their profits by putting bleach, chalk, and other nonfood additives into powdered milk given to children. It was rumored that thousands of gas tanks used by Egyptians to cook food in their homes were faulty and could explode at any time. Five men suffocated when they entered a manhole in the street without protective equipment and were overcome by sewer fumes.[15] An eight-year-old girl died of sunstroke when she and her class were forced – along with thousands of other people – to line the streets of an upper Egyptian town in anticipation of a senior governorate official passing through.[16] An ambulance crew was subject to criminal action if it drove down a road when a senior regime official was on his way to work.[17] Repeated concerns were raised about the quality of drinking water,[18] particularly in Giza governorate, where it was reported that hazardous waste was found in the groundwater.[19] Newspaper editorials reflected anger about government selling of land to foreigners in a series of corrupt scams and deals.[20] Low-quality Chinese crockery – untested by the government – was decorated with lead paint.[21] These were the news reports and subjects of conversation during a relatively short period of time. Everyday acts of government neglect and corruption are the source of both frustration and incredible disappointment for many Egyptians.

In particular, citizens are angered by the failure of the state to provide them with basic protection from some of the by-products of economically based corruption. Increasingly, concerns about public safety are creating an important problem for the regime. Tarek al-Bishri, retired judge and intellectual, has said in an interview:

> Security is limited almost exclusively to protecting the regime, while the safety and security of ordinary citizens is ignored. This makes the future worrying, inasmuch as there will come a time when the state is faced with a certain situation [and it won't be able to act]. A couple of years ago a cargo train left Alexandria without functioning brakes. The driver reported the problem but was told only to drive slowly. Of course he couldn't control the train and when he reached Kafr al-Dawwar station the train derailed, destroying near-by shops. There were no ambulances to take the injured to hospital so they were

---

[14] Interview with 'Ali Fatah al-Bab, Muslim Brotherhood parliamentarian, September 25, 2005.
[15] *Egyptian Gazette*, May 16, 2007.
[16] *Egyptian Gazette*, May 27, 2007.
[17] Ibid.
[18] *Egyptian Gazette*, May 27, 2007.
[19] *Al-Masry Al-Youm*, May 26, 2007.
[20] *Al-Masry Al-Youm*, May 31, 2007.
[21] *Egyptian Gazette*, May 31, 2007.

placed in a truck. When they got to the hospital there were no doctors. When doctors finally arrived there was no blood. You see how many sectors were put to test and failed?[22]

Acts of government neglect and corruption have the ability to mobilize Egyptians who are increasingly frustrated with their treatment at the hands of government. When a person dies crossing the street in an area that should have a pedestrian walkway, locals will often rise up in protest (Ismail 2006, 161–2). When whole villages in Kafr al-Shaykh were forced to go without water, thousands of angry peasants forced a closure of the Cairo–Alexandria Road in a bid to draw officials' attention to their plight.[23] Nearly 150 hepatitis C patients rallied outside a major state hospital to protest a delay in the dispersal of their medication.[24] Egypt has the highest prevalence of hepatitis C in the world; the conventional explanation for this is that needles used by state sector medical personnel were routinely reused without proper sterilization.

Acts of protest are related to a popular perception that the regime is not concerned with the safety and well-being of the citizenry.[25] The widely publicized deaths of children being treated in public hospitals have led to increased scrutiny of the entire public health system.[26] A scandal erupted in 2008 after it was discovered that the national high school exit examination was leaked to powerful individuals, including a member of parliament, members of the ruling party, and police officers.[27] The corruption of both high- and low-level officials and the constant need for mediation has led Carrie Wickham to write that "the single greatest problem facing Egyptian society was its normlessness" (2002, 159). This sense of normlessness is perhaps the biggest threat to the future of the Egyptian regime. Although the regime has established both informal norms and more formal institutions to govern treatment of the elite, less of an effort has been made to provide assurances to the everyday Egyptians.

Clearly, the way that these quasi parameters – like corruption and its by-products – interact with the existing equilibrium is a subject that demands

---

[22] *Al-Ahram Weekly*, December 28, 2006–January 3, 2007.

[23] *Egyptian Gazette*, July 7, 2007.

[24] *Al-Masry Al-Youm*, February 20, 2008.

[25] One related form of protest is what might be called the "not in my backyard" protest. In 2008, protests erupted in Damietta governorate to protest the building of a fertilizer factory by a Canadian company. Fearful of the environmental consequences of the plant, demonstrators from across the country descended on the planned site in the hope of convincing the government to build the installation elsewhere. During some of the protests, participants shouted slogans against President Mubarak. According to press reports, it will cost the company $500 million to move the $1.2 billion project, and the Canadian firm has asked the Egyptian government to compensate it for expenses associated with relocation. See *Al-Masry Al-Youm*, April 15, 2008, *Al-Masry Al-Youm*, April 18, 2008, *Egyptian Gazette*, April 28, 2008, and *Al-Ahram Weekly*, June 26–July 2, 2008 for more details.

[26] *Al-Ahram Weekly*, July 12–18, 2007.

[27] *Egyptian Gazette*, June 19, 2008.

greater investigation. There is little doubt, however, that over the long term some of the conditions that are at the very core of this system have the potential to undermine its continued durability. This suggests that the institutional equilibrium that has evolved persists in the context of a continuing dialectic between the regime and the citizenry – and growing tension between the ruler and the ruled.

Bibliography

Abaza, Mona. 2000. *Tanwir* and Islamization: Rethinking the struggle over intellectual inclusion in Egypt. Discourses in Contemporary Egypt: Politics and Social Issues. *Cairo Papers in Social Science* 22(4).

Abdel Aal, Mohamed H. 2002. Agrarian reform and tenancy in Upper Egypt. In: *Counter-Revolution in Egypt's Countryside: Land and Farmers in the Era of Economic Reform.* Ray Bush, editor. London: Zed Books.

Abdel Khalek, Gouda. 1979. The open door economic policy in Egypt: A search for meaning, interpretation, and implication. Studies in Egyptian Political Economy. *Cairo Papers in Social Science* 3.

Abdel Latif, Omayma. 2007. Syria: Elections without politics. *Arab Reform Bulletin* 5(3).

Abdel Maguid, Wahid. 2003. *Egypt's Gama'ah Islamiyah: The Turnabout and Its Ramifications.* Cairo: Al-Ahram Center for Political and Strategic Studies.

Abdelnasser, Gamal. 2004. Egypt: Succession politics. In: *Arab Elites: Negotiating the Politics of Change.* Volker Perthes, editor. Boulder: Lynne Rienner.

Abdelrahman, Maha M. 2004. *Civil Society Exposed: The Politics of NGOs in Egypt.* Cairo: American University in Cairo Press.

Abdo, Geneive. 2000. *No God but God: Egypt and the Triumph of Islam.* Oxford: Oxford University Press.

Abed-Kotob, Sana. 1995. The accommodationists speak: Goals and strategies of the Muslim Brotherhood of Egypt. *International Journal of Middle East Studies* 27(3).

el-Abnoudy, Ateyat. 1996. *Days of Democracy: Egyptian Women and the 1995 Parliamentary Election* (documentary film). Seattle: Arab Film Distribution [in Arabic].

Abu-Lughod, Lila. 1995. Movie stars and Islamic moralism in Egypt. *Social Text* 42.

———. 2003. *Dramas of Nationhood: The Politics of Television in Egypt.* Cairo: American University in Cairo Press.

Achen, Christopher. 2000. Why lagged dependent variables can suppress the explanatory power of other independent variables. Presented at the Annual Meeting of Political Methodology, Los Angeles, CA.

Acemoglu, Daron and James Robinson. 2006. *Economic Origins of Dictatorship and Democracy.* Cambridge: Cambridge University Press.

Adams, Richard H. Jr. 1993. Agricultural bureaucracy in rural Egypt. In: *The Political Economy of Food and Nutrition Policies*. Per Pinstrup-Andersen, editor. Baltimore: Johns Hopkins University Press.

Aghrout, Ahmed. 2008. Parliamentary and presidential elections in Mauritania, 2006 and 2007. *Electoral Studies* 27(2).

Ajami, Fouad. 1998. *Dream Palace of the Arabs: A Generation's Odyssey*. New York: Pantheon.

Ake, Claude. 1996. Rethinking African democracy. In: *The Global Resurgence of Democracy*. Larry Diamond and Marc Plattner, editors. Baltimore: Johns Hopkins University Press.

Akerlof, George. 1976. The economics of caste and of the rat race and other woeful tales. *Quarterly Journal of Economics* 90(4).

Albrecht, Holger. 2005. How can opposition support authoritarianism? Lessons from Egypt. *Democratization* 12(3).

———. 2007. Authoritarian opposition and the politics of challenge in Egypt. In: *Debating Arab Authoritarianism: Dynamics and Durability in Nondemocratic Regimes*. Oliver Schlumberger, editor. Stanford: Stanford University Press.

Albrecht, Holger and Eva Wegner. 2006. Autocrats and Islamists: Contenders and containment in Egypt and Morocco. *Journal of North African Studies* 11(2).

Alesina, Alberto, Reya Baqir, and William Easterly. 1999. Public goods and ethnic divisions. *Quarterly Journal of Economics* 114(4).

Alesina, Alberto and David Dollar. 2000. Who gives foreign aid to whom and why? *Journal of Economic Growth* 5(1).

Alesina, Alberto, Nouriel Roubini, and Gerald Cohen. 1997. *Political Cycles and the Macroeconomy*. Cambridge: MIT Press.

Alexander, Christopher. 1997. Back from the democratic brink: Authoritarianism and civil society in Tunisia. *Middle East Report* 205.

Ali, Sonia and Richard H. Adams Jr. 1996. The Egyptian food subsidy system: Operation and effects on income distribution. *World Development* 24(11).

Alvarez, Sonia. 1990. *Engendering Democracy in Brazil: Women's Movements in Transition Politics*. Princeton: Princeton University Press.

Aly, Abdel Moneim Said. 2006. An ambivalent alliance: The future of US–Egyptian relations. Analysis Paper. Saban Center for Middle East Policy at the Brookings Institution, 6.

Ames, Barry. 1987. *Political Survival*. Berkeley: University of California Press.

el-Amrani, Issandr. 2005. Controlled reform in Egypt: Neither reformist nor controlled. *Middle East Report*.

Ansari, Hamied. 1986. *Egypt, the Stalled Society*. Albany: State University of New York Press.

Arce, Daniel and Todd Sandler. 2005. Counterterrorism: A game-theoretic analysis. *Journal of Conflict Resolution* 49(2).

al-Aswany, Alaa. 2004. *The Yacoubian Building* (translated by Humphrey Davies). Cairo: American University in Cairo Press.

Auda, Gehad. 1991. Egypt's uneasy party politics. *Journal of Democracy* 2(2).

Auyero, Javier. 1999. From the client's point(s) of view: How poor people perceive and evaluate political clientelism. *Theory and Society* 28(2).

———. 2001. *Poor People's Politics: Peronist Survival Networks and the Legacy of Evita*. Durham: Duke University Press.

al-Awadi, Hesham. 2004. *In Pursuit of Legitimacy: The Muslim Brothers and Mubarak, 1982–2000.* Library of Modern Middle East Studies 46. London: I.B. Tauris.

al-Awadi, Hesham. 2005. Mubarak and the Islamists: Why did the "honeymoon" end? *Middle East Journal* 59(1).

Ayubi, Nazih. 1980. *Bureaucracy and Politics in Contemporary Egypt.* London: Ithaca Press.

———. 1988. Arab Bureaucracies: Expanding size, changing roles. In: *Beyond Coercion: The Durability of the Arab State.* Adeed Dawisha and I. William Zartman, editors. London: Croom Helm.

———. 1989. *Government and the State in Egypt: Egypt under Mubarak.* Charles Tripp and Roger Owen, editors. London: Routledge.

———. 1995. *Overstating the Arab State: Politics and Society in the Middle East.* London: I.B. Tauris.

Azarva, Jeffrey. 2007. From cold peace to Cold War? The significance of Egypt's military buildup. *Middle East Review of International Affairs* 11(1).

Baaklini, Abdo, Guilain Denoeux, and Robert Springborg. 1999. *Legislative Politics in the Arab World: The Resurgence of Democratic Institutions.* Boulder: Lynne Rienner.

Badran, Wadouda and Azza Wahby, editors. 1996. *Privatization in Egypt: The Debate in the People's Assembly.* Cairo: Konrad Adenauer Stiftung.

Bach, Kirsten. 2002. Rural Egypt under stress. In: *Counter-Revolution in Egypt's Countryside: Land and Farmers in the Era of Economic Reform.* Ray Bush, editor. London: Zed Books.

Baker, Raymond. 1978. *Egypt's Uncertain Revolution under Nasser and Sadat.* Cambridge: Harvard University Press.

———. 1990. *Sadat and After: Struggles for Egypt's Political Soul.* Cambridge: Harvard University Press.

———. 1991. Afraid for Islam: Egypt's Muslim centrists between pharaohs and fundamentalists. *Daedalus* 120(3).

———. 2003. *Islam without Fear: Egypt and the New Islamists.* Cambridge: Harvard University Press.

Bank, Andre and Oliver Schlumberger. 2004. *Jordan: Between Regime Survival and Economic Reform. Arab Elites: Negotiating the Politics of Change.* Boulder: Lynne Rienner.

Bar, Shmuel. 2006. Bashar's Syria: The regime and its strategic worldview. *Comparative Strategy* 25.

Baram, Amazia. 1989. The ruling political elite in Ba'thi Iraq, 1968–1986: The changing features of a collective profile. *International Journal of Middle East Studies* 21.

———. 1997. Neo-tribalism in Iraq: Saddam Hussein's tribal policies, 1991–1996. *International Journal of Middle East Studies* 29(1).

Barkey, Karen. 1997. *Bandits and Bureaucrats: The Ottoman Route to State Centralization.* Ithaca: Cornell University Press.

Barro, Robert J. 1999. Determinants of democracy. *Journal of Political Economy* 107(6).

Bates, Robert. 1981. *Markets and States in Tropical Africa: The Political Basis of Agricultural Policies.* Berkeley: University of California Press.

al-Batran, Hamdi. 1997. Yawmiyāt ẓābit fil Aryāf *(Diary of an Officer in the Countryside).* Cairo: *Dār al-Hilāl.*

el-Batran, Manal and Christian Arandel. 1998. A shelter of their own: Information settlement expansion in greater Cairo and government responses. *Environment and Urbanization* 10(1).

Bayat, Asef. 1996. Cairo's poor: Dilemmas of survival and solidarity. *Middle East Report* 202.

———. 1997. *Street Politics: Poor People's Movements in Iran*. New York: Columbia University Press.

Bayat, Asef and Eric Denis. 2000. Who is afraid of Ashwaiyaat? Urban change and politics in Egypt. *Environment and Urbanization* 12.

Beattie, Kirk. 1991. Prospects for democratization in Egypt. *American-Arab Affairs* 36.

———. 2000. *Egypt during the Sadat Years*. New York: Palgrave Macmillan.

Beinin, Joel. 2007. The militancy of Mahalla al-Kubra. *Middle East Report Online*. September 29.

———. 2008. Underbelly of Egypt's neoliberal agenda. *Middle East Report Online*. April 5.

Beinin, Joel and Hossam el-Hamalawy. 2007. Strikes in Egypt spread from center of gravity. *Middle East Report Online*. May 9.

Beinin, Joel and Zachary Lockman. 1988. *Workers on the Nile: Nationalism, Communism, Islam, and the Egyptian Working Class, 1882–1954*. Cairo: American University in Cairo Press.

Beinin, Joel and Joe Stork, editors. 1997. What does the Gama'a Islamiyya want? Tal'at Fu'ad Qasim interview with Hisham Mubarak. In: *Political Islam: Essays from Middle East Report*. Berkeley: University of California Press.

Bellin, Eva. 2002. *Stalled Democracy: Capital, Labor, and the Paradox of State-Sponsored Development*. Ithaca: Cornell University Press.

———. 2005. Coercive institutions and coercive leaders. In: *Authoritarianism in the Middle East: Regimes and Resistance*. Marsha Pripstein Posusney and Michele Penner Angrist, editors. Boulder: Lynne Rienner.

Bengio, Ofra. 1998. *Saddam's Word: Political Discourse in Iraq*. Oxford: Oxford University Press.

Benstead, Lindsay. 2008. Representation as bargaining in multiple arenas: How regime preferences shape member behavior in Morocco and Algeria. Paper presented at the annual meeting of the Middle East Studies Association.

Berger, Johannes and Claus Offe. 1982. Functionalism vs. rational choice? Some questions concerning the rationality of choosing one or the other. *Theory and Society* 11(4).

Bianchi, Robert. 1989. *Unruly Corporatism: Associational Life in Twentieth-Century Egypt*. Oxford: Oxford University Press.

Bicchieri, Cristina. 1993. *Rationality and Coordination*. Cambridge: Cambridge University Press.

Bicchieri, Cristina and John Duffy. 1997. Corruption cycles. *Political Studies* 45.

Bicchieri, Cristina and Carlo Rovelli. 1995. Evolution and revolution: The dynamics of corruption. *Rationality and Society* 7.

Binder, Leonard. 1966. Political recruitment and participation in Egypt. In: *Political Parties and Political Development*. Joseph LaPalombera and Myron Weiner, editors. Princeton: Princeton University Press.

———. 1978. *In a Moment of Enthusiasm: Political Power and the Second Stratum in Egypt*. Chicago: University of Chicago Press.

———. 1988. *Islamic Liberalism: A Critique of Development Ideologies*. Chicago: University of Chicago Press.

Bin Nefisa, Sara and Alaa al-Din Arafat. 2005. Al-Intikhābāt wal Zabā'nīya al-Siyāsīya fī Miṣr: Tajdīd al-Wusaṭā' wa 'Audat al-Nākhib *(Elections and Political Clientelism in Egypt: Renewal of the Intermediary and the Return of the Voter)*. Cairo: Center for Human Rights Studies.

al-Bishri, Tariq. 1983. al-Ḥaraka al-Siyāsīya fī Miṣr 1945–1952 *(The Political Movement in Egypt 1945–1952)*, 2nd edition. Cairo: *al-Shurūq*.

Blais, Andre. 2000. *To Vote or Not to Vote: The Merits and Limits of Rational Choice Theory*. Pittsburgh: University of Pittsburgh Press.

Blaydes, Lisa. 2005. *Al-Mu'assasāt al-siyāsīya al-rasmīya wa-ghair al-rasmīya fī Miṣr* [Formal and informal political institutions in Egypt]. al-Dimuqrāṭīya [*Democracy Review*] (in Arabic and English), October.

Blaydes, Lisa and Mark Kayser. 2007. Counting calories: Democracy and distribution in the developing world. Paper presented at the annual meeting of the American Political Science Association.

Blaydes, Lisa and Lawrence Rubin. 2008. Ideological reorientation and counterterrorism: Confronting militant Islam in Egypt. *Terrorism and Political Violence* 20(4).

Blaydes, Lisa and Safinaz el-Tarouty. 2009. Women's electoral participation in Egypt: The implications of gender for voter recruitment and mobilization. *Middle East Journal* 63.

———. 2008. *Al-Tanāfusīya al-ḥizbīya al-dakhīlīya: Dirāsat ḥāla lil-ḥizb al-waṭanī al-dimuqrātī fī Miṣr* [Intraparty competition and Egypt's National Democratic Party] (with Safinaz El-Tarouty). al-Dimuqrāṭīya [*Democracy Review*] (in Arabic and English), April.

Block, Steven. 2002. Political business cycles, democratization, and economic reform: The case of Africa. *Journal of Development Economics* 67.

Blum, Roberto. 1997a. Corruption and complicity: Mortar of Mexico's political system? *Trends in Organized Crime* 3(1).

———. 1997b. The weight of the past. *Journal of Democracy* 8(4).

Boix, Carles. 2003. *Democracy and Redistribution*. Cambridge: Cambridge University Press.

Boix, Carles and Milan Svolik. 2007. Non-tyrannical autocracies. Paper presented at the UCLA Comparative Politics Seminar.

el-Borei, Negad. 1995. Democracy jeopardized: Nobody "passed" the elections. *Account of the Egyptian Parliamentary Elections 1995*. Cairo: Egyptian Organization for Human Rights.

Bouandel, Youcef. 2003. Political parties and the transition from authoritarianism: The case of Algeria. *Journal of Modern African Studies* 41(1).

———. 2008. Election of the legislature in Algeria, May 2007. *Electoral Studies* 27(3).

Bouandel, Youcef and Yahia Zoubir. 1998. Algeria's elections: The prelude to democratization. *Third World Quarterly* 19(2).

Boutaleb, Assia. 2002. The parliamentary elections of year 2000 in Egypt: A lesson in political participation. Elections in the Middle East: What do they mean? Iman A. Hamdy, editor. *Cairo Papers in Social Science* 12(1/2).

Bradley, John. 2008. *Inside Egypt: The Land of the Pharaohs on the Brink of a Revolution*. New York: Palgrave Macmillan.

Brand, Laurie. 1998. *Women, the State, and Political Liberalization: Middle Eastern and North African Experiences*. New York: Columbia University Press.

Brandt, Patrick and John Williams. 2000. A linear Poisson autoregressive model. *Political Analysis* 9(2).

Brandt, Patrick, John Williams, Benjamin Fordham, and Brian Pollins. 2000. Dynamic modeling for persistent event-count time series. *American Journal of Political Science* 44(4).

Bratton, Michael, Robert Mattes, and E. Gyimah-Boadi. 2005. *Public Opinion, Democracy, and Market Reform in Africa*. Cambridge: Cambridge University Press.

Brommelhorster, Jorn and Paes Wolf-Christian. 2003. *The Military as an Economic Actor: Soldiers in Business*. New York: Palgrave Macmillan.

Brown, Nathan J. 1990. *Peasant Politics in Modern Egypt: The Struggle against the State*. New Haven: Yale University Press.

Brown, Nathan J. and Amr Hamzawy. 2008. The draft party platform of the Egyptian Muslim brotherhood: Foray into political integration or retreat into old positions. Carnegie Papers. Carnegie Endowment for International Peace 89. At http://www.carnegieendowment.org/publications/.

Brown, Nathan J., Amr Hamzawy, and Marina Ottaway. 2006. Islamist movements and the democratic process in the Arab world: exploring the gray zones. Carnegie Papers. Carnegie Endowment for International Peace 67. At http://www.carnegieendowment.org/publications/.

Brownlee, Jason. 2002. The decline of pluralism in Mubarak's Egypt. *Journal of Democracy* 13(4).

———. 2004. Ruling parties and durable authoritarianism. CDDRL Working Paper.

———. 2005. Political crisis and restabilization: Iraq, Libya, Syria, and Tunisia. In: *Authoritarianism in the Middle East: Regimes and Resistance*. Marsha Pripstein Posusney and Michele Penner Angrist, editors. Boulder: Lynne Rienner.

———. 2007. *Authoritarianism in an Age of Democratization*. Cambridge: Cambridge University Press.

Brumberg, Daniel. 2002. The trap of liberalized autocracy. *Journal of Democracy* 13(4).

———. 2005. Islam is not the solution (or the problem). *Washington Quarterly* 29(1).

Brusco, Valeria, Mara Marcelo Nazareno, and Susan C. Stokes. 2004. Vote buying in Argentina. *Latin American Research Review* 39(2).

Bueno de Mesquita, Bruce and Alastair Smith. 2007. Foreign aid and policy concessions. *Journal of Conflict Resolution* 51(2).

Bueno de Mesquita, Bruce, Alastair Smith, Randolph M. Siverson, and James D. Morrow. 2003. *The Logic of Political Survival*. Cambridge: MIT Press.

Bueno de Mesquita, Ethan. 2005a. The quality of terror. *American Journal of Political Science* 49(3).

———. 2005b. The terrorist endgame: A model with moral hazard and learning. *Journal of Conflict Resolution* 49(2).

———. 2005c. Conciliation, commitment, and counterterrorism. *International Organization* 59(1).

———. 2005d. Politics and the suboptimal provision of counterterror. Paper presented at the Annual Meeting of the Midwest Political Science Association.

Bueno de Mesquita, Ethan and Eric Dickson. 2004. The propaganda of the deed: Terrorism, counterterrorism, and mobilization. Paper presented at the Annual Meeting of the American Political Science Association.

Burrowes, Robert and Catherine Kasper. 2007. The Salih regime and the need for a credible opposition. *Middle East Journal* 61(2).

Bush, Ray. 2002a. Land reform and counter-revolution. In: *Counter-Revolution in Egypt's Countryside: Land and Farmers in the Era of Economic Reform*. Ray Bush, editor. London: Zed Books.

————. 2002b. More losers than winners in Egypt's countryside: The impact of changes in land tenure. In: *Counter-Revolution in Egypt's Countryside: Land and Farmers in the Era of Economic Reform.* Ray Bush, editor. London: Zed Books.

Calvo, Ernesto and Maria Victoria Murillo. 2004. Who delivers? Partisan clients in the Argentine electoral market. *American Journal of Political Science* 48(4).

Campana, Joel. 1996. From accommodation to confrontation: The Muslim Brotherhood in the Mubarak years. *Journal of International Affairs* 50(1).

Carapico, Sheila. 1993. Elections and mass politics in Yemen. *Middle East Report* 185.

————. 1998. *Civil Society in Yemen: The Political Economy of Activism in Modern Arabia.* Cambridge: Cambridge University Press.

————. 2003. How Yemen's ruling party secured an electoral landslide. *Middle East Report Online.* May 16.

Case, William. 1992. Semi-democracy in Malaysia: Pressures and prospects for change. Regime Change and Regime Maintenance in Asia and the Pacific. Discussion Paper Series 8. Australian National University.

————. 2001. Malaysia's resilient pseudodemocracy. *Journal of Democracy* 12(1).

Cavatorta, Francesco. 2002. The failed liberalization of Algeria and the international context: A legacy of stable authoritarianism. *Journal of North African Studies* 7.

Central Agency for Public Mobilization and Statics. (Multiple years). Cairo: Census of Building and Housing Characteristics.

Chhibber, Pradeep and Infan Noorudiin. 2004. Do party systems matter? The number of parties and government performance in the Indian states. *Comparative Political Studies* 37(2).

Cho, Wendy Tam. 1998. If the assumption fits . . . : A comment on the King ecological inference solution. *Political Analysis* 7(1).

————. 2004. The limits of ecological inference: The case of split-ticket voting. *American Journal of Political Science* 48(1).

Chong, Dennis. 1991. *Collective Action and the Civil Rights Movement.* Chicago: University of Chicago Press.

Clark, Janine A. 2004. *Islam, Charity, and Activism: Middle-Class Networks and Social Welfare in Egypt, Jordan, and Yemen.* Bloomington: Indiana University Press.

Clark, Janine A. and Remonda Bensabat Kleinberg, editors. 2000. *Economic Liberalization, Democratization, and Civil Society in the Developing World.* New York: Palgrave Macmillan.

Collombier, Virginie. 2007. The internal stakes of the 2005 elections: The struggle for influence in Egypt's National Democratic Party. *Middle East Journal* 61(1).

Cook, Steven. 2003. The military enclave: Islam and state in Egypt, Turkey, and Algeria. University of Pennsylvania doctoral dissertation.

————. 2007. *Ruling but not Governing: The Military and Political Development in Egypt, Algeria, and Turkey.* Baltimore: Johns Hopkins University Press.

Cooper, Mark N. 1982. *The Transformation of Egypt.* London: Croom Helm.

Corstange, Dan. 2008. Why Sunni votes are cheap in Lebanon but dear in Yemen. Working paper.

Cox, Gary. 2008. Authoritarian elections and leadership succession, 1975–2000. Working paper, UCSD.

Cox, Gary and Matthew McCubbins. 1986. Electoral politics as a redistributive game. *Journal of Politics* 48.

Crenshaw, Martha. 1991. How terrorism declines. *Terrorism and Political Violence* 3(3).

Crystal, Jill. 1990. *Oil Politics in the Gulf: Rulers and Merchants in Kuwait and Qatar.* Cambridge: Cambridge University Press.

Darden, Keith A. 2001. Blackmail as a tool of state domination: Ukraine under Kuchma. *East European Constitutional Review* 10(2/3).

Davenport, Christian. 1996. The weight of the past: Exploring lagged determinants of political repression. *Political Research Quarterly* 49(2).

Dawisha, Adeed and I. William Zartman, editors. 1988. *Beyond Coercion: The Durability of the Arab State.* London: Croom Helm.

Debs, Alexandre. 2007. The wheel of fortune: Agency problems in dictatorships. Working paper, Department of Economics, MIT.

de Figueiredo, Rui and Barry Weingast. 2001. Vicious cycles: Endogenous political extremism and political violence. Working paper, Institute of Governmental Studies, University of California at Berkeley.

Dekmajian, R. Hrair. 1971. *Egypt under Nasir: A Study in Political Dynamics.* Albany: State University of New York Press.

Della Porta, Donatella and Alessandro Pizzorno. 1996. The business politicians: Reflections from a study of political corruption. *Journal of Law and Society* 23(1).

DeNardo, James. 1985. *Power in Numbers.* Princeton: Princeton University Press.

Desposato, Scott. 2006. How informal electoral institutions shape the Brazilian legislative arena. In: *Informal Institutions and Democracy: Lessons from Latin America.* Gretchen Helmke and Steven Levitsky, editors. Baltimore: Johns Hopkins University Press.

Dessouki, Ali E. Hillal. 1981. Policy making in Egypt: A case study of the open door economic policy. *Social Problems* 28(4).

Detalle, Renaud. 1993. The Yemeni elections up close. *Middle East Report* 185.

Dethier, Jean-Jacques and Kathy Funk. 1987. The Language of food: PL 480 in Egypt. *Middle East Report* 145.

Diamond, Larry. 1989. Preface. *Democracy in Developing Countries: Asia.* Larry Diamond, Juan Linz, and Seymour Martin Lipset, editors. Boulder: Lynne Rienner.

———. 2002. Elections without democracy: Thinking about hybrid regimes. *Journal of Democracy* 13(2).

Diaz-Cayeros, Alberto, Beatriz Magaloni, and Barry Weingast. 2003. Tragic brilliance: Equilibrium hegemony and democratization in Mexico. Working paper, Stanford University.

Diaz-Cayeros, Alberto, Federico Estevez, and Beatriz Magaloni. 2007. Strategies of Vote Buying: Poverty, Democracy, and Social Transfers in Mexico. Book manuscript.

Dillman, Bradford. 2003. Parliamentary elections and the prospects for political pluralism in North Africa. *Government and Opposition* 35(2).

Dixit, Avinash and John Londregan. 1996. The determinants of success in special interests in redistributive politics. *Journal of Politics* 58(4).

Dowell, Andrew. 1999. Pound seen stable post-election. *Business Monthly*, September. American Chamber of Commerce Egypt.

Dreher, Axel. 2002. The development and implementation of IMF and World Bank conditionality. Hamburg Institute of International Economics Discussion Paper 165.

Dresch, Paul. 2000. *A History of Modern Yemen.* Cambridge: Cambridge University Press.

Dresch, Paul and Bernard Haykel. 1995. Stereotypes and political styles: Islamists and tribesfolk in Yemen. *International Journal of Middle East Studies* 27(4).

Droz-Vincent, Phillipe. 1997. Challenges to the military in Egypt. *Middle East Policy.*

Dumke, David T. 2006. Congress and the Arab heavyweights: Questioning the Saudi and Egyptian alliances. *Middle East Policy* 13(3).

———. 2003. *Democracy in Contemporary Egyptian Public Discourse*. Amsterdam: John Benjamins Publishing.

Dunne, Michelle. 2007. Time to pursue democracy in Egypt. Middle East Program Policy Outlook. Carnegie Endowment for International Peace.

Dunning, Thad. 2004. Conditioning the effects of aid: Cold War politics, donor credibility, and democracy in Africa. *International Organization* 58(2).

———. 2008. *Crude Democracy: Natural Resource Wealth and Political Regimes*. Cambridge: Cambridge University Press.

Durac, Vincent. 2009. The impact of external actors on the distribution of power in the Middle East: The case of Egypt. *Journal of North African Studies* 14(1).

Easterly, William. 2001. *The Elusive Quest for Growth: Economists' Adventures and Misadventures in the Tropics*. Cambridge: MIT Press.

Egorov, Georgy, Sergei Guriev, and Konstantin Sonin. 2006. Media freedom, bureaucratic incentives, and the resource curse. Working paper.

Egorov, Georgy and Konstantin Sonin. 2006. Dictators and their viziers: Endogenizing the loyalty-competence trade-off. Working paper.

Ehab, John. 2005. Battle for Bab Al Shaariya. *Cairo Magazine*, November.

Ehteshami, Anoushiravan and Emma Murphy. 1996. Transformation of the corporatist state in the Middle East. *Third World Quarterly* 17(4).

Eickelman, Dale. 2002. Inside the Islamic reformation. In: *Everyday Life in the Muslim Middle East*, 2nd edition. Donna Lee Bowen and Evelyn A. Early, editors. Bloomington: Indiana University Press.

Elster, Jon. 1979. *Ulysses and the Sirens: Studies in Rationality and Irrationality*. Cambridge: Cambridge University Press.

———. 1982. Marxism, functionalism, and game theory: The case for methodological individualism. *Theory and Society* 11(4).

———. 1989. *Solomonic Judgements: Studies in the Limitations of Rationality*. Cambridge: Cambridge University Press.

———. 1992. *Local Justice: How Institutions Allocate Scarce Goods and Necessary Burdens*. New York: Russell Sage Foundation.

Elyachar, Julia. 2005. *Markets of Dispossession: NGOs, Economic Development, and the State in Cairo*. Durham: Duke University Press.

Erdle, Steffan. 2004. Tunisia: Economic transformation and political restoration. In: *Arab Elites: Negotiating the Politics of Change*. Volker Perthes, editor. Boulder: Lynne Rienner.

Esposito, John L. and John O. Voll. 1996. *Islam and Democracy*. Oxford: Oxford University Press.

Fahmy, Ninette. 2002. *The Politics of Egypt*. London: Routledge.

———. 2004. Informal settlements and the debate over the state–society relationship in Egypt. *Middle East Journal* 58(4).

Fandy, Mamoun. 1994. Egypt's Islamic group: Regional revenge? *Middle East Journal* 48(4).

Fearon, James. 1994. Domestic political audiences and the escalation of international disputes. *American Political Science Review* 88.

———. 1999. Electoral accountability and the control of politicians: Selecting good types versus sanctioning poor performance. In: *Democracy, Accountability, and Representation*. Adam Przeworski, Susan Stokes, and Bernard Manin, editors. Cambridge: Cambridge University Press.

————. 2006. Self-enforcing democracy. Paper presented at the Annual Meeting of the American Political Science Association, Philadelphia, PA, August 31–September 3.

Fish, Steven M. 2002. Islam and authoritarianism. *World Politics* 55(1).

Fish, Steven M. and Omar Choudhry. 2007. Democratization and economic liberalization in the postcommunist world. *Comparative Political Studies* 40(3).

[FAO] Food and Agriculture Organization. 2001. *Food Balance Sheets: A Handbook.* Rome: United Nations.

Friedman, Elisabeth. 1998. The paradoxes of gendered political opportunity in the Venezuelan transition to democracy. *Latin American Research Review* 33(3).

Frisch, Hillel. 2001. Guns and butter in the Egyptian army. *Middle East Review of International Affairs* 5(2).

Fukuyama, Francis and Michael McFaul. 2007. Should democracy be promoted or demoted? *Washington Quarterly* 31(1).

Gandhi, Jennifer. 2008. *Political Institutions under Dictatorship.* Cambridge: Cambridge University Press.

Gandhi, Jennifer and Adam Przeworski. 2001. Dictatorial institutions and the survival of dictators. Paper presented at the Annual Meeting of the American Political Science Association.

————. 2006. Cooperation, cooptation, and rebellion under dictatorship. *Economics and Politics* 18(1).

Gandhi, Jennifer and Ellen Lust-Okar. 2009. Elections under authoritarianism. *Annual Review of Political Science* 12.

Gause, F. Gregory III. 1994. *Oil Monarchies: Domestic and Security Challenges in the Arab Gulf States.* New York: Council on Foreign Relations Press.

Geddes, Barbara. 1999. Authoritarian breakdown: Empirical test of a game theoretic argument. Paper presented at the Annual Meeting of the American Political Science Association.

————. 2004. Minimum-winning coalitions and personalization in authoritarian regimes. Paper presented at the Annual Meeting of the American Political Science Association.

————. 2005. Why parties and elections in authoritarian regimes? Paper presented at the Annual Meeting of the American Political Science Association.

————. 2008. Party creation as an autocratic survival strategy. Working paper.

Geddes, Barbara and John Zaller. 1989. Sources of popular support for authoritarian regimes. *American Journal of Political Science* 33(2).

Gehlbach, Scott and Philip Keefer. 2007. Investment without democracy: Ruling-party institutionalization and credible commitment in autocracies. Working paper, University of Wisconsin.

Gehlbach, Scott, Konstantin Sonin, and Ekaterina Zhuravskaya. 2007. Businessmen candidates. Working paper, University of Wisconsin.

Gerges, Fawaz A. 2000. The end of the Islamist insurgency in Egypt? Costs and prospects. *Middle East Journal* 4.

Ghannam, Farha. 2002. *Remaking the Modern: Space, Relocation, and the Politics of Identity in a Global Cairo.* Berkeley: University of California Press.

el-Ghobashy, Mona. 2005. The metamorphosis of the Egyptian Muslim Brothers. *International Journal of Middle East Studies* 37(3).

————. 2006. Egypt's paradoxical elections. *Middle East Report* 238.

Gibson, Edward L. 1997. The populist road to market reform policy and electoral coalitions in Mexico and Argentina. *World Politics* 49(3).

Giddens, Anthony. 1982. Commentary on the debate. *Theory and Society* 11(4).

Gilley, Bruce. 2003. The limits of authoritarian resilience. *Journal of Democracy* 14(1).

Glad, Betty. 2002. Why tyrants go too far: Malignant narcissism and absolute power. *Political Psychology* 23(1).

Glain, Stephen. 2006. The Brotherhood: How far will Egypt's Islamists go? *Boston Review*, May/June.

Golden, Miriam and Eric C. C. Chang. 2001. Competitive corruption: Factional conflict and political malfeasance in postwar Italian Christian democracy. *World Politics* 53(4).

Goldschmidt, Arthur Jr. and Robert Johnston. 2004. *Historical Dictionary of Egypt*, revised edition. Cairo: American University in Cairo Press.

Gomez, Edmund Terence and K. S. Jomo. 1999. *Malaysia's Political Economy: Politics, Patronage and Profits*. Cambridge: Cambridge University Press.

Gonzalez, Maria de los Angeles. 2002. Do changes in democracy affect the political budget cycle? Evidence from Mexico. *Review of Development Economics* 6(2).

Greene, Kenneth. 2007. *Why Dominant Parties Lose: Mexico's Democratization in Comparative Perspective*. Cambridge: Cambridge University Press.

Greene, William H. 2000. *Econometric Analysis*, 4th edition. Upper Saddle River: Prentice Hall.

Greenwood, Scott. 2008. Bad for business? Entrepreneurs and democracy in the Arab world. *Comparative Political Studies* 41(6).

Greif, Avner and David Laitin. 2004. A theory of endogenous institutional change. *American Political Science Review* 98(4).

Grier, Robin M. and Kevin B. Grier. 2000. Political cycles in nontraditional settings: Theory and evidence from the case of Mexico. *Journal of Law and Economics* 43(1).

Grofman, Bernard. 1993. Is turnout the paradox that ate rational choice theory? In: *Information, Participation, and Choice: An Economic Theory of Democracy in Perspective*. Bernard Grofman, editor. Ann Arbor: University of Michigan Press.

Guazzone, Laura. 1995. *The Islamist Dilemma: The Political Role of Islamist Movements in the Contemporary Arab World*. London: Ithaca Press.

Gupta, Dipak, Harinder Singh, and Tom Sprague. 1993. Government coercion of dissidents: Deterrent or provocation? *Journal of Conflict Resolution* 37(2).

Gupta, Sanjeev, Hamid Davoodi, and Rosa Alonso-Terme. 2002. Does corruption affect income inequality and poverty? *Economics of Goverance* 3.

Haber, Stephen. 2002. The political economy of crony capitalism. In: *Crony Capitalism and Economic Growth in Latin America: Theory and Evidence*. Stephen Haber, editor. Stanford: Hoover Institution Press.

————. 2006. Authoritarian government. In: *The Oxford Handbook of Political Economy*. Barry R. Weingast and Donald Wittman, editors. Oxford: Oxford University Press.

Haber, Stephen, Armando Razo, and Noel Maurer. 2003. *The Politics of Property Rights: Political Instability, Credible Commitments, and Economic Growth in Mexico, 1876–1929*. Cambridge: Cambridge University Press.

Hafez, Mohammed. 2003. *Why Muslims Rebel: Repression and Resistance in the Islamic World*. Boulder: Lynne Rienner.

Hafez, Sherine. 2003. The terms of empowerment: Islamic women activists in Egypt. *Cairo Papers in Social Science* 24(4).

Haggard, Stephan and Robert Kaufman. 1995. *The Political Economy of Democratic Transitions*. Princeton: Princeton University Press.

Hagopian, Frances. 1996. *Traditional Politics and Regime Change in Brazil*. Cambridge: Cambridge University Press.

Halliday, Fred. 1990. Tunisia's uncertain future. *Middle East Report* 163.

el-Hamalawy, Hossam. 2007. Comrades and brothers. *Middle East Report* 242.

Hamdan, Gamal. 1967. *Shakhsiat Misr (The Personality of Egypt)*. Cairo: Dār al-Hilāl.

Hamdy, Iman. 2002. Elections in the Middle East: What do they mean? *Cairo Papers in Social Science* 12(1/2).

Hamed, Osama. 1981. Egypt's open door economic policy: An attempt at economic integration in the Middle East. *International Journal of Middle East Studies* 13.

Hammond, Andrew. 2007. *What the Arabs Think of America*. Oxford: Greenwood World.

Hammoudi, Abdellah. 1997. *Master and Disciple: The Cultural Foundations of Moroccan Authoritarianism*. Chicago: University of Chicago Press.

Hamzawy, Amr and Nathan Brown. 2005. Can Egypt's troubled elections produce a more democratic future? Carnegie Endowment for International Peace Policy Outlook.

Hamzawy, Amr, Marina Ottaway, and Nathan Brown. 2007. What Islamists need to be clear about: The case of the Egyptian Muslim Brotherhood. Carnegie Endowment for International Peace Policy Outlook.

Handoussa, Heba and Nivine El Oraby. 2004. Civil service wages and reform: The case of Egypt. Working paper no. 98, Egyptian Center for Economic Studies.

Harik, Iliya. 1973. The single party as a subordinate movement: The case of Egypt. *World Politics* 26(1).

——. 1974. *The Political Mobilization of Peasants: A Study of an Egyptian Community*. Bloomington: Indiana University Press.

Hatem, Mervat F. 1992. Economic and political liberalization in Egypt and the demise of state feminism. *International Journal of Middle East Studies* 24.

Heberer, Thomas. 2006. Institutional change and legitimacy via urban elections? People's awareness of elections and participation in urban neighborhoods (Shequ). Duisburg Working Papers on East Asia Studies 68.

Heikal, Mohamed. 1983. *Autumn of Fury: The Assassination of Sadat*. London: Andre Deutsch.

Helmke, Gretchen. 2002. The logic of strategic defection: Court–executive relations in Argentina under dictatorship and democracy. *American Political Science Review* 96(2).

Helmke, Gretchen and Steven Levitsky. 2003. Informal institutions and comparative politics: A research agenda. Working paper no. 307, Kellogg Institute for International Studies, University of Notre Dame.

Helmy, Omneia A. 2008. The impact of budget deficit on inflation in Egypt. Working paper no. 141, Egyptian Center for Economic Studies.

Hendriks, Bertus. 1985. Egypt's elections, Mubarak's bind. *Middle East Report* 129.

——. 1987. A report from the election campaign: Egypt's new political map. *Middle East Report* 147.

Herb, Michael. 1999. *All in the Family: Absolutism, Revolution, and Democracy in the Middle Eastern Monarchies*. Albany: State University of New York Press.

——. 2002. Democratization in the Arab world? Emirs and parliaments in the Gulf. *Journal of Democracy* 13(4).

_____. 2004. Princes and parliaments in the Arab world. *Middle East Journal* 58(3).

_____. 2009. A nation of bureaucrats: Political participation and economic diversification in Kuwait and the United Arab Emirates. *International Journal of Middle Eastern Studies* 41(3).

Hermet, Guy, Richard Rose, and Alain Roouquie. 1978. *Elections without Choice*. New York: Wiley.

Heydemann, Steven. 2004. Networks of privilege: Rethinking the politics of economic reform in the Middle East. In: *Networks of Privilege in the Middle East: The Politics of Economic Reform Revisited*. Steven Heydemann, editor. New York: Palgrave Macmillan.

_____. 2007a. Upgrading authoritarianism in the Arab world. Saban Center for Middle East Policy Analysis Paper 13.

_____. 2007b. Social pacts and the persistence of authoritarianism in the Middle East. In: *Debating Arab Authoritarianism: Dynamics and Durability in Nondemocratic Regimes*. Oliver Schlumberger, editor. Stanford: Stanford University Press.

Hibbs, Douglas A. 1987. *The American Political Economy*. Cambridge: Harvard University Press.

Hinnebusch, Raymond Jr. 1988a. *Egyptian Politics under Sadat: The Post-populist Development of an Authoritarian-Modernizing State*, updated edition. Boulder: Lynne Rienner.

_____. 1988b. Political parties in the Arab state: Libya, Syria, and Egypt. In: *Beyond Coercion: The Durability of the Arab State*. Adeed Dawisha and I. William Zartman, editors. London: Croom Helm.

_____. 1994. Liberalization in Syria: The struggle of economic and political rationality. In: *Contemporary Syria: Liberalization between Cold War and Cold Peace*. Eberhard Kienle, editor. London: British Academic Press.

_____. 1997. Syria: The politics of economic liberalization. *Third World Quarterly* 18(2).

_____. 2001a. The politics of economic liberalization: Comparing Egypt and Syria. In: *The State and Global Change: The Political Economy of Transition in the Middle East and North Africa*. Hassan Hakimian and Ziba Moshaver, editors. Surrey: Curzon.

_____. 2001b. *Syria: Revolution from Above*. London: Routledge.

_____. 2006. Authoritarian persistence, democratization theory, and the Middle East: An overview and critique. *Democratization* 13(3).

_____. 2007. Authoritarian persistence, democratization theory, and the Middle East: An overview and critique. In: *Democratization in the Muslim World: Changing Patterns of Power and Authority*. Frederic Volpi and Francesco Cavatorta, editors. London: Routledge.

Hirschkind, Charles. 2006. *The Ethical Soundscape: Cassette Sermons and Islamic Counterpublics*. New York: Columbia University Press.

Hiskey, Jonathan. 1999. Does democracy matter? Electoral competition and local development in Mexico. Doctoral dissertation, University of Pittsburgh.

Hoehn, John P. and Douglas J. Krieger. 2000. The economic analysis of water and wastewater investments in Cairo, Egypt. *Evaluation Review* 24.

Honaker, James. 2004. Unemployment and violence in Northern Ireland: A missing data model for ecological inference. Paper presented at the Annual Meeting of the Midwest Political Science Association.

Hoodfar, Homa. 1997. *Between Marriage and the Market: Intimate Politics and Survival in Cairo*. Berkeley: University of California Press.

Hoover, Dean and David Kowalewski. 1992. Dynamic models of dissent and repression. *Journal of Conflict Resolution* 36(1).

Hopkins, Nicholas and Reem Saad. 2004. *Upper Egypt: Identity and Change.* Cairo: American University in Cairo Press.

Hopkins, Nicholas S. and Kirsten Westergaard, editors. 1998. *Directions of Change in Rural Egypt.* Cairo: American University in Cairo Press.

Hopwood, Derek. 1985. *Egypt: Politics and Society 1945–1984.* Boston: Allen and Unwin.

Howard, Marc Morje and Philip Roessler. 2006. Liberalizing electoral outcomes in competitive authoritarian regimes. *American Journal of Political Science* 50(2).

Hudson, Michael. 1991. After the Gulf War: Prospects for democratization in the Arab world. *Middle East Journal* 45(3).

Humphreys, R. Stephen. 2005. *Between Memory and Desire: The Middle East in a Troubled Age,* updated edition. Berkeley: University of California Press.

Huntingon, Samuel. 1968. *Political Order in Changing Societies.* New Haven: Yale University Press.

————. 1991. *The Third Wave: Democratization in the Late Twentieth Century.* Norman: University of Oklahoma Press.

Huntington, Samuel P. and Joan M. Nelson. 1976. *No Easy Choice: Political Participation in Developing Countries.* Cambridge: Harvard University Press.

Hussein, Adel, Rifaat Al-Said, and Mustapha Kamel Al-Sayyid. 1998. Twenty years of multi-partyism in Egypt: A debate. *Cairo Papers in Social Science* 21(3).

Hwang, In-Won. 2003. *Personalized Politics: The Malaysian State under Mahatir.* Singapore: Institute of Southeast Asian Studies.

Ibrahim, Nageh et al. 2003. Nahr al-Ḍikrayāt (*River of Memories*). Cairo: *Maktabat al-Turāth al-Islāmī.*

Ibrahim, Saad Eddin. 1980. Anatomy of Egypt's militant Islamic groups: Methodological note and preliminary findings. *International Journal of Middle East Studies* 12.

Ichino, Nahomi. 2005. Local politicians and clientelism: Political tournaments in Nigeria. Paper presented at the Annual Meeting of the American Political Science Association.

IDEA. 2005. *Building Democracy in Yemen: Women's Political Participation, Political Party Life, and Democratic Elections.* Stockholm: International IDEA.

Inter-Parliamentary Union. 2006. Parliamentary immunity. Background paper, UNDP.

Ismail, Salwa. 2003. *Rethinking Islamist Politics: Culture, the State, and Islamism.* London: I.B. Tauris.

————. 2006. *Political Life in Cairo's New Quarters: Encountering the Everyday State.* Minneapolis: University of Minnesota Press.

Jackman, Robert. 1987. Political institutions and voter turnout in the industrialized democracies. *American Political Science Review* 81(2).

al-Jawadi, Mohammed. 2001. al-Muḥafiẓūn (*The Governors*). Cairo: *al-Hai'a al-Misrīya al-'Amma lil-Kutāb.*

Kalyvas, Stathis. 1998. Democracy and religious politics: Evidence from Belgium. *Comparative Political Studies* 31(3).

————. 2000. Commitment problems in emerging democracies: The case of religious parties. *Comparative Politics* 32(4).

Kamrava, Mehran. 1998. Non-democratic states and political liberalization in the Middle East: A structural analysis. *Third World Quarterly* 19(1).

Karam, Azza M. 1998. *Women, Islamisms, and the State: Contemporary Feminisms in Egypt.* New York: St. Martin's Press.

el-Karanshawy, Samer. 1997. Class, family, and power in an Egyptian village. *Cairo Papers in Social Science* 20(1).

Karawan, Ibrahim. 2005. Radical Islam: Egypt's experience. Conference paper, the Aspen Institute.

Karklins, Rasma. 1986. Soviet elections revisited: Voter abstention in noncompetitive voting. *American Political Science Review* 80.

Kassem, Maye. 1999. *In the Guise of Democracy: Governance in Contemporary Egypt.* Ithaca: Ithaca Press.

———. 2002. The 2000 elections: New rules, new tactics. *Cairo Papers in Social Science* 12(1/2)

———. 2004. *Egyptian Politics: The Dynamics of Authoritarian Rule.* Boulder: Lynne Rienner.

Kepel, Gilles. 1985. *The Prophet and the Pharaoh: Muslim Extremism in Egypt.* London: Al Saqi Books.

———. 2002. Jihad: *The Trail of Political Islam.* Cambridge: Harvard University Press.

Keshavarian, Arang. 2009. Regime loyalty and Bazari representation under the Islamic Republic of Iran: Dilemmas of the society of Islamic coalition. *International Journal of Middle Eastern Studies* 41(2).

Khalil, Magdi. 2006. Egypt's Muslim Brotherhood and political power: Would democracy survive? *Middle East Review of International Affairs* 10(1).

Khattab, Mokhtar. 1999. Constraints on privatization: The Egyptian experience. Working paper no. 38, Egyptian Center for Economic Studies.

Khawaja, Marwan. 1993. Repression and popular collective action: Evidence from the West Bank. *Egyptian Center for Economic Studies, Sociological Forum* 8(1).

Khwaja, Asim Ijaz and Atif Mian. 2005. Do lenders favor politically connected firms? Rent provision in an emerging financial market. *Quarterly Journal of Economics* 120(4).

Kienle, Eberhard. 2001. *A Grand Delusion: Democracy and Economic Reform in Egypt.* London: I.B. Tauris.

———. 2004. Reconciling privilege and reform: Fiscal policy in Egypt, 1991–2000. In: *Networks of Privilege in the Middle East: The Politics of Economic Reform Revisited.* Steven Heydemann, editor. New York: Palgrave Macmillan.

———. 2007. Democracy promotion and the renewal of authoritarian rule. In: *Debating Arab Authoritarianism: Dynamics and Durability in Nondemocratic Regimes.* Oliver Schlumberger, editor. Stanford: Stanford University Press.

King, Gary. 1997. *A Solution to the Ecological Inference Problem: Reconstructing Individual Behavior from Aggregate Data.* Princeton: Princeton University Press.

King, Gary and Will Lowe. 2003. An automated information extraction tool for international conflict data with performance as good as human coders: A rare events evaluation design. *International Organization* 57(3).

King, Stephen J. 2003. *Liberalization against Democracy: The Local Politics of Economic Reform in Tunisia.* Bloomington: Indiana University Press.

———. 2007. *Tunisia: Countries at the Crossroads.* Washington, DC: Freedom House.

Kitschelt, Herbert and Steven I. Wilkinson. 2007. Citizen-politician linkages: An introduction. In: *Patrons, Clients, and Policies: Patterns of Democratic Accountability and Political Competition.* Herbert Kitschett and Steven Wilkinson, editors. Cambridge: Cambridge University Press.

Klemperer, Paul. 1999. Auction theory: A guide to the literature. *Journal of Economic Surveys* 13(3).

Knack, Stephen. 2004. Does foreign aid promote democracy? *International Studies Quarterly* 48.

Kocan, Gurcan and Simon Wigley. 2005. Democracy and the politics of parliamentary immunity in Turkey. *New Perspectives on Turkey* 33.

Koehler, Kevin. 2008. Authoritarian elections in Egypt: Formal and informal mechanisms of rule. *Democratization* 15(5).

Korayem, Karima. 1995. Structural adjustment, stabilization policies, and the poor in Egypt. *Cairo Papers in Social Science* 18(4).

———. 1997. Egypt's Economic Reform and Structural Adjustment (ERSAP). Working paper no. 19, Egyptian Center for Economic Studies.

Krueger, Anne and I. Turan. 1993. The politics and economics of Turkish policy reform in the 1980s. In: *Political and Economic Interactions in Economic Policy Reform*. Robert Bates and Anne Krueger, editors. Oxford: Blackwell.

Kuran, Timur. 1995. *Private Truths, Public Lies: The Social Consequences of Preference Falsification*. Cambridge: Harvard University Press.

Kurizaki, Shuhei. 2005. Efficient secrecy: Public versus private threats in crisis diplomacy. Paper presented at the Annual Meeting of the International Studies Association.

Kurzman, Charles. 2008. *Democracy Denied: 1905–1915: Intellectuals and the Fate of Democracy*. Cambridge: Harvard University Press.

Land Center for Human Rights, Cairo. 2002. Farmer struggles against Law 96 of 1992. In: *Counter-Revolution in Egypt's Countryside: Land and Farmers in the Era of Economic Reform*. Ray Bush, editor. London: Zed Books.

Landolt, Laura K. 2007. USAID, population control, and NGO-led democratization in Egypt: The fate of the ICPD Programme of Action. *Democratization* 14(4).

Langohr, Vickie. 2000. Cracks in Egypt's electoral engineering: The 2000 vote. *Middle East Report Online*. November 7.

———. 2004. Too much civil society, too little politics: Egypt and liberalizing Arab regimes. *Comparative Politics* 36(2).

Lawson, Fred. 2007. Intraregime dynamics, uncertainty, and the persistence of authoritarianism in the contemporary Arab world. In: *Debating Arab Authoritarianism: Dynamics and Durability in Nondemocratic Regimes*. Oliver Schlumberger, editor. Stanford: Stanford University Press.

Leiken, Robert and Steven Brooke. 2007. The moderate Muslim Brotherhood. *Foreign Affairs*, March/April.

Levitsky, Steven. 2007. From populism to clientelism? The transformation of labor-based party linkages in Latin America. In: *Patrons, Clients, and Policies: Patterns of Democratic Accountability and Political Competition*. Herbert Kitschett and Steven Wilkinson, editors. Cambridge: Cambridge University Press.

Levitsky, Steven and Lucan Way. 2002. The rise of competitive authoritarianism. *Journal of Democracy* 13(2).

———. 2003. Autocracy by democratic rules: The dynamics of competitive authoritarianism in the post–Cold War era. Working paper.

———. 2005. International linkage and democratization. *Journal of Democracy* 16(3).

———. 2010. *Competitive Authoritarianism: Hybrid Regimes after the Cold War*. Cambridge: Cambridge University Press.

Lichbach, Mark. 1987. Deterrence or escalation? The puzzle of aggregate studies of repression and dissent. *Journal of Conflict Resolution* 31(2).

Lilla, Mark. 2001. *The Reckless Mind: Intellectuals in Politics.* New York: New York Review Books.

Lindbeck, Assar and Jorgen Weibull. 1987. Balanced-budget redistribution as the outcome of political competition. *Public Choice* 52(3).

Lindsey, Ursula. 2003. Amid continuing inflation, precise data still proves wanting. American Chamber of Commerce Egypt. *Business Monthly*, September.

Linz, Juan. 2000. *Totalitarian and Authoritarian Regimes.* Boulder: Lynne Rienner.

Lipton, Michael. 1997. *Why Poor People Stay Poor: Urban Bias in World Development.* Cambridge: Harvard University Press.

Lohmann, Susanne. 1998. Rationalizing the political business cycle: A workhouse model. *Economics and Politics* 10(1).

————. 1994. Dynamics of informational cascades: The Monday demonstrations in Leipzig, East Germany, 1989–1991. *World Politics* 47.

Longley, April. 2007. The high water mark of Islamist politics? The case of Yemen. *Middle East Journal* 61(2).

Longley, April and Abdul Ghani al-Iryani. 2008. Fighting brushfires with batons: An analysis of the political crisis in South Yemen. *Middle East Institute Policy Brief* 7.

Lorentzen, Peter. 2006. Regularized rioting: Strategic toleration of popular protest in China. Working paper.

Luciani, Giacomo. 1987. Allocation vs. production states: A theoretical framework. In: *The Rentier State.* Hazem Beblawi and Giacomo Luciani, editors. London: Croom Helm.

————. 2007. Linking economic and political reform in the Middle East: The role of the bourgeoisie. In: *Debating Arab Authoritarianism: Dynamics and Durability in Nondemocratic Regimes.* Oliver Schlumberger, editor. Stanford: Stanford University Press.

Lupsha, Peter and Stanley Pimentel. 1997. The nexus between crime and politics: Mexico. *Trends in Organized Crime* 3(1).

Lust-Okar, Ellen. 2005. *Structuring Conflict in the Arab World: Incumbents, Opponents, and Institutions.* Cambridge: Cambridge University Press.

————. 2006. Elections under authoritarianism: Preliminary lessons from Jordan. *Democratization* 13(3).

————. 2008. Competitive clientelism in Jordanian elections. In: *Political Participation in the Middle East.* Ellen Lust-Okar and Saloua Zerhouni, editors. Boulder: Lynne Rienner.

————. 2009a. Competitive clientelism: Rethinking elections in the MENA and the prospects for democracy. In: *Global Democracy and Its Difficulties.* Anthony J. Langlois and Karol Edward Soltan, editors. London: Routledge.

————. 2009b. Reinforcing informal institutions through authoritarian elections: Insights from Jordan. *Middle East Law and Governance* 1.

Lust-Okar, Ellen and Amaney Jamal. 2002. Rulers and rules: Reassessing the influence of regime type on electoral law formation. *Comparative Political Studies* 35(3).

Lust-Okar, Ellen and Saloua Zerhouni, editors. 2008. *Political Participation in the Middle East.* Boulder: Lynne Rienner.

Lynch, Marc. 2007. Young brothers in cyberspace. *Middle East Report*, The Politics of Youth 245.

Magaloni, Beatriz. 2006. *Voting for Autocracy: The Politics of Party Hegemony and Its Demise*. Cambridge: Cambridge University Press.

———. 2008. Credible power-sharing and the longevity of authoritarian rule. *Comparative Political Studies* 41(4–5).

Magaloni, Beatriz, Alberto Diaz-Cayeros, and Federico Estevez. 2007. Clientelism and portfolio diversification: A model of electoral investment with application to Mexico. In: *Patrons, Clients, and Policies: Patterns of Democratic Accountability and Political Competition*. Herbert Kitschelt and Steven I. Wilkinson, editors. Cambridge: Cambridge University Press.

Magaloni, Beatriz, Barry Weingast, and Alberto Diaz-Cayeros. 2006. Why authoritarian regimes sabotage economic growth: Land reform in Mexico. Working paper, Stanford University.

Mahmood, Saba. 2004. *Politics of Piety: The Islamic Revival and the Feminist Subject*. Princeton: Princeton University Press.

Mahoney, James. 2000. Path dependence in historical sociology. *Theory and Society* 29.

Makram-Ebeid, Mona. 1989. The role of the official opposition. In: *Egypt under Mubarak*. Charles Tripp and Roger Owen, editors. London: Routledge.

———. 2002. Elections in Egypt: Rumblings for change. In: Elections in the Middle East: What do they mean? Iman A. Hamdy, editor. *Cairo Papers in Social Science* 12(1/2).

Manion, Melanie. 2004. *Corruption by Design: Building Clean Government in Mainland China and Hong Kong*. Cambridge: Harvard University Press.

Marr, Phebe. 1988. Iraq: Its revolutionary experience under the Bath. In: *Ideology and Power in the Middle East: Studies in Honor of George Lenczowski*. Peter Chelkowski and Robert Pranger, editors. Durham: Duke University Press.

———. 2004. *The Modern History of Iraq*. Boulder: Westview.

Marty, Marianne. 2002. Mauritania: Political parties, neo-patrimonialism, and democracy. *Democratization* 9(3).

Masoud, Tarek. 2006a. Dr. Heshmat goes to Cairo. *Foreign Policy*, July/August.

———. 2006b. Peasants and the politics of faith. Paper presented at the Annual Meeting of the American Political Science Association.

———. 2008a. Are they democrats? Does it matter? *Journal of Democracy* 19(3).

———. 2008b. Why Islam wins electoral ecologies and economies of political Islam in contemporary Egypt. Yale University doctoral dissertation.

———. 2008c. Why do important social movements run in rigged elections for seats in rubber-stamp legislatures? Paper presented at the Annual Meeting of the Middle East Studies Association.

———. 2010. How the Brothers win. Paper presented at the Harvard University Middle East Politics Workshop, February 2010.

Mayfield, James. 1996. *Local Government in Egypt: Structure, Process, and the Challenges of Reform*. Cairo: American University in Cairo Press.

McCubbins, Mathew and Thomas Schwartz. 1984. Congressional oversight overlooked: Police patrols versus fire alarms. *American Journal of Political Science* 28.

McDermott, Anthony. 1988. *Egypt from Nasser to Mubarak: A Flawed Revolution*. London: Croom Helm.

McFaul, Michael. 2002. The fourth wave of democracy and dictatorship: Noncooperative transitions in the postcommunist world. *World Politics* 54(2).

McMillan, John. ND. Using markets to help solve public problems. Stanford Graduate School of Business, unpublished manuscript.

El-Meehy, Asya. 2009. "Your big dream... starts with a small loan": The social fund, politics, and the poor in Egypt. Paper presented at the Cornell University Institute for the Social Sciences Conference.

Meltzer, Allan and Scott Richard. 1981. A rational theory of the size of government. *Journal of Political Economy* 89.

el-Menoufi, Kamal and Ali al-Sawi, editors. 2004. *Are Businessmen Lawmakers Business Oriented?* Parliamentary Program, Faculty of Economics and Political Science, Cairo University.

Mezey, Michael L. 1983. The functions of legislatures in the Third World. *Legislative Studies Quarterly* 8(4).

Migdal, Joel. 1988. *Strong Societies and Weak States: State–Society Relations and State Capabilities in the Third World*. Princeton: Princeton University Press.

el-Mikaway, Noha. 1999. *The Building of Consensus in Egypt's Transition Process*. Cairo: American University in Cairo Press.

———. 2000. Perceptions of the social role of the state in Egypt. Discourses in contemporary Egypt: Politics and social issues. *Cairo Papers in Social Science* 22(4).

Milgrom, Paul. 1989. Auctions and bidding: A primer. *Journal of Economic Perspectives* 3(3).

Mitchell, Richard P. 1969. *The Society of the Muslim Brothers*. London: Oxford University Press.

Mitchell, Timothy. 2002. *Rule of Experts: Egypt, Techno-Politics, Modernity*. Berkeley: University of California Press.

Moehler, Devra C. 2005. Free and fair or fraudulent and forged: Elections and legitimacy in Africa. *Afrobarometer Working Papers* 55.

Moore, Clement Henry. 1974. Authoritarian politics in unincorporated society: The case of Nasser's Egypt. *Comparative Politics* 6(2).

———. 1986. Money and power: The dilemma of the Egyptian infitah. *Middle East Journal* 40(4).

Moore, Pete W. 1994. The international context of liberalization and democratization in the Arab world. *Arab Studies Quarterly* 16(3).

Moustafa, Tamir. 2000. Conflict and cooperation between the state and religious institutions in contemporary Egypt. *International Journal of Middle East Studies* 32(1).

———. 2007. *The Struggle for Constitutional Power: Law, Politics, and Economic Development in Egypt*. Cambridge: Cambridge University Press.

Mozaffar, Shaheen. 2002. Patterns of electoral governance in Africa's emerging democracies. *International Political Science Review* 23(1).

Mubarak, Hisham. 1996. What does the Gama'a Islamiyya want? *Middle East Report* 198.

Mufti, Malik. 1999. Elite bargains and the onset of political liberalization in Jordan. *Comparative Political Studies* 32(1).

Murphy, Caryle. 1995. The business of political change in Egypt. *Current History* 94(588).

———. 2002. *Passion for Islam: Shaping the Modern Middle East – The Egyptian Experience*. New York: Scribner.

Murphy, Emma. 1999. *Economic and Political Change in Tunisia: From Bourguiba to Ben Ali*. New York: St. Martin's Press.

———. 2001a. Economic reform and the state in Tunisia. In: *The State and Global Change: The Political Economy of Transition in the Middle East and North Africa*. Hassan Hakimian and Ziba Moshaver, editors. Surrey: Curzon.

_____. 2001b. The state and the private sector in North Africa: Seeking specificity. *Mediterranean Politics* 6(2).

Musolf, Lloyd D. and J. Fred Springer. 1977. Legislatures and divided societies: The Malaysian parliament and multi-ethnicity. *Legislative Studies Quarterly* 2(2).

Mustafa, Hala and Augustus Richard Norton. 2007. Stalled reform: The case of Egypt. *Current History* 106(696).

Myerson, Roger. 2008. The autocrat's credibility problem and foundations of the constitutional state. *American Political Science Review* 102(1).

Najjar, Fauzi. 2000. Islamic fundamentalism and the intellectuals: The case of Nasr Hamid Abu Zayd. *British Journal of Middle Eastern Studies* 27(2).

Nalepa, Monika. 2010. *Skeletons in the Closet: Transitional Justice in Post-Communist Europe*. Cambridge: Cambridge University Press.

N'Diaye, Boubacar. 2001. Mauritania's stalled democratization. *Journal of Democracy* 12(3).

_____. 2006. Mauritania, August 2005: Justice and democracy, or just another coup? *African Affairs* 105(420).

Nedoroscik, Jeffrey A. 2002. Extremist groups in Egypt. *Terrorism and Political Violence* 14(2).

Nichter, Simeon. 2008. Vote buying or turnout buying? Machine politics and the secret ballot. *American Political Science Review* 102(1).

Nielsen, Hans Christian Korsholm. 2004. Tribal identity and politics in Aswan governorate. In: *Upper Egypt: Identity and Change*. Nicholas Hopkins and Reem Saad, editors. Cairo: American University in Cairo Press.

Noel, Hans. 2006. The coalition merchants: How ideologues shape parties in American politics. University of California, Los Angeles, doctoral dissertation.

_____. 2007. Listening to the coalition merchants: Measuring the intellectual influence of academic scribblers. *Forum* 5(3).

Nordhaus, William. 1975. The political business cycle. *Review of Economic Studies* 42.

North, Douglass. 1993. Institutions and credible commitment. *Journal of Institutional and Theoretical Economics* 149(1).

O'Donnell, Guillermo and Phillipe Schmitter. 1986. *Transitions from Authoritarian Rule: Tentative Conclusions about Uncertain Democracies*. Baltimore: Johns Hopkins University Press.

Oldham, Linda, Haguer El Hadidi, and Hussein Tamaa. 1987. Informal communities in Cairo: The basis of a typology. *Cairo Papers in Social Science* 10(4).

Ottaway, Marina. 2003. *Democracy Challenged: The Rise of Semi-Authoritarianism*. Washington, DC: Carnegie Endowment for International Peace.

Ottaway, Marina and Thomas Carothers. 2004. Think again: Middle East democracy. *Foreign Policy*, November/December.

Ouda, Jihad, Negad El-Borai, and Hafez Abu Seada. 2002. *A Door onto the Desert: The Egyptian Parliamentary Elections of 2000*. Cairo: Friedrich Neumann Foundation.

Ould-Mey, Mohameden. 1996. *Global Restructuring and Peripheral States: The Carrot and the Stick in Mauritania*. London: Littlefield Adams.

Owen, Roger. 1983. Egypt gropes for political direction. *Middle East Report* 116.

_____. 2004. *State, Power, and Politics in the Making of the Modern Middle East*. London: Routledge.

Palmer, Glenn, Scott B. Wohlander, and T. Clifton Morgan. 2002. Give or take: Foreign aid and foreign policy substitutability. *Journal of Peace Research* 39(1).

Pape, Robert. 2003. The strategic logic of suicide bombing. *American Political Science Review* 97(3).

Parikh, Sunita and Barry Weingast. 2003. Partisan politics and the structure and stability of federalism, Indian style. Working paper, Washington University in St. Louis.

Pazzanita, Anthony. 1996. The origins and evolution of Mauritania's Second Republic. *Journal of Modern African Studies* 34(4).

———. 1997. State and society in Mauritania in the 1990s. *Journal of North African Studies* 2(1).

Pepinsky, Thomas. 2007. Autocracy, elections, and fiscal policy: Evidence from Malaysia. *Studies in Comparative International Development* 42.

Persson, Torston and Guido Tabellini. 2002. Do electoral cycles differ across political systems? Working paper.

Perthes, Volker. 1991. The bourgeoisie and the Ba'th. *Middle East Report* 170.

———. 1992. Syria's parliamentary elections: Remodeling Asad's political base. *Middle East Report* 174.

———. 1997. *The Political Economy of Syria under Asad*. New York: St. Martin's Press.

———. 2004a. *Syria under Bashar al-Asad: Modernisation and the Limits of Change*. Oxford: Oxford University Press.

———. 2004b. Syria: Difficult inheritance. In: *Arab Elites: Negotiating the Politics of Change*. Boulder: Lynne Rienner.

———. 2004c. Elite change and systems maintenance. In: *Arab Elites: Negotiating the Politics of Change*. Boulder: Lynne Rienner.

Pfeifer, Karen. 1999. How Tunisia, Morocco, Jordan and even Egypt became IMF "success stories" in the 1990s. *Middle East Report* 210.

Pfeiffer, Silke. 2004. *Vote Buying and Its Implications for Democracy: Evidence from Latin America*. Transparency International Global Corruption Report 2004. London: Pluto Press.

Picard, Elizabeth. 1978. Syria returns to democracy: The May 1973 legislative elections. In: *Elections without Choice*. Guy Hermet, Richard Rose, and Alain Rouqui, editors. London: Macmillan.

Pierson, Paul. 2004. *Politics in Time: History, Institutions, and Social Analysis*. Princeton: Princeton University Press.

Pioppi, Daniela. 2007. Privatization of social services as a regime strategy: The revival of Islamic endowments (Awqaf) in Egypt. In: *Debating Arab Authoritarianism: Dynamics and Durability in Nondemocratic Regimes*. Oliver Schlumberger, editor. Stanford: Stanford University Press.

Poggi, Gianfranco. 1978. *The Development of the Modern State: A Sociological Introduction*. Stanford: Stanford University Press.

Post, Erika. 1987. Egypt's elections. *Middle East Report* 147.

Posusney, Marsha Pripstein. 1997. *Labor and the State in Egypt: Workers, Unions, and Economic Restructuring*. New York: Columbia University Press.

———. 1998. Behind the ballot box: Electoral engineering in the Arab world. *Middle East Report* 209.

———. 1999. Egyptian privatization: New challenges for the left. *Middle East Report* 210.

———. 2004. Enduring authoritarianism: Middle East lessons for comparative theory. *Comparative Politics* 36(2).

Powers, Timothy and J. Timmons Roberts. 1995. Compulsory voting, invalid ballot, and abstention in Brazil. *Political Research Quarterly* 48(4).

Przeworski, Adam. 1991. *Democracy and the Market: Political and Economic Reforms in Eastern Europe and Latin America.* Cambridge: Cambridge University Press.

Przeworski, Adam, Susan Stokes, and Bernard Manin, editors. 1999. *Democracy, Accountability, and Representation.* Cambridge: Cambridge University Press.

Puryear, Jeffrey. 1994. *Thinking Politics: Intellectuals and Democracy in Chile, 1973–1988.* Baltimore: Johns Hopkins University Press.

Quandt, William. 2002. Democratization in the Arab world? Algeria's uneasy peace. *Journal of Democracy* 13(4).

Redissi, Hamadi. 2009. Tunisia: Do elections have meaning? *Arab Reform Bulletin* 7(8).

Reed, Steven. 2001. Impersonal mechanisms versus personal networks in the distribution of central grants-in-aid to local governments in Japan. In: *Local Governments in Post-War Japan.* Michio Muramatsu, Jkuo Kume, and Farruku Iqbal, editors. Oxford: Oxford University Press.

Reeves, Edward. 1990. *The Hidden Government: Ritual, Clientelism and Legitimation in Northern Egypt.* Salt Lake City: University of Utah Press.

Remmer, Karen. 1993. The political economy of elections in Latin America, 1980–1991. *American Political Science Review* 87(2).

Richards, Alan. 1984. Ten years of infitah: Class, rent, and policy stasis in Egypt. *Journal of Development Studies* 20(4).

Riker, William. 1976. The number of political parties: A reexamination of Duverger's law. *Comparative Politics* 9.

Riker, William and Peter Ordeshook 1968. A theory of the calculus of voting. *American Political Science Review* 62.

Roberts, Hugh. 1992. The Algerian state and the challenge of democracy. *Government and Opposition* 27(4).

———. 1998. Algeria's contested elections. *Middle East Report* 209.

———. 2002. Musical chairs in Algeria. *Middle East Report Online.* June 4.

———. 2003. *The Battlefield Algeria 1988–2002.* London: Verso.

Roberts, Kenneth M. and Moisés Arce. 1998. Neoliberalism and lower-class voting behavior in Peru. *Comparative Political Studies* 31(2).

Roeder, Philip. 1989. Electoral avoidance in the Soviet Union. *Soviet Studies* 41.

Rogoff, Kenneth. 1990. Equilibrium political budget cycles. *American Economic Review* 80.

Rogoff, Kenneth and Anne Silbert. 1988. Elections and macroeconomic policy cycles. *Review of Economic Studies* 55.

Rosberg, James. 1995. Roads to the rule of law: The emergence of an independent judiciary in contemporary Egypt. Ph.D. dissertation, Massachusetts Institute of Technology.

Rosendorff, Peter and Todd Sandler. 2004. Too much of a good thing: The proactive response dilemma. *Journal of Conflict Resolution* 48(5).

Ross, Jeffrey Ian. 1993. Structural causes of oppositional political terrorism: Towards a causal model. *Journal of Peace Research* 30(3).

Ross, Michael. 2001. Does oil hinder democracy? *World Politics* 53(3).

Rothchild, Donald and Michael W. Foley. 1988. African states and the politics of inclusive coalitions. In: *The Precarious Balance: State and Society in Africa.* Donald Rothchild and Naomi Chazan, editors. Boulder: Westview.

Roy, Olivier (translated by Carol Volk). 1994. *The Failure of Political Islam.* Cambridge: Harvard University Press.

Rubin, Barry. 2007. *The Truth about Syria.* New York: Palgrave Macmillan.

Rutherford, Bruce. 2006. What do Egypt's Islamists want? Moderate Islam and the rise of Islamic constitutionalism. *Middle East Journal* 60(4).

———. 2008. *Egypt after Mubarak: Liberalism, Islam, and Democracy in the Arab World.* Princeton: Princeton University Press.

Ryan, Curtis R. 2002. *Jordan in Transition: From Hussein to Abdullah.* Boulder: Lynne Rienner.

Saad, Reem. 2002. Egyptian politics and the tenancy law. In: *Counter-Revolution in Egypt's Countryside: Land and Farmers in the Era of Economic Reform.* Ray Bush, editor. London: Zed Books.

Sadiki, Larbi. 2000. Popular uprisings and Arab democratization. *International Journal of Middle East Studies* 32(1).

———. 2002. Bin Ali's Tunisia: Democracy by non-democratic means. *British Journal of Middle Eastern Studies* 29(1).

Sadowski, Yahya. 1988. Bathist ethics and the spirit of state capitalism: Patronage and party in contemporary Syria. In: *Ideology and Power in the Middle East: Studies in Honor of George Lenczowski.* Peter Chelkowski and Robert Pranger, editors. Durham: Duke University Press.

———. 1991. *Political Vegetables: Businessman and Bureaucrat in the Development of Egyptian Agriculture.* Washington, DC: Brookings Institution.

Sagiv, David. 1995. *Fundamentalism and Intellectuals in Egypt, 1973–1993.* London: Frank Cass.

Sartori, Giovanni. 1976. *Parties and Party Systems: A Framework for Analysis.* Cambridge: Cambridge University Press.

Sater, James N. 2007. Changing politics from below? Women parliamentarians in Morocco. *Democratization* 14(4).

al-Sawy, Ali, Ali Moussa, and Ajlan Ibrahim. 2005. *Kaifa tuzawir al-intikhābāt? (How Are Elections Forged?).* Cairo.

al-Sayyid, Mustapha K. 2003. The other face of the Islamist movement. Working paper, Democracy and Rule of Law Project. Washington, DC: Carnegie Endowment for International Peace.

———. 2007. International dimensions of Middle Eastern authoritarianism: The G8 and external efforts at political reform. In: *Debating Arab Authoritarianism: Dynamics and Durability in Nondemocratic Regimes.* Oliver Schlumberger, editor. Stanford: Stanford University Press.

Schady, Norbert R. 2000. The political economy of expenditures by the Peruvian Social Fund (FONCODES), 1991–95. *American Political Science Review* 94(2).

Schaffer, Frederic C. 1998. *Democracy in Translation: Understanding Politics in an Unfamiliar Culture.* Ithaca: Cornell University Press.

———. 2004. *Vote Buying in East Asia: Transparency International Global Corruption Report 2004.* London: Pluto Press.

———. 2007. *Elections for Sale: The Causes and Consequences of Vote Buying.* Boulder: Lynne Rienner.

Schamis, Hector and Christopher Way. 2003. Political cycles and exchange-rate based stabilization. *World Politics* 56.

Schatz, Edward. 2006. Access by accident: Legitimacy claims and democracy promotion in authoritarian Central Asia. *International Political Science Review* 27(3).

Schedler, Andreas. 2002. Elections without democracy: The menu of manipulation. *Journal of Democracy* 13(2).

——. 2006. *Electoral Authoritarianism: The Dynamics of Unfree Competition.* Boulder: Lynne Rienner.

Scheiner, Ethan. 2006. *Democracy without Competition in Japan: Opposition Failure in a One-Party Dominant State.* Cambridge: Cambridge University Press.

Schelling, Thomas. 1960. *The Strategy of Conflict.* Cambridge: Harvard University Press.

Schlumberger, Oliver. 2008. Structural reform, economic order, and development: Patrimonial capitalism. *Review of International Political Economy* 15(4).

Schuessler, Alexander. 2000. *A Logic of Expressive Choice.* Princeton: Princeton University Press.

Schultz, Kenneth. 1998. Domestic opposition and signaling in international crises. *American Political Science Review* 92.

——. 1999. Do democratic institutions constrain or inform? Contrasting two institutional perspectives on democracy and war. *International Organization* 52.

Schultz, Kenneth. 1995. The politics of the political business cycle. *British Journal of Political Science* 25.

Schwartz, Joel, et al. 1996. Methodological issues in studies of air pollution and daily counts of deaths or hospital admissions. *Journal of Epidemiology and Community Health* 50(1).

Schwedler, Jillian. 2002. Democratization in the Arab World? Yemen's aborted opening. *Journal of Democracy* 13(4).

——. 2006. *Faith in Moderation: Islamist Parties in Jordan and Yemen.* Cambridge: Cambridge University Press.

Scott, James C. 1985. *Weapons of the Weak: Everyday Forms of Peasant Resistance.* New Haven: Yale University Press.

Seale, Patrick. 1989. *Asad: The Struggle for the Middle East.* London: I.B. Tauris.

Searle, Peter. 1999. *The Riddle of Malaysian Capitalism: Rent Seekers or Real Capitalists?* Honolulu: University of Hawai'i Press.

Seddon, David. 1990. The politics of adjustment: Egypt and the IMF, 1987–1990. *Review of African Political Economy* 17(47).

——. 1996. The political economy of Mauritania: An introduction. *Review of African Political Economy* 23(68).

Sederberg, Peter. 1995. Conciliation as counter-terrorist strategy. *Journal of Peace Research* 32(3).

Seligson, Mitchell. 2002. The impact of corruption on regime legitimacy: A comparative study of four Latin American countries. *Journal of Politics* 64(2).

Sfakianakis, John. 2002. In search of bureaucrats and entrepreneurs: The political economy of the export agribusiness sector in Egypt. In: *Counter-Revolution in Egypt's Countryside: Land and Farmers in the Era of Economic Reform.* Ray Bush, editor. London: Zed Books.

——. 2004. The whales of the Nile: Networks, businessmen, and bureaucrats during the era of privatization in Egypt. In: *Networks of Privilege in the Middle East. The Politics of Economic Reform Revisited.* Steven Heydemann, editor. New York: Palgrave Macmillan.

al-Shawarby, Sherine. 2008. Measuring inflation in Egypt: Assessment of the CPI accuracy. Working paper no. 132, Egyptian Center for Economic Studies.

Shefa, A. 2006. Egyptian intellectuals speak out against the Muslim Brotherhood movement and its slogan "Islam Is the Solution." *MEMRI Inquiry and Analysis Series,* Report 268.

Shehata, Samer. 2008. Inside an Egyptian parliamentary campaign. In: *Political Participation in the Middle East*. Ellen Lust-Okar and Saloua Zerhouni, editors. Boulder: Lynne Rienner.

Shepsle, Kenneth and Barry Nalebuff. 1990. The commitment to seniority in self-governing groups. *Journal of Law, Economics and Organization* 6.

Shi, M. and J. Svensson. 2002a. Conditional political budget cycles. CEPR discussion paper 3352.

———. 2002b. Political business cycles in developed and developing countries. Working paper.

Shi, Tianjian. 1999. Voting and nonvoting in China: Voting behavior in plebiscitary and limited choice elections. *Journal of Politics* 61(4).

Shorbagy, Manar. 2007. Understanding Kefaya: The new politics in Egypt. *Arab Studies Quarterly* 29(1).

al-Shoubaki, Amr. 2006. *Mustaqbal Jam'īya al-Ikhwān al-Muslimīn* (Future of the Muslim Brotherhood). Ahram Center for Political and Strategic Studies 163.

Siddiqa, Ayesha. 2007. *Military Inc.: Inside Pakistan's Military Economy*. London: Pluto Press.

Sims, David. 2003. *Understanding Slums: Case Studies for the Global Report on Human Settlements*. Cairo: United Nations Human Settlements Program.

Singerman, Diane. 1995. *Avenues of Participation: Family, Politics, and Networks in Urban Quarters of Cairo*. Princeton: Princeton University Press.

Slater, Dan. 2003. Iron cage in an iron fist: Authoritarian institutions and the personalization of power in Malaysia. *Comparative Politics* 36(1).

———. 2005. Ordering power: Contentious politics, state-building, and authoritarian durability in Southeast Asia. Ph.D. dissertation, Emory University, Department of Political Science.

Smith, Alastair. 2008. The perils of unearned income. *Journal of Politics* 70(3).

Smith, Benjamin. 2005. Life of the party: The origins of regime breakdown and persistence under single-party rule. *World Politics* 57.

Soliman, Ahmed M. 1996. Legitimizing informal housing: Accommodating low-income groups in Alexandria, Egypt. *Environment and Urbanization* 8.

Soliman, Samer. 2006. *Al-Mushāraka al-Siyāsīya fī al-Intikhabāt al-Niyābīya 2005*. Cairo: EACPE.

Sonbol, Amira El-Azhary. 2000. *The New Mamluks: Egyptian Society and Modern Feudalism*. Syracuse: Syracuse University Press.

Springborg, Robert. 1982. *Family Power and Politics in Egypt: Sayed Bey Marei – His Clan, Clients, and Cohorts*. Philadelphia: University of Pennsylvania Press.

———. 1988. Approaches to the understanding of Egypt. In: *Ideology and Power in the Middle East: Studies in Honor of George Lenczowski*. Peter Chelkowski and Robert Pranger, editors. Durham: Duke University Press.

———. 1989. *Mubarak's Egypt: Fragmentation of the Political Order*. Boulder: Westview.

Stacher, Joshua. 2004. Parties over: The demise of Egypt's opposition parties. *British Journal of Middle Eastern Studies* 31(2).

Stasavage, David. 2005. Democracy and education spending in Africa. *American Journal of Political Science* 49(2).

Stokes, Susan C. 2005. Perverse accountability: A formal model of machine politics with evidence from Argentina. *American Political Science Review* 99(3).

Stone, Peter. 2007. Why lotteries are just. *Journal of Political Philosophy* 15(3).

———. 2008. Rationality, functionalism, and social criticism. Working paper, Stanford University.

Stone, Randall. 2002. *Satellites and Commissars: Strategy and Conflict in the Politics of Soviet-Bloc Trade*. Princeton: Princeton University Press.

Stork, Joe. 1981. Massive arrests precede Sadat's assassination. *Middle East Report* 100/101.

Sullivan, Denis. 1994. *Private Voluntary Organizations in Egypt: Islamic Development, Private Initiative, and State Control*. Gainesville: University of Florida Press.

Sullivan, Denis and Sana Abed-Kotob. 1999. *Islam in Contemporary Egypt: Civil Society vs. the State*. Boulder: Lynne Rienner.

Sullivan, Earl L., editor. 1984. Impact of development assistance on Egypt. *Cairo Papers in Social Science* 7(4).

Tadros, Mariz. 2005. Egypt's election all about image, almost. *Middle East Report Online*. September 6.

———. 2009. Vicissitudes in the entente between the coptic Christian church and the state in Egypt (1952–2007). *International Journal of Middle Eastern Studies* 41(2).

Taher, Nadia Adel. 1986. Social identity and class in a Cairo neighborhood. *Cairo Papers in Social Science* 9(4).

Tahi, Mohand Salah. 1995. Algeria's democratization process: A frustrated hope. *Third World Quarterly* 16(2).

Tal, Nachman. 2005. *Radical Islam in Egypt and Jordan*. Brighton: Sussex Academic Press.

el-Tarouty, Safinaz. 2004. Institutionalization and reform: The case of the National Democratic Party in Egypt. American University in Cairo, MA thesis.

Tessler, Mark and Eleanor Gao. 2005. Gauging Arab support for democracy. *Journal of Democracy* 16(3).

Teti, Andrea, Gennaro Gervasio, and Raffaella Rucci. 2006. Shayfeenkum! We see you!...So what? The 2005 Egyptian elections and the ambiguities of (de) liberalization. Working paper.

Tetreault, Mary Ann. 2000. *Stories of Democracy: Politics and Society in Contemporary Kuwait*. New York: Columbia University Press.

Tezcur, Gunes Murat. 2008. Intra-elite struggles in Iranian elections. In: *Political Participation in the Middle East*. Ellen Lust-Okar and Saloua Zerhouni, editors. Boulder: Lynne Rienner.

Thompson, Mark R. 2005. "Democratizing" theories of revolution: Why and how democrats rebel. In: *Democratization and Political Culture in Comparative Perspective*. Norbert Kersting and Lasse Cronqvist, editors. Wiesbaden: VS Verlag.

Tomz, Michael. 2007. Domestic audience costs in international relations: An experimental approach. *International Organization* 61(4).

Tripp, Charles. 2000. *A History of Iraq*. Cambridge: Cambridge University Press.

———. 2001. States, elites, and the "management of change." In: *The State and Global Change: The Political Economy of Transition in the Middle East and North Africa*. Hassan Hakimian and Ziba Moshaver Surrey, editors. Curzon.

Tripp, Charles and Roger Owen, editors. 1989. *Egypt under Mubarak*. London: Routledge.

Tsai, Lily. 2007. *Accountability without Democracy: Solidary Groups and Public Goods Provision in Rural China*. Cambridge: Cambridge University Press.

Tschirgi, Dan. 1999. Marginalized violent internal conflict in the age of globalization: Mexico and Egypt. *Arab Studies Quarterly* 21.

Tsebelis, George. 2002. *Veto Players: How Political Institutions Work*. Princeton: Princeton University Press.

Tucker, Judith. 1978. While Sadat shuffles: Economic decay, political ferment in Egypt. *MERIP Reports 65*.

Tufte, Edward. 1978. *Political Control of the Economy*. Princeton: Princeton University Press.

Tullock, Gordon. 1987. *Autocracy*. Dordrecht: Kluwer Academic Publishers.

USAID. 2006. *Parliamentary Immunity Brief: A Summary of Case Studies of Armenia, Ukraine, and Guatemala*. USAID.

Valeri, Marc. 2007. State building, liberalization from above, and political legitimacy in the sultanate of Oman. In: *Debating Arab Authoritarianism: Dynamics and Durability in Nondemocratic Regimes*. Oliver Schlumberger, editor. Stanford: Stanford University Press.

Van Dam, Nikolaos. 1981. *The Struggle for Power in Syria: Sectarianism, Regionalism and Tribalism in Politics, 1961–1980*. London: Croom Helm.

Van de Walle, Nicolas. 2007. Meet the new boss, same as the old boss? The evolution of political clientelism in Africa. In: *Patrons, Clients, and Policies: Patterns of Democratic Accountability and Political Competition*. Herbert Kitschett and Steven Wilkinson, editors. Cambridge: Cambridge University Press.

Vatikiotis, P. J. 1961. *The Egyptian Army in Politics: Pattern for New Nations?* Bloomington: Indiana University Press.

———. 1992. *The History of Modern Egypt*, 4th edition. Baltimore: Johns Hopkins University Press.

Volpi, Frèdèric. 2006. Algeria's pseudo-democratic politics: Lessons for democratization in the Middle East. *Democratization* 13(3).

Vreeland, James. 2002. Institutional determinants of IMF agreements. Working paper.

Wahba, Mourad Magdi. 1994. *The Role of the State in the Egyptian Economy: 1945–1981*. London: Ithaca Press.

Wantchekon, Leonard. 2003. Clientelism and voting behavior: Evidence from a field experiment in Benin. *World Politics 55*.

Waterbury, John. 1973. Endemic and planned corruption in a monarchical regime. *World Politics 25(4)*.

———. 1978. *Egypt: Burdens of the Past, Options of the Future*. Bloomington: Indiana University Press.

———. 1983. *The Egypt of Nasser and Sadat: The Political Economy of Two Regimes*. Princeton: Princeton University Press.

———. 1985. The "soft state" and the open door: Egypt's experience with economic liberalization, 1974–1984. *Comparative Politics* 18(1).

———. 1993. *Exposed to Innumerable Delusions: Public Enterprise and State Power in Egypt, India, Mexico, and Turkey*. Cambridge: Cambridge University Press.

Weaver, Mary Anne. 2000. *A Portrait of Egypt: A Journey through the World of Militant Islam*. New York: Farrar, Straus and Giroux.

Weber, Robert James. 1985. Auctions and competitive bidding fair allocation. H. Peyton Young, editor. *Proceedings of Symposia in Applied Mathematics, American Mathematical Society* 33. Providence: American Mathematical Society.

Wedeen, Lisa. 1998. Acting "as if": Symbolic politics and social control in Syria. *Comparative Studies in Society and History* 40(3).

———. 1999. *Ambiguities of Domination: Politics, Rhetoric, and Symbols in Contemporary Syria*. Chicago: University of Chicago Press.

———. 2007. The politics of deliberation: Qat chews as public spheres in Yemen. *Public Culture* 19(1).

———. 2008. *Peripheral Visions: Publics, Power, and Performance in Yemen*. Chicago: University of Chicago Press.

Weinbaum, Marvin G. 1986. *Egypt and the Politics of U.S. Economic Aid*. Boulder: Westview.

Weingast, Barry. 1993. Constitutions as governance structures. The political foundations of secure markets. *Journal of Institutional and Theoretical Economics* 149.

Weiss, Dieter and Ulrich Wurzel. 1998. *The Economics and Politics of Transition to an Open Market Economy*. Paris: OECD.

Werenfels, Isabelle. 2004. Algeria: System continuity through elite change. In: *Arab Elites: Negotiating the Politics of Change*. Boulder: Lynne Rienner.

———. 2007. *Managing Instability in Algeria: Elites and Political Change since 1995*. London: Routledge.

Weyland, Kurt. 1998. The politics of corruption in Latin America. *Journal of Democracy* 9(2).

Weyland, Petra. 1993. *Inside the Third World Village*. London: Routledge.

Wickham, Carrie Rosefsky. 2002. *Mobilizing Islam: Religion, Activism, and Political Change in Egypt*. New York: Columbia University Press.

Wigley, Simon. 2003. Parliamentary immunity: Protecting democracy or protecting corruption? *Journal of Political Philosophy* 11(1).

Willis, Michael. 2002. Political parties in the Maghrib: The illusion of significance? *Journal of North African Studies* 7(2).

Winegar, Jessica. 2006. *Creative Reckonings: The Politics of Art and Culture in Contemporary Egypt*. Stanford: Stanford University Press.

Wittfogel, Karl. 1957. *Oriental Despotism: A Comparative Study of Total Power*. New Haven: Yale University Press.

Wright, Joseph. 2008. Do authoritarian institutions constrain? How legislatures affect economic growth and investment. *American Journal of Political Science* 52(2).

Wurzel, Ulrich. 2004. Patterns of resistance: Economic actors and fiscal policy reform in Egypt in the 1990s. In: *Networks of Privilege in the Middle East: The Politics of Economic Reform Revisited*. Steven Heydemann, editor. New York: Palgrave Macmillan.

Young, H. Peyton. 1994. *Equity: In Theory and Practice*. Princeton: Princeton University Press.

Zaalouk, Malak. 1989. *Power, Class, and Foreign Capital in Egypt: The Rise of a New Bourgeoisie*. London: Zed Books.

Zaki, Moheb. 1995. *Civil Society and Democratization in Egypt: 1981–1994*. Cairo: Konrad Adenauer Stiftung.

———. 1998. *Egyptian Business Elite: Their Visions and Investment Behavior*. Cairo: Konrad Adenauer Stiftung.

Zaller, John. 1992. *The Nature and Origins of Mass Opinion*. Cambridge: Cambridge University Press.

Zartman, I. William. 1988a. Opposition as support of the state. In: *Beyond Coercion: The Durability of the Arab State*. Adeed Darwisha and I. William Zartman, editors. London: Croom Helm.

———. 1988b. Introduction. In: *Beyond Coercion: The Durability of the Arab State*. Adeed Darwisha and I. William Zartman, editors. London: Croom Helm.

Zeghal, Malika. 2008. *Islamism in Morocco: Religion, Authoritarianism, and Electoral Politics*. Princeton: Markus Wiener Publishers.

Zerhouni, Saloua. 2004. Morocco: Reconciling continuity and change. In: *Arab Elites: Negotiating the Politics of Change*. Boulder: Lynne Rienner.

———. 2008. The Moroccan parliament. In: *Political Participation in the Middle East*. Ellen Lust-Okar and Saloua Zerhouni, editors. Boulder: Lynne Rienner.

Ziblatt, Daniel. 2008. Does landholding inequality block demcratization? A test of the "bread and democracy" thesis and the case of Prussia. *World Politics* 60(4).

Zisenwine, Daniel. 2007. Mauritania's democratic transition: A regional model for political reform? *Journal of North African Studies* 12(4).

Zisser, Eyal. 2001. *Asad's Legacy: Syria in Transition*. London: Hurst and Company.

Zuhur, Sherifa. 2003. Women and empowerment in the Arab world. *Arab Studies Quarterly* 25(4).

Index

CPSIA information can be obtained at www.ICGtesting.com
Printed in the USA
LVOW082150010313

322371LV00003B/5/P

9 781107 000551